PSYCHOLOGY
AND
MENTAL HEALTH

MAGILL'S CHOICE

PSYCHOLOGY AND MENTAL HEALTH

VOLUME I
Abnormality — Grief and Guilt

edited by

Jaclyn Rodriguez, Ph.D.
Occidental College

project editor
Tracy Irons-Georges

SALEM PRESS, INC.
PASADENA, CALIFORNIA   HACKENSACK, NEW JERSEY

Most of the essays in *Magill's Choice: Psychology and Mental Health* originally appeared in *Magill's Survey of Social Science: Psychology*, 1993, edited by Dr. Frank N. Magill and Jaclyn Rodriguez; some of them were updated for *Magill's Choice: Psychology Basics*, 1998. The remainder of the essays were taken from *Magill's Medical Guide: Revised Edition 1998*. All bibliographies have been updated, and some formats have been changed.

∞ The paper used in these volumes conforms to the American National Standard for Permanence of Paper for Printed Library Materials, Z39.48-1992 (R1997).

Library of Congress Cataloging-in-Publication Data
Psychology and mental health / edited by Jaclyn Rodriguez ; project editor Tracy Irons-Georges.
     p.   cm. — (Magill's choice)
Includes bibliographical references and index.
     ISBN 0-89356-066-9 (set : alk. paper). — ISBN 0-89356-167-7 (vol. 1 : alk. paper). — ISBN 0-89356-068-5 (vol. 2 : alk. paper)
     1. Psychology, Pathological—Encyclopedias. 2. Mental illness— Encyclopedias. 3. Mental health—Encyclopedias. I. Rodriguez, Jaclyn. II. Irons-Georges, Tracy. III. Series.

     RC437 P795 2001
     616.89'003—dc21

                                                 00-046312

First Printing

TABLE OF CONTENTS

PUBLISHER'S NOTE

From the earliest history, humans have sought explanations for seemingly abnormal thoughts and actions. Some behaviors were attributed to possession by gods or demons, others to an imbalance of theoretical "humors" in the body. It was not until modern times, with the advent of the science of psychology, that the influence of physical disease, genetic makeup, and emotional or psychological trauma on mental health has been identified. *Psychology and Mental Health* examines this field as it continues to unravel the origins of mental illness and psychological disorders and the means to prevent or alleviate their symptoms.

Of the 107 essays in this work, 83 first appeared in *Magill's Survey of Social Science: Psychology* (1993); 16 of them were updated and reprinted in *Psychology Basics* (1998). The other 24 essays were published in *Magill's Medical Guide, Revised Edition 1998*. All bibliographies have been updated with the latest editions and most recent scholarship in the field.

Many of the entries in *Psychology and Mental Health* consider psychopathologies. Some of these conditions can pose a serious threat to the safety and functionality of the patient, such as schizophrenia, Alzheimer's disease, anorexia nervosa, or autism. Other psychic-emotional and learning disorders have a lesser but still significant impact on a patient's mental health and emotional condition, such as depression, dyslexia, sibling rivalry, or sexual dysfunction. A number of entries discuss various treatment options, from electroconvulsive therapy and lobotomy to play therapy and psychoanalysis.

All entries begin with the standard information "Type of psychology" and "Fields of study." A brief definition of the topic follows. Next comes a list of "Principal terms" with concise definitions. Entries on mental illness or lesser psychological impairments have a section "Causes and Symptoms," which defines the condition and describes its origins and possible manifestations in patients, and a section "Treatment and Therapy," which explores the various treatments available to alleviate symptoms or effect a cure. More general entries feature the sections "Overview" and "Applications." The last section of all entries is "Perspective and Prospects," which places the topic in a larger context within psychology. For example, an entry on a psychopathology may cover the earliest known investigation into that condition, the evolution of its treatment over time, and promising areas of research for a greater understanding of its causes and cure. Every entry ends with a "Bibliography" of sources to consult for further study and a list of cross-references to related articles within *Psychology and Mental Health*. All essays are signed by the author.

At the end of volume 2 is a list of entries by category: abnormality, anxiety disorders, childhood and adolescent disorders, depression, developmental issues, diagnosis, emotional disorders, learning disorders, organic disorders, personality disorders, schizophrenias, sexual disorders, sleep disorders, stress, substance abuse, and treatment. A comprehensive subject Index of people and concepts concludes the volume.

The contributors to this work are academicians from psychology, medicine, and other disciplines in the life sciences; their names and affiliations are listed in the front matter to volume 1. We thank them for sharing their expertise with general readers. The charts of possible symptoms and signs that appear in some entries were taken from National Mental Health Association factsheet from 1996 and 1997.

CONTRIBUTOR LIST

Norman Abeles
Michigan State University

Steven C. Abell
Loyola University of Chicago

Bruce Ambuel
Medical College of Wisconsin

Stephen M. Auerbach
Virginia Commonwealth University

Bruce E. Bailey
Stephen F. Austin University

Iona C. Baldridge
Lubbock Christian University

Donald G. Beal
Eastern Kentucky University

Alan J. Beauchamp
Northern Michigan University

Brett L. Beck
Bloomsbury University

Paul F. Bell
The Medical Center, Beaver, Pennsylvania

Christiane Brems
University of Alaska

Louis A. Cancellaro, M.D.
Veteran Affairs Medical Center, Mountain Home, Tennessee

Rebecca M. Chesire
University of Hawaii—Manoa

Richard G. Cormack
Independent Scholar

Arlene R. Courtney
Western Oregon State College

Thomas E. DeWolfe
Hampton-Sydney College

Ted Eilders
American Psychological Association

Russell Eisenman
McNeese State University

Mary C. Fields
Collin County Community College

Robin Franck
Southwestern College

Alan K. Gibson
Southern California College

Virginia L. Goetsch
West Virginia University

Dolye R. Goff
Lee College

L. Kevin Hamberger
Medical College of Wisconsin

Ronald C. Hamdy, M.D.
James H. Quillen College of Medicine

Peter M. Hartmann, M.D.
York Hospital, Pennsylvania

James Taylor Henderson
Wingate College

Katherine H. Houp
Midway College

Larry Hudgins, M.D.
Veteran Affairs Medical Center, Mountain Home, Tennessee

Mark E. Johnson
University of Alaska, Anchorage

Jonathan Kahane
Springfield College

William B. King
Edison Community College

Terry Knapp
University of Nevada, Las Vegas

Kevin T. Larkin
West Virginia University

Joseph C. LaVoie
University of Nebraska at Omaha

Scott O. Lilienfeld
State University of New York at Albany

Deborah R. McDonald
New Mexico State University

Linda E. Meashey
Pennsylvania State University, Harrisburg

Laurence Miller
Western Washington University

Paul Moglia
St. Joseph's Hospital and Medical Center, Paterson, New Jersey

John Panos Najarian
William Paterson University

John W. Nichols
Tulsa Junior College

Shirley A. Albertson Ownes
Southern California College

Oliver Oyama
Duke/Fayetteville Area Health Education Center

Linda J. Palm
Edison Community College

Keith Krom Parker
Western Montana College of the University of Montana

Carol Moore Pfaffly
Fort Collins Family Medical Center

Vicky Phares
University of Connecticut

Nancy A. Piotrowski
University of California, Berkeley

Layne A. Prest
University of Nebraska Medical Center

Judith Primavera
Fairfield University

R. Christopher Qualls
Emory and Henry College

Paul August Rentz
South Dakota State University

Ronald G. Ribble
University of Texas at San Antonio

Cheryl A. Rickabaugh
University of Redlands

Denise S. St. Cyr
New Hampshire Technical College

Elliott P. Schuman
Long Island University

Susan J. Shapiro
Indiana University East

Michael F. Shaughnessy
Eastern New Mexico University

Sanford S. Singer
University of Dayton

Genevieve Slomski
Independent Scholar

Gerald Sperrazzo
University of San Diego

Stephanie Stein
Central Washington University

Leland C. Swenson
Loyola Marymount University

Richard G. Tedeschi
University of North Carolina at Charlotte

Gerald T. Terlep
Bon Secours Hospital System

Leslie V. Tischauser
Prairie State College

James T. Trent
Middle Tennessee State University

Lois Veltum
University of North Dakota

Scott R. Vrana
Purdue University

Elaine F. Walker
Emory University

Ann L. Weber
University of North Carolina at Asheville

Edward R. Whitson
State University of New York, College at Genesco

Mark A. Williams
University of Mississippi

Russell Williams
University of Arkansas for Medical Sciences

Bradley R. A. Wilson
University of Cincinnati

Gregory L. Wilson
Washington State University

Karen Wolford
State University of New York, College at Oswego

Frederic Wynn
County College of Morris

PSYCHOLOGY
AND
MENTAL HEALTH

ABNORMALITY

Type of psychology: Psychopathology
Fields of study: Models of abnormality

Abnormality means behavior, thinking processes, or feelings deemed undesirable and therefore subject to control or change. Differing points of view about theoretical orientation, tolerance for deviance, where to draw the line between normal and abnormal, and the use of labeling lead to differences in the criteria used for definitions. Important criteria include subjective discomfort, disability or inefficiency, and deviance, especially bizarre or reality-distorting deviance.

Principal terms

BEHAVIORAL VIEW: a perspective that emphasizes understanding a person in terms of his or her objectively measured behavior; normal, in this view, is functioning well

DEVIANCY: the quality of having a condition or engaging in behavior that is different from the typical in a social group and is considered undesirable

DISTORTIONS OF REALITY: beliefs that distort universally accepted assumptions such as those about time, space, cause and effect, or life and death; delusions

MEDICAL MODEL: a view in which abnormality consists of a number of diseases which originate in bodily functions, especially in the brain, and have defined symptoms, treatments, and outcomes

PHENOMENOLOGICAL VIEW: a perspective that emphasizes understanding a person from his or her own viewpoint; normal, in this view, is feeling satisfied with oneself

PSYCHODYNAMIC VIEW: a perspective that emphasizes understanding a person in terms of how he or she copes with unconscious feelings and conflicts; normal, in this view, is understanding and controlling the feelings and conflicts

STATISTICAL DEFINITION: a definition of abnormality as a condition that is different from the average or mean of the characteristic or trait

Overview

Abnormality is a term applied to behaviors, thinking processes, or feelings that are viewed by the individual and/or by society as undesirable and requiring control or change, and viewed as deficits which may or may not have a clear etiology but which should be compensated for by the individual and society. Psychologists or other mental health professionals are enlisted to test and/or interview individuals to determine whether a condition is abnormal, and to facilitate change or advise in delineating compensation. There are three typical standards, or criteria, that are used by mental health professionals to decide whether the condition is abnormal: discomfort, disability, and deviance.

The first two of these criteria have some similarity to the general indicators of a physical disease. Just as physical disease may be marked by pain, the major symptom that brings most private patients to a psychotherapist is a chronic psychological pain or discomfort. Just as a physical impairment, such as a broken leg, usually leads to problems in daily living, so the second condition that defines abnormality is some sort of difficulty in functioning, a disability or impairment. Both discomfort and disability are often evaluated by one's personal standards. One is feeling discomfort because of problems one knows best oneself, or one is inefficient compared to what one expects of oneself.

The third major criterion for abnormality, deviance, is based not on personal standards but on the standards of society. Deviance is behavior that is undesirably different from social expectations; such behavior is most likely to be considered psychologically abnormal if it is unpredictable, bizarre, or dangerous.

Each of these three major criteria that collectively define psychological abnormality can range greatly in quality and degree, and each summarizes a large number of symptoms and conditions. Any deviancy or discomfort is more likely to be defined as abnormal if disability or impairment in function is present. The impairment can be judged based on the typical performance of others, or it can be judged based upon the individual's own potential or subjective expectation. The impairment may sometimes be based on a physical condition such as retardation or brain injury. Even if the condition itself cannot be changed, a psychologist can help determine the degree of the problem and help facilitate useful compensations.

Although one can catalog the suggested criteria for abnormality, there are broad theoretical disagreements about which of these criteria should be emphasized in practice. For example, there are phenomenologists who argue that problems do not exist unless they are perceived by the individual and reflected in personal distress. There are behaviorists who argue equally vehemently that only overt behavior should be treated. Such theoretical differences are a primary reason for differences in definitions.

A second core issue is the quantitative one, the question of how much deviance, bizarreness, inefficiency, or distress constitutes "abnormality." Many of those who use the medical model assume a dichotomy between those who have a specific mental disease and the vast majority of normals who are disease free. An alternative view is that the dimensions defining illness are continuous ones ranging from abnormality through mere adequacy to equally rare degrees of supernormality.

Defining categories of deviancy as "abnormal" presents the particularly thorny problem of the relativity of cultural standards. The actions society considers deviant seem limited to particular cultures at particular times. For example, in Victorian times, young women who had children out of wedlock were sometimes committed to hospitals for the "morally insane." Such deviant actions of one generation may later be ignored or even approved by society. A common solution to this dilemma is to distinguish deviancies requiring correction and treatment from others. Deviancies that are dangerous, harmful to others, or accompanied by personal distress are examples of the former.

A final issue pertains to the value placed on the defining process itself. According to the medical model, the definition of abnormality is all-important, central to understanding the cause of the disease and to planning treatment. Any disease should be diagnosed as soon as possible. A sharply contrasting view, held by some sociologists, is that defining, or labeling, has mostly harmful effects. Not only does labeling a person as abnormal relegate him or her to the stigma of being undesirably different, but the label itself creates a self-fulfilling prophecy as others pay particular attention to symptoms of the person's deviancy. The process is also challenged because it focuses on symptoms of the individual that may really result from difficulties in the family, the community, or even the society.

Applications

Each criterion for abnormality referred to above can be applied to many varieties of abnormality, differing in quality and degree. One important feeling of discomfort is sadness, which is called "depression" when it is considered abnormal. Another typical feeling of discomfort is anxiety: a chronic, vague, fearlike feeling of impending doom. When depression or anxiety is chronic, intense, and interferes with functioning, it is much more likely to be considered abnormal than when it is the temporary or mild feeling everyone has from time to time. These feelings are also much more likely to be considered abnormal if there is no real-life stress or crisis to explain them.

Another major criterion of abnormality is deviance, characterized by a condition or behavior that is undesirably different from that of the significant cultural group. This is not necessarily the same as being statistically different from the average of the group, as one can be statistically different in unimportant or even desirable ways. (Wolfgang Amadeus Mozart and Albert Einstein were statistically different from the average.) Rather, deviance is always different in some significant way and is undesirable.

To classify conditions as psychologically abnormal simply because they are deviant is an expansive use of the concept of abnormality that is highly controversial. There are, nevertheless, particular types of deviants that are practically always thought of as abnormal, particularly those that seem bizarre.

The key discriminator, bizarreness, involves behavior, thoughts, or feelings that do not seem consistent with any recognized social role. The deviant individual may distort reality in that he holds beliefs that violate universal assumptions about time, space, selfhood, and cause and effect. Belief in bizarre plots, seeing things that are not there, or hearing imaginary voices are all examples of such distortions. It should be pointed out that this sort of behavior seems to be accepted as abnormal in practically every known culture, although some cultures have valued such bizarreness as religious experiences.

Definitional questions are involved whenever a psychologist considers the question of whether a patient is suitable for treatment and, if so, what sorts of treatment are appropriate. Typical cases sometimes involve the referral of a case that fits only one of the criteria above. A successful lawyer, married and with an attractive family, sees his career as one of only playing silly games. Adequate and conforming, he is abnormal only by the standard of subjective discomfort. A student promoted to the fourth grade seems conscientious and hardworking, but cannot seem to do much more than first-grade work. A psychologist finds that she tests within the retarded range of intelligence. Her problem is an impairment in functioning. A youth who has wounded an owner of a jewelry store during a robbery is interviewed by a psychologist in a detention center. He explains that he did not do anything wrong, really, because the store owner could have simply collected from his insurance company and should have minded his own business. This young man, who can easily rationalize almost any behavior, feels good about himself. He is abnormal in the sense of being deviant and dangerous.

Psychodynamic or phenomenologically oriented psychologists would consider the first patient ideal; behavioral psychologists might help the second develop useful compensations. The approach to the deviant would be largely a matter of external controls.

Most cases seen by psychologists would be abnormal by more than a single criterion. A young man who cannot start the day without a couple of shots of vodka begins developing family problems and staying away from work. He both is a deviant (alcoholic) and shows an impairment in functioning. A woman in a deep depression considers herself worthless and feels she is guilty of unforgivable sins. She also moves very slowly and has stopped eating. She experiences discomfort, shows impairment, and her feelings of guilt seem to distort reality. A middle-aged accountant becomes preoccupied with the fact that he feels estranged from his wife. He thinks so much about this that his performance ratings drop. Like most of the milder cases seen by mental health professionals, subjective discomfort here results in an impairment in efficiency.

Many symptoms that could be diagnosed from a psychiatric manual may not really be considered significant or abnormal if they do not interfere with the individual's functioning. A phobia concerning flying would not be significant for those who never travel; such a phobia might be highly significant for someone who has to travel in work.

Definitional questions are also involved in collective decisions of the American Psychiatric Association (APA) when they revise their *Diagnostic and Statistical Manual of Mental Disorders* (DSM), first published in 1952. At each revision, new syndromes are proposed and borderline ones discussed. As the third edition was being prepared, homosexuality became the focus of a major controversy. Some psychodynamically oriented psychiatrists argued that homosexuality involves an impairment in mature sexual functioning, and so is inherently abnormal. The argument that homosexuals function adequately and sometimes extremely well in important areas of life and that any discomfort is largely the result of discrimination, however, prevailed. Homosexuality was removed from the DSM-III (1980) as a mental disorder.

Perspective and Prospects

Modern mental health professionals deal with an enormously varied assortment of problems. Definitions of abnormality offer a guideline as to what conditions should be treated in whom. In contrast, the pioneers of the mental health professions served limited groups of dramatically different populations in different settings.

One such limited group was the hospitalized psychotic population on which the medically oriented Emil Kraepelin, about 1900, commenced his work of classifying the behavior of patients. He hypothesized discrete diseases, each of which presumably had a specific course, outcome, and cause within the brain. Advocates of the medical model still hold that real abnormalities are brain conditions. Even in cases of such real brain impairment, it is usually behavior that reveals the abnormality.

Sigmund Freud, a pioneer of psychodynamic theory and a contemporary of Kraepelin, saw ambulatory middle-class patients who were suffering from anxiety and irrational rigidity in their behavior. Freud identified the causes as impulsive desires with various defensive strategies to keep these from awareness. The defining symptoms that brought the patients to Freud, however, were the anxiety (subjective discomfort) and the rigid, defensive behavior (impairment).

Around the middle of the twentieth century, phenomenologist Carl Rogers identified the basic problem of many of his bright young college students as a lack of self-esteem. This was caused, he believed, by the client's adopting of the artificial, unrealistic standards of others. Rogers paid attention to the client's subjective comfort, or inner attitude toward self. To the phenomenologist, a person, however deviant, who knows and likes himself, is normal. Rogers, like Freud, had faith in insight into oneself and the world "as it really is" as the key to normality.

About the same time in mid-century, the behavioral psychology of B. F. Skinner developed in the animal laboratory, and was applied to the treatment of humans. To Skinner, abnormality consisted of adjustive behavior that had not been learned (impairment) and maladjustive behavior that had been learned (deviance). Inner torment was not, to the behaviorist, a problem.

Definitions of abnormality allowed the practitioner to know the conditions appropriate for treatment and clarified the differences among practitioners. In the late twentieth century, criticism from several sources has led to a fine-tuning of these definitions. The tendency to extend the illness model to many conditions when there is no hard evidence of brain pathology and to assert medical control over these conditions was challenged by Thomas Szasz. Sociologists pointed out the negative effects of labeling as well as the relevance of family and community to problems that are defined by psychologists as individual abnormality. In contrast to widely held assumptions, research by Shelley Taylor and associates suggested that the most robust, altruistic people were not the most "realistic" and open to experience, but were rather biased toward a belief in their own good traits and good fortunes. Research and new technology in the field of medical psychology has led to an understanding of genetic or physiological components in conditions previously known only by behavior.

The mental health professions have begun to absorb this research and technology to extend an understanding of abnormalities outward to the community and inward toward underlying genetic or brain pathology. Criteria for the conditions which they define within the domain of psychology will remain the same: discomfort, disability, and deviance.

Bibliography

Altrocchi, John. *Abnormal Behavior*. New York: Harcourt Brace Jovanovich, 1980. Practically every textbook of abnormal behavior contains a discussion of the definitional problem. Altrocchi's chapter 1 offers a particularly thorough discussion, put in the historical context of alternative nonmedical approaches to abnormal conditions. Written on the introductory college level.

Carson, Robert C., James N. Butcher, and Susan Mineka. *Abnormal Psychology and Modern Life*. 11th ed. Boston: Allyn & Bacon, 2000. An up-to-date reference work on pathological psychology. A bibliography and an index are included.

Gilbert, Daniel T., Susan T. Fiske, and Gardner Lindzey, eds. *The Handbook of Social Psychology*. 4th ed. 2 vols. Boston: McGraw-Hill, 1998. Presents a general review of deviance from the perspective of several sociologists. A discussion of the variety of conditions which have been defined as deviant at different times and places, and the negative consequences of labeling. Puts the issue in a sociological perspective. Heavy going but worth it.

Jahoda, Marie. *Current Concepts of Positive Mental Health*. New York: Basic Books, 1958. Reviews and classifies the many different views of mental health, with an emphasis upon those offered by psychotherapists. Argues for attention to "psychological health," which Jahoda views as a "positive striving," not the mere absence of illness. Good as a review of the early literature on the specific problem of definition. Thorough, but some knowledge of personality theories helps.

Lazarus, Arnold A., and Andrew M. Colman, eds. *Abnormal Psychology*. New York: Longman Group, 1995. This text in pathological psychology includes bibliographical references and an index.

Phares, E. Jerry, and Timothy J. Trull. *Clinical Psychology: Concepts, Methods, and Profession*. 5th ed. Pacific Grove, Calif.: Brooks/Cole, 1997. This text for college psychology students contains a thorough description of standards for judging normality. These are discussed from the viewpoint of famous psychologists and applied to problems in psychological diagnosis. Cases of the sort found in clinical practice illustrate and help the reader comprehend the issues. Quite readable by the introductory-level student.

Wechsler, Henry, Leonard Solomon, and Bernard M. Kramer, eds. *Social Psychology and Mental Health*. New York: Holt, Rinehart and Winston, 1970. Each of the first ten papers in this edited volume consists of arguments for one of the alternative definitions of abnormality, each by a leading proponent. The papers, particularly those for and against the medical model, are classics. One would otherwise have to comb many journals to find so many important papers from a variety of perspectives.

Widiger, T. A., and T. J. Trull. "Diagnosis and Clinical Assessment." In *Annual Review of Psychology* 42. Stanford, Calif.: Annual Reviews, 1991. This article applies a consideration of definitions of abnormality to the continuing problem of specifically what sorts of disabling or distressful conditions should be included in the APA's revised diagnostic manual. Shows that psychiatrists take the definitional issue seriously.

Wilson, G. Terence, et al. *Abnormal Psychology: Integrating Perspectives*. Boston: Allyn & Bacon, 1996. A comprehensive look at the nature and treatment of psychopathologies. Accompanied by case histories, *Diagnostic and Statistical Manual of Mental Disorders: DSM-IV* tables, and critical thinking exercises.

Thomas E. DeWolfe

See also:

Abnormality: Behavioral Models; Abnormality: Biomedical Models; Abnormality: Cognitive Models; Abnormality: Family Models; Abnormality: Humanistic-Existential Models; Abnormality: Legal Models; Abnormality: Psychodynamic Models; Abnormality: Sociocultural Models.

ABNORMALITY
Behavioral Models

Type of psychology: Psychopathology
Fields of study: Behavioral and cognitive models; models of abnormality

Behavioral models of abnormal behavior use principles of learning to explain how maladaptive behaviors develop. Learning-based explanations have proved useful for both conceptualizing the development of abnormality and developing effective treatments for abnormal behaviors.

Principal terms

ABNORMALITY: a pattern of behavior that is maladaptive for the individual or society

BEHAVIOR THERAPIES: treatment approaches for abnormal behavior that are derived from principles of learning

CLASSICAL CONDITIONING: a learning principle used to explain how emotional and physiological responses can be learned

EXTINCTION: a process by means of which the probability of a behavior occurring is decreased; applies to both classical and operant conditioning and involves the unlearning of a response

OPERANT CONDITIONING: a learning principle used to explain how voluntary behavior can be learned; states that behavior is a function of its consequences

STIMULUS GENERALIZATION: the ability of stimuli that are similar to other stimuli to elicit a response that was previously elicited only by the first stimuli

Overview

The behavioral model asserts that normal as well as abnormal behaviors are acquired through learning. Unlike biomedical or psychodynamic models, which view abnormal behavior as symptoms of underlying pathology (biochemical disturbance and psychological conflicts, respectively), the behavioral model does not postulate underlying causes.

Behavioral explanations state that behavior is determined by the environment. Genetically or biologically determined variations in abilities are accepted. Apart from this, however, the behavioral model asserts that specific behavioral characteristics are acquired through learning experiences. Therefore, the same individual has the potential to develop numerous different characteristics. For example, the factors that determine whether one will become a criminal or a priest are the learning experiences one has.

Behavioral models of abnormal behavior have emerged from two basic learning processes: classical conditioning and operant conditioning. Classical conditioning is typically used to explain how emotional and physiological responses can be brought under the control of cues in the environment. For example, the emotional (for example, fear) and physiological (for example, increased heart rate) responses elicited by the presentation of a dog to an individual with cynophobia (an extreme, unrealistic fear of dogs) can be explained by classical conditioning. "Voluntary" behaviors, however, such as running away when a dog is seen, can be explained by operant conditioning.

The classical conditioning model states that by pairing a neutral stimulus with a stimulus that produces an unlearned emotional or physiological response (called the unconditioned response), the neutral stimulus (now called the conditioned stimulus) can take on properties that allow it to elicit a response (called the conditioned response) that is similar to the unconditioned response. Stimulus generalization is said to occur when stimuli that are similar to the conditioned stimulus take on the ability to elicit a conditioned response. Principles derived from the study of classical conditioning have led to the development of useful conceptualizations of fear-based abnormal behaviors.

Whereas the classical conditioning model has been useful in demonstrating how "nonvoluntary" (emotional and physiological) reactions can be learned, principles of operant conditioning have been useful in explaining goal-directed, "voluntary" behaviors. The basic assumption of the operant conditioning model is that behaviors are controlled by their consequences. Positive reinforcers are consequences that, when presented following the performance of a target behavior, result in the increased occurrence of that target behavior in the future. Negative reinforcers are consequences that allow the escape from aversive situations and result in an increase in avoidance and escape behaviors in the future. Punishers are consequences that result in the decreased occurrence of the punished behavior in the future. The operant conditioning model views the consequences of behaviors as responsible for shaping behavior, both normal and abnormal.

Behavioral explanations have been presented to explain nearly all classes of abnormal behaviors. The usefulness of this model in accounting for the etiology of the vast range of abnormal behaviors is, however, varied. Behavioral explanations have been most useful in accounting for maladaptive behaviors characterized by relatively discrete, overt responses that are considered abnormal because of their excessive, deficient, or inappropriate expression. Examples include phobias, psychophysiological disorders (abnormal physical responses not caused by physical pathology), paraphilias (abnormal sexual arousal toward nonhuman objects), and conduct disturbances (such as oppositional or delinquent behaviors). Empirical evidence exists that demonstrates the process of learning and unlearning these abnormal responses.

Abnormal behaviors that are characterized by abnormal covert processes, such as disturbances in attention, perception, thought, and emotion, do not lend themselves to behavioral explanations. For example, schizophrenia is an abnormal behavior characterized by the presence of bizarre behavior, unrealistic thoughts, auditory or visual hallucinations, and inappropriate emotional expressions. The biomedical model, which postulates underlying brain pathology, provides a more useful general explanation for the development of schizophrenia than that provided by the behavioral model.

Although the behavioral model is not useful as a general explanation for the development of some disorders, it is helpful in explaining individual differences in overt behavior across all types of abnormality. Despite the likely contribution of biological factors in the formation of some classes of abnormal behavior, environmental-learning factors also continue to be influential. Principles of classical and operant conditioning are just as responsible for shaping the behaviors of schizophrenics as they are for shaping the behaviors of everyone else. Although the environment affects persons differently (partly as a result of biological differences between individuals), it does not cease to control behavior. Thus, in many cases behavioral models offer good general explanations for abnormal behaviors, while in other cases behavioral explanations must be combined with other models to produce useful explanations.

Applications

The behavioral model of abnormal behavior has probably been credited most with providing a useful explanation for the development of phobias. A phobia is defined as a strong, persistent fear that is out of proportion to any real threat that may be present.

To explain the development of phobias, the behavioral model uses both classical and operant conditioning principles. Take, for example, the development of cynophobia. According to the classical conditioning model, the presence of a dog becomes associated with an extremely frightening situation. One such experience may be enough to cause the dog to become a conditioned stimulus for a fear reaction. A child who has never touched a dog before and who has the unfortunate experience of attempting to pet a dog that barks ferociously may develop cynophobia. The dog's ferocious bark represents the unconditioned stimulus that, without prior learning, elicits a fear response (the unconditioned response). The dog (conditioned stimulus) is the primary neutral stimulus that becomes associated with the frightening situation. The next time the child sees the same dog, he or she may respond with extreme fear even if the dog does not bark ferociously.

The principle of stimulus generalization accounts for the observation that the child has developed a phobia not only for the ferocious dog that initially frightened the child but also for all dogs and perhaps even other furry creatures such as cats and squirrels. This explanation of the development of phobias has received much empirical support. On average, 60 percent of phobic individuals can recall a traumatic event that precipitated the development of their phobia.

The second aspect of phobias that any model must explain is the fact that they tend to be persistent. The classical conditioning model predicts that the phobic response should extinguish (gradually weaken) after a few trials of facing the dog (conditioned stimulus) in the absence of ferocious barking (unconditioned stimulus). In order to explain the absence of extinction (or persistence of the phobia), the principle of negative reinforcement is used.

The principle of negative reinforcement states that any behavior that is immediately followed by escape from or avoidance of an aversive consequence will be strengthened. Phobias are persistent because individuals actively avoid or escape from situations in which the phobic object is present. The fear reduction that escape and avoidance behaviors produce results in these behaviors being strengthened in the future. Therefore, extinction trials are not given an opportunity to take place.

Behavioral therapies for phobias are also derived from learning principles. The most common therapies involve procedures that are designed to make the phobic individual face the feared object in the absence of any real danger so that extinction can take place. One procedure, which is called modeling, involves having the phobic individual observe another person (the model) performing the feared tasks. In the case of a cynophobic, the model would pet the dog in the presence of the phobic individual. As that individual becomes less frightened, he or she approaches the dog until eventually he or she is able to interact with the dog without being overwhelmed by fear.

The behavioral model has also been useful in explaining disorders of conduct, such as juvenile delinquency. Most treatment programs for conduct disorders are based upon behavioral principles. These programs provide delinquent youths with structured environments that are designed in such a way that prosocial behaviors are reinforced and antisocial or delinquent behaviors are punished. These programs have demonstrated that, by systematically controlling the consequences for prosocial as well as problem behaviors, delinquent behaviors can be controlled. Unfortunately, when the child is returned home, the old behavior-consequence contingencies may still be present, and as a result, the old behavior patterns will return.

Behavioral models have been used in combination with other models to explain the etiology of some abnormal behaviors. For example, autism, a disorder that is first expressed in childhood, is characterized by disturbed language development, a lack of interpersonal responsiveness, odd and repetitive behaviors, and resistance to changes in the environment. Although little is known about the specific etiology of this disorder, the most promising model currently is the biomedical model. This model accounts for autism by referring to disturbed neurological functioning. The behavioral model has been useful in demonstrating that, despite the presence of an apparent neurological disturbance, principles of learning also apply to these individuals. The most effective treatments for autism have been based upon principles of classical and operant conditioning. For example, language skills and appropriate social behaviors have been effectively taught by systematically using such operant-conditioning principles as positive and negative reinforcement.

Perspective and Prospects

Behavioral models of abnormality began to gain a following in the academic arena in the 1920's, after John B. Watson, commonly considered the founder of behaviorism, published a series of works on that subject. Watson argued that the focus of a scientific psychology should be overt behavior. He rejected the study of mental entities such as thoughts as useless, because such entities cannot be measured objectively and reliably. Watson proposed a model for understanding behavior that was based upon Ivan Pavlov's principles of classical conditioning. During the same decade, Pavlov published reports on what he called "experimental neurosis." In these reports, Pavlov explained how "neurotic" or abnormal behavior could be taught to dogs by using the principles of conditioning.

Two psychologists, John Dollard and Neal Miller, published a book entitled *Personality and Psychotherapy: An Analysis in Terms of Learning, Thinking, and Culture* (1950), which used principles of conditioning to explain how abnormal behavior develops and how it can be changed. This book was important in expanding the behavioral influence outside academic circles and into the applied areas of case conceptualization and treatment. At the same time that behaviorism was becoming a powerful force among academic psychologists, clinical psychologists, who were in great demand, began to provide treatment for disturbed individuals. The role of treatment provider had previously been restricted to psychiatrists. The influx of psychologists into treatment was followed by an increased influence of behavioral psychology on conceptualizing and treating abnormal behavior. In the 1950's, new treatment approaches based upon learning theories began to multiply. These treatments are referred to collectively as "behavior therapies."

Behavioral models of abnormality provide useful explanations for the etiology and treatment of numerous types of abnormal behaviors. The experimental methodology from which behaviorism has developed has also influenced other models of abnormality. This has been seen, for example, in the increased interest among psychoanalytic theorists in developing empirical tests to evaluate their theories.

Behavioral models will continue to be developed and evaluated. It is likely that interdisciplinary models will become more common in the future. For example, behavioral models have recently been combined with models from developmental psychology. Developmental psychologists study the psychological development of normal individuals across the life span. Knowledge gained from developmental psychology about the abilities and characteristics of children at different ages has been helpful in refining behavioral therapies for children. This trend shows promise for the development of more effective treatment interventions for children and adolescents.

Bibliography

Dollard, John, and Neal E. Miller. *Personality and Psychotherapy: An Analysis in Terms of Learning, Thinking, and Culture.* New York: McGraw-Hill, 1950. This classic work was very influential in bringing behavioral theories into the applied realm of explaining and treating abnormal behaviors. Phenomena such as defense mechanisms, which are concepts from psychoanalytic theory, are examined and explained within a behavioral framework. This book should be read only after the reader has gained a basic knowledge of psychoanalytic and behavioral models of abnormality.

Masters, John C., et al. *Behavior Therapy: Techniques and Empirical Findings.* 3d ed. San Diego: Harcourt Brace Jovanovich, 1987. Provides an exhaustive review of behavioral therapies. Theoretical explanations as well as reviews of empirical finding are presented. This text offers an introductory yet complete presentation of behavior therapy. Useful as a reference text for specific behavior therapies.

Plaud, Joseph J., and Georg H. Eifert, eds. *From Behavior Theory to Behavior*

Therapy. Boston: Allyn & Bacon, 1998. A discussion of behavioral theories and therapies. Includes bibliographical references and an index.

Rosenhan, David L., and Martin E. P. Seligman. "The Environmentalist Model: Behavioral and Cognitive Approaches." In *Abnormal Psychology.* 3d ed. New York: W. W. Norton, 1995. This chapter provides an easy-to-read introduction to behavioral models of abnormality. The basic assumptions of behavioral models are discussed, and interesting case conceptualizations from a behavioral perspective are given. This is a good source for the reader who is interested in a brief yet informative presentation of behavioral models of abnormality.

Skinner, B. F. *Science and Human Behavior.* New York: Free Press, 1953. This book is considered a classic among behavioral psychologists. Skinner presents the principles of operant conditioning and then uses them to explain human behavior at the private, social, and cultural levels. The depth of presentation precludes this book from being a good reference book. For the serious student of behaviorism, however, this is required reading.

Weissman, Myrna M., John C. Markowitz, and Gerald L. Klerman. *Comprehensive Guide to Interpersonal Psychotherapy.* New York: Basic Books, 2000. This text in basic behavorial science discusses depression and other mental disorders, interpersonal relations, and methods of psychotherapy. A bibliography and an index are provided.

Wolpe, Joseph. *Psychotherapy by Reciprocal Inhibition.* Stanford, Calif.: Stanford University Press, 1958. Wolpe's development of a treatment technique called systematic desensitization led to a rapid acceptance of behaviorally based interventions. In this classic book, Wolpe provides a learning-based explanation for abnormal behaviors. Clinical and experimental support is given for behavioral interventions. The chapters are arranged in such a way that the book can be used as a reference for varying principles in the behavioral model.

Mark A. Williams

See also:

Abnormality; Agoraphobia and Panic Disorders; Anxiety Disorders; Aversion, Implosion, and Systematic Desensitization Therapies; Behavioral Assessment and Personality Rating Scales; Behavioral Family Therapy; Operant Conditioning Therapies; Phobias.

ABNORMALITY
Biomedical Models

Type of psychology: Psychopathology
Fields of study: Models of abnormality; organic disorders

Biomedical models of abnormality examine the roles of medical, neurological, and biochemical factors in creating psychological disturbances. Psychologists have come to realize that many disturbances have a significant biomedical component or are, in some cases, primarily organic. This had led to the development of more effective biomedical therapies, such as drug therapies, for these disorders.

Principal terms

ANTIDEPRESSANT DRUGS: drugs such as iproniazid, imipramine, and amitriptyline that are used to treat depression

ANTIPSYCHOTIC DRUGS: drugs such as chlorpromazine and clozapine that alleviate the symptoms of schizophrenia; also called neuroleptics

BIOGENIC AMINES: a class of neurotransmitter chemicals in the brain, including dopamine, norepinephrine, and serotonin

DIFFERENTIAL DIAGNOSIS: distinguishing between two or more illnesses that have the same or very similar symptoms

LIMBIC SYSTEM: a system of structures in the brain that regulates emotional responsiveness and plays a role in learning and memory

NEUROTRANSMITTER: a chemical that is secreted from one nerve cell and stimulates receptors on another nerve cell, thus transmitting a message between them

PRIMARY DISORDER: the principal disorder, not the result of some other medical condition, as opposed to a secondary disorder, in which the disorder and its symptoms result from some other medical condition

TRANQUILIZERS: drugs such as Librium and Valium that are used to treat anxiety disorders; also called antianxiety drugs or anxiolytics

Overview

The study of biomedical bases for mental illnesses and their treatment is called biological psychiatry or biopsychiatry. A basic premise of biopsychiatry is that psychiatric symptoms occur in many conditions—some psychological and some medical.

Inherent in this viewpoint is a new outlook on mental illness. Faced with a patient who is lethargic, has lost his or her appetite, cannot sleep normally, and feels sad, traditional psychotherapists may diagnose him or her as suffering from one of the depressive disorders. Usually, the bias is that this illness is psychological in origin and calls for treatment with psychotherapy. Biopsychiatrists, however, see depression not as a diagnosis, but as a description of the patient's condition. The task of diagnosing—of finding the underlying illness—remains to be done.

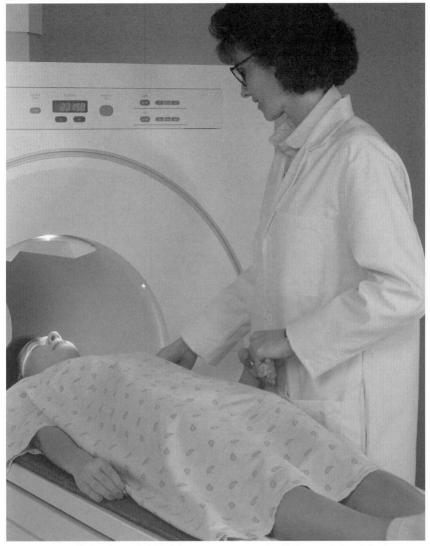

A computed tomography (CT) scan is recommended to rule out possible organic causes of psychiatric distress. (Digital Stock)

After examining the patient and doing a battery of medical tests, the biopsychiatrist, too, may conclude that the condition is a primary mood disorder. Further tests may reveal whether it is caused by life stresses, in which case psychotherapy is called for, or by biochemical imbalances in the brain, in which case drug therapy—perhaps in concert with psychotherapy—is called for. The medical tests may indicate that the depression is secondary to a medical condition—such as Addison's disease or cancer of the pancreas—in which case medical treatment of the primary condition is called for.

An important distinction must be made between psychiatric conditions resulting from the psychological stress of having a serious illness and psychiatric conditions resulting from chemical imbalances or endocrine disturbances produced by the illness. For example, the knowledge that one has pancreatic cancer can certainly lead to depression. This is a primary mood disorder that can be treated with psychotherapy. According to Mark Gold, a leading biopsychiatrist, however, depression occurs secondarily to pancreatic cancer in up to three-quarters of patients who have the disease and may precede physical symptoms by many years. In such a case, psychotherapy not only would be pointless but also would actually put the patient's life at risk if it delayed diagnosis of the underlying cancer.

According to Gold, there are at least seventy-five medical diseases that can produce psychiatric symptoms. Among these are endocrine disorders, including diseases of the thyroid, adrenal, and parathyroid glands; disorders of the blood and cardiovascular system; infectious diseases, such as hepatitis and syphilis; vitamin-deficiency diseases caused by niacin and folic acid deficiencies; temporal-lobe and psychomotor epilepsies; drug abuse and side effects of prescription drugs; head injury; brain tumors and other cancers; neurodegenerative diseases such as Alzheimer's, Huntington's, and Parkinson's diseases; multiple sclerosis; stroke; poisoning by toxic chemicals, such as metals or insecticides; respiratory disorders; and mineral imbalances.

After medical illnesses are ruled out, the psychiatric symptoms can be attributed to a primary psychological disorder. This is not to say that biomedical factors are unimportant. Compelling evidence indicates that the more severe psychotic disorders are caused by biochemical imbalances in the brain.

The evidence of genetic predispositions for schizophrenia, major depressive disorder, and manic-depressive disorder is strong. The function of genes is to regulate biochemical activity within cells, which implies that these disorders are caused by biochemical abnormalities.

Research suggests that schizophrenia, in most cases, results from an abnormality in the dopamine neurotransmitter system in the brain. All drugs that effectively treat schizophrenia block the action of dopamine, and the more powerfully they do so, the more effective they are therapeutically. Furthermore, overdoses of drugs, such as amphetamines, that strongly stimulate the dopamine system often cause a schizophrenialike psychosis. Finally, studies show that, in certain areas of the brain in schizophrenic patients, tissues are abnormally sensitive to dopamine.

In major depressive disorders, the biogenic amine theory is strongly supported. Biogenic amines, among which are dopamine, norepinephrine, and serotonin, are neurotransmitters in the brain that are concentrated in the limbic system, which regulates emotional responses. Biogenic amines were originally implicated by the observation that drugs that deplete them in the brain, such as reserpine, frequently cause depression, whereas drugs that stimulate them, such as amphetamines, cause euphoria. Studies of cerebrospinal fluid have revealed abnormalities in the biochemical activity of these amines in some depressed patients. In many suicidally depressed patients, for example, serotonin activity in the brain is unusually low. In other depressed patients, norepinephrine or dopamine activity is deficient. These patients often respond well to antidepressant medications, which increase the activity of the biogenic amine neurotransmitter systems.

Less severe neurotic, emotional disturbances may also have biochemical explanations in some patients. Research suggests that mild or moderate depressions often result from learned helplessness, a condition in which the person has learned that his or her behavior is ineffective in controlling reinforcing or punishing consequences. Experiments show that this produces depletion of norepinephrine in the brain, as do other psychological stressors that cause depression. These patients also are sometimes helped by antidepressant drugs.

Finally, many anxiety disorders may result from biochemical imbalances in the brain. Drugs that alleviate anxiety, such as Librium (chlordiazepoxide) and Valium (diazepam), have powerful effects on a brain neurotransmitter called gamma aminobutyric acid (GABA), as do other tranquilizers, such as alcohol and barbiturates. GABA is an inhibitory neurotransmitter that acts to keep brain activity from running away with itself, so to speak. When GABA is prevented from acting, the result is agitation, seizures, and death. Positron emission tomography (PET) scans of the brains of people suffering from panic attacks show that they have abnormally high activity in a part of the limbic system called the parahippocampal gyrus, an effect that might be caused by a GABA deficiency there.

Applications

Understanding the biomedical factors that cause illnesses with psychiatric symptoms leads directly to improved diagnoses and subsequent patient care. Numerous studies have shown that psychiatric disorders are misdiagnosed between 25 percent and 50 percent of the time, the most persistent bias being toward diagnosing medical problems as psychological illnesses. A study published in 1981 by Richard Hall and colleagues found that, of one hundred psychiatric patients admitted consecutively to a state hospital, eighty had a physical illness that required medical treatment but had not been diagnosed in preadmission screening. In twenty-eight of these patients, proper medical treatment resulted in rapid and dramatic clearing of their psychiatric symptoms. In another eighteen patients, medical treatment resulted in substantial improvement of their psychiatric conditions. In an earlier study, Hall and colleagues found that 10 percent of psychiatric outpatients—those whose conditions were not severe enough to require hospitalization—had medical disorders that caused or contributed to their psychiatric illnesses.

Psychiatric symptoms are often among the earliest warning signs of dangerous, even life-threatening, medical illnesses. Thus, proper physical evaluation and differential diagnosis, especially of patients with psychiatric symptoms not obviously of psychological origin, are critical. In other cases, psychiatric illnesses result from biochemical imbalances in the brain. In any case, patients and therapists alike must be wary of uncritically accepting after-the-fact psychological explanations. A psychological bias can all too easily become a self-fulfilling prophecy, to the detriment of the patient's health and well-being.

Hall and colleagues found that a medical workup consisting of psychiatric and physical examinations, complete blood-chemistry analysis, urinalysis and urine drug screening, electrocardiography (ECG or EKG), and electroencephalography (EEG) successfully identified more than 90 percent of the medical illnesses present in their sample of one hundred psychiatric patients. The authors recommend that such a workup be done routinely for all patients admitted to psychiatric hospitals.

E. Fuller Torrey makes similar recommendations for patients admitted to psychiatric hospitals because of schizophrenia. He recommends that a thorough examination include a careful and complete medical history and mental-status examination, with assistance from family members and friends if necessary. Physical and neurological examinations are also recommended. A blood count, blood-chemical screen, and urinalysis should be done to reveal conditions such as anemia, metal poisoning, endocrine or metabolic imbalances, syphilis, and drug abuse. A computed tomography (CT) scan may be necessary to clarify suspicions of brain abnormalities. Some doctors recommend that a CT scan be done routinely to detect conditions such as brain tumors, neurodegenerative diseases, subdural hematomas (bleeding into the brain resulting from head injuries), viral encephalitis, and other conditions that might be missed upon initial neurological screening. Torrey also recommends a routine examination of cerebrospinal fluid obtained by lumbar puncture, which can reveal viral infections, brain injury, and biochemical abnormalities in the brain, and a routine electroencephalogram, which can reveal abnormal electrical activity in the brain caused by infections, inflammations, head injury, or epilepsy.

If any medical disorder is discovered, it should be treated appropriately. If this does not result in clearing the psychiatric symptoms, Torrey recommends that antipsychotic medications be given. If the initial drug trial is unsuccessful, then the dosage may have to be adjusted or another drug tried, since a patient's response to medication can be quite idiosyncratic. About 5 percent of patients react adversely to medication, in which case it may have to be discontinued.

Mark Gold makes parallel recommendations for patients with depressive and anxiety disorders. In patients who have depressive symptoms, tests for thyroid function are particularly important. Perhaps 10 to 15 percent of depressed patients test positive for thyroid disorder. Hypothyroidism, especially before the disease is fully developed, may present only psychiatric, particularly depressive, symptoms. Hyperthyroidism may be indicated by depression, mania, or psychosis. Blood and urine screens for drug abuse are also indicated for patients with depression.

Patients who are found to have a primary mood disorder may be candidates for antidepressant drug therapy. Since responses to these medications are highly idiosyncratic, careful monitoring of patients is required. Blood tests can determine whether the drug has reached an ideally effective concentration in the body.

In some cases, even biological depressions can be treated without drugs. Seasonal affective disorder (SAD), also called winter depression, may be treated with exposure to full-spectrum lights that mimic sunlight, a process called phototherapy. Studies suggest that this alters activity in the pineal gland, which secretes melatonin, a hormone that has mood-altering effects. Similarly, some depressions may result from biological rhythms that are out of synchronization. Exposure to lights is often helpful in such cases, as is sleep deprivation.

In anxious patients, tests for endocrine function, especially hyperthyroidism, are called for, as are tests of the cardiovascular system and tests for drug abuse. In patients in whom no primary medical disorder is identified, the use of antianxiety medications may be indicated. Patients on medication should be closely monitored. Psychotherapy, such as behavior therapy for avoidant behaviors engendered by panic attacks and phobias, is also indicated.

As the public becomes more knowledgeable about the biomedical factors in psychiatric illnesses, malpractice lawsuits against therapists who misdiagnose these illnesses or who misapply psychotherapy and psychoactive drug therapy are becoming more common. In the future, it is likely that all manner of mental health providers will have to become more medically sophisticated and rely more on medical testing for the purpose of the differential diagnosis of illnesses presenting psychiatric symptoms.

Perspective and Prospects

Theories of abnormal behavior have existed since prehistoric times. At first, these centered on supernatural forces. Behavior disturbances were thought to result from invasion by evil spirits. Treatment was likely to consist of trephining—drilling a hole in the skull to allow malevolent spirits to escape. The threat of trephination must have motivated many psychotic individuals to stay out of public view or to comply as nearly as possible with social expectations.

In the fourth century B.C.E., the Greek physician Hippocrates proposed the first rudimentary biomedical theory. He proposed that illnesses, including mental illnesses, resulted from imbalances in vital bodily fluids. His break with supernatural explanations resulted in more humane treatment of the mentally ill. Unfortunately, this trend proved to be abortive. By medieval times, theories of abnormality had reverted to demonology. Mental illness was often attributed to demoniac possession, and "treatment" was sometimes little less than torture.

The Renaissance, with its revival of learning and interest in nature, initially saw little change in this attitude. People whose behavior was considered peculiar were often accused of witchcraft or of conspiring with the devil. As knowledge of the human organism increased, however, superstitions again gave way to speculation that "insanity" resulted from physical illness or injury. The mentally ill were consigned to asylums where, it was hoped, they would be treated by physicians. In most cases, unfortunately, asylums were essentially prisons, and medical treatment, when available, was rarely effective.

Two historical movements were responsible for restoring humane treatment to the mentally ill. The first was a moral reform movement ushered in by such individuals as Phillipe Pinel in France, William Tuke in England, and Dorothea Dix in America.

The second was continuing research in chemistry, biology, and medicine. By the nineteenth century, the brain was recognized as the seat of human reasoning and emotion. Once thought to be a place of supernatural happenings, the brain was finally revealed to be an organ not unlike the liver. Like the liver, the brain is subject to organic disturbances, and the result of these is similarly predictable—namely, psychological abnormalities. Discovery of diseases, such as advanced syphilis, that cause brain deterioration and are characterized by psychological symptoms, supported this organic model.

By the mid-twentieth century, little reasonable doubt remained that some psychological disturbances have biomedical causes. Interest centered especially on schizophrenia, major depressive disorder, and manic-depressive psychosis (later called bipolar disorder). Genetic studies strongly indicated that organic factors existed in each of these illnesses, and research was directed toward finding the biomedical fault and effecting a cure.

Paradoxically, effective treatments were found before medical understanding of the disorders was achieved. Therapeutic drugs were developed first for schizophrenia, then for depression, and finally for anxiety. These drugs proved to be important research tools, leading directly to discovery of neurotransmitter systems in the brain and helping to elucidate the biochemical nature of brain functioning. Much neuroscience research is still motivated by the desire for a better biomedical understanding of psychological disorders, which will ultimately lead to more effective treatments and patient care for these conditions.

Bibliography

Andreasen, Nancy C. *The Broken Brain: The Biological Revolution in Psychiatry.* New York: Harper & Row, 1984. An excellent introduction to biopsychiatry for the general reader. Andreasen's summary of brain structure and function, and their relationship to mood and behavior, is one of the best in a book of this type. Highly recommended.

Bellenir, Karen, ed. *Mental Health Disorders Sourcebook: Basic Consumer Health Information About Anxiety Disorders, Depression, and Other Mood Disorders.* 2d ed. Detroit: Omnigraphics, 2000. A volume on mental illness in the health reference series. Includes a bibliography and an index.

Buckley, Peter F., and John L. Waddington, eds. *Schizophrenia and Mood Disorders: The New Drug Therapies in Clinical Practice.* Woburn, Mass.: Butterworth-Heinemann, 2000. A volume on psychopharmacology. Includes bibliographical references and an index.

Gold, Mark S. *The Good News About Depression: Cures and Treatments in the New Age of Psychiatry.* New York: Random House, 1986. Written in a light, easy-to-read style, this book discusses the myriad biomedical conditions that can lead to depression and describes how they can be diagnosed and treated. Especially valuable for someone who is contemplating psychiatric treatment for depression or who has a loved one who is.

_____. *The Good News About Panic, Anxiety, and Phobias.* New York: Random House, 1989. Written for the nontechnical reader, this book offers a good general summary of anxiety disorders, their diagnosis (and misdiagnosis), and their treatment. The second half deals specifically with the biopsychiatric approach to anxiety. Gold's books also include extensive bibliographies and state-by-state listings of experts in the field.

Gottesman, Irving I. *Schizophrenia Genesis: The Origins of Madness.* New York:

W. H. Freeman, 1991. An excellent, well-written resource on the causes of schizophrenia that can be understood without a technical background. Highly recommended.

Torrey, E. Fuller. *Surviving Schizophrenia: A Manual for Families, Consumers, and Providers.* 3d ed. New York: HarperPerennial, 1995. An excellent book for the general reader on schizophrenia. It should be read by everyone interested in the disorder, including every mental health worker.

Willner, Paul. *Depression: A Psychobiological Synthesis.* New York: John Wiley & Sons, 1985. This book was written for the specialist in the field but is not beyond the reach of readers with a solid background in science, especially chemistry (but keep a medical dictionary close by). The bibliography is very extensive.

William B. King

See also:

Abnormality; Agoraphobia and Panic Disorders; Anxiety Disorders; Depression; Madness: Historical Concepts; Manic-Depressive Disorder; Psychoactive Drug Therapy; Schizophrenia; Schizophrenia: High-Risk Children; Seasonal Affective Disorder.

ABNORMALITY
Cognitive Models

Type of psychology: Psychopathology
Fields of study: Behavioral and cognitive models; cognitive processes; models of
abnormality

The cognitive perspective on psychopathology asserts that faulty thinking in the
form of irrational or illogical thought processes leads to abnormal behavior;
although the cognitive approach has been criticized for overlooking biological or
genetic influences, it has led to effective treatments for anxiety and depression.

Principal terms

APPRAISAL: a short-term cognitive process; an automatic evaluation of an event
based on past experience
ATTRIBUTION: a short-term cognitive process in which the cause of an event is
assigned to someone or something
COGNITIONS: thoughts believed to lead to certain behavioral responses
COGNITIVE BEHAVIOR THERAPY: therapy that integrates principles of learning
theory with cognitive strategies to treat disorders such as depression, anxiety,
and other behavioral problems (smoking, obesity)
COGNITIVE BIAS: the particular way in which one sees the world and forms a basis
for interpreting or misinterpreting events from a certain perspective
COGNITIVE EXPECTANCY: the belief that something done by oneself or others will
lead to a certain outcome
COGNITIVE PROCESSES: the processes a person uses to become aware of events or
things and their mental representations: learning, memory, images, reason, and
problem solving

Overview

Cognitive models of abnormality assume that the way a person interprets and
evaluates experience through his or her thoughts leads directly to emotional and
behavioral consequences. These units of thought are called cognitions. Activities
involving reasoning, memory, imagining, problem solving, and decision making
form the mental representations of events in one's life and are called cognitive
processes. Short-term cognitive processes are referred to as "expectations, attributions, and appraisals," and long-term cognitive processes are called "beliefs."
When viewing psychopathology (the study of abnormal behavior) from a cognitive
perspective, illogical, erroneous, or irrational thoughts are seen as the cause of the
maladaptive behavioral responses.

Behaviorists believe that maladaptive behavior is learned through the principles
of conditioning and reinforcement; however, cognitive psychologists note that
phobias, fear reactions, or aggressive behavior can be acquired through observa-

tion or modeling alone, without any direct experience, as Albert Bandura demonstrated in the case of aggression. Bandura conducted a study in which children observed and then imitated adult "parental models" whom they viewed punching and kicking an inflatable "Bobo" doll. It became increasingly apparent that strict behavioral explanations for abnormal behavior were inadequate. Cognitive psychologists began to look for the intervening variable and proposed that the key to behavioral responses is the way people think about and perceive events. The children who imitated the parental models probably thought, "If a grown-up can kick and punch that doll, then I can too."

Dissonant cognitions and their contribution to anxiety disorders or neurotic behavior was explained by Carl Rogers in the early 1960's. Rogers believed that the stronger the magnitude or perception of threat, the more likely it is that a person will resort to denying or distorting the event. This happens as the person attempts to cope with information that is dissonant (does not fit) with his or her expectations. As a result of this process, Rogers suggested, one's self-image lowers as coping strategies for anxiety begin to fail.

Aaron T. Beck and Donald Meichenbaum both developed comprehensive theories regarding the influence of cognitive processes on the onset and maintenance of psychiatric disorders such as anxiety and depression. Beck systematically studied the illogical or negative thought processes of an individual that occur in response to stimuli through a process called rational analysis. He set up a series of homework assignments, designed to be accomplished easily, to assist the client in changing maladaptive thoughts and behaviors. By encouraging the client to engage in behaviors he or she has previously avoided, Beck demonstrated the ability to change the irrational beliefs that had inhibited those behaviors in the first place.

Beck's cognitive interpretation of anxiety disorders is the following: Such a disorder has occurred when a person has a negative, distorted view (schema) of some event, thing, or person and responds with anxiety when exposed to the feared situation or stimulus because of this distorted view. These cognitive errors are thought to be based on early experiences, and they lead to negative attributions, such as "I did not get promoted because I cannot handle any stress," or to negative appraisals, such as "I am a nervous person." Expectations are other forms of short-term cognitions; they include "outcome expectations" that refer to the desired outcome and "efficacy expectations" that refer to whether the person has the capacity to accomplish a behavior that produces a desired outcome. Attributions, or automatic explanations for events, can be global ("I am a failure at everything") or specific ("I am not good at football"). They can be stable (fixed), as in "I will always be unhappy," or unstable (changing), as in "I am having a bad day but tomorrow will be better," and can be internal, as in "It is my fault I had an accident; I should have seen the car coming through the stop sign," or external, as in "The other person ran the stop sign and hit my car." A cognitive therapist tries to get clients to adjust their attributions to be specific, unstable, and external in order to improve problems such as anxiety.

Beck used the cognitive model to understand how depression arises and is maintained. He proposed the existence of a "negative cognitive triad" that consists of negative thoughts about the present, the past, and the future. This negative triad forms a vicious circle of thinking that leads to the hopelessness and helplessness associated with depressive disorders. A cognitive therapist would intervene at any point in the triad to change the pessimistic outlook and to help the client increase involvement in positive rewarding experiences.

Donald Meichenbaum, a cognitive therapist, explored a client's illogical beliefs and used an interview style he called "Columbo style interviewing," in which the therapist encourages the client to assist in solving the mystery of why illogical thoughts are allowed to influence the client's behavior. Meichenbaum, in a supportive but gently confrontational manner, engaged the client in the therapeutic task. Most cognitive psychologists use techniques such as "thought substitution" and "behavioral substitution" to replace negative thoughts and behaviors with more appropriate behaviors. The process of changing the negative or illogical thought processes has been called cognitive restructuring. For example, Meichenbaum might say to a client, "Maybe you think you have no friends or that no one likes you, but that cannot be true, because you just named six people with whom you socialize regularly. I wonder if you can help me figure this puzzle out?"

Albert Ellis used a form of cognitive therapy he called rational-emotive therapy to accomplish the corrective process. Ellis used a technique called disputation to help a person replace damaging thoughts such as "I should always be perfect" or "Everyone must always love me" with more realistic ideas. Ellis's belief that people are ruled by their "shoulds" and "musts" and need to become aware of this to live happier and fuller lives led to his treatment approach.

Cognitive processes have been examined as contributors to childhood psychopathology. Developmental psychologists focus on cognitive functions as organizing capacities for children's ego functions. This model uses an information-processing analogy for the various ego functions (reasoning, problem solving, and so on). As the child progresses developmentally and cognitively, the cognitive information-processing functions become more complex and sophisticated. Individuals who have difficulty with these cognitive functions may be more vulnerable to experiencing psychopathology, since their ego functions are not as flexible or adaptive as those of a person who has achieved higher developmental levels of cognitive functioning. Children who have major psychiatric disorders such as schizophrenia may have immature, egocentric ego capacity, compared to mentally healthy children. This cognitive information-processing model has been expanded to adult psychopathology by Michael F. Basch in his book *Understanding Psychotherapy* (1988).

Applications

David Shapiro applied the theory of different levels of cognitive organization to personality styles. His book *Neurotic Styles* (1965) illustrates with intriguing examples the psychopathological forms of experiencing, perceiving, and relating to the world that accompany depressive, obsessive-compulsive, paranoid, and other personality styles.

Many other types of psychiatric problems have been addressed by the cognitive model. Alan Marlatt used the cognitive approach to explain the addictive cycle of alcohol "craving" and chronic drinking. A person's cognitive expectancy that alcohol will reduce anxiety or help him or her get through a difficult social situation fuels the person's desire for alcohol or other addictive substances. Marlatt's work has been utilized in the treatment of obesity, in which the addictive substance is food, and the process of craving and cognitive expectancy is thought to be in some ways similar to that of alcohol abuse. If a person who is obese can change the automatic negative thoughts that accompany a lapse (a temporary reversion to maladaptive habits), such as "I binged once this week; therefore I am a failure at managing my weight, so why bother trying to lose any more weight?" to more positive thoughts, such as "Well, I have only binged once this week, I can compensate with more exercise," it allows him or her to regain control over his or her behavior and resume positive weight-management strategies. If an obese individual does not regain control cognitively and behaviorally over his or her eating habits, the risk of relapse becomes greater.

Cognitive-behavioral approaches have been applied in group settings with eating-disordered populations and in couples therapy for marital problems. Meichenbaum applied the cognitive approach to stress management in a treatment approach outlined in his book *Stress Inoculation Training: A Clinical Guidebook* (1985). In this application, he developed a short manual designed to help a therapist take a person through the steps of preparing for and coping with various stressors.

Self-help programs are available and are increasing in popularity for individuals who have discrete problems such as having difficulty relaxing or difficulty with smoking cessation, test anxiety, stress management, or chronic headache. These programs, often on audiotapes or in books, utilize cognitive strategies to address negative thought patterns associated with these problems and substitute more appropriate thoughts and behaviors in a process called cognitive restructuring. In addition, these self-help programs use practice homework assignments—daily logs or journals to document and record behavior change toward the targeted goal.

A set of audiotapes, developed in 1991 by Thomas Cash, utilizes cognitive strategies to identify cognitive distortions and correct distorted body image. He found a total of twelve cognitive errors that people make that affect body image negatively, such as "magnification of flaws," "overlooking assets," and "comparing oneself to more beautiful others." Cash's research found that as many as 40 percent of normal-weight women and 30 percent of normal-weight men are dissatisfied with some aspects of their physical appearance. If normal-weight individuals have difficulty with body image, then one can imagine the problems someone with an eating disorder has with accepting his or her body. In fact, one of the most difficult aspects to treat in individuals with eating disorders is the cognitive problem of body-image distortion.

Perspective and Prospects
The cognitive model was born out of a dissatisfaction with models of "radical behaviorism" of the 1950's. Cognitive psychologists believed that there was more to understanding abnormal behavior than just looking at the connection between

an environmental event or stimulus and the resulting behavior—the approach used by the most prominent behavioral psychologist at the time, B. F. Skinner. In other words, cognitive psychologists believe that understanding the way people interpret or evaluate events in their lives is the key to correcting faulty thinking and abnormal behavior. The cognitive psychology movement in relation to understanding and treating psychopathology is relatively new, starting sometime in the early 1960's; many important studies were conducted in the 1970's and 1980's.

Aaron T. Beck began publishing his work on the cognitive aspects of depression in the 1960's. Continuing that line of research, he expanded it into the cognitive understanding of anxiety disorders and their treatment. Beck's studies on hopelessness and suicide spanned the decades from the 1970's to the 1990's. He found that the single best predictor for future suicide was the cognitive variable of hopelessness, and he developed the Beck Depression Inventory (BDI) to measure the cognitive, behavioral, motivational, and physical aspects of depression. Treatment of personality-disordered individuals from the cognitive perspective was introduced by Beck in his book *Cognitive Therapy of Personality Disorders* (1990). For a long time, many in the helping professions thought that individuals with personality disorders (long-standing maladaptive ways of perceiving and behaving) were untreatable. There have been some effective approaches for understanding and treating characterological problems with psychodynamic methods, but these have been criticized for being time-consuming and expensive. Beck's cognitive therapy for personality disorders holds the promise of utilizing briefer forms of treatment for people with personality disorders.

Donald Meichenbaum published *Cognitive-Behavior Modification: An Integrative Approach* (1977) and presented numerous workshops on the cognitive treatment of depression to professional therapists and counselors from virtually every mental health discipline. Arnold Lazarus developed the multimodal approach to treatment in the 1970's, which consists of the following components, referred to as the "basic id": behavioral, affective, sensation, interpersonal, cognitive, imaging, and drugs (for psychotropic medication). Lazarus demonstrated success with his multimodal comprehensive treatment approach for individuals with severe disorders such as schizophrenia. Lazarus and Alan Fay applied the cognitive-behavioral approach to the treatment of couples in marital therapy and wrote a number of useful books on this subject. Some are designed for the general public as self-help reference tools to be used as an adjunct to therapy.

Wallace Wilkins, like Beck, applied cognitive psychotherapy principles to the treatment of mood disorders. He used an approach that he called personal empowering strategies for improving moods, which works on the principle of increasing self-enhancing thoughts to improve mood and behavior. Wilkins outlined a three-step process: building a foundation, identifying self-limiting thoughts, and perishing thoughts. His list of perishable thoughts is long and includes black-or-white thinking; catastrophic thinking; shoulds, oughts, and musts; perfectionistic evaluation standards; and many others. He helped clients change two critical processes: externalizing causes for success and internalizing causes for failure.

Beginning in the late 1980's, the area of developmental psychopathology gained a foothold and a new momentum in the study of abnormality. This discipline represents the marriage of clinical and developmental psychology in the joint effort to understand the development and maintenance of psychiatric disorders. New models for comprehending abnormal psychology, particularly in children but also in adults, have been generated from this approach. Philip Cowan developed the "nine-cell model," which represents a three-by-three matrix for the conceptualization of psychopathology. He incorporated biological, environmental, and interactive aspects on the horizontal axis, with individual, psychological (cognitive), and relationship aspects on the vertical axis. The resulting framework of nine cells allows the reader to understand the interrelationship of multidimensional contributors to psychopathology and shows the many ways one can intervene in any of the cells to begin the corrective treatment process. Each cell contains a theoretical cause for the disorder and a proposed treatment. In the future, comprehensive models such as Cowan's nine-cell model may further clarify the interconnection of cognitive processes with behavioral, biological, interpersonal, environmental, and genetic variables.

Bibliography

Beck, Aaron T., and Gary Emery. *Anxiety Disorders and Phobias: A Cognitive Perspective*. New York: Basic Books, 1985. This book gives the reader a more in-depth understanding of the specific cognitive aspects that are involved in the development and maintenance of anxiety disorders. There is a focus on phobias, one of the most common types of anxiety disorders experienced by both children and adults in Western society.

Beck, Aaron T., A. J. Rush, B. F. Shaw, and Gary Emery. *Cognitive Therapy of Depression*. New York: Guilford Press, 1979. One of the most helpful resources in bringing the reader to an awareness of how specific types of cognitive-behavioral therapeutic interventions can be utilized to treat depression. Depression has been called the "common cold" of emotional disorders and has affected as many as one out of every ten to twenty people in the United States.

Holmes, David S. "Theoretical Perspectives." In *Abnormal Psychology*. New York: Harper Collins, 1991. Holmes reviews the major theoretical perspectives and models that aid in understanding abnormal psychology in this abnormal psychology textbook. Provides a critique of cognitive and other models and gives examples that illustrate the models.

McCullough, James P., Jr. *Treatment for Chronic Depression: Cognitive Behavioral Analysis System of Psychotherapy (CBASP)*. New York: Guilford Press, 2000. Discusses the diagnosis of and therapy for depressive disorder. Includes bibliographical references and an index.

McMullin, Rian E. *The New Handbook of Cognitive Therapy Techniques*. Rev. ed. New York: W. W. Norton, 2000. A manual discussing cognitive therapies. Includes bibliographical references and an index.

Meichenbaum, Donald. *Cognitive-Behavior Modification: An Integrative Approach*. New York: Plenum Press, 1977. Explains the process and technique of cognitive-behavioral therapy in an easy-to-understand way. The author presents illustrative examples and is able to bring to life the types of problems that people are likely to have and the corresponding interventions from which they may benefit.

_____. *Stress Inoculation Training: A Clinical Guidebook*. New York: Pergamon Press, 1985. This brief, concise manual covers the areas of stress reactions and outlines the strategies that can be used to intervene or to prevent negative reactions to stressful experiences.

Willerman, Lee, and D. B. Cohen. *Psychopathology*. New York: McGraw-Hill, 1990. Provides a general introduction to psychopathology with a more sophisticated discussion of theoretical facets of abnormality, psychiatric disorders, and their treatments.

Karen Wolford

See also:

Abnormality; Addictive Personality and Behaviors; Aggression: Definitions and Theoretical Explanations; Aggression: Reduction and Control; Alcoholism; Anorexia Nervosa and Bulimia Nervosa; Cognitive Behavior Therapy; Cognitive Therapy; Eating Disorders; Rational-Emotive Therapy; Reality Therapy; Transactional Analysis.

ABNORMALITY
Family Models

Type of psychology: Psychopathology
Fields of study: Interpersonal relations; models of abnormality

Dysfunctional family communications and structures have been regarded as contributing to psychopathology of family members. These faulty communications and structures can lead to the scapegoating and labeling of vulnerable family members. In certain families, significant psychopathology in either or both parents can lead to disturbed family communications including double-bind messages, denial or injection of meaning, and distortion of meaning.

Principal terms

DOUBLE-BIND COMMUNICATION: a statement that contains two independent and contradictory messages; results in a "no-win" situation for the recipient of the communication

DYSFUNCTIONAL FAMILY: a family grouping that is characterized by the presence of disturbed interactions and communications; an abusive, incestuous, or alcoholic family

SCAPEGOATING: the targeting of one member of a family, usually a child, by the other members as the "problem child" or "identified patient"

SCHISMATIC FAMILY STRUCTURE: a disturbed family structure that is created when there is marital hostility and the child or children are forced to mediate between the parents or choose sides in the marital problem

SCHIZOPHRENOGENIC: a term that refers to a parent whose communication style is dominated by double-bind or contradictory communications to the child

SKEWED FAMILY STRUCTURE: a disturbed family structure formed when a parent is mentally ill and the other parent and members of the family "adopt" the distorted view of the mentally ill parent to keep peace in the home

SYMBIOTIC RELATIONSHIP: an overprotective, often enmeshed relationship between a parent and child

Overview

A certain amount of conflict, stress, and disagreement is common in most family systems. It has even been jokingly suggested that no one has been reared in a "functional family." Yet there are a significant number of families whose family structures or systems are definitely thought to be pathological, or dysfunctional, when viewed by standards set by mental health professionals or representatives of other social agencies. Families in which significant substance abuse is present, such as alcoholic family settings, are an example of where pathological family dynamics would be likely to occur. In addition, families in which child abuse (emotional or physical), incest, or other forms of victimization and scapegoating occur are also described as dysfunctional.

Family models of abnormality include those studied in relation to the hypothesized development of schizophrenia. Most researchers now regard schizophrenia as a biological disease, a major psychiatric disorder which is caused by a biochemical imbalance or structural brain disorder. In the early views of investigators who studied family interaction, certain family structures were thought to foster psychosis. Three early family models thought to contribute to schizophrenia were schizophrenogenic, schismatic, and skewed family structures.

Schizophrenogenic referred to settings in which parents (usually the mother) communicate to their children using "double-bind" messages. A double-bind message refers to communication containing two contradictory, opposing messages. An example is when a mother says to a child, "Come here and give me a hug and show me you love me," and then, when the child complies, pushes him or her away and says, "Don't touch me, you'll mess up my clothes." One can easily see that a child who complies with such a communication is in a "no-win" situation in which anything the child does will meet with dissatisfaction. Another double-bind communication is when the parent makes a comment such as "You should not do that," but says it in a tone of voice that is permissive. The child is left in a state of confusion about the real message and what is expected of him or her.

A second type of disturbed family structure is referred to as a schismatic family structure. Schismatic families are those in which there are significant marital problems that are not being addressed within the marital dyad. Instead, the children are triangulated into the marital relationship and often serve as go-betweens for marital communication. There may be an attempt on the part of one parent to get the child to align with that parent against the other parent. This results in confusion and guilt in the child, who is forced to choose sides and align against a parent.

The third disturbed family structure is the skewed family. In this family, one member, usually one of the parents, has a major mental illness. The rest of the family adopts the disturbed view of the world in order to keep peace at home. For example, in the case of a family in which the father has chronic paranoid schizophrenia, the family members, including the healthy spouse, assist in not letting others into the home, keep the drapes closed, and generally do not trust outsiders. All of this is designed to keep the fears of the disturbed parent at a minimum. Additional pathological communications found in disturbed families include messages in which one person tries to tell another how the other person thinks or feels. Denial of meaning, for example, refers to one person telling another that the other person is not really angry or depressed when in fact the person is. Distortion of meaning occurs when the first person tells the second person that the second person really *means* to say something other than what the person has said; injection of meaning is telling someone else what he or she thinks.

Margaret Mahler, a psychoanalytic theorist, studied childhood and family development in the early 1950's and proposed a developmental stage theory for the healthy development of the self. If parental behaviors and communications are disturbed, the child's development can be adversely affected. This can be manifested in enmeshed, symbiotic relationships in which the mother intrudes on her child and literally invades the child's autonomy or development of the self. A mother who develops a symbiotic relationship with a child may not give adequate room for the child to develop or adequate privacy and respect to the child's own ideas. A child in this type of relationship will not learn to trust his or her own ideas and may remain dependent on the parent into the adult years.

Theodore Lidz, who studied family interactions in the 1960's, also found that the parents' personalities and the marital coalition strongly influenced the effectiveness of their children's ability to negotiate the outside world. In some cases, the child's mental illness can appear to have been learned from the parent's mental illness and pathological behaviors. Both chaotic families, which lack a stable figure with whom the child can identify, and rigid families, which permit only superficial, stereotyped communications and behaviors, have been the breeding grounds for disturbed children, particularly children with schizophrenia; however, many normal children have also come from these homes. Research is increasingly focusing on these resilient children, those who are able to emerge from pathological families relatively emotionally intact.

Applications
Applications of the knowledge that has been gathered regarding disturbed family systems and family communications have been plentiful. One area has been the development of a parental support group called Parents Anonymous. This program has been developed on the twelve-step approach of Alcoholics Anonymous (AA). Often, these groups are sponsored by an agency and may have a professional counselor as a leader. Parents Anonymous has been successful in helping some parents gain advice, support, and understanding of their parenting behaviors. It is a proactive approach that assists all parents, and especially parents who feel that they may harm their children either emotionally or physically. Along this line of prevention, child abuse hotlines and family crisis day care centers have been established in many communities. Parents who are under stress can call for assistance or go to a crisis center and receive counseling while someone else takes over the child care.

Thomas Gordon wrote a book that has been widely read entitled *Parent Effectiveness Training: The Tested New Way to Raise Responsible Children* (1972). This is a guide for all parents that presents positive alternatives for discipline and scheduling of family activities. Communication patterns are suggested that do not negate the child but make the desired behaviors clear and easy to understand. The book has been used as an aid to family therapy and for adjunctive parent counseling of parents whose children may be in therapy.

Family therapy itself has been a growing area. Multigroup family therapy has also been developed to bring families together in this process. Filial therapy was developed as a unique approach established on the principle of using parents as therapists for their own children. Lawrence Hornsby and Alan Applebaum expanded on the approach in the late 1970's to involve the parents in therapy themselves as well as in the play therapy with their own children. Hornsby and Applebaum then supervise the direction of the play therapy. Six to eight sessions are conducted to train the parents, who then continue the play therapy in their home on a weekly basis.

There has been an increasing focus on the nuclear family structure and on the single-parent family. These family structures have disadvantages that can lead to increased stress on the parents and the children. Without an extended family network of support, many times the focus on maintaining a career competes with the needs of the children. Third parties such as day care centers, schools, churches, and babysitters become key influences on the development of the children, and parents have been cautioned to choose such settings and caregivers wisely. Research has suggested that quality programs and caregivers can enhance the child's development; however, there have been numerous problems with unqualified, overburdened, or even pathological third-party caregivers who may contribute to disturbed child development.

The rise of addiction as a major form of pathology has also led to applications of family work with the complementary components of AA such as Al-Anon, Alateen, and ACOA (Adult Children of Alcoholics) support groups. There are now also support groups for victims of anorexia and bulimia and their family members. Most clinical treatment programs for these addictive or habit disorders require the family to be involved in the treatment and healing process. Sexual abuse and incest victim support groups can aid members in overcoming the devastating effects of growing up in a pathological, abusive environment.

Perspective and Prospects

Margaret Mahler, Frieda Fromm-Reichmann, Theodore Lidz, and other dynamic theorists noted the difference between normal and pathological family communications and structures in the mid 1900's. Faulty communications between child and parent, as well as disturbed family structures, have been correlated with disturbance in some offspring. The majority of children coming from pathological homes remain intact, however, which suggests these are not causal factors in mental illness but may be contributing factors. Some children may be vulnerable to such dynamics or may be singled out or scapegoated for abuse. For example, Lidz and others, in the mid 1950's, wrote about the effect of a remote or distant father on the subsequent development of schizophrenic or homosexual behavior in some children. Role reversals in family structure in which there is a weak, ineffective male model and a strong, overbearing female model have also been linked to variations in development of sexual identity in children.

Family therapy itself has been a growing area in the decades that followed. Salvador Minuchin, Virginia Satir, Jay Haley, Murray Bowen, and Carl Whittaker all made significant contributions to the field of family therapy and family systems theory in the decades that followed. Minuchin is credited, because of his work at the Philadelphia Child Guidance Center, with leading the movement toward family therapy during the decade of the 1970's. His "structural family therapy" approach uses systems theory to resolve family pathology. If the family system is changed, Minuchin feels, then the individual family members will also change and take on more adaptive roles within the new system.

Haley has focused on the particular meaning of certain communications and wrote extensively in the 1970's about techniques for therapeutic intervention in disturbed family interactions. Haley and his colleagues often prescribe homework and specific exercises designed to break through family resistance to change. In fact, Haley will sometimes direct a family *not* to change in hopes that "going with the resistance" will eventually lead to effective improvement in the family interaction. This type of intervention has been called a paradoxical approach because of its ambiguous nature. Haley believes that an individual's psychopathology is a key component in the family system and that the individual's disturbance and symptoms cannot change unless the family also changes. From this understanding, the term "identified patient" was derived, which refers to the identification of one problem member in the family as being a symptom of the family pathology.

In the late 1960's, Virginia Satir's popular approach to family therapy was called conjoint family therapy. In order to develop a family system that better met the emotional needs of the family members, Satir focused on improving impaired communications and interactions as well as impaired relationships among family members. Also in this time period, family therapist Carl Whittaker demonstrated his intergenerational approach to family therapy in a film entitled *A Different Kind of Caring*. In this demonstration, Whittaker works with an entire family, focusing on both the parents and their needs and on the children, and on how the two generations influence each other. Whittaker often shares his own observations, using humor and anecdotes to "break the ice." Family therapy work is often difficult, and many therapists undertake it with a cotherapist to balance the therapeutic interchange.

In the late 1970's, Peter Steinglass studied the effects of specific communications and relapse rates of schizophrenia. His work, published in 1980, highlighted the importance of what Steinglass termed high expressed emotion (EE). EE refers to negative, hostile, often rejecting communications of the family directed toward a mentally ill (usually schizophrenic) member. Relapse rates have been 40 percent higher for clients returning to these types of hostile households after psychiatric hospitalization. Family work to educate the members about the effects of these types of communications is necessary to prevent relapse. If the family is so dysfunctional that it does not change to improve the home environment, alternate living arrangements for the client may be pursued.

Family dynamics, communication, and structure are key components in attempts to alleviate psychopathology. This work, although challenging, is expected to grow and continue to benefit both families and society well into the future.

Bibliography

Arnold, L. Eugene. *Helping Parents Help Their Children.* New York: Brunner/Mazel, 1978. Outlines general principles of parent guidance. Details are provided about family therapy, including filial therapy (Hornsby and Applebaum's approach). Specific problems of children, such as mental retardation, learning disabilities, hyperactivity, and so on are addressed, as are specific problems of parents, such as the abusing parent, teenage motherhood, adoptive parenthood, and more.

Bowen, Murray. *Family Therapy in Clinical Practice*. New York: Jason Aronson, 1978. Bowen is well respected as a family therapist and presenter of workshops. Here he shows his application of family therapy in the clinical setting.

Brown, Fredda Herz, ed. *Reweaving the Family Tapestry: A Multigenerational Approach to Families*. New York: W. W. Norton, 1991. Gives an overview of the work done by the Family Institute of Westchester. This approach is important not only from the multigenerational perspective, but also because extremely important issues of race, class, gender, and ethnicity are incorporated into clinical analysis and treatment.

Figley, Charles R., ed. *Treating Stress in Families*. New York: Brunner/Mazel, 1989. In today's stress-focused society, this book makes an important contribution. Observations are provided from scientific studies of families regarding how they not only cope with but also produce and react to stress. Interventions for prevention are explored.

Horne, Arthur M., et al. *Family Counseling and Therapy*. 3d ed. Itasca, Ill.: F. E. Peacock, 2000. An up-to-date volume on family psychotherapy. Includes bibliographies and indexes.

Minuchin, Salvador. *Families and Family Therapy*. Cambridge, Mass.: Harvard University Press, 1974. A leader in family therapy interventions and techniques writes about his work and experiences treating families at the Philadelphia Child Guidance Center.

Ramsey, Christian N., Jr., ed. *Family Systems in Medicine*. New York: Guilford Press, 1989. A landmark book that expands what is known about family dysfunction and its effects on family members to the field of medicine. Reviews family systems theory, including a family stress model developed by Joan M. Patterson. Family systems research, immunology, endocrinology, biology, health, chronic illness, and behavioral disorders are all covered thoroughly. Suggestions for future directions of research are offered.

Simon, Richard, et al., eds. *The Art of Psychotherapy: Case Studies from the Family Therapy Networker*. New York: John Wiley & Sons, 1999. A text that discusses marital and family psychotherapy. Includes case studies.

Skynner, A. C. Robin. *Systems of Family and Marital Psychotherapy*. New York: Brunner/Mazel, 1976. A systems approach to marital and family communication that integrates gender and role as well as relationship and sexuality to complete the picture of the influence of the marital relationship on the family.

Karen Wolford

See also:

Abnormality; Anorexia Nervosa and Bulimia Nervosa; Behavioral Family Therapy; Child Abuse; Codependent Personality; Couples Therapy; Divorce and Separation: Adult Issues; Divorce and Separation: Children's Issues; Domestic Violence; Eating Disorders; Jealousy; Sibling Rivalry; Strategic Family Therapy; Teenage Suicide.

ABNORMALITY
Humanistic-Existential Models

Type of psychology: Psychopathology
Fields of study: Humanistic-phenomenological models; models of abnormality

The humanistic-existential approach views psychopathology as stemming from feelings of meaninglessness, valuelessness, and alienation; lack of commitment, will, and responsibility; and failure to grow and to realize potentials. This paradigm has led to therapies that emphasize awareness, authenticity, free will, choice, integration, human growth, and fulfillment.

Principal terms

EXISTENTIALISM: a viewpoint emphasizing human existence and situation in the world, and giving life meaning through the free choice of mature values and commitment to goals

HIERARCHY OF NEEDS: a sequence of basic human needs, including (from more to less powerful) physiological needs, safety and security, love and belongingness, esteem and respect, and self-actualization needs

HUMANISTIC PSYCHOLOGY: a branch of psychology that emphasizes the human tendencies toward growth and fulfillment, autonomy, choice, responsibility, and ultimate values such as truth, love, and justice

INCONGRUENCE: the possession of false aspects of the self-concept; lack of genuineness

PHENOMENOLOGY: an approach that stresses openness to direct experience in introspective or unsophisticated ways

SELF: the unified and integrated center of one's experience and awareness, which one experiences both subjectively, as an actor, and objectively, as recipient of actions

SELF-ACTUALIZATION: a constructive process of functioning optimally and fulfilling one's potential; characterized by acceptance, autonomy, accurate perceptions, creativity, high ethics, personal growing, and societal contributions

Overview

Humanistic-existential models provide a way of understanding psychopathology that is an alternative to those offered by the biological, psychoanalytic, and behavioral and social learning paradigms. In contrast to explaining abnormal behavior through biological or physiological defects or anomalies (the medical or illness model), or through unconscious intrapsychic conflict and unresolved psychosexual developmental issues from the first six years of life (the psychoanalytic model), or as a result of past conditioning or reinforcement history or observational learning (the learning paradigm), humanistic-existential models essentially maintain that abnormality reflects and results from a failure to grow and to realize one's potentials.

The humanistic viewpoint emphasizes that all people have the human potential to grow and the capacity for full functioning; given the proper conditions for growth, people will be self-determining, will exercise choice and responsibility, and will fulfill their potential and be self-actualizing.

Abnormality is the failure of such growth and development to be realized. Thus, in the humanistic model, health is not necessarily the absence of disease, but is instead something positive. Whereas the medical or illness model has traditionally stressed movement or change from sickness to normalcy, the humanistic model emphasizes change from normalcy or deficiency in growth to full functioning. The humanistic model also maintains that people must develop values and make their choices freely, based on their own experiences. If a person blindly accepts others' values and choices, then the person will lose a sense of self and become incongruent. Such incongruence is equivalent to abnormality.

The self is a central theme for humanistic psychologists. Carl Rogers postulated that all people have an actualizing tendency to maintain and enhance themselves, including their self-concept. Rogers described an organismic valuing process: What is experienced as satisfying is consistent with the actualizing tendency, and what is unsatisfying is not in accord with this tendency. When people distort or even deny experiences in conscious awareness, they have given up using their self or their organismic valuing process. Instead, they adopt conditions of worth that have been imposed by parents or other significant people. By becoming what others want them to be, or evaluating according to others' perceptions or experience, they obtain the positive regard and caring that is so important, but they sacrifice accurate and efficient perception of reality, and ultimately lose their true selves.

Failure to satisfy basic needs leads to deficiency and is another source of psychopathology. Abraham Maslow's motivational theory described a hierarchy of basic needs. Ranging from the more powerful to the less prepotent higher needs, these are physiological requirements, safety and security, love and belongingness, esteem and regard, aesthetic and cognitive, and self-actualization needs. In healthy, self-actualizing individuals, all the lower needs in the hierarchy are or have at one time been adequately satisfied; thus, these individuals can express more of their self-actualizing needs and motives (which include values such as truth, justice, beauty, and wholeness).

People are not self-actualizing if they are motivated primarily by lower deficiency needs, such as for safety, belongingness, or esteem; the self-actualization or growth motivation is the weakest of all the needs in the hierarchy. Maslow and other humanistic psychologists have identified other reasons why so few individuals may be self-actualizing. The force of habit, the tendency to stay where one is (inertia), and the fear of becoming all that one can be (which Maslow called the Jonah complex) are some psychological forces that conspire against growth. The misfortunes of poverty, poor parenting, or other sociocultural barriers can prevent growth motivation from being central. The tremendous power of culture, which can greatly inhibit deviation from the norm, or societal sanctions that can punish (socially or otherwise) those who stray too far beyond what society dictates as normal or acceptable prevent many from realizing their true self-expression and potentials. Certain political freedoms are also basic requisites for human fulfillment.

According to Maslow, when a person does not function according to growth motivation and the various self-actualization needs (truth, beauty, justice, and others), then he or she suffers from various kinds of spiritual disorders such as cynicism, nihilism, or emptiness. Spiritual or existential disorders are also highlighted by the existential perspective. All humans must have the courage, commitment, and will to use their freedom to choose values that guide life, give life its meaning, and emphasize obligations to others. Failure to choose, to create one's essence, or to deal with normal guilt (awareness of not fulfilling potentials) or normal existential anxiety (stemming from challenges to one's values and from awareness of one's ultimate death or nonbeing) results in existential despair and frustration. An existential disorder or crisis is often a reflection of perceived meaninglessness, isolation, alienation, or valuelessness.

Both Rogers and Maslow characterized the actualizing tendency or self-actualization need as positive, constructive, rational, trustworthy, and in the direction of growth and harmony. Existentialists, not quite so optimistically, place additional emphasis on irrational forces and the potentiality of evil in the normal human personality.

Optimal health, full functioning, self-actualization, or existential being can be difficult to realize; Maslow spoke of the "psychopathology of the average," meaning that most normal people are content to be adjusted to their social group of society, and do not truly grow and realize their full potentials as human beings. Indeed, Maslow suggested that perhaps only 1 percent of the American population might be self-actualizing. Existential crises, problems of values and meaning, stunted growth, and lack of fulfillment are not uncommon among materially comfortable people.

Applications

Humanistic and existential models are appropriately applied in situations in which clients desire not merely symptomatic relief, but also to become more aware of self and of existential conflicts and to achieve greater personal growth. Indeed, the humanistic paradigm has been particularly dissatisfied with pathology-centered conceptualizations, which have several disadvantages. One problem is that the illness model stresses the need (rather than the desirability) for treatment; the decision concerning need for therapy is often made by someone other than the person herself or himself. A second disadvantage is that therapists tend to be elevated above the patient, often in an authoritarian, parent-type role, rather than functioning in a more egalitarian therapeutic relationship. A third problem involves reinforcing the belief that people are sick and cannot really care for themselves or take an active and responsible role in their treatment. The humanistic model presents an alternative, one which would increase client choice and responsibility and focus on positive goals of fostering strengths rather than simply getting rid of illness or weakness. Humanistic theorists have observed that the goal of much counseling and psychotherapy is more than eliminating pathology and achieving a state of normalcy.

Humanistic and existential therapists place great emphasis on the nature of the therapist-client relationship. Existential thinkers such as Martin Buber and Karl Jaspers stressed the tremendous importance and impact of therapists providing a full human presence, an authentic encounter, an "I-Thou" relationship with their clients. Such a deep encounter of intimacy and authenticity allows clients to gain access to their inner worlds through the unfolding of their real feelings, experiences, and potentials. Buber emphasized "unfolding" as the desired approach for both therapists and educators.

One of the leading existential analysts was Viktor Frankl, who developed an approach that he called logotherapy. By examining each person's unique way of "being there," in relation to the physical world, social world, and self, and by engaging in intimate, open, authentic therapeutic encounter, the logo therapist allows clients through their basic freedom to take responsibility for creating a life with meaning. Frankl emphasized techniques such as de-reflection and paradoxical intention. De-reflection involves taking attention away from oneself and one's problems and symptoms and focusing instead on activities that could be done, on experiences that can be enjoyed, and on other people. Paradoxical intention involves the client's engaging in and even exaggerating symptoms; by thus magnifying and even ridiculing the symptoms, the client can understand his or her control over the neurotic behaviors and symptoms, and can choose different responses. Logotherapy, like most humanistic-existential approaches, stresses authenticity and working with immediacy on issues and experience in the present; it is especially useful for people dealing with existential crises or boundary situations (such as confrontation with one's own death, major changes in life that highlight one's ultimate aloneness, or situations that challenge one's values or that give one a feeling of meaninglessness).

Gestalt therapy, developed by Fritz and Laura Perls, is yet another approach that is phenomenological and existential in form and process. Centrally important are awareness and dialogue, using the direct phenomenological experience of therapist and client. Process (what and how) in the present (here and now) is amplified and experienced through contact and existential dialogue, and clients are able in such an environment to assume responsibility for their choices and values. Gestalt therapists help patients focus on present experience, reexperience emotions or enact feelings or thoughts in the present, visualize, act out elements of a dream or parts of a conflict, exaggerate gestures or bodily symptoms—all to increase client self-awareness and integration through organismic self-regulation. Various specialized Gestalt techniques to increase awareness, to resolve splits or conflicts within the self, and to achieve integration have been developed; the therapist balances frustration and support to achieve these goals. This approach is particularly useful for people who tend to live in the past or the anticipated future, and for those who overemphasize intellectual functions and restrain or neglect their feelings and bodily experiences.

The person-centered approach is perhaps humanistic psychology's most practiced and influential system of psychotherapy. Developed as a process of counseling troubled individuals, it has extended to groups, to human relations training programs, and even to institutional change. The emphasis of the approach is squarely on the relationship. Grounded in trust, and with the therapist providing the necessary facilitative conditions of genuineness, unconditional positive regard for the client, and accurate empathy (deeply listening and reflecting the client's feelings and meanings without interpretation or judgment), the relationship is intended to allow the client to become more genuine and use the self as the basis for evaluating experience and behavior. The negative feelings, discouragement, and conflicts typically experienced in early therapy sessions give way to increased hope and self-acceptance and ultimately to reaching out to others and living a more flexible, adaptable, existential, constructive, full-functioning life. This approach is particularly helpful for those who seem to have lost their sense of who they are, or who are troubled because of external or internal blockages of their growth.

Rogers, Perls, Maslow, and other humanistic psychologists contributed greatly to the growth of the human potential movement, which promoted sensitivity training, encounter groups, and other forms of growth groups and workshops. Such notions and emphases as the self, growth, free will, choice, autonomy, commitment, responsibility, awareness, positive self-regard, integration, congruence, authenticity, immediacy, encounter, and human potential are also common to group and institutional applications of the humanistic-existential approach.

Perspective and Prospects

The biological or medical model of human health had rapidly gained ascendance during and after the Renaissance, and it dominated psychopathology during the 1800's. This medical approach continues to be a well-established and even entrenched model; types of maladjustment or problems in living such as depression, anxiety disorders, eating disorders, and alcoholism are often viewed essentially and sometimes exclusively as diseases, notwithstanding limited evidence of biological factors in many instances of these disorders.

Within contemporary psychopathology, the first comprehensive psychologically oriented approach for conceptualizing abnormality was Sigmund Freud's psychoanalysis. This model, like the medical model, sees the person as a patient, is pathology centered, implies little free will, and offers limited responsibility and choice. It has been criticized as being reductionistic (a person is reduced to drives and intrapsychic conflicts), mechanistic (a person is viewed as a machine would be), deterministic (a person has little freedom in creating himself or herself), and pessimistic (a person is motivated by irrational forces, including instincts for aggression, unrestrained sexuality, and self-destruction). The psychoanalytic approach inadequately accounts for human potentials or existential concerns. Yet until the humanistic-existential approaches developed, the psychoanalytic was the predominant psychotherapy system available.

The classical conditioning work of Ivan Pavlov, the tremendous influence of John B. Watson, and B. F. Skinner's subsequent monumental contributions in instrumental learning led the behavioral approach to rival the psychoanalytic in explaining abnormality. Viewing psychopathology as the failure to learn adaptive responses or the learning of maladaptive ones, behaviorists utilize the scientific method with precise theoretical formulations and careful observation and measurement to test and advance their views. Their experimental approach, however, is also reductionistic (a person is reduced to stimulus-response bonds or a product of reinforcement history), mechanistic, and deterministic; Skinner disavowed freedom and even the possibility of dignity.

The humanistic-existential paradigm presented an alternative: a holistic, organismic, optimistic approach emphasizing innate growth tendencies, potentials, and freedom. Many instances of abnormality were viewed as failures to grow, and as resulting from perceived isolation and alienation in an increasingly technological and bureaucratic world, or as problems concerning values and meaning. In these cases, applying the other paradigms meant that people simply were not being understood or helped.

The humanistic-existential model emerged as a significant contemporary paradigm for explaining and treating psychopathology during the 1940's and 1950's, and became increasingly influential during the next two decades. Carl Rogers formulated client-centered therapy during the 1940's as an alternative to psychoanalytic techniques. Abraham Maslow devoted much of his professional life to the study of self-actualization. Ludwig Binswanger developed existential analysis during the 1940's; Rollo May and Irvin Yalom became highly influential developers of existential therapy. Fritz Perls's first book was published in the 1940's. Thus, both the humanistic and existential branches of this approach were developing simultaneously as coherent, interrelated perspectives.

Many humanistic and existential writers believe that their approach will be successful to the degree that their notions, emphases, and procedures are incorporated into the underlying attitudes, techniques, and approaches of the other major models. If this be the measure, then humanistic-existential writers have already been quite successful. From behavioral medicine to contemporary psychodynamic approaches to cognitive-behavioral strategies, many theorists and therapists have broadened their conceptualizing and enhanced the therapy process by incorporating at least some of the insights, concepts, techniques, and approaches championed by the major humanistic and existential writers. Given that the true origins of these insights and notions undoubtedly go back to the philosophers and religious leaders of antiquity, this important model has achieved another measure of success by penetrating to a large segment of the lay community. This paradigm points to and confronts dimensions of each person's existence and humanity that had previously been ignored by the other perspectives; in these ways, the humanistic-existential model has enhanced people's understanding of normality and abnormality, and of themselves.

Bibliography

Fagan, Joen, and Irma Lee Shepherd, eds. *Gestalt Therapy Now*. Palo Alto, Calif.: Science and Behavior Books, 1970. Contains articles by several leading Gestalt therapists, who discuss the theory of this therapy approach, various Gestalt techniques, and applications. Includes a bibliography of Gestalt books and materials.

Frankl, Viktor Emil. *The Doctor and the Soul: From Psychotherapy to Logotherapy.* 2d expanded ed. New York: Alfred A. Knopf, 1965. Highlights how the spiritual and existential domains have been neglected by psychoanalysis and earlier therapeutic systems. Focusing on the "will to meaning," Frankl discusses the meaning of life, death, suffering, work, and love. Examines existential analyses of several types of psychopathology, and presents the therapeutic technique of logotherapy.

May, Rollo. *Power and Violence: A Search for the Sources of Violence.* New York: W. W. Norton, 1972. An existential analysis of power, self-affirmation, self-assertion, aggression, and violence. May argues that feelings of impotence, powerlessness, and insignificance underlie aggression and violence, and argues strongly against innocence and for power in terms of psychological and spiritual valuing of self, assuming responsibility, and acknowledging people's potentiality for evil.

May, Rollo, Ernest Angel, and Henri F. Ellenberger, eds. *Existence: A New Dimension in Psychology and Psychiatry.* New York: Basic Books, 1958. A historically important book that helped initiate existential psychology in the United States. The first two essays and some case studies (including that of Ellen West) are quite readable and rewarding, but some articles may be rather difficult reading.

Moss, Donald, ed. *Humanistic and Transpersonal Psychology: A Historical and Biographical Sourcebook.* Westport, Conn.: Greenwood Press, 1999. A volume in the series Schools of Psychological Thought. Includes bibliographical references and an index.

Perls, Frederick S. *The Gestalt Approach and Eye Witness to Therapy.* Ben Lomond, Calif.: Science and Behavior Books, 1973. One of the better-written and more accessible of Perls's efforts to describe Gestalt therapy. Describes foundations, theory, and techniques; offers verbatim excerpts of filmed transcripts of introductory Gestalt work. Provides a good description of Perls's style and approach.

Rogers, Carl R. *Client-Centered Therapy.* Boston: Houghton Mifflin, 1951. Rogers's first book on the person-centered approach to therapy is very readable and affords a good introduction. Includes discussion of the necessary therapist characteristics, the nature of the therapy relationship and the therapeutic process, theory of therapy, training of therapists, and applications in counseling, teaching, and administration.

Valle, Ron, ed. *Phenomenological Inquiry in Psychology: Existential and Transpersonal Dimensions.* New York: Plenum Press, 1998. Discusses phenomenological, existential, and transpersonal psychologies. Includes bibliographical references and indexes.

Yalom, Irvin D. *Existential Psychotherapy.* New York: Basic Books, 1980. A clinically oriented book that describes abnormality in terms of how one deals with one's own mortality, isolation, lack of fulfilling potential, feelings of meaninglessness, and freedom. Also applies theory to clinical practice and examines implications of the approach.

Edward R. Whitson

See also:

Abnormality; Abnormality: Cognitive Models; Abnormality: Sociocultural Models; Gestalt Therapy; Person-Centered Therapy.

ABNORMALITY
Legal Models

Type of psychology: Psychopathology
Fields of study: Models of abnormality

The law assumes rationality. Abnormality is a departure from this rationality, including the incapacity to have criminal intent (insanity) and the inability to understand legal responsibilities (incompetence). The law protects citizens from those who are dangerous and protects harmless incompetents from themselves; psychological research has influenced a broadening of the "insanity" rule and a limitation on involuntary commitment.

Principal terms

INCOMPETENCY: the legally established lack of sufficient knowledge and judgment to perform a given right or responsibility

INSANITY: the condition of having a mental disease or defect so great that criminal intent or responsibility and punishability are not possible

M'NAGHTEN RULE: the traditional insanity rule, which holds that a person incapable of knowing the nature, quality, and wrongfulness of his or her act is legally "insane"

MENS REA: the possession of intent to commit a crime; intent must be present as well as the legal offense itself before a punishable crime exists (literally, "guilty mind")

PARENS PATRIAE: the power of the state to act as guardian of those people who cannot take care of themselves (literally, "parent of the country")

PSYCHOSIS: a mental condition involving distortion of universal assumptions about time, space, cause and effect, or "reality"

RATIONALITY: the capability of thinking logically so that one is aware of the consequences (rewards and costs) of actions

Overview

In the United States, three broadly based legal principles and their elaboration by judicial interpretation (case law) and by legislatures (statutory law) reflect the law's core assumptions about normal and abnormal behavior. These principles are rationality, the protection of the incompetent, and protection from the dangerous.

The first of these concerns is the importance of rational understanding. The normal person is, the law assumes, sufficiently rational that the person can base his or her choices and actions upon a consideration of possible consequences, of benefits and costs. In the civil law, two people making a contract or agreement are expected to be "competent" to understand its terms. In the criminal law, a destructive act is deemed much worse and punishable if it is intentional and deliberate. Concern about motivation extends through the normal range of illegal acts, and offenses resulting from malice (that is, intentional offenses) are generally dealt with more harshly than those that result from mere negligence. Under the civil law, those incapable of understanding simple business transactions with ordinary prudence may be deemed "incompetent." Under the criminal law, in a principle that dates back to Roman times, persons who are deprived of understanding are considered incapable of intent and the corresponding guilty mind (*mens rea*). In the words of the 1843 M'Naghten rule (named for Daniel M'Naghten, also spelled McNaughton), if the accused is laboring under such a defect of reason from a disease of the mind as not to know the nature and quality of the act he was doing, or, if he did know it, he did not know what he was doing was wrong, then this accused person is "insane" and cannot be found guilty.

Two other basic legal principles justify society's special attention to helpless people and to dangerous people. The doctrine of *parens patriae* as early as 1324 authorized King Edward II of England to protect the lands and profits of "idiots" and "lunatics." Under this doctrine, the state may appoint a guardian for the harmless but helpless mentally ill—that is, those incapable of managing their ordinary business affairs. Since the mentally incompetent cannot make an informed decision about their need for treatment, the protection of the state allows the "commitment" of such people to hospitals, regardless of their own wishes.

The third doctrine which has been applied to the abnormal is the "police power" of the state. Inherent in the very concept of a state is a duty to protect its citizens from danger to their personal safety or property. This duty is considered to include the right to remove from society those abnormal people who are dangerous and to segregate them in institutions. In the United States, the laws of all fifty states authorize the restraint and custody of persons displaying aberrant behaviors that may be dangerous to themselves or others.

These principles of law, all based upon logically derived exemptions from assumptions concerning rational intent and understanding, have changed slowly in response to influences from the public and from the mental health professions. In institutionalization decisions, the *parens patriae* power of the state became more widely used beginning in the mid-nineteenth century as judges and the public became more accepting of the mental health enterprise. Hospitals were considered protective, nonstressful environments where the harmless insane would be safe.

In the decade of the 1960's, the arguments of critics of these views became widely known. Psychiatrist Thomas Szasz argued that mental illnesses were little more than crude metaphors for "problems in living," myths that were used, harmfully, to deprive individuals of their feelings of responsibility. Erving Goffman charged that institutionalization was a degrading, dependency-producing process. As a result of these criticisms, the institutionalization of individuals for their own welfare (*parens patriae*) became less common. Dangerousness became the major reason for involuntary commitment.

The insanity exemption from legal responsibility also has been adjusted and modified. The central concern of the professionals was that strict M'Naghten-rule "insanity" included only the small minority of offenders who had no understanding whatsoever that their offense was unlawful, the sort of offender who shot the victim thinking he was a tree. An offender could be mentally ill by psychiatric standards but still be considered sane. As a response to these criticisms, new legal tests that expanded the meaning of insanity were somewhat experimentally adopted by a few courts. The "irresistible impulse" rule, stating that a person would not be considered responsible if driven by an impulse so strong it would have occurred had there been "a policeman at his elbow," supplemented the M'Naghten rule in some states. In 1954, the federal courts, in the case of the *United States v. Durham*, adopted an even simpler rule: Insanity involves simply the illegal act being "the product of mental disease or defect." This Durham rule was quickly attacked for turning a legal decision over to mental health professionals, some of whom seemed to consider virtually all deviancy a disease. Stung by such criticisms, the federal courts, along with twenty-six states, adopted a rule proposed by the American Law Institutes (the ALI rule) that seemed to incorporate aspects of each of the preceding rules: Because of mental disease or defect (Durham rule), the defendant lacks the substantial capacity to appreciate the criminality of his or her conduct (a softening of M'Naghten "know"), or to conform this act to the requirements of law (the substance of the "irresistible impulse test").

As a result of public fears that manipulative villains would use the insanity defense as a way of escaping punishment, some states have adopted the alternative of allowing "guilty but mentally ill" verdicts or abolishing the insanity plea entirely.

Applications
Abstract models of abnormality represented in the law often present many complexities when applied to an actual case. Before such concepts as insanity or dangerousness can be implemented, many commonsense and often implicit assumptions are added to the legal definitions.

Studies of the deliberations of mock (simulated) juries and the decisions of real juries in various types of cases suggest that a successful insanity plea would have a number of characteristics. The offender would have a record of psychiatric contact before the offense, preferably hospitalization. His or her offense would not seem to make sense—that is, it would involve a trivial reward and poor or no planning. His or her stated reasons for the offense would sound fantastic to others. He or she would initially be found incompetent to stand trial. The crime with which he or she was charged would not be murder and especially would not be seen as a heinous offense. Curiously enough, most of these factors are considered by juries regardless of the legal rule in effect. Most of the factors are involved in the 80 percent of all successful insanity pleas which seem sufficiently clear that they are not contested by the prosecution. Most defendants found not guilty by reason of insanity remain in mental institutions as long as they would have otherwise served in prison if convicted.

A case that displays most of the ambiguities that sometimes occur in the process, and that shifted public opinion against the legitimacy of the insanity plea, was the trial of John Hinckley, a young man who attempted to assassinate President Ronald Reagan and gravely wounded Reagan's press secretary. Hinckley's act had many

Abnormality: Legal Models

of the elements of an "insane" one. Hinckley identified very closely with a character in a popular motion picture, a loner who stalks the president and engages in a rescue attempt that ends in a bloody gun battle. So involved was Hinckley with the film that he seemed controlled by his fantasy and unaware of his own identity. Diagnosed a schizophrenic, a condition in which fantasies cannot be separated from reality, he had wandered aimlessly for years and had consulted psychiatrists. On the other hand, he had clearly planned the act, bought special bullets, and given every indication he knew the act was illegal. Under strict M'Naghten-rule standards, he would probably have been found to "know" right from wrong. Under the more liberal ALI standard, however, it was felt that he both had a mental disease and was driven to the act by his fantasy; he lacked the capacity to conform his behavior to the law. He was found "insane" and committed to locked facilities in a hospital.

Aside from illustrating the complexity of an actual case at law, the Hinckley case illustrates an implicit assumption of the public: A notorious offense against a popular leader seems to justify punishment. In other famous cases, the offenders appeared clearly schizophrenic as well, but "insanity" was not used successfully as a defense. Serial killer David Berkowitz received instructions from a dog; Herbert Mullin killed at random whenever instructed by mysterious voices. Both were found sane in spite of obvious symptoms. Heinous crimes seem to require punishment regardless of the mental state of the offender.

The investigation of the meaning of the term "dangerousness" offers an example of how a term can be operationalized by experience. This term has been elaborated by the laws of the various states. It usually includes dangerousness against oneself as well as others. It can include threats against the property of others or even, sometimes, unintended harm caused by incompetence. A retarded person wandering onto a busy highway might be a case of this last condition. Often the word "dangerousness" is used in connection with other aberrant behavior.

John Monahan, refining the word "dangerousness" to imply the prediction of future violent behavior, has reviewed several studies that have spoken to the question of the accuracy of such predictions. If one excludes that minority of such individuals who have already committed violent acts, the post hospitalization rate of violent acts of former mental patients seems approximately similar to the rate of violent acts in the public in general. In a typical study, offenders at a Massachusetts facility were evaluated for dangerousness by clinical examinations and by the careful construction of their life record. Of 435 patients released during a ten-year period, approximately 50 were evaluated as dangerous. The rate of commission of a new violent (assaultive) act was 35 percent among those predicted dangerous but only 8 percent among those judged nondangerous and ready for release: There was sufficiently more violence among the predicted group. This research was interpreted to indicate that such predictions could be made for groups. Nevertheless, two-thirds of those predicted as dangerous failed to commit another violent act during the five-year follow-up period. Were it not for a judicial order, they would have been incarcerated for what a team of mental health evaluators had to say about their potential—for what they were expected to do in the future. It should be added that among the most valid predictors was the presence of overt violent acts in the past.

Perspective and Prospects

Legal models of abnormality were formulated in Western civilization many centuries before psychology existed as a science. The models were based upon principles concerning human beings that evolved in folk wisdom and in religion. The normal person was expected to be able to undertake important actions intentionally and to be aware of the consequences. Abnormality was any condition that involved the incapacity to make intentional decisions with awareness of the consequences. There was, by necessity, a sharp dividing line between the normal and abnormal, as a lack of competence made an agreement invalid. The degree of rationality needed was a minimal one involving only an understanding of the direct and immediate consequences of an act. The rest of the law concerning abnormality involved two additional considerations: the protection of the harmless insane, and protection of citizens from those who were "dangerous." For centuries, the legal system merely fine-tuned these basic principles: The M'Naghten rule expressed proof of the lack of criminal intent more precisely; state laws often provided in greater detail just what was meant by dangerousness.

The legal model evolved as a separate system and was little influenced by the academic psychology of the early twentieth century. Since about 1950, the legal model has been influenced by some general insights from the behavioral sciences. The broadening of the insanity rule and the narrowing of the justification for institutionalization were the direct effects of such influences.

Psychological models of abnormality, in contrast to legal models, tend to be less narrowly focused on thinking processes, look for causes and consequences that are hidden or far removed, and see abnormality as a matter of degree. Almost inevitably, psychological models are biased against seeing a criminal action entirely as the result of a decision made a few minutes before and in favor of determination by external events. A few psychologists have publicly extended the concept of mental illness to cover such conditions as "television intoxication." Public reactions to broadening the concept of abnormality, along with the Hinckley case, have led to pressures to eliminate the insanity defense altogether.

Psychology is well positioned to continue its contributions to legal models by helping to make clear the meaning of legal terms which sometimes imply predictions or refer to quantifiable dimensions. The skills involved in "competence to stand trial" or "legal responsibility" have been quantified in standardized interviews that yield numerical scores. This can bring greater objectivity to a process that has largely been intuitive. A better than chance prediction of future violent acts can be made only for those who have already committed violent acts. Further study of these violent actors might advance understanding of motivational factors that lead to the repetition of violence.

Psychological criticism of the legal system is sometimes little more than disguised criticism of the assumption of free will and responsibility on which the law is based. Psychology (and other behavioral sciences) generally looks for causes of external events that are far removed from the point at which individual decisions are made.

The law, on the other hand, assumes that an individual can at any given moment exercise a choice, "free will." Any foreseeable consequences that come from that choice are "caused" by the individual who makes it. The assumption of free choice and responsibility found in the law is an assumption necessary to an ordered system of justice. For this reason, rational intent will continue to be an intrinsic part of the law, as will special treatment for those who lack the capacity to make this choice.

Bibliography

Bartol, Curt R. *Psychology and the American Law*. Belmont, Calif.: Wadsworth, 1983. Reviews both the criminal law and the civil law as they deal with concepts of competence, dangerousness, and legal responsibility. Contains a thorough presentation of the historic origin of the rules pertaining to civil commitment. Chapters 4 and 5 are particularly relevant. Written on an introductory level.

Monahan, J. "The Prediction of Violent Behavior: Developments in Psychology and Law." In *The Master Lecture Series: Psychology and the Law*, edited by C. James Scheirer and Barbara L. Hammonds. Vol. 2. Washington, D.C.: American Psychological Association, 1983. Reviews the arguments for psychologists to play a role in predicting violence, and the evidence on how well this can be done. The conclusion is that predictions of violent behavior tend to predict a considerable amount of violence that never occurs. Relevant because "dangerousness" is the primary reason for involuntary commitment.

Szasz, Thomas Stephen. *Law, Liberty, and Psychiatry*. New York: Macmillan, 1963. A discussion of what Szasz considers the "psychiatrization" of the law. Argues that due process protections and responsibility are eroded by loose "mental illness" standards. Well written, one-sided, somewhat polemical in style. Very readable and informative.

Hess, Allen K., and Irving B. Weiner, eds. *The Handbook of Forensic Psychology*. 2d ed. New York: John Wiley & Sons, 1999. Each chapter was written by an expert in the variety of areas related to psychology and the law, including the assessment of criminal responsibility, civil competency, the competence of juries, competency to stand trial, diminished responsibility, predicting violence, and psychotherapy with criminal offenders. Sometimes heavy going, but worth it.

Wrightsman, Lawrence S. *Psychology and the Legal System*. Monterey, Calif.: Brooks/ Cole, 1987. Contains a review of the legal rules concerning insanity, placed in a historical context, and the rules pertaining to civil commitment. Particularly strong in summarizing a number of court cases in which the insanity defense was employed and in reviewing current arguments for and against this defense. Written on the level of a college introductory text.

Thomas E. DeWolfe

See also:

Abnormality; Abnormality: Behavioral Models; Abnormality: Biomedical Models; Abnormality: Sociocultural Models; Antisocial Personality; Juvenile Delinquency; Madness: Historical Concepts; Psychosis; Schizophrenia.

ABNORMALITY
Psychodynamic Models

Type of psychology: Psychopathology
Fields of study: Models of abnormality; psychodynamic and neoanalytic models

Psychodynamic models of psychopathology contribute much to the investigation of abnormality and to the study of personality in general. The psychodynamic view pivots around the strong influence of the unconscious and internal psychological conflict on human emotions and behavior and in the development of psychiatric disorders. Neoanalytic models such as ego analytic, ego psychology, and self/object relations models have gained increasing popularity.

Principal terms

CONVERSION DISORDER: a disorder in which unconscious conflicts are transformed into physical symptoms such as blindness, loss of function, or paralysis
DEFENSE MECHANISMS: coping strategies that distort reality to some degree and are used to deal with anxiety aroused by internal conflict
EGO: the fundamental part of the mind that mediates among the reality of the world, id forces, and superego forces
FIXATION: an inability to progress to the next level of psychosexual development because of overgratification or undergratification of desires at a particular stage
ID: the part of the mind that operates on the pleasure principle; contains unconscious biological drives for sex, hunger, and aggression
IDENTIFICATION: the internalization of parental or societal values, behaviors, and attitudes
PSYCHOSEXUAL STAGES: the stages of psychosexual (personality) development; they are the oral, anal, phallic, latency, and genital stages
SUPEREGO: the process in the mind that is commonly thought of as one's conscience

Overview

Psychoanalytic theory forms the basis for the psychodynamic model as developed by Sigmund Freud in the early 1900's. Freud and the other psychodynamic theorists of his time believed strongly in the principle of psychic determinism. This principle is founded on the belief that men and women are not free to choose their behaviors; rather, behaviors, both normal and abnormal, are determined or caused by a combination of intrapsychic forces, which Freud named the id, ego, and superego. These processes interact in the execution of internal mental activities that are both conscious and unconscious. Unsuccessfully resolved conflicts within the mind can lead to abnormal behavior. The ego, which operates on the reality principle, must negotiate between the desires generated by the id, the controls of the superego, and the demands of the real world. Successful negotiation can be illustrated by the following example. An ice cream truck drives through Michelle's suburban neighborhood every day at dinner time. Michelle's parents have forbidden her to buy a Popsicle, however, because it will ruin her appetite. Michelle approaches her parents and says, "Can I buy a Popsicle now and put it in the freezer until after dinner? I promise I will clean my plate." In this example, the ego has arrived at an acceptable compromise between the id, which operates on the pleasure principle ("I want the Popsicle now") and the superego or conscience ("Mom and dad will be angry at me unless I wait until after dinner"). Partial or incomplete resolution of internal conflicts is thought to lead to psychopathology.

In 1905, Freud proposed that personality development progresses through a series of "psychosexual stages." Disorders such as schizophrenia, according to some psychoanalytic theorists, are thought to be a result of an individual's "regression," or return to an earlier, more primitive level of psychosexual development, such as the oral stage. This regression can signal that the patient is not ready to cope with the demands of adult sexuality or responsibility and may be unconsciously designed to elicit caregiving or nurturing from others. Some psychoanalysts have advocated a type of "reparenting therapy" to encourage resolution of early conflicts about being cared for and to encourage the patient to return to higher developmental levels of functioning. In the case of schizophrenia, symptoms such as symbolic language and bizarre gestures may represent the patient's distorted attempt to communicate the underlying conflict or trauma. Some patients who have experienced schizophrenic regression and withdrawal and recovered have reported that they knew people were talking to them but could not respond or look at them because of overwhelming fears, such as that the world would end. The intense, overwhelming anxiety and the accompanying difficulties in being able to communicate with others often make it more difficult to reach out to the individual who is suffering. The book *The Eden Express* (1975), by Mark Vonnegut, presents a personal account of the experience of developing schizophrenia and recovering from the disorder.

Many professionals believe that some major psychiatric disorders such as depression and schizophrenia result from both internal psychological conflict or trauma and biochemical changes or abnormalities. Combination treatments that utilize psychotropic medication to calm the overwhelming anxiety or treat the depression can often make the patient better able to benefit from psychodynamic therapies. Depression, according to psychoanalysts, may result from anger turned inward on the self. The self forms a love attachment to an idealized other in a close relationship; when the relationship is over, that part of the self that identified and internalized the image of the other turns the anger of rejection in on those parts of itself. Psychodynamic interventions would seek to help the depressed person release this anger in appropriate ways rather than internalize it.

The development of some personality disorders or traits is thought to have origins in the early (pregenital) psychosexual stages. Freud hypothesized that toilet training that was too harsh or too lax could lead to "fixation" in the anal stage. If someone became fixated at this or any other pregenital stage, Freud believed that he or she would be thwarted in achieving mature personality development. He proposed the "anal character" (such as the obsessive-compulsive personality) to describe an adult who may be excessively sloppy or neat, depending on the nature of the toilet training the person experienced. Similarly, the oral character is a person who was fixated at the oral stage and may show symptoms such as chain smoking, overeating, or other excessive oral habits. Although this idea is intriguing, there has been little empirical support for these hypotheses.

Some of the anxiety disorders are thought to originate in the phallic stage. For example, a little boy who develops a phobia or irrational fear of adult men might have been thought to have displaced the castration anxiety he had experienced from his father to all adult men. The internal conflict related to sexuality results in anxiety and avoidance. If the central conflict of this period was resolved successfully, the child would progress to the next stage of development, the latency period. Partial resolution of any of the conflicts associated with the stages could lead to other psychiatric disorders. Freud believed that conflicts over sexuality and traumatic experiences would be repressed or eliminated from conscious awareness because they were too unpleasant and caused too much tension and anxiety if the person became conscious of these memories or thoughts. This reliance on repression can lead to dissociative disorders such as fugue states or multiple personality disorder, in which entire periods of a person's life are blocked out of conscious awareness. Although there is controversy over the existence of multiple personality disorder, a dissociative disorder in which alternate identities are formed through dissociation and a form of self-hypnosis as a defense against abuse or trauma, many clinicians believe they have treated individuals with this disorder.

Freud's last stage of development, the genital stage, represents the highest level of psychosexual development. Adults who have successfully negotiated the tasks of this stage are able to sublimate sexual and aggressive energy. Sublimation refers to the ability to channel these energies into socially acceptable activities. In this stage, mature sexuality and altruistic (nonselfish) love evolve. Persons who can function normally are thought to have reached this level of development; however, Sigmund Freud believed that even emotionally healthy people use defense mechanisms to cope with anxiety.

Anna Freud, his daughter, further developed and refined the list of defense mechanisms that were originally proposed. Each time one uses a defense mechanism, however, one gives up or distorts a little of the true reality one experiences. For example, a college student fails to attend class regularly, thinking he or she can pass the course anyway, but flunks the first test. The student then says to his or her roommate, "I would have passed the exam if the professor had given a fair test." In this example, the student uses the defense of denial, essentially disregarding his or her failure to attend class as a contributing factor in the poor academic outcome. It also demonstrates rationalization, or making up an excuse that is not accurate but is acceptable to one's self-esteem.

Freud treated the neurotic or anxiety disorders exhibited by his patients with the method of psychoanalytic psychotherapy. Clients, or patients, as they were referred to then, would lie on a couch, with Freud seated at the head, looking away from the client. Then the first step of psychoanalysis, called free association, would begin; the patient was encouraged to say anything that came to his or her mind.

Each thought or memory was believed to trigger subsequent memories and tap into the stream of unconscious thought. During the free association period, early childhood experiences were relived and their anxiety was released in a process called catharsis. This represented a cleansing of the mind through the release of repressed (forgotten) traumas. Repression, previously mentioned, is a defense mechanism that has a central place in psychodynamic theory; it is thought to occur at the unconscious level to block memories that are too painful for the person to remember. Freud used the psychoanalytic technique to treat a common disorder of the times, which was then called "hysteria." This disorder was thought by Freud to be caused by repressed memories that led to the expression of various symptoms such as temporary loss of vision, temporary paralysis, and anxiety.

The psychoanalytic model and the method of psychoanalysis have been criticized for several reasons. Neo-Freudians considered the psychodynamic model to be too focused on psychosexual development, determinism, sexuality, and aggression; however, most did believe that the model was viable for explaining the development of various psychiatric disorders. Psychoanalysis, as a method of treatment, has been criticized as being too time-consuming and expensive, often taking years to accomplish its goal. Proof of its effectiveness as a therapeutic approach has not been unequivocally documented by outcome research. Neoanalytic theorists (or ego psychologists, as some have been termed) developed psychodynamic theory further to focus more on the development of the self. Important contributors to modified versions of psychodynamic theory were Carl Jung, Alfred Adler, Karen Horney, and Harry Stack Sullivan. Important ego psychologists included Heinz Hartmann and Erik Erikson. Margaret Mahler, Heinz Kohut, Melanie Klein, James Masterson, and Otto Kernberg have also been contributors to self or object relations theory, another psychodynamic stage theory that refers to the development of mental representations of one's emotional attachments to significant others.

Applications

Psychoanalytic models have had widespread influence on the field of psychology and have strongly influenced contemporary thinking, especially in the area of marketing to consumers. Although there has been mixed empirical support for the advertising technique referred to as "subliminal persuasion," this technique has been used to market products to consumers in the form of subliminal messages flashed on television screens, subliminal audio messages played over piped-in music in stores, and pictures secretly embedded in magazine ads. Subliminal persuasion is designed to influence the unconscious mind in order to get people to purchase certain products without their conscious or direct awareness. Subliminal messages are also used in self-help programs produced on audiocassette tapes to help people relax or to raise their self-esteem. The unconscious subliminal messages are embedded in background sounds such as music and are not audible to the listener.

The most direct applications of the psychodynamic model have been in the ability to understand psychopathology and personality development. The use of this model to develop forms of short-term psychodynamic psychotherapy has played a significant role in the area of psychotherapy. Short-term therapy refers to a treatment approach that is more focused and goal-oriented than traditional, classical psychoanalysis, with a maximum time limit of twenty sessions or six months. This approach has been popular with third-party reimbursement agencies such as insurance companies, who often impose limits on reimbursement.

The following case example illustrates the use of short-term psychodynamic treatment of a conversion disorder. Michael had been playing ball with a friend when the friend ran out into the street to retrieve the ball. The friend was hit by a car and became paralyzed and confined to a wheelchair. After a few weeks, Michael, who had been traumatized by witnessing the event and who felt guilty about having thrown the ball, lost the function of his legs and became unable to walk. Physical examination showed no organic cause for his paralysis, and he was referred to a psychodynamic therapist. A complete history was taken, which included recent events. His parents reported the incident with his friend; Michael, however, had repressed it and did not recall what had happened. One day in a therapy session, Michael noticed a picture in the office of a famous baseball player. He then remembered for the first time witnessing the accident (a memory he had previously found too anxiety provoking). After several more sessions in which Michael expressed his guilt and remorse over the accident, he began to realize that he did not intentionally want his friend to be hurt. Sometime later, Michael regained the use of his legs. The treatment took two months, with weekly one-hour sessions. In this case, the symptom of paralysis of Michael's legs represented the unconscious conversion of his intense internal anxiety into a physical symptom. The memory lapse for the incident represented repression and dissociation.

Art therapists have used psychodynamic models to understand the meaning underlying artwork created by emotionally disturbed children. This application is often referred to as art therapy or expressive therapy. The "kinetic house, tree, person" drawings and "draw a person" tests utilize principles of art therapy using psychoanalytic theory as the basis for interpreting the drawings and discovering the developmental level and psychological defenses of the child. Determining the presence of unconscious conflicts such as a child's difficulty with aggressive or sexual impulses has also been accomplished with these interpretive methods.

Hilde Bruch studied eating disorders, particularly anorexia nervosa and bulimia nervosa, for three decades and was a proponent of the ego-analytic approach to explain the underlying problem central to eating disorders. Bruch believed that the central problem in individuals with eating disorders was the failure to develop an autonomous self. According to her theory, women with anorexia seek to control their bodies as a substitute for their lack of control in making their own decisions and because they have not been able to develop mature ego functions as a result of parental overprotection or domination. Bruch's work has had a significant influence on the successful treatment of clients with eating disorders and represents a lasting contribution to the field of psychology.

Perspective and Prospects
Sigmund Freud has been described as the father of psychoanalysis, the forerunner of modern psychotherapy. He originally studied hypnosis and trained under Josef

Breuer. Freud was educated as a physician, with a specialty in neurology; he was also influenced by the theories of Charles Darwin, particularly *The Descent of Man* (1871). Freud's heritage was Jewish, and he was originally from Germany. He fled Germany to escape the Nazis, an event that undoubtedly had a strong influence on his perspective. He settled in Vienna, Austria, which became the seat of development of many psychoanalytic theoreticians of late Victorian times; however, because of the social setting (upper-middle-class Vienna) and the time period (Victorian), Freud's theories met with strong objection. Particularly offensive was his focus on infant sexuality as well as adult sexuality. During this period, society in Vienna was very strict and repressive regarding sexuality. Women, especially, were discouraged from expressing or even acknowledging sexual desires and impulses. The society was strongly patriarchal, with the male head of the household holding a dominant position of authority, under which the wife and children were seen as possessions. Thus, Freud's theory was not popular with the public; in fact, it was originally rejected by other professionals as well.

The Neo-Freudians, dissatisfied with the deterministic approach of psychoanalytic theory, began to branch out and broaden the psychodynamic perspective. Carl Jung, a Swiss psychiatrist, believed that Freud's theory was too negative and narrow. Jung proposed that the mind houses a "collective unconscious" that consists of archetypes, which are symbols of the experience common to all humans. In addition, Jung's therapy operated on the integration of conflicting or opposite aspects of the self, such as masculinity and femininity.

Another contemporary and colleague of Freud, Alfred Adler, disagreed with the part of drive theory that emphasized sexuality. Adler preferred to emphasize the ego, or the self, and one's relationships to others and society. He believed that humans suffer from feelings of inferiority, and thought that the important drive determining actions is a drive for dominance over others. In the early and mid-1900's, Harry Stack Sullivan and Karen Horney continued this emphasis on the importance of social relationships, specifically the importance of the parenting relationship. They suggested that poor parenting during early childhood leads to anxiety and poor self-concept in later adult years.

In this same period, Heinz Hartmann, credited with being the founding father of the contemporary school of ego psychology, proposed the existence of the "conflict-free sphere" of ego functioning. Hartmann believed that the ego not only negotiates between the opposing forces of the id and superego but also has independent, free functions of its own. Erik Erikson developed a theory of psychosocial development that outlined and defined the formation of "ego identity" achieved through a conflict resolution of crises presented at eight stages of development. For example, in the first stage, from birth to age two, the child has to learn whether it can trust its caretakers. If not, the child will have a basic mistrust that will influence subsequent development and relationships.

Margaret Mahler became one of the most influential object relations theorists. Object relations are defined as the mental representations of one's emotional attachments to significant others. Mahler developed a stage theory that outlines the development of the psychological birth of an individual. The stages are autism, symbiosis, separation-individuation, and on-the-way-to-object-constancy. The end product of the progression through these stages is an individual who can function independently and hold mental representations of others as whole persons with both good and bad qualities. Mahler's separation-individuation stage has been one of the most important contributions to object relations theory; children who do not complete the tasks of the stage will never develop into fully independent adults. Object relations approaches and short-term psychodynamic therapy are widely used to treat individuals who suffer from personality disorders.

Bibliography
Alloy, Lauren B., Neil S. Jacobson, and Joan Acocella. *Abnormal Psychology: Current Perspectives*. 8th ed. New York: McGraw-Hill, 1998. This abnormal psychology text reviews the psychoanalytic perspective in clear, understandable terms with meaningful examples. In the section on psychiatric disorders, the contribution of the psychodynamic model to underlying causes and to treatment of certain disorders is explained.

Bruch, Hilde. *The Golden Cage: The Enigma of Anorexia Nervosa*. Cambridge, Mass.: Harvard University Press, 1978. Bruch explains the central dilemma in anorexia as a failure in the autonomous or independent development of the self. Her work is based on clinical experience, and the case examples show the reader the reality of anorexia and its impact on individuals and their families.

Frank, Ellen, ed. *Gender and Its Effects on Psychopathology*. Washington, D.C.: American Psychiatric Press, 2000. Examines sex differences in mental disorders. Includes bibliographical references and an index.

Hersen, Michel, and Alan S. Bellack, eds. *Psychopathology in Adulthood*. 2d ed. Boston: Allyn & Bacon, 2000. Discusses various mental disorders that occur among adults. Includes bibliographical references and indexes.

Vonnegut, Mark. *The Eden Express*. New York: Praeger, 1975. A personal description of the experience of developing schizophrenia. Gives readers insight into the dynamics underlying some cases of the disorder.

Wertheimer, Michael. *A Brief History of Psychology*. 3d ed. New York: Holt, Rinehart and Winston, 1987. Provides a brief historical overview of various approaches to psychological study including gestalt, behavioral, and psychodynamic. The facts regarding the history of each movement are concise and interesting.

Willerman, Lee. *Psychopathology*. New York: McGraw-Hill, 1990. Provides a general introduction to psychopathology, with a fairly sophisticated discussion of theoretical facets of abnormality, psychiatric disorders, and their treatments.

Karen Wolford

See also:
Abnormality; Amnesia, Fugue, and Multiple Personality; Antisocial Personality; Behavioral Assessment and Personality Rating Scales; Borderline, Histrionic, and Narcissistic Personalities; Hypochondriasis, Conversion, Somatization, and Somatoform Pain; Projective Personality Traits; Psychoanalysis.

ABNORMALITY
Sociocultural Models

Type of psychology: Psychopathology; social psychology
Fields of study: Models of abnormality

A sociocultural approach to abnormal psychology examines how cultural factors determine what behavior is labeled abnormal within different societies; in addition, it investigates how societal values promote certain types of psychological abnormality.

Principal terms

CROSS-CULTURAL RESEARCH ON ABNORMALITY: a comparison of different cultures' practices of labeling behavior as abnormal

CULTURAL FACTORS: the standards and expectations of a particular society that influence the labeling of behavior as abnormal

PSYCHIATRIC DIAGNOSIS: the label applied to an individual whose behavior is thought to be the result of a specific mental disorder

STEREOTYPIC GENDER ROLES: a society's expectations of individuals' behavior based on their gender

STIGMATIZATION: the practice of discrediting or discriminating against someone because of a past or present psychological disorder

Overview

A sociocultural viewpoint of abnormality is one of several approaches used in attempting to explain the causes of abnormal behavior. Unlike other approaches to abnormality, this perspective places great emphasis not only on the causes of abnormality but also on the reasons behind why certain behaviors are labeled abnormal. Supporters of this approach assert that cultural factors are at work within each society determining why certain behaviors are considered normal while others are not. Therefore, a sociocultural perspective uses research from areas such as anthropology, sociology, and political science as well as psychology in studying abnormality.

There is a large range of opinion regarding what should be considered abnormal behavior even among those who take a sociocultural viewpoint. Certain investigators consider the concept of psychological abnormality to be a complete myth. Thomas Szasz and R. D. Laing, both psychiatrists, are two examples of such individuals. Szasz, in *The Myth of Mental Illness* (1961), rejected the idea that people have mental illnesses in the same way that individuals have physical disorders such as cancer or heart disease. Szasz contended that behavior said to be the result of mental illness is nothing more than an individual's way of managing the problems of living.

R. D. Laing expressed a similar viewpoint and extended it to the condition of schizophrenia. Considered by most mental health professionals to be one of the most severe psychological disorders, schizophrenia is characterized by symptoms which include auditory or visual hallucinations (hearing voices or seeing visions of people or things not physically present), delusions (beliefs not based in reality), and deterioration in areas such as work or school, interpersonal relationships, and hygiene. Laing asserted that certain individuals enact these schizophrenic symptoms as a reasonable response to an unreasonable living situation. That is, individuals who are diagnosed as schizophrenic perceive their current environment as unlivable and face it by adopting schizophrenia. Laing concluded that these individuals are diagnosed as schizophrenic because of their violation of particular social standards, not because they have an underlying physical disease that causes their behavior (Richard Evans, 1976).

Most investigators who endorse a sociocultural view of abnormal behavior are not as radical as Szasz or Laing. More moderate advocates of a sociocultural perspective do not deny the existence of factors other than societal standards (for example, biological influences) that cause the development of abnormality. The goal of sociocultural researchers, however, is to illustrate how societal standards dictate what behavior is labeled abnormal.

Cross-cultural investigations are one way of examining the influence that societal factors have on determining the behaviors which are considered abnormal. Cross-cultural research has shown that societal factors are important in determining not only what is diagnosed as psychologically abnormal, but also what is labeled physically abnormal. For example, dyschromic spriochaetosis, a disfiguring disease characterized by multicolored spots on the skin, is so common among members of a South American tribe that those who do *not* have it were long considered abnormal. To a greater extent, societal standards also determine which behaviors are considered psychologically abnormal. For example, until recently, every winter near the southeastern Canadian region of the Saint Lawrence River, male residents of all ages engaged in a yearly ritual of clubbing to death baby seals for their pelts. Even though more humane ways were available to kill the seals, citizens of this region viewed clubbing the seals to death as normal because of the tradition surrounding the practice. This treatment of animals within most parts of American society would be considered cruel, and it is likely that those who participated in it would be labeled as abnormal. In summary, cross-cultural studies demonstrate that what is considered abnormal behavior differs across societies depending on the values and customs of a particular culture.

The sociocultural approach proposes that, across different societies, there are certain types of action likely to be viewed as abnormal. One type of conduct that is likely to be viewed as abnormal is behavior that violates societal expectations. Each society has expectations about what is appropriate and inappropriate behavior for a given setting. For example, if in the middle of a college lecture a student were to strip down to a bathing suit, most Americans would believe that this behavior was the result of a psychological disorder. If the same student were to undress in a similar fashion on a public beach, however, minimum disruption would occur, and few, if any, fellow sunbathers would consider this conduct abnormal. This example illustrates how a particular society's expectations regarding what is appropriate behavior for a particular situation determine what is considered normal or abnormal.

A second type of behavior likely to be termed abnormal is behavior that is disturbing enough to others that they want it changed (Leonard Krasner, Author Houts, and Leonard Ullmann, 1992). Children who are diagnosed as having attention-deficit disorder (ADD) would fit this criterion. In the classroom, ADD children have difficulty remaining seated and waiting their turns, often blurt out answers, talk excessively, and do not follow instructions. These behaviors are often so disturbing to their peers and teachers that children who engage in them are frequently referred to mental health professionals because they are considered abnormal and in need of treatment.

A final type of behavior that is likely to be labeled abnormal is behavior that appears irrational, self-defeating, or maladaptive. For example, imagine the reaction most people would have if they were to view a man walking along a downtown street, shabbily dressed and foul smelling, and talking to himself about Martian invaders sent to Earth to steal his mind. It is likely that most observers of this individual would consider him to be crazy. In this connection, persons who exhibit the symptoms of schizophrenia, as illustrated in this example, seem to most observers to be engaging in actions that are irrational and maladaptive.

Applications

Researchers who advocate a sociocultural perspective are very concerned with the potential weaknesses and misuses of labeling certain people abnormal. Psychiatric diagnoses are obtained through a psychiatrist's or other mental health professional's labeling of someone as having a mental disorder based on that person's reported or observed behavior. In practice, diagnosing involves taking the reported and observed behavior of an individual and comparing it to the conditions listed in the American Psychiatric Association's *Diagnostic and Statistical Manual of Mental Disorders*, or DSM; new editions are published periodically. The manual contains a sanctioned system for diagnosing behavior. A now-classic study conducted by David Rosenhan, "On Being Sane in Insane Places" (1973), demonstrated several potential problems with correctly diagnosing people as psychologically abnormal. In Rosenhan's experiment, he and seven associates from Stanford University presented themselves to mental hospitals under false identities and complained of hearing voices saying "empty," "hollow," and "thud." All eight were admitted to the hospitals; seven were diagnosed as schizophrenic, and the eighth person was diagnosed as having another severe psychological disorder. After being admitted to the hospital, the pseudopatients behaved as normally as they did before their admission and stopped complaining of hearing voices.

During their hospital stay, some of the patients recorded information in notebooks. This note-taking behavior, as well as other normal behavior, was listed in their medical records as further evidence of their mental disorder. In spite of their normality, the average patient was hospitalized for nineteen days and typically released with the diagnosis of "schizophrenia in remission." That is, although the pseudopatients did not exhibit schizophrenic behavior at the time of their discharge, they were labeled as having an underlying psychological disorder that could recur in the future. Rosenhan's study illustrates several potential limitations to declaring people abnormal. First, people are often labeled as abnormal with insufficient supporting evidence. Second, once a person is designated as abnormal, much of his or her behavior, whether otherwise normal or not, is seen as part of his or her abnormality. Third, the label of being abnormal is difficult to discard. That is, even though the pseudopatients were discharged, they were released carrying psychiatric diagnoses.

In addition to the potential problems with accurately diagnosing abnormality, the label of abnormality is often intentionally used to harm or discredit individuals. One graphic example of how the concept of psychological abnormality has been misused is the practice of leaders in some countries diagnosing political dissidents as mentally ill in order to banish them to psychiatric hospitals for "treatment," thus silencing their protests. Andrei Sakharov, regarded as a prominent nuclear physicist within the Soviet Union until he began to criticize the Communist party, wrote about how political opponents of the Communist government were often diagnosed as schizophrenic and sent to mental hospitals. Once hospitalized, these dissidents often were given powerful psychiatric medications and kept from the public as a means of quieting their protesting.

In America, individuals diagnosed with psychological disorders such as depression may be refused access to benefits such as health insurance and employment. In addition, those diagnosed as having mental disorders are often stigmatized. Stigmatization is the practice of discrediting or discriminating against someone because of having a past or present psychological disorder. An example of stigmatization occurred in the 1972 presidential campaign, when Democratic vice presidential candidate Thomas Eagleton was pressured into withdrawing from the race because of the revelation that he had received treatment for depression.

In addition to pointing out the potential misuses of labeling someone as abnormal, sociocultural investigators are interested in identifying the larger societal influences responsible for creating behaviors that are labeled abnormal. Among these suggested sociocultural causes of abnormal behavior are factors such as stereotypical gender roles and poverty. Stereotypic gender roles are the types of behaviors and attitudes that are expected from individuals because they are either males or females. Each society has its own set of stereotypic gender roles. These expectations based on gender place both males and females at higher risk for exhibiting different types of abnormal behavior. For example, males are at much higher risk to develop pedophilia, a disorder characterized by recurrent sexual arousal toward children, and frequently accompanied by attempts to have sexual relations with children. A sociocultural perspective on pedophilia would highlight the cultural factors that promote pedophilia, such as society's frequent depiction of men as dominating women and children, and the belief that men have a right to satisfy their sexual desires even at the expense of others.

Women also are at greater risk for developing certain psychological disorders as a result of particular cultural factors. For example, women are approximately nineteen times more likely than men to develop anorexia nervosa. Anorexia nervosa is an eating disorder in which the individual is extremely underweight because of self-imposed starvation, sees herself as fat even though she is underweight, and is fearful of becoming obese. One prominent sociocultural factor that is suggested as making women more vulnerable to developing anorexia is society's emphasis on women being thin in order to be considered attractive. A study by David Garner and colleagues, published in 1980, illustrated this increased emphasis on thinness within today's society by analyzing the weight of women depicted in *Playboy* centerfolds from 1959 to 1978. The results of this analysis revealed that the average weight of the centerfolds decreased significantly over the twenty-year period. This finding indicated that the ideal woman, as defined by Western society, has become thinner even as the weight of the average American woman has continued to rise. Supporters of a sociocultural viewpoint state that these contradictory events have placed women under pressure to be thin even at extreme costs to their health and happiness.

Poverty is another sociocultural factor that places particular members of society at greater risk for developing psychological disorders. For example, children reared in impoverished environments experience an increased number of stressful events such as witnessing violence. This high level of stress increases the likelihood that these children will develop psychological disorders such as post-traumatic stress disorder (PTSD). PTSD develops as a reaction to a traumatic stressor (for example, witnessing the murder of one's parents) and consists of symptoms such as experiencing recurrent nightmares regarding the traumatic event, withdrawing from one's family and friends, and having difficulty concentrating.

Perspective and Prospects

The sociocultural approach to examining abnormal psychology was spurred on by criticisms made by Thomas Szasz and R. D. Laing in the early 1960's. Both these men had personal reasons to react against the practice of labeling people as psychologically abnormal. Laing was aware that some of his own personal experiences would be considered by many to be abnormal. For example, Laing reported that he was able to sleep one hour a night for a week's time, without the use of drugs, by altering his own state of mind. Laing also described his participation in mystical experiences of altered consciousness which he regarded as similar to a schizophrenic's hallucinations. Because of his own experience of altered states of mind and his realization of his normality, Laing was adamant in his denunciation of assigning labels to people whose behavior is different from that of the typical person.

More recently, those offering a sociocultural perspective on abnormality have grown concerned over the increase in the number of labels available to diagnose someone as having a mental disorder. Between the introduction of the first edition of the *Diagnostic and Statistical Manual of Mental Disorders* in 1952 and its third revised edition in 1987, the number of psychiatric labels roughly tripled, from approximately one hundred to three hundred. Not by coincidence, sociocultural advocates contend, the number of mental health workers increased fourfold during the same approximate time period. This suggests that the rapid expansion of diagnostic labels has greatly added to the number of people who can be labeled abnormal, thus creating an increased market for mental health professionals.

As a consequence of the proliferation in the number of diagnostic labels, the number of people being diagnosed as suffering from a mental disorder also has increased. Sociocultural advocates are concerned with this trend, given the possibility that someone may be discriminated against because of being diagnosed as mentally ill. The potential stigmatization that could occur as a result of being labeled mentally ill should give all reason to reflect on the usefulness and validity of the current practice of psychiatric labeling.

In addition to its important criticism of the manner in which people are often diagnosed as abnormal, the sociocultural approach is useful in that it alerts individuals to societal pressures that might promote psychological disorders. An awareness of these societal pressures allows for the initiation of efforts to prevent the development of certain psychological disorders. For example, if it is acknowledged that society's overemphasis on thinness for women is behind certain women developing anorexia nervosa, then steps such as educational efforts within school systems can be taken to challenge the attitude that women must be thin to be attractive.

Bibliography

Bayer, Ronald. *Homosexuality and American Psychiatry: The Politics of Diagnosis.* New York: Basic Books, 1981. A through examination of the politics involved in the removal in 1980 of homosexuality from the third edition of the *Diagnostic and Statistical Manual of Mental Disorders* (DSM-III), the official guide of psychiatric diagnoses. An important illustration of how political processes become involved in determining what behavior, in this case homosexuality, is designated normal or abnormal. Very readable work.

Brumberg, Joan Jacobs. *Fasting Girls: The Emergence of Anorexia Nervosa as a Modern Disease.* Cambridge, Mass.: Harvard University Press, 1988. Brumberg, a historian, presents the history of anorexia nervosa from a sociocultural perspective. This book provides an in-depth examination of how societal values operate to increase the prevalence of a specific psychological disorder. A well-researched and very readable book.

Evans, Richard Isadore. *R. D. Laing: The Man and His Ideas.* New York: E. P. Dutton, 1976. A series of discussions with Laing regarding his views on the concept of mental illness. In this readable work, Laing outlines his objections to the diagnostic and treatment approaches of the mental health establishment.

Group for the Advancement of Psychiatry. *Homosexuality and the Mental Health Professions: The Impact of Bias.* Hillsdale, N.J.: Analytic Press, 2000. Discusses views of homosexuality within psychiatry. Includes bibliographical references and an index.

Krasner, Leonard, Arthur C. Houts, and Leonard P. Ullmann. *A Psychological Approach to Abnormal Behavior: Invention and Discovery.* Englewood Cliffs, N.J.: Prentice-Hall, 1992. This textbook differs from other abnormal psychology texts in that it examines each category of psychiatric disorders from a sociocultural perspective. Provides an excellent historical overview of the development of the concept of psychological abnormality. Also examines the politics involved in the decision-making process by which behaviors are labeled abnormal.

Lask, Bryan, and Rachel Bryant-Waugh, eds. *Anorexia Nervosa and Related Eating Disorders in Childhood and Adolescence.* 2d ed. Hove, East Sussex, England: Psychology Press, 2000. This volume examines, in seventeen parts, the origins and treatment of eating disorders in young people.

Offer, David, and Melvin Sabshin. "Culture, Values, and Normality." In *Normality and the Life Cycle.* New York: Basic Books, 1984. Provides an excellent sociocultural perspective on abnormality; it gives numerous examples from ancient and modern times regarding the influence of societal standards in dictating which behavior is labeled abnormal. A readable chapter.

Peplau, Letitia Anne, and Shelley E. Taylor, eds. *Sociocultural Perspectives in Social Psychology: Current Readings.* Upper Saddle River, N.J.: Prentice Hall, 1997. Discusses the relationship between ethnicity and social science research. Includes bibliographical references.

Rosenhan, David L. "On Being Sane in Insane Places." *Science* 179 (January 19, 1973): 250-258. Provides the findings of a classic study investigating the pitfalls of labeling people as abnormal. Extremely well written, and easily understood even by psychological novices.

Szasz, Thomas S. *The Myth of Mental Illness.* New York: Dell Books, 1961. A classic work in which Szasz provides his objections to the concept of "mental illness." An ageless critique of the practice of psychiatric diagnosis; for the advanced reader.

R. Christopher Qualls

See also:

Abnormality; Abnormality: Behavioral Models; Abnormality: Biomedical Models; Abnormality: Psychodynamic Models; Community Psychology; Madness: Historical Concepts.

Addictive Personality and Behaviors

Type of psychology: Psychopathology
Fields of study: Attitudes and behavior; critical issues in stress; substance abuse

The effects of an addictive personality are harmful to the afflicted individual and are often harmful to others. Addictive behaviors seem to be at least partly caused by a need to self-medicate and by low self-esteem; study of these behaviors involves attempts to identify, predict, and treat them.

Principal terms

ADDICTION: a condition of slavery to a habit, or a very strong inclination concerning it
COMPULSION: an impulse that is difficult to resist
DEPENDENCY: the state of relying on another for support or existence
OBSESSION: a compelling idea or feeling, usually irrational, over which a person has little conscious control
PERSONALITY: the total physical, intellectual, and emotional structure of an individual, exhibited through consistent patterns of behavior
SYMPTOM: a sign or indication of a problem; it is not necessarily noticeable to the untrained individual

Causes and Symptoms

Some researchers have asked whether there is a single psychological predisposition or a multilevel series of complications involved in the addictive personality—or whether virtually any personality is vulnerable. Researchers administering the Minnesota Multiphasic Personality Inventory, an objective personality test, to addicted individuals have found that they have distinctive personality traits; sometimes these traits precede the addiction, and sometimes they seem to be caused by or exacerbated by the addiction. These findings are highly controversial and have fueled many heated discussions.

A surplus of aggressive energy seems to be at the core of most addictions. Indulgence in the addictive behavior is accompanied by the release of aggressive impulses, resulting in a feeling of euphoria. This feeling of relief is then associated with the outlet used, and it seduces the user to attempt a duplication of the original process, thus reexperiencing the euphoria.

Inadequate self-esteem is another psychological predisposition thought to be a common source of imperceptible pain, and the inability to handle the pain can lead to striving for a pain-reducing outlet. The addictive personality seems to have the desire to control the pain but lacks the necessary social, psychological, and biological tools to follow through. Other symptoms of the addictive personality that show up early enough to allow preventive measures to be taken include poor impulse control; intolerance and low frustration level, leading to a need for control; a strong sense of denial in everyday situations; and rigidness and extremes in action and thoughts.

Psychic and/or physical dependence on a release can occur. This dependence can take the form of an addiction to drugs, food, work, sex, gambling, exercise, or any number of other compulsive behaviors. Problems such as manipulation, denial of responsibility, displacement of emotions, and general dishonesty in lifestyle may provoke the process. The addictive process can be periodic, cyclic, sporadic, or continuous, depending upon a person's life patterns.

Different personality theories have conflicting ideas on addiction, adding to the controversy surrounding this topic. The psychoanalytic group believes that the addictive personality is a result of unconscious conflicts and of fixation on the pleasure principle, which states that one's energy in life is directed toward reducing pain and that one's innate drives control one's actions. Although some neo-Freudians disagreed with the cause of the pain, most agreed with the basic concept. Social learning and behavioral psychologists believe that an addictive personality is molded through shaping—the slow and continual development of a behavior, with continuous reinforcement along the way, based on the social mores prevalent when the individual grew up. The need to be accepted becomes the driving force.

The cognitive group holds that an addictive personality is formulated by the way a person receives, processes, stores, and retrieves information received through the senses. If the action taken produces a positive effect, then the person is likely to repeat the process so that the effect can be duplicated. In essence, people become addicted to the pleasurable results before they become addicted to the particular path taken to achieve them. The humanistic group concentrates on the here and now, focusing on the fact that people have choices, yet many people do not know how to make them because of a trauma they experienced while growing up. To the humanist, the idea of the family becomes very important, particularly how love was expressed and experienced, because through love, a person can believe in himself or herself enough to be able to make a positive choice. The proponents of trait theory contend that people are born with certain tendencies and preferences of action, which may or may not be genetic; the evidence is inconclusive. Trait theorists seem to agree, however, that society and the family have a strong influence on people and that some people are predisposed toward compulsive behavior from an early age.

Biological studies have been conducted to explore the suspected link between addictive behavior and genes, suggesting that, at least in part, the addictive personality may be inherited. Studies suggest that certain people may have inherited an impaired neurological homeostasis, which is partly corrected by their addiction—such as to alcohol. The sons of alcoholic fathers have a higher "body sway" than do nonalcoholics; it decreases when they are intoxicated. Sons of alcoholics have a higher rate of addiction than do daughters, no matter which parent reared the children.

People with "familial essential tremor," an inherited disorder, have less tremor when drinking and have a higher rate of alcohol dependence. Also, while alcohol-dependent people do not have higher levels of arousal at rest, they become more aroused when stressed, as measured by heart rate, and are slower to return to rest.

Other studies have suggested that people who are at high risk have abnormal brain-wave activity, suggesting an inability to concentrate or a reduced brain capacity. High-risk people have shown normal to slightly above normal intelligence quotient (IQ) test scores, but low scores on verbal subscales and attention. They also show delayed language development. Moreover, they seem to produce a heroinlike tranquilizing substance which is released and soothes the person when using an addictive substance or pursuing addictive behavior.

The majority of controlled scientific studies on genetics have been conducted on the alcoholic population; because of this, they are inconclusive when discussing the addictive personality overall. They do, however, add evidence to the possible link between biology and behavior.

It seems clear from the research that addiction is a multilevel problem with complex roots, dispersed throughout psychology, sociology, biology, and genetics. A look at three of the symptoms of this disorder will help provide a clearer picture of the observable behavior that results from whatever combination of earlier experiences and inherited traits causes it. Among the symptoms of addictive behavior are a strong need to self-medicate, low self-esteem, and a tendency toward excessiveness.

A strong need to self-medicate, or to stop the pain, seems to be found in most addicts. Whether the pain is real or perceived does not seem to matter; most addicts have both a low tolerance and a strong need to get their way, which reduces the pain for them.

This tendency can be traced back to childhood and used as a warning sign so that an effort can be made to alter the child's first impulse and slowly, over time and with much positive reinforcement, show the child alternative, acceptable behavior. When the child can be taught to achieve the self-medication in a positive way, according to his or her society, there is a better chance for positive achievement as an outcome. Sigmund Freud called this mechanism sublimation—the rechanneling of a socially unacceptable trait or feeling into a socially acceptable outlet. As an example of self-medication, Alice, a five-year-old child in a typical suburban community, is experiencing considerable anxiety because of going to school for the first time. She is swinging her legs back and forth while she sits in her chair as her mother speaks to the teacher on the first day. Her fingers encircle her thumbs and her head is down. The swinging of Alice's legs is a form of self-medication to relieve the anxiety of starting school; it is perfectly normal in this situation and is appropriate for a child of Alice's age.

If this same self-medicating style shows up in other areas of Alice's life, however, in less appropriate situations, then it becomes a symptom and deserves to be watched. At this time, steps can be taken to help Alice feel more confident, which could relieve much of the anxiety and could reduce the need to self-medicate. Children's body language can tell much about their inner feelings and give adults time to alter a potential problem before it gets out of control.

If it is not addressed at this time and Alice is allowed to get into the habit of self-medicating in this relatively harmless way, she may develop a tolerance for this behavior; as she approaches puberty, she might change her habits to include more powerful self-medicating forms such as alcohol, sex, or overeating, which may also be more popular with her age group. She would then need to be taught socially appropriate tools to handle her anxiety. As one can readily see, the deeper the anxiety, the more powerful the self-medicating outlet, and the more difficult it is to turn around.

Another warning sign that seems to appear most of the time in addictive people is low self-esteem. Research has shown that self-esteem is based on a gradual shaping of many small experiences into a general feeling of power—the ability to have a positive effect on one's environment and the people within it. The addictive person translates a feeling of powerlessness into pain, and then must self-medicate to alleviate this condition.

The channel taken to ease the pain may be the one that is easiest to reach or that is most acceptable in the social group that surrounds the individual or that the individual wishes to enter. Therefore, the addictive personality may reach out through work, gambling, sex, eating, dieting, substance use, exercising, competition, or many other ways that can eventually get out of control and lead to destructive patterns of behavior. Self-esteem, or a general feeling of worth, begins at birth. (Some say that it begins while the child is still in the womb, around the sixth or seventh month, but this idea is controversial.)

Children seem to pick up the behaviors and concepts shown them by the society in which they grow up. Socially, a child becomes what society teaches him or her to become. Sarah, for example, is one of three children being reared by an upwardly mobile family interested only in what is best for their children. All her life, Sarah has received a double message: "I love you when you do what I want, and I am disappointed with you when you do what you want to do."

Sarah, like any healthy child, wants to please her parents, so she concentrates on doing what they want; however, it does not seem to be enough, and over the years she begins to numb herself from the pain of rejection and failure. She begins to believe that she is not worth loving, except when she does what others want—and when she does, it is not enough, so she does not see why she should bother. She looks for a group outside her home that will accept her for who she is, or she withdraws or becomes defiant in order to get attention. Sarah is now vulnerable to any self-medicating outlet that comes her way, as she seeks to relieve the pain of her perceived rejection. It does not matter if the pain is justified or is falsely perceived; to the addictive personality, it is real and must be soothed. Sarah's siblings may not experience their family or surroundings in the same way and therefore may not have the need to self-medicate; not all children in an addictive family follow addictive behavior patterns.

Another precursor to addictive behavior seems to be an ever-growing need to get a little more from whatever task is giving one pleasure at the time; this has been called excessiveness, and it is a controversial issue. Many therapists have heard clients discuss a seemingly insatiable appetite for pleasure, in whatever form; they do not know when to stop and simply feel gratitude for the pleasure they have experienced. In the beginning of most addictions, there is sufficient relief to encourage the further use of an acquired outlet, whether it be positive or negative at this time. Because addictive people have a strong sense of denial, they seem to be unable to envision the inevitably destructive phase of their choice for relief.

One question that arises regarding excessiveness is how to teach a person balance when American society in general does not know how to achieve this goal. The United States has been called a nation of overachievers for profit, success, and power. People are rewarded highly for these motives and are considered well-adjusted by their fellow citizens if they achieve them. A problem arises when one considers that addictive personalities are a mass of excessive desires to begin with. They lack impulse control, and there is a strong need to achieve self-validation any way they can.

A thirteen-year-old boy who is growing up in a city atmosphere finds that there is constant stimulation and temptation around him. A normal, healthy boy wishes to be accepted by those who are important to him, and he wishes to have fun. In a city, stimulation is vast, and inappropriate stimulation may easily be overpowering to a child who lacks impulse control, may have a low self-esteem, and probably has already found a way to self-medicate. Even to a thirteen-year-old child without addictive personality tendencies, city stimulation can be overpowering. Some researchers say that at age thirteen, life in general is overpowering and that the child needs strong but nurturing guidance. At this age, a child will look to society for guidance and approval; in his or her role models is the hope for the tools necessary to create a balance between what is available and what the child needs in order to function and mature.

Treatment and Therapy

A concentrated effort was made in Ohio in 1935 by Robert Smith and William Wilson to help the addictive personality through the organization of Alcoholics Anonymous (AA) a self-help group of alcoholics in various stages of recovery.

The success of Alcoholics Anonymous is world renowned, and it is considered by most professionals and nonprofessionals who have contact with it to be one of the more complete recovery programs in the world. The twelve-step program, an idea that AA started, transcends the boundaries of alcohol abuse and has been applied to many addictions. AA is run by recovering alcoholics who are nonprofessionals—simply individual humans helping others. Yet it was not until the early 1970's that addictive people gained national and international attention.

In 1971, the National Institute on Alcohol Abuse and Alcoholism conducted research that showed addiction to be threatening American society. A concentrated effort was made to study the addictive person and attempt to find symptoms that could predict high-risk individuals. The federally funded studies, it was hoped, would find ways to help prevent and reduce the tremendous health, social, and economic consequences of addiction in the United States. Assessing dependence potential and discovering vulnerability or high-risk factors through demographic characteristics, psychological status, and individual drug history became its focus. The funding of these studies has become a critical component in the fight to better understand the addictive personality. National programs were begun to attempt to show individuals and communities how to deal with the behavioral aftermath of addictive thinking.

David M. Murco, of the Psychiatric Research Center, University of Maryland School of Medicine, and Lawrence J. Hatterer, a psychiatrist at New York Hospital, Cornell Medical Center, both leaders in the area of addictive personalities, have obtained similar findings in their individual research. They conclude that neglect from parents, absence of family support, and inconsistent or permissive behavior on the parents' part can place children in the high-risk category. With the further sophistication of genetic studies, researchers are slowly compiling an addictive profile which may lend itself to early intervention and prevention.

Perspective and Prospects

Addictions and their victims have been studied and described at least since the beginning of written language, and probably since humanity first communicated by storytelling. Fascination with the idea of an addictive personality and related behavior dates back to 950 B.C., to the works of Homer, the Greek poet, and perhaps before that to the writings of Lao-tzu, a Chinese philosopher and imperial adviser. These men studied human nature and sometimes wrote about the uncontrollable allure of certain desires which led to behaviors that were likely to cause personal and cultural destruction.

The implications of the effect on society of negative addiction are far reaching. Each year more accidents are being caused by people who are under the influence of alcohol or other drugs; more strokes and heart attacks are caused by overwork, lack of sufficient exercise, and improper nutritional habits. More babies are being born addicted than ever before. On the other hand, there is the idea of a positive addiction, or compulsive behavior that actually enriches the individual and the society in which that person lives. (Even this behavior can get out of control when a person who has problems with setting healthy limits attempts to use it.)

Whether addictive behavior is learned for survival, genetically passed on, or an intricate combination of both, there appears to be a set of symptoms which can predispose a person toward addiction—or, at the least, can place a person in a high-risk group. If these symptoms can be identified early enough, the chance to teach potential addicts the path toward balance increases, and the compulsive lifestyle can be decreased or channeled in a healthy way. Yet it does seem that American society values addictive behavior in the form of overachievers and rewards them accordingly, therefore actually encouraging a form of addiction. As long as addictive behavior is encouraged in any form, there will be a part of the population that has trouble differentiating excess from balance.

Internationally, it has been surmised that advanced, technological societies seem to give rise to more kinds of dependency than do more slowly developing countries, a fact which could help researchers focus on some societal misconceptions of overall health. For example, in the United States and some other technologically advanced societies, there seems to be a belief pattern, propagated by the mass media, that supports instant gratification. If one is tense, one should take a pill; if one is lonely, one can call a certain number for conversation. If one is bored, have an alcoholic drink. If one wants to be part of the in-crowd, smoke; if one is unhappy, eat. People who are addicted to a negative anxiety releaser have been described as "committing suicide on the installment plan." Societies, governments, and researchers must unite in a desire to unveil all possible symptoms of addiction, to identify those at high risk toward them, and to employ successful recovery methods.

Bibliography

Berger, Gilda. *Addiction: Its Causes, Problems, and Treatments*. New York: Frank-lin Watts, 1982. Berger, a former special education teacher, writes with sensitivity and depth about the subject of addiction and its problems with sensitivity and depth. She fully explores the idea of compulsive dependency on pleasure-giving substances such as alcohol, illegal drugs, tobacco, caffeine, and food. She also provides insight into causes, treatments, and societal attitudes.

McCance-Katz, Eilnore F., and Thomas R. Kosten, eds. *New Treatments for Chemical Addictions*. Washington, D.C.: American Psychiatric Press, 1998. Discusses the diagnosis and treatment of alcoholism, tobacco abuse, and opioid use. Includes bibliographical references and an index.

McCrady, Barbara S., and Elizabeth E. Epstein, eds. *Addictions: A Comprehensive Guidebook*. New York: Oxford University Press, 1999. Discusses alcoholism and other forms of substance abuse. Includes bibliographical references and an index.

May, Rollo. *The Meaning of Anxiety*. New York: Ronald Press, 1950. This classic work by one of the masters of humanism is well-written, clear, and concise. It covers the subject of anxiety, an intricate component of most addictive behaviors, from modern interpretation to management of clinical analysis. Included are self-testing devices in the appendices, an extensive bibliography, and clear and informative notes.

Mule, S. Joseph, ed. *Behavior in Excess: An Examination of the Volitional Disorders*. New York: Free Press, 1981. This set of nineteen chapters is a must for the beginning student of addictive personalities and behavior. Explains the many drugs of choice available to the addictive person as well as the societal addictions of eating, work, gambling, sports, television, sex, and smoking. Explores the environment influence on excessive behaviors and psychodynamic and behavioral treatments. An excellent group of writings.

Oxford, Jim. *Excessive Appetites: A Psychological View of Addictions*. New York: John Wiley & Sons, 1985. This internationally focused, easily read book begins by proclaiming that the author himself is an addict in recovery—a workaholic. It is well organized into two parts, one dealing with the topic of the excessive appetite and the other with psychological viewpoints on causes and treatments. The summary at the end draws most of the central themes together in an easily accessible format.

Wilson, Bill. *Alcoholics Anonymous*. 3d ed. New York: Alcoholics Anonymous World Services, 1976. In this compilation of stories, words of wisdom, and insights into the world of the addicted person, the cofounders of Alcoholics Anonymous have been the impetus for an inspiring group of writings. Together with one of their original associates, Sister Ignatia of St. Thomas Hospital in Akron, Ohio, and many others, they have put into words the heart and soul of an addictive person's behavior—physically, emotionally, and spiritually. An essential part of any student's reading in the field of compulsive behavior.

Frederic Wynn

See also:
Alcoholism; Codependent Personality; Substance Abuse.

AGGRESSION
Definitions and Theoretical Explanations

Type of psychology: Social psychology
Fields of study: Aggression

Aggression is conceptualized as a diverse category of behaviors that are intended to injure or harm another. Psychological theories of aggression seek to explain, and ultimately to control, people's hostile or antisocial behaviors. Generally, psychological theories address the relative influences of biological factors (such as aggressive instincts or physiological arousal) and situational factors associated with aggression in animals and humans.

Principal terms

CATHARSIS: a reduction of psychological tension and/or physiological arousal

DEFENSE MECHANISM: according to Sigmund Freud, a psychological strategy by which an unacceptable sexual or aggressive impulse may be kept from conscious thought or expressed in a disguised fashion

DISPLACEMENT: according to Freud, a defense mechanism by which a person redirects his or her aggressive impulse onto a target that may substitute for the target that originally aroused the person's aggression

HOSTILE AGGRESSION: aggressive behavior that is associated with anger and is intended to harm another

INSTINCTIVE AGGRESSIVE BEHAVIOR: aggressive behavior that does not result from learning experiences; such behavior is expressed by each member of a species with little variation in its expression

INSTRUMENTAL AGGRESSION: aggressive behavior that is a by-product of another activity; instrumental aggression occurs only incidentally, as a means to another end

SUBLIMATION: according to Freud, a defense mechanism by which a person may redirect aggressive impulses by engaging in a socially sanctioned activity

Causes and Symptoms

Aggression is any antisocial behavior that is harmful or injurious to another. This may include overt physical and verbal behaviors (for example, firing a gun or screaming at someone in anger) as well as nonverbal behaviors, such as the display of obscene gestures. Psychologists consider aggression to be a category of diverse behaviors under which two subordinate categories of behaviors can be subsumed. The first category, instrumental aggression, consists of aggressive behaviors that are simply a means to another end. Hence, the primary goal of instrumental aggression is not necessarily to injure another person; aggression is used to attain a desired outcome. For example, a soccer player might knock her teammate down as they both run to tackle a ball. The girl's aggressive behavior was not intended to harm her teammate; rather, her goal was to gain possession of the ball and to score. The second category, hostile aggression, is often the result of anger, and its sole purpose is to injure or harm its target. Hostile aggression includes cases of physical assault, verbal abuse, and other antisocial behaviors. Most of the theoretical perspectives and empirical studies of aggression in psychology are concerned with hostile aggression.

There are three major psychological perspectives on aggression. The first perspective adopts a strongly biological stance on the development and maintenance of aggression in the human species. The second perspective takes the position that aggression is a result of the buildup of psychological frustration. The third perspective argues that aggression is a learned social behavior.

The first theoretical perspective, instinct theories, adopts the position that human nature includes an inborn drive for aggression. The ethologist Konrad Lorenz studied the instinctive nature of aggression in animals and humans. According to his work, aggression is a species-specific impulse that builds within the body and is eventually released by specific stimuli that elicit aggression. For example, an aggressive impulse might be unleashed by the presence of one's enemy. In some cases, however, the expression of this instinct may be inhibited by certain stimuli (for example, a parent may become angered by a child's behavior but not strike the child). Ethologists argue that the "babyish" facial characteristics of infants and young children serve as stimuli that inhibit the expression of aggressive behavior by adults.

Another instinct theory, psychoanalytic theory, posits that the seeds of aggression lie in the human personality. According to Sigmund Freud, a significant portion of one's unconscious psychological processes are governed by Thanatos. Thanatos, or the death instinct, is a reservoir of aggressive, and often self-destructive, tendencies that Freud considered to be part of the human species' evolutionary heritage. The psychic energy dedicated to Thanatos is thought to build over time until it is released in aggressive behavior. Periodic discharge, or catharsis, of this psychic energy is necessary for psychological health. Catharsis can occur either directly through overt aggression or indirectly through a number of disguised avenues. Many of Freud's defense mechanisms allow for a safe outlet of a person's aggressive impulses. For example, a man might be angered by his abusive employer's demands. Instead of accosting his employer directly, however, he might drive to his health club and "blow off steam" by sparring with a boxing partner. His aggressive urge is thus reduced through displacement of his aggressive impulse. As another example, an angry and sarcastic young girl may become a prosecuting attorney upon reaching adulthood. By aggressively prosecuting accused criminals and interrogating defense witnesses, a necessary part of her profession, this woman may be sublimating her aggressive tendencies.

The second theoretical perspective was introduced by John Dollard and his colleagues' early work investigating S-R (stimulus-response) theory. Their theory of aggression consisted of two simple propositions. First, aggression must always

Ethologist Konrad Lorenz studied the instinctive nature of aggression in animals and humans. (©The Nobel Foundation)

result from frustration. Second, frustration always leads to aggression. Thus, aggression was thought to be attributable to the thwarting of one's purpose or being prevented from attaining a valued goal. This theory, the frustration-aggression hypothesis, was later revised by Leonard Berkowitz, who argued that the frustration-aggression relationship was not quite so clear-cut. He posited that frustration simply makes a person ready to be aggressive. Aggression will result from frustration if, and only if, a cue for aggressive behavior is present. Aggressive cues are social stimuli, such as potential weapons, that have been associated with aggression in the past. Thus, the revised frustration-aggression hypothesis posits that aggressive tendencies will accumulate as a response to frustration. Catharsis is likely to occur when situational cues support an aggressive response.

The final perspective, social learning theory, emphasizes the role of social and situational factors in the learning and expression of aggressive behaviors. According to Albert Bandura, aggressive behaviors can be learned through two primary avenues, direct experience and observational learning. Learning by direct experience involves the actual enactment of aggressive behavior. If aggression is rewarded, then it is likely to recur. If aggression is punished, then it is likely to be suppressed, especially in the presence of the punishing agent. Observational learning, on the other hand, involves a process whereby people attend to the behaviors of people in their environment and the consequences of these behaviors. Bandura stated that people are most likely to attend to, and thus learn from, the behaviors of three salient model categories: families, subcultures, and the media. For example, a young boy may observe the aggressive behavior exhibited by the fellow members of his neighborhood gang. This modeling by other gang members not only may teach him novel behaviors but also may lower his inhibitions on being aggressive. Thus, when this boy becomes aroused by an aversive event, such as a taunt from a rival gang member, he will be likely to respond in an aggressive manner.

Treatment and Therapy
Much of the psychological research investigating the nature of aggression has been focused on the control of aggression. Of particular interest to researchers is the notion that allowing limited expression of low levels of aggression (catharsis) might play an important role in controlling the expression of high levels of aggression and antisocial behavior. The concept of catharsis is a central component of both psychoanalytic theory and the frustration-aggression hypothesis. Further, the idea of catharsis is intuitively appealing to many people who feel that periodically "blowing off steam" is important to positive mental health.

Psychologists Russell Geen, David Stonner, and Gary Shope designed a laboratory study to define the role that catharsis plays in aggression. In this study, male college students were angered and then administered electric shock by a confederate of the experimenters. When these subjects were allowed to retaliate against the confederate, they experienced a drop in their blood pressure (defined by the experimenters as a cathartic release). At this point in the experiment, the role of catharsis in moderating physiological arousal was supported. The experimenters, however, also wanted to know the effect of catharsis on subjects' subsequent behavior, so they next provided subjects with an opportunity to administer shocks to the confederate. Geen and his colleagues found that the subjects who had experienced catharsis (reductions in blood pressure) actually delivered higher levels of shock to the confederate. Thus, while catharsis was reflected in decreased physiological arousal, it was associated with higher, not lower, levels of actual aggression. These researchers concluded that they were unable to find support for psychoanalytic theory or the frustration-aggression hypothesis, both of which would predict that catharsis would reduce subsequent aggression.

Laboratory studies have been subjected to a number of criticisms because they isolate people from their natural social environments and perhaps encourage the expression of artificial behavior. Laboratory studies of aggression are particularly vulnerable to such criticism, because they may provide subjects with a safe arena within which they may be encouraged to behave in an unnaturally aggressive manner. In response to these critics, many psychologists have studied the aggressive behavior of adults and children in typical social environments. Leonard Eron and his associates investigated the role that television might play in modeling aggressive behavior for a sample of elementary school children. First, the children's viewing habits were observed, to establish the nature of the programming they preferred and the amount of time they spent watching television. These children were followed up twenty-two years later to observe the effect their television viewing habits might have had on their behavior. Eron and his colleagues found that the amount of television these children had watched was significantly related to their level of aggressive behavior in young adulthood. The criminal records of certain children revealed that the more serious crimes were committed by the children who had been the heaviest consumers of violent television programming. The researchers interpreted these results to support social learning theory; that is, the media may be effective models of aggression, both immediate and long-term.

Proponents of handgun legislation point to studies such as these to argue for the control of privately owned firearms. They point to violent models in the media that may be related to the high rate of homicides in the United States. Additionally, they argue that the presence of a handgun itself may serve as a cue that elicits aggression and that the use of a handgun allows the aggressor to distance himself or herself physically from the victim. At firing range, the cues that elicit empathy and inhibit aggression are not so readily apparent. The influence of gun control on homicide rates was studied by a group of physicians led by John Henry Sloan. This team selected two cities for comparison. One city, Vancouver, British Columbia, had adopted restrictive handgun regulations. The comparison city, Seattle, Washington, was similar to Vancouver on a number of important demographic variables, but had no handgun control. The crime rates for both cities were compared for six years (1980 through 1986). Although the rates in both cities for burglary, robbery, and assault were not significantly different, the homicide rate was significantly higher in Seattle. They found that the citizens of Seattle had a 4.8 times higher risk of being killed with a handgun than did the citizens of Vancouver. These researchers concluded their report with the suggestion that handgun control legislation might reduce community homicide rates.

Perspective and Prospects

Early psychological theories of aggression were quite pessimistic in the inferences they made about human nature. Much of Sigmund Freud's writings about the nature of Thanatos and the expression of aggression in humans occurred against the backdrop of the two world wars that he experienced in Europe. Becoming increasingly pessimistic about human nature and civilization, he revised his theory of the libido to include not only the sexual instinct, Eros, but also the aggressive instinct, Thanatos. Other theorists of that time entertained similar views of aggression as an instinct. For example, social psychologist William McDougall included aggression in his taxonomy of innate human instincts.

During the 1930's John Dollard and his colleagues at Yale attempted to reformulate psychoanalytic theory by use of S-R theory. These researchers were concerned with the mentalistic nature of Freud's theory, and they attempted to test his propositions by reconceptualizing libidinal impulses as biological drives. The frustration-aggression hypothesis grew out of this research program and generated a considerable amount of empirical research for a number of years. Interest in this concept then flagged, for the most part, until the 1960's, when Leonard Berkowitz published his revised frustration-aggression hypothesis that acknowledged the important role of social cues in the instigation of aggression.

Berkowitz's revision of the frustration-aggression hypothesis reflected the increased focus of American psychologists on social learning theory. Albert Bandura's classic studies of the social learning of aggressive responses, published in the early 1960's were influential in two ways. First, they generated considerable empirical research. Second, they provided a theoretical framework and methodology by which the effects of a relatively new social phenomenon, television, could be studied. Since then, more than two thousand studies have looked at the role of television in the modeling and maintenance of aggression in adults and children.

That is not to say that the instinct theories have fallen into disfavor. Konrad Lorenz's influential book, *On Aggression*, published in 1966, again brought instinct theories into the public eye. His book captured the interest not only of the comparative psychologists who studied aggression in other species but of the general reading public as well.

Bibliography

Bandura, Albert. *Aggression: A Social Learning Analysis*. Englewood Cliffs, N.J.: Prentice-Hall, 1973. Bandura presents a thorough overview of his social learning theory of aggression. He outlines the important antecedents of aggression and the critical factors in the instigation and maintenance of aggressive behavior. He also describes relevant social learning principles and applies those principles that are useful techniques for behavioral change. Accessible to the college-level reader.

Baumeister, Roy F. *Evil: Inside Human Cruelty and Violence*. New York: W. H. Freeman, 1997. Examines the psychological aspects of good and evil. Includes bibliographical references and an index.

Berkowitz, Leonard. *Aggression: A Social-Psychological Analysis*. New York:

McGraw-Hill, 1962. This classic volume presents the frustration-aggression hypothesis. Contrasts the frustration-aggression hypothesis with instinct theories of aggression and discusses situational factors implicated in the expression and inhibition of aggression. The role of catharsis in aggression is also discussed.

_____. "Biological Roots: Are Humans Inherently Violent?" In *Psychological Dimensions of War*, edited by Betty Glad. Newbury Park, Calif.: Sage Publications, 1990. This is an excellent, easy-to-read critique of instinct theories of aggression. Berkowitz presents the frustration-aggression hypothesis and applies this theory to an analysis of international conflict. The role of aggression in the human condition and international relations is thoroughly discussed.

Denfeld, Rene. *Kill the Body, the Head Will Fall: A Closer Look at Women, Violence, and Aggression*. Foreword by Katherine Dunn. New York: Warner Books, 1997. The author examines her experiences as a boxer and argues that women are not less aggressive than men.

Geen, Russell G. *Human Aggression*. Pacific Grove, Calif.: Brooks/Cole, 1990. The author, a prominent researcher in the field, provides a solid empirical and theoretical discussion of the concept of aggression. Individual differences in aggression are discussed as well as interpersonal and environmental factors that mediate the actual expression of aggressive behavior.

Groebel, Jo, and Robert A. Hinde, eds. *Aggression and War: Their Biological and Social Bases*. New York: Cambridge University Press, 1989. This edited volume presents a lively discussion of the biological, psychological, and cultural factors in human aggression. Physiological and individual differences in aggression are presented in addition to social and situational forces that are useful in the control of aggression and the encouragement of pro-social behaviors. Cultural and political issues relevant to aggression are discussed.

Lloyd, Sally A., and Beth C. Emery. *The Dark Side of Courtship: Physical and Sexual Aggression*. Thousand Oaks, Calif.: Sage Publications, 2000. This volume in the Sage Series on Close Relationships examines dating violence. Includes bibliographical references and an index.

Lorenz, Konrad. *On Aggression*. New York: Methuen, 1966. This easy-to-read classic is a comparative study of aggression in a number of species. Lorenz documents the evolutionary significance of aggression and describes its expression in fish, animals, and humans. He argues that aggression plays an important social role in same-species interactions.

Luschen, Gunther. "Psychological Issues in Sports Aggression." In *Sports Violence*, edited by Jeffrey H. Goldstein. New York: Springer-Verlag, 1983. Describes the cathartic role of sports in both athletes' and spectators' aggressive behaviors. The author summarizes the central role that catharsis plays in several psychological and philosophical perspectives on aggression, then presents the results of empirical studies investigating the links between sports and aggression.

Segall, Marshall H. "Cultural Roots of Aggressive Behavior." In *The Cross-Cultural Challenge to Social Psychology*, edited by Michael Harris Bond. Newbury

Park, Calif.: Sage, 1988. Segall presents a summary and critique of important cross-cultural studies of aggression. His presentation focuses on the manner in which gender roles, biology, and cultural forces interact in the socialization of aggression across the globe. An intriguing and quite accessible article.

Cheryl A. Rickabaugh

See also:

Aggression: Reduction and Control; Antisocial Personality; Child Abuse; Domestic Violence; Juvenile Delinquency; Stress: Behavioral and Psychological Responses; Stress: Physiological Responses.

AGGRESSION
Reduction and Control

Type of psychology: Social psychology
Fields of study: Aggression

Aggressive behavior has been a problem for humans since before the beginning of recorded history. Psychologists have developed many theories of aggression, and there are many different ideas as to how—or whether—aggression might be controlled.

Principal terms

BEHAVIORISM: a school of psychology which holds that learning, centering on a stimulus, a response, and reinforcement, is central to behavior

CATHARSIS: the idea that experiencing aggression or violence vicariously will relieve an individual's aggressive drives

FRUSTRATION-AGGRESSION HYPOTHESIS: a concept pioneered by John Dollard stating that aggressive behavior is born of frustration in attempting to reach a goal

SOCIAL LEARNING THEORY: a theory introduced by Albert Bandura stating that behavior is learned by observing others model that behavior

SOCIOBIOLOGY: a field of biology that views behavior as being extensively based on inherited characteristics

Overview

Aggression has been humankind's steady companion throughout history—in life, literature, and art. Many hypotheses have been suggested by psychologists and other scientists concerning the nature of aggression; some have suggested that it is learned behavior, others that it is an innate, genetically inherited drive. The fields of ethology and sociology have mustered evidence to support the evolutionary (genetic) basis of aggression. Theories based on these viewpoints hold that at some point in humankind's past, aggressiveness was an adaptive trait—that is, aggression helped ensure the survival of the individual who possessed that quality, thereby enabling the aggressive trait to be passed on to future generations. Social psychologists, on the other hand, have studied the effects of modeling aggressive behavior. When children, for example, have been exposed to aggressive behavior modeled (acted out or demonstrated in some way) by others, they have shown an increase in aggressive behavior. In other words, the children observe and learn the behavior. Albert Bandura's social learning theory describes this concept of aggression.

The frustration-aggression hypothesis, as described by John Dollard, holds that both violence and aggression are the result of being frustrated in an attempt to reach a goal. When basic needs have been thwarted, aggression appears. As

Leonard Berkowitz stated it in *Roots of Aggression* (1969), "If a person is aggressive, he has been frustrated. If a person is frustrated, he has become aggressive." Negative environmental factors are also believed by many to have a major impact on aggression. Studies have found links, for example, between a high number of violent crimes and high air temperature. Overcrowding and economic hard times are also associated with higher crime rates. These studies tend to support negative affect theory, which holds that exposure to stimuli that create discomfort leads to aggression.

The amount of hope one holds for the possibility of reducing or controlling aggression depends, to some extent, on the theory of aggression that one believes to be most accurate. If aggressive behavior is an integral part of the genetic makeup of the human species, the outlook is not nearly as promising as it is if aggression is primarily a behavior learned from others and reinforced by certain rewards. In the former case, aggressive actions can perhaps be controlled by societal strictures, but the aggressive instinct will always remain within. In the latter case, decreasing the modeling of aggression or increasing the modeling of and rewards for nonaggressive behavior could conceivably produce effective results. Different studies have produced different results concerning the effectiveness of various attempts to reduce aggressive behavior.

Another complication in understanding and controlling aggression is that different people will react very differently when in similar circumstances. When frustrated, some people will react aggressively, while others will become withdrawn and depressed. Depression itself can lead to aggression, however, and this type of delayed aggression can produce seemingly unpredictable acts of violence. Psychologists simply do not have all the answers to why some people react aggressively and others do not when faced with identical predicaments.

Applications

Psychologists Matthew McKay, Martha Davis, and Patrick Fanning (1981) adapted Donald Meichenbaum's concept of stress inoculation training to produce one technique that allows an aggressive person to control his or her own aggressive behavior. McKay and his colleagues present simple, concise, step-by-step directions to deal with aggression. Since aggression is often fueled by emotional distress, they offer a technique of "covert assertion" through the development of two separate skills: thought interruption and thought substitution. When becoming angry or frustrated, the potential aggressor thinks of the word "stop" or some other interrupting device. The void suddenly created is then filled with a reserve of previously prepared positive, nonaggressive thoughts. This technique can be mastered, the authors maintain, if it is practiced conscientiously throughout the day for three days to a week.

The creation of an "aggression stimulants structure" gives the individual who is compelled to be negatively aggressive the opportunity to take a personal inventory of who (or what) the targets of his or her aggression are, what the feelings associated with those people are, and what would occur if a plan of "attack" against them were to be put into action. This type of analysis lends itself well to self-accountability; it allows the individual to "own" the problem and to believe that it can be controlled if he or she chooses to control it. It also allows, through its identification of specific targets and imaging of the act of aggression, a global perspective on what can otherwise seem a very fragmented problem.

Aggression in the work environment can be damaging and disruptive both for individuals and for organizations. In an article in the *Journal of Occupational Psychology*, Philip L. Storms and Paul E. Spector (1987) claimed that high frustration levels of organizational employees were positively related to interpersonal aggression, sabotage, and withdrawal. Suggestions for dealing with aggression in the workplace have included such strategies as training courses and the use of humor to defuse tensions. Diane Lamplugh notes that aggression in this arena can range from whispered innuendo to harassment to violence. She maintains that a training course that focuses on tension control, relaxation techniques, customer-relations orientation, assertiveness practice, aggression-centered discussions, and self-defense training can be helpful. She also states that support from management in identifying problem areas and formulating guidelines for staff support is crucial. William A. Kahn promotes humor as a means for organizational members to make statements about themselves, their groups, or their organization. Humor, he notes, is a nonthreatening vehicle that allows people to say things that might otherwise insult or offend coworkers, thereby making them defensive and threatening working relationships.

Written or unwritten laws, rules, and codes of conduct are established in an attempt to curb unacceptably aggressive behavior. A company may terminate an employee who does not adhere to certain standards of behavior; athletes are benched for aggression or violence. Society as a whole formulates laws to control its members' aggressive behavior. When individuals act in ways that are damagingly aggressive to other people or to the property of others, law enforcement agencies step in to safeguard the population. Perpetrators are fined or sentenced to prison terms.

Studies disagree as to the most effective means of rehabilitating offenders, but many studies do suggest that rehabilitation is possible. One avenue that is frequently explored is the use of various techniques founded in behaviorism. In *Psychological Approaches to Crime and Its Correction* (1984), edited by Irving Jacks and Steven G. Cox, for example, Stanley V. Kruschwitz investigates the effectiveness of using a voluntary token reinforcement procedure to change the behavior of inmates who are difficult to manage. In the same volume, Albert F. Scheckenbach makes an argument for behavior modification as it relates to adult offenders. Modeling positive behaviors and holding group discussions have been found at least somewhat effective in rehabilitating juvenile delinquents, as has the development of behavioral contracts. John Lochman and his colleagues (1987), using what they called an "anger coping mechanism," explored cognitive behavioral techniques for reducing aggression in eleven-year-old boys. The boys treated with this procedure showed vast improvements—a reduction of disruptive classroom behavior and an increase in perceived social competence. Such techniques, used with young people, might reduce their high-risk status for later difficulties.

Perspective and Prospects

Acts of aggression have been central in human history, myth, literature, and even religion. In the biblical account, for example, humankind has barely come into existence when Cain kills his brother Abel. Almost as old are questions concerning the causes of aggression and the debate over how to control it.

Sigmund Freud saw aggression as the result of struggles within the psyche of the individual; the tension produced in the struggle between the life instinct and the death instinct creates outward aggression. Alfred Adler, another psychodynamic theorist, stated that aggression represents the most general human striving and is a necessity of life; its underlying principle is self-assertion. Humanistic theorist Rollo May notes that attention to aggression has nearly universally focused on its negative aspects. In *Power and Innocence* (1972), May wrote that "we have been terrified of aggression, and we assume—delusion though it is—that we can better control it if we center all our attention on its destructive aspects as though that's all there is."

It was first the behaviorists, then social learning theorists (such as Albert Bandura), who explored ways to reduce and control aggression. The frustration-aggression hypothesis, for example, was developed in the 1930's. Behaviorists tended to approach aggressive behavior in terms of stimuli, responses, and reinforcement. In a general sense, any approaches that seek to punish unacceptably aggressive behavior or to reward positive behavior are related to the behavioral view. Bandura and other social learning theorists found that, in some situations, children would respond to viewing aggressive acts by performing aggressive acts themselves. The implications of this have been widely argued and debated; one aspect concerns the effects of viewing television and motion-picture violence. Viewing violence on television does seem to cause increased aggressive behavior, although because of the nature of the types of studies most often performed, it can be difficult to draw unarguable cause-and-effect relationships.

The debate over whether aggression is learned, innate, or both (and, if both, over the relative importance of the two aspects) is not likely to end soon. Debates over how to control aggression will also continue. As in many areas of psychology, bridging the gap between the theoretical and the practical is difficult. As only one example, negative affect theory suggests that noxious environmental stimuli can produce negative emotions and, therefore, aggression; however, it is virtually impossible to remove such stimuli, except on a very small scale. Yet another area that will be increasingly explored is the relationship between aggression and biochemical factors. Studies have found correlations, for example, between aggressiveness and high levels of norepinephrine and low levels of serotonin, two important neurotransmitters. The significance of such chemical findings remains to be ascertained.

Bibliography

Bach, George R., and Herb Goldberg. *Creative Aggression.* New York: Avon Books, 1975. A guidebook for people who cannot confront conflict as well as for those who choose to seek conflict. Helps the reader to assess himself or herself honestly and to approach aggressiveness in new ways.

Berkowitz, Leonard, ed. *Roots of Aggression*. New York: Atherton Press, 1969. Revisits the frustration-aggression hypothesis. Examines such areas as catharsis, frustration, and conditions facilitating the occurrence of aggression.

Boyd, Neil. *The Beast Within: Why Men Are Violent*. New York: Greystone Books, 2000. An examination of aggressiveness in men. Includes bibliographical references and an index.

Dworetzky, John P. *Psychology*. 6th ed. Pacific Grove, Calif.: Brooks/Cole, 1997. This text has a strong research base and contains extensive detail to reinforce the material presented. Good discussion of aggression.

Fishbein, Diana H., ed. *The Science, Treatment, and Prevention of Antisocial Behaviors: Application to the Criminal Justice System*. Kingston, N.J.: Civic Research Institute, 2000. Relates criminal activity to such topics as genetics, brain dysfunction, sexual abuse, addiction, and attention-deficit disorder. Includes bibliographical references and an index.

Jacks, Irving, and Steven G. Cox, eds. *Psychological Approaches to Crime and Its Correction*. Chicago: Nelson-Hall, 1984. Covers a wide range of topics related to aggression and positivistic points of view in the face of crime. Examines the modification of aggressive behavior.

May, Rollo. *Power and Innocence*. New York: W. W. Norton, 1972. Probes the sources of violence. Advances solutions for contemporary society, examining the concept of innocence and challenging traditional views of aggression.

Denise S. St. Cyr

See also:

Aggression: Definitions and Theoretical Explanations; Biofeedback and Relaxation; Stress: Behavioral and Psychological Responses; Stress: Coping Strategies; Stress: Physiological Responses; Stress: Prediction and Control.

Agoraphobia and Panic Disorders

Type of psychology: Psychopathology
Fields of study: Anxiety disorders; biology of stress

Panic disorder with agoraphobia is a condition characterized by the presence of severe anxiety attacks coupled with avoidance of a wide range of situations. Considerable progress has been made toward understanding its cause and treatment.

Principal terms

DEPERSONALIZATION: a feeling of unreality regarding oneself or one's body
DEREALIZATION: a feeling of unreality regarding the external world
FLOODING: prolonged and intense exposure to feared stimuli
HABITUATION: a process by which physiological or psychological responses decline in intensity with repeated stimulation
HYPERVENTILATION: overly rapid or deep breathing
PALPITATION: pronounced pounding of the heart
PARESTHESIA: numbness or tingling, particularly in the extremities
SOCIAL PHOBIA: a condition characterized by fear of the possible scrutiny or criticism of others

Causes and Symptoms

Panic disorder is a condition characterized by frequent panic attacks—that is, intense surges of anxiety. These attacks of anxiety often occur unexpectedly or "out of the blue"; the individual frequently is unable to identify an external trigger for them. Between attacks, the panic-disorder patient often ruminates about the possibility of additional attacks.

Panic attacks tend to be accompanied by a number of physical symptoms. Hyperventilation—overly rapid or deep breathing—is common, as are choking and smothering sensations, dizziness, faintness, and paresthesias—sensations of numbness and tingling, particularly in the extremities. Other common symptoms during panic attacks are sweating, trembling, nausea, abdominal distress, hot or cold flashes, accelerated heart rate, chest pain, and palpitations (feeling one's heart pound). Not surprisingly, many individuals who are having a panic attack believe that they are experiencing a heart attack.

Panic attacks are also frequently characterized by a number of psychological symptoms. Depersonalization and derealization are among the most common of these symptoms. Depersonalization is marked by feelings of unreality regarding oneself or one's body—sensations of being "disconnected" from oneself or of "watching" oneself as would an outside observer are frequent. Derealization refers to feelings of unreality concerning the external world; objects or people may seem somehow "strange" or unfamiliar. Also common during panic attacks are fears of dying (for example, from a heart attack or stroke), losing one's mind, or performing embarrassing behaviors (such as screaming uncontrollably).

The difficulties of many patients with panic disorder do not end here, however; many, but not all, of these patients develop an often debilitating syndrome known as agoraphobia. Agoraphobia is a fear of

POSSIBLE SYMPTOMS OF PANIC DISORDER

- ❖ pounding heart
- ❖ sweating
- ❖ feeling weak, faint or dizzy
- ❖ numbness or tingling feeling in hands
- ❖ feeling flushed or chilled
- ❖ chest pain or smothering sensations
- ❖ sense of unreality
- ❖ fear of impending doom or loss of control
- ❖ fear of a heart attack or a stroke
- ❖ fear of losing one's mind
- ❖ fear of dying

situations in which escape is difficult, inconvenient, or potentially embarrassing, or in which assistance might not be readily available. Specifically, what appears to occur is that many panic patients, dreading the possibility of a future attack, begin to fear and (in many cases) avoid situations that might precipitate such an attack. The situations feared or avoided by agoraphobics are extremely varied, but they include public transportation, open spaces, shopping malls, supermarkets, large social gatherings, elevators, driving in heavy traffic, passing over bridges or through tunnels, standing in long lines, and sitting in crowded theaters or churches.

In mild cases, agoraphobics may experience moderate discomfort while traveling or shopping alone, and may avoid those situations in only certain cases. In severe cases, agoraphobics may be unwilling to leave their houses unaccompanied. The fears of agoraphobics are generally alleviated by the presence of another individual, particularly one close to the patient. This is probably because this person would presumably be available to provide help in the event of an emergency, such as a heart attack.

The prevalence of panic disorder with agoraphobia in the general population of the United States has been estimated to be approximately 5 percent; an additional 2 percent have been estimated to have panic disorder without agoraphobia. Thus, panic disorder is relatively common and is perhaps the most frequent reason individuals seek outpatient psychiatric care. In addition, isolated panic attacks occur frequently among individuals in the general population. G. Ron Norton and his colleagues, for example, have found that approximately 34 percent of college students experience occasional panic attacks.

Panic disorder and agoraphobia have been reported to occur more frequently among females than males, although this difference is probably more marked for agoraphobia than for panic disorder. In addition, the prevalence of panic disorder appears to decline with age; its frequency has generally been reported to be highest among individuals under thirty and lowest among individuals over sixty-five. The course of panic disorder tends to be chronic but fluctuating. In other words, its symptoms often persist for many years, but they typically wax and wane depending upon the level of life stress and other factors.

In addition, panic disorder patients appear to have an elevated rate of several medical conditions. A subset of these patients, for example, has been reported to have mitral valve prolapse syndrome (MVPS), a condition in which the heart's mitral valve bulges into the atrium. Because MVPS results in physical symptoms such as palpitations and chest pain, it may be a risk factor for panic disorder in some individuals. In addition, a subset of panic patients appear to have disturbances of the vestibular system, an apparatus in the inner ear responsible for maintaining balance. As dizziness is a common symptom of panic attacks, vestibular dysfunction may be an important precipitant of some panic attacks.

A number of psychiatric conditions are commonly found among patients with panic disorder and agoraphobia. Depression is a particularly frequent complication of both syndromes; in many cases it probably results from the distress produced by panic attacks and the constriction of activities produced by agoraphobia. This depression may have tragic consequences; panic disorder patients have been reported to be at greatly increased risk for suicide compared with individuals in the general population. In addition, many panic disorder patients turn to alcohol or other substances to alleviate their anxiety. Also commonly associated with panic disorder is social phobia, a condition characterized by fears of the possible scrutiny or criticism of others. Like panic disorder patients, many social phobics experience panic attacks. Nevertheless, in social phobia these attacks are almost invariably triggered by situations in which the patient is the perceived focus of others' attention.

A variety of models have been proposed for the causation of panic disorder and agoraphobia. Early explanations tended to focus largely or exclusively on physiological factors. In the 1960's, Donald Klein and his colleagues reported that panic disorder improved following administration of imipramine, a drug traditionally used to treat depression, whereas more sustained and long-lasting ("generalized") anxiety did not. Based upon this finding, Klein and his coworkers argued that panic is biologically distinct from other forms of anxiety. Although Klein's observation was important, it should be noted that making inferences about the nature of a disorder from the treatment of that disorder is logically flawed: A condition's treatment bears no necessary implications for its cause (for example, one would not be justified in concluding that headaches are caused by a lack of aspirin).

Nevertheless, it seems likely that physiological factors play an important role in panic disorder. Identical twins (who share all the same genes) with panic disorder are more likely than are fraternal twins (who share only half of their genes, on average) to have co-twins with panic disorder, suggesting that genetic factors play at least some role in this disorder. It is not known, however, whether these genetic factors predispose a person to panic disorder per se or to anxiety in general. In addition, there is evidence that the locus coeruleus, a structure in the pons (which is located at the back of the brain), is overactive during panic attacks. This is important because the locus coeruleus is a major center for norepinephrine, a chemical transmitter in the nervous system that appears to play a major role in the genesis of arousal and anxiety. Finally, it has been found that, in contrast to normals, many panic disorder patients develop panic attacks following infusion of certain substances, such as sodium lactate and caffeine. It is possible, however, that this is simply attributable to greater arousal on the part of panic disorder patients; the infusion of these substances may provoke attacks in these patients because they are already on the verge of panicking.

Many subsequent models of the causation of panic disorder have attempted to move beyond physiological abnormalities to examine how panic disorder patients react to and construe their environment. One of the most influential of these might be termed the "fear of fear" model. According to Dianne Chambless, Alan Goldstein, and other proponents of this model, individuals who are afraid of their own anxiety are particularly prone to the development of panic disorder. During frightening experiences, this "fear of fear" can spiral into a panic attack.

A more recent theory of panic disorder is the "cognitive model" of David Clark, Aaron Beck, and other researchers. According to this model, panic attacks result from the catastrophic misinterpretation of unusual or unexpected bodily sensations. In other words, panic attacks may occur when a physical symptom (such as rapid heartbeat or dizziness) is misinterpreted as presaging a disastrous outcome (heart attack or stroke). Interestingly, many of the physical symptoms of anxiety, such a rapid heartbeat, can themselves be exacerbated by anxiety, as anyone who has felt his or her heart race uncontrollably while giving a speech can attest. Thus, the misinterpretation of certain physical sensations may set in motion a cycle in which these sensations progressively increase in intensity, giving rise to further misinterpretations and ultimately culminating in a panic attack. The cognitive model is also consistent with the evidence, mentioned earlier, that some panic patients have physiological abnormalities, such as MVPS and vestibular dysfunction. These abnormalities might be chronically misinterpreted by some individuals as indicative of serious consequences, and thereby provide a repeated trigger for panic attacks.

Treatment and Therapy

There is good evidence that many cases of panic disorder and agoraphobia are treatable by means of either medication or psychotherapy. Imipramine, as well as several other antidepressant drugs, appears to ameliorate the symptoms of these syndromes. It is not clear, however, whether these drugs actually exert their impact upon panic or whether they instead work by alleviating the depressive symptoms so common to these patients. Alleviating depressive symptoms may then provide agoraphobics with the energy and confidence needed to confront previously avoided situations.

Panic disorder and agoraphobia also are amenable to interventions involving confrontation with feared situations. For example, many panic patients improve following flooding, a technique involving prolonged and intense exposure to feared stimuli. In the case of panic disorder, the patient is typically exposed, in graduated fashion, to increasingly anxiety-producing situations. The patient is typically encouraged to remain in the situation until his or her anxiety subsides.

The efficacy of flooding and related treatments for panic disorder and agoraphobia can be explained in at least two ways. One possibility is that flooding works by a process known as habituation. Habituation is a process in which physiological or psychological responses decline in intensity with repeated stimulation. For example, many parachute jumpers find that their anxiety reactions gradually decrease with each succeeding jump; habituation may be the basis of this phenomenon. A second possibility is that flooding works by means of the cognitive model. That is, prolonged exposure to feared stimuli may demonstrate to patients that these stimuli are not as dangerous as they had believed.

Perspective and Prospects

The term "panic" derives from the Greek god Pan, who let out a terrifying scream whenever he was awakened by passersby. Most of the earliest accounts of panic attacks emphasized their physiological nature. In 1871, Jacob DaCosta described a syndrome he termed "irritable heart," which was characterized by palpitations, shortness of breath, dizziness, and other symptoms now recognized as typical of panic disorder. DaCosta observed this condition both in Civil War soldiers and in individuals not involved in military combat. Irritable heart syndrome became a frequent diagnosis among anxiety-stricken soldiers in the Franco-Prussian and Boer wars. Other early terms for this syndrome were "effort syndrome" and "neurocirculatory asthenia"; again, both of these terms emphasized overexertion of the heart and circulatory system as the principal causes of panic symptoms.

At approximately the same time, Sigmund Freud was describing a syndrome he called "anxiety neurosis." Freud noted that this neurosis could occur in a diffuse, long-lasting form (what would today be called generalized anxiety) or in sudden, discrete attacks marked by symptoms such as excessive heartbeat and respiration (what would today be called panic disorder). In contrast to DaCosta and other writers of this period, Freud emphasized unconscious psychological factors as the primary determinants of panic disorder. According to Freud, anxiety attacks resulted from a massive damming up ("repression") of sexual impulses. In his later writings, Freud revised his position to assert that anxiety served as a signal to the individual that sexual impulses needed to be repressed. According to this later view, anxiety (including panic) is a cause, rather than a result, of the repression of sexual urges. Although many psychologists did not concur with Freud's conjectures, by World War II there was increasing appreciation that many of the panic reactions seen among soldiers were largely of psychogenic origin.

The term "agoraphobia" stems from the Greek *agora*, meaning marketplace. As noted earlier, however, although agoraphobics fear marketplaces and similar situations, their fears tend to be extremely varied. "Agoraphobia" was coined by Alexander Westphal in 1871, who observed that many patients experienced anxiety while walking across open spaces or deserted streets. Interestingly, Moritz Benedikt had observed a similar syndrome in 1870; he labeled in *Platzschwindel* (dizziness in public places), a term that presaged findings of vestibular dysfunction in some of these patients.

For many years, panic disorder and agoraphobia were believed to be two quite different, although often overlapping, conditions. In the third edition of the American Psychiatric Association's *Diagnostic and Statistical Manual of Mental Disorders* (DSM-III, 1980), for example, panic disorder and agoraphobia were listed as

separate disorders. Nevertheless, research has increasingly indicated that agoraphobia is, in most cases, a consequence of panic attacks. Therefore, in the 1987
revision of DSM-III, a new diagnosis called "panic disorder with agoraphobia"
was christened.

Bibliography

Barlow, David H. *Anxiety and Its Disorders: The Nature and Treatment of Anxiety
and Panic*. New York: Guilford Press, 1988. In this comprehensive and well-
written volume, Barlow surveys the major theoretical issues relevant to anxiety
(such as the relation of anxiety to other emotions, the biological origins of
anxiety, and the classification of anxiety disorders) and discusses the literature
on each anxiety disorder. This is one of the finest and most complete sources on
anxiety disorders.

Chambless, Dianne L., and Alan J. Goldstein, eds. *Agoraphobia: Multiple Perspectives on Theory and Treatment*. New York: John Wiley & Sons, 1982. Contains
several chapters on more specialized topics than are found in other texts on
agoraphobia, such as agoraphobia and the marital relationship, and the association between agoraphobia and obsessions. Chambless's chapter, which summarizes the typical characteristics of agoraphobics, and Goldstein's chapter, which
includes several detailed case histories, are especially useful.

Craske, Michelle G. *Anxiety Disorders: Psychological Approaches to Theory and
Treatment*. Boulder, Colo.: Westview Press, 1999. This volume in the series
Perspectives in Clinical Psychology addresses the diagnosis and treatment of
anxiety disorders. Includes bibliographical references and an index.

Dumont, Raeann. *The Sky Is Falling: Understanding and Coping with Phobias,
Panic, and Obsessive-Compulsive Disorders*. New York: W. W. Norton, 1996.
A popular work on common anxiety-causing conditions. Includes bibliog-
raphical references and an index.

Goodwin, Donald W., and Samuel B. Guze. "Panic Disorder (Anxiety Neurosis)."
In *Psychiatric Diagnosis*. New York: Oxford University Press, 1989. A brief but
excellent introduction to the most important psychiatric research on panic
disorder. The reader will find a clear discussion of topics such as diagnosis,
family studies, and differentiating panic disorder from other conditions. The
reference section is a good resource for readers wishing to pursue research on
panic disorder in greater depth.

Mathews, Andrew M., Michael G. Gelder, and Derek W. Johnston. *Agoraphobia:
Nature and Treatment*. New York: Guilford Press, 1981. The authors review the
literature on the symptomatology, assessment, and pharmacological treatment
of agoraphobia, and discuss the behavioral treatment of this syndrome in depth.
The appendices, which include a detailed self-help manual for agoraphobics
and a brief package of assessment materials, will be of particular interest to
many readers.

Walker, John R., G. Ron Norton, and Colin A. Ross, eds. *Panic Disorder and
Agoraphobia: A Comprehensive Guide for the Practitioner*. Pacific Grove,
Calif.: Brooks/Cole, 1991. This edited volume provides a thorough overview of

the literature on the diagnosis, causation, and treatment of panic disorder and agoraphobia. The coverage of material on assessment and on psychotherapeutic and pharmacological interventions is especially complete. Although intended for the clinician, this volume is also a good reference for the layperson.

Scott O. Lilienfeld

See also:

Abnormality: Behavioral Models; Abnormality: Cognitive Models; Anxiety Disorders; Cognitive Therapy; Phobias; Post-traumatic Stress; Stress; Stress: Behavioral and Psychological Responses; Stress: Physiological Responses.

ALCOHOLISM

Type of psychology: Psychopathology
Fields of study: Substance abuse

Alcoholism, the compulsive chronic or periodic drinking of alcoholic beverages, is a widespread substance-abuse problem that can lead to irreversible brain damage, other tissue damage, and death. It also causes crime and many fatal traffic accidents. The causes of alcoholism are not clearly understood; it can be arrested but not cured.

Principal terms

CIRRHOSIS: a chronic liver disease symptomized by destruction of liver cells and their replacement by nonfunctional tissue; it ultimately causes blocked blood circulation, liver failure, and death

DELIRIUM TREMENS: a severe alcohol withdrawal syndrome that includes anxiety attacks, confusion, depression, delirium, and terrifying hallucinations; as it worsens, tremors can develop

KORSAKOFF SYNDROME: alcohol-induced brain damage that causes disorientation, impaired long-term memory, and production of false memories to fill memory gaps

MANIC-DEPRESSIVE DISORDER: a psychiatric condition involving rapidly alternating manic elation and melancholic depression

NEURITIS: an inflammation of a nerve that causes pain, loss of reflexes, and muscular atrophy

PSYCHOSIS: any severe mental disorder characterized by deterioration of normal intellectual and social function and partial or complete withdrawal from reality

SUBSTANCE ABUSE: excessive use of any controlled substance—such as alcohol—that leads to physical dependence and psychological abnormalities

Causes and Symptoms

Pure ethyl alcohol is a colorless, mild-smelling liquid that boils at 79 degrees centigrade and evaporates quickly at room temperature. It is made either by fermentation of grain mashed and suspended in water or fruit juice, followed by the distillation (boiling) of the beer or wine that is produced, or by chemical synthesis from the petrochemical ethylene. Ethyl alcohol—usually simply called alcohol—has many uses, including the sterilization of surgical instruments and inclusion in the fuel gasohol; it is the liquid in which many medicines are dissolved, serves as the main component of perfumes and colognes, and is used in the manufacture of many useful chemicals. The best-known use of alcohol, however, is in alcoholic beverages, viewed by many as recreational beverages because of the mood-altering properties of the alcohol they contain.

It is believed that alcoholic beverages have been made since prehistoric times. The oldest records of widespread brewing of beer and production of wine have been found in what were ancient Babylon and Egypt, respectively. According to historians, the main reasons for the preparation of alcoholic beverages by early civilizations were that their antimicrobial properties kept grape juice and other food sources from which they were prepared from spoiling, and the fact that drinking sparing amounts of fermented beverages was a preventive of many illnesses that people contracted from contaminated drinking water or from other unfermented beverages.

The abuse of alcoholic beverages has certainly occurred since their discovery; however, it became widespread during the Middle Ages, when the art of distillation became more universal, producing hard liquors (containing five to ten times the alcohol of beer and wine) that made it much easier to attain alcoholic euphoria and stupor. It has been estimated that nearly 70 percent of Americans use alcoholic beverages and that more than ten million of these people are involved in severe abuse of alcohol. These last people are called alcoholics; their compulsive alcohol abuse makes it difficult for them to retain a job, obtain an education, or perform responsible societal roles. Ultimately, alcoholics damage their brains and other body tissues irreversibly, often dying of the affliction or by suicide.

Unlike with nonalcoholics, once an alcoholic takes a drink, self-control is lost and a drinking spree begins that ends only in stupor, when intoxication is complete. Continued alcoholism over a long time period affects many body organs. Among them is the brain, where related mental disorders include delirium tremens (the DTs), acute alcoholic hallucinations, and Korsakoff syndrome. Both the DTs—

A drawing from 1885 illustrates the nineteenth century attitude toward alcoholism: "The sins of the drunken father are visited on the heads of the children—a thief and woman of shame visit their lunatic father in the criminal lunatic asylum." (Library of Congress)

characterized by hallucinations and other psychotic symptoms—and Korsakoff syndrome may be accompained by physical debility that can require hospitalization.

Alcoholic neuritis will develop when alcohol is the sole substance consumed. In addition, alcoholism damages the liver (causing cirrhosis that can be lethal), the kidneys, the heart, and the pancreas. In fact, a large percentage of diseases of these organs stems from alcohol abuse. Furthermore, evidence suggests that severe alcoholism, combined with excessive cigarette smoking, greatly enhances the incidence of cancer of the mouth and throat.

There is no clear physical explanation for the development of alcoholism. Rather, it is most often proposed that alcoholism develops as the result of social problems and psychological stress. Much support is given to the high likelihood of alcoholism arising in the socioeconomic groups where consumption of alcoholic beverages is equated with manliness or sophistication. Other major bases proposed for the development of alcoholism include domineering parents, adolescent peer pressure, personal feelings of inadequacy, loneliness, job pressures, and marital discord.

Treatment and Therapy

There is no known cure for alcoholism. A thorough review of the literature led Diane M. Riley and coworkers to the conclusion that "treatments for alcohol problems with demonstrated enduring effectiveness do not exist, regardless of treatment orientations or treatment goals." It is a disease that can be handled only by total abstinence from alcoholic beverages, medications that contain alcohol, and any other potential sources of alcohol in the diet. A single contact with alcohol from any source frequently leads to a relapse. Its recognition as a medical problem has led to many alcohol-rehabilitation treatment centers, where psychiatric treatment, medication, and physical therapy—in various combinations—provide valuable treatments. Furthermore, many experts believe that Alcoholics Anonymous (AA) programs are effective deterrents to a return to alcohol abuse.

As pointed out by Andrew M. Mecca, before 1935 the main opinion on alcoholism was that it was criminal behavior that merited punishment. Around 1935, the identification of the problem as a disease began. Crucial to the successful treatment of alcoholism was the advent of Alcoholics Anonymous, founded in that year. This organization operates on the premise that abstinence is the best course of treatment for alcoholism—an incurable disease that can be arrested by cessation of all alcohol intake. The goal of the organization is sobriety: the permanent stoppage of a person's drinking.

The methodology of Alcoholics Anonymous is psychosocial. It brings alcoholics to the realization that they cannot use alcoholic beverages without succumbing to alcoholism. It identifies the need for help from a higher power, and it develops a support group of people with the same condition. As stated by Mecca, "Alcoholics Anonymous never pronounces the disease cured. . . . [I]t is arrested." Estimates of the membership of the organization are between 1.5 and 3 million, meaning that up to a third of American alcoholics are affected by its tenets. These people achieve results ranging from periods of sobriety (usually lasting longer and longer as membership in the organization continues) to lifelong sobriety. A deficit of sole utilization of Alcoholics Anonymous for treatment—according to many experts—is a lack of medical, psychiatric, and trained sociological counseling.

As to medical treatment aiming at abstinence via therapeutic drugs, two well-known drugs for enforcing sobriety are disulfiram (Antabuse) and citrated calcium carbonate (Abstem). These drugs may be given to alcoholics who wish to avoid using any alcoholic beverages and who require a deterrent to help them stop drinking. Neither drug should ever be given in secret by well-meaning family or friends because of the serious danger they cause in the presence of alcoholic beverages.

These dangers are attributable to the biochemistry of alcohol utilization via the enzymes (biological protein catalysts) alcohol dehydrogenase and aldehyde dehydrogenase. Normally, alcohol dehydrogenase converts alcohol to the toxic chemical acetaldehyde, then aldehyde dehydrogenase quickly converts acetaldehyde to acetic acid, the main biological fuel of the body. Abstem or Antabuse turns off aldehyde dehydrogenase. This causes acetaldehyde buildup in the body, when alcohol is consumed, and quickly leads to violent headache, flushing, nausea, dizziness, heart palpitation, and vertigo. Consumption of alcohol in several drinks (or even in cough medicines) in the presence of either drug can be fatal. An interesting sidelight is the view of some researchers, such as Cleamond D. Eskelson, that abstinence from alcohol may be genetically related to the presence of too much alcohol dehydrogenase and/or too little aldehyde dehydrogenase in the body, producing enough acetaldehyde to cause aversion to alcohol consumption.

Other therapeutic drugs that have been utilized to treat alcoholics include lithium (more often given to manic-depressive psychiatric patients), and tranquilizers. Their usual function is to soften the severe discomfort of alcohol withdrawal on the alcoholic patient. Lithium treatment, which must be done with great care because lithium can become toxic, appears to be effective only in a subset of alcoholics who drink because of depression or manic-depressive psychosis.

The use of tranquilizers (and related sedative hypnotics) must also be done with great care, under the close supervision of a physician. There are two main reasons for this: many of these drugs can be addicting, and their abuse can simply substitute another drug dependence for alcoholism; and alcohol and some of these drugs have additive effects that can be fatal if an alcoholic backslides during therapy.

The great value of the psychiatrist in alcoholism therapy has been identified by various sources. David H. Knott, in his book *Alcohol Problems: Diagnosis and Treatment* (1986), points out that while a psychotherapist cannot perform miracles, psychotherapy can be very valuable in helping the alcoholic patient by identifying factors leading to "destructive use of alcohol"; exploring and helping to rectify problems associated with alcohol abstinence; providing emotional support that helps many patients to rebuild their lives; and interfacing in referring patients to Alcoholics Anonymous and other long-term support efforts. The psychotherapist also has irreplaceable experience with psychoactive therapeutic drugs, behavioral modification techniques, and identifying whether a given individual requires institutionalization.

Knott also points out the importance of behavioral modification as a cornerstone of alcohol psychotherapy and makes it clear that a wide variety of choices is available to alcoholics desiring psychosocial help. An interesting point made by A. E. Bennet, in *Alcoholism and the Brain* (1977), is that autopsy and a variety of sophisticated medical techniques, including computed tomography (CT) scans, identify atrophy of the cerebral cortex of the brain in many alcoholics. This damage is viewed as a factor in the inability of alcoholics to stop drinking, as well as in loss of motor skills and eventual development of serious conditions such as Korsakoff syndrome.

Perspective and Prospects

The excessive use of alcoholic beverages, with resultant alcoholism, has occurred for many centuries. In recent years, however, the problem of alcoholism has assumed epidemic proportions; it affects more than ten million Americans. Two societal observations that are particularly disturbing are the estimates that 10 to 25 percent of American high school students get drunk once a week and the observation that alcoholism appears to be self-perpetuating: More than 50 percent of alcoholics are the offspring of alcoholic parents.

Modern efforts to deal with alcoholism are often considered to have begun in the early twentieth century, with the activities of the American temperance movement that culminated with Prohibition upon the passage of the 1919 Volstead Act by the U.S. Congress. The idea behind the Volstead Act was that making liquor impossible to obtain would force sobriety on the nation. Prohibition turned out to be self-defeating, however, and several sources point out that it actually increased the incidence of alcoholism in the potential problem drinker. It was repealed in 1933.

The next, and much more useful, effort to combat alcoholism was the psychosocial approach of Alcoholics Anonymous, started in 1935 and still operating well. Yet that organization does not reach the majority of alcoholics, so other efforts needed to evolve as treatment methodologies. Among these have been the wide use of psychiatric counseling, alcohol rehabilitation centers, family counseling, and alcohol management programs in the workplace.

These options—alone or in various combinations—have had considerable success in reaching alcoholics, and combined alcoholism therapy seems to work best; however, it has not yet been possible to stem the tide of increasing alcoholism or to cure the disease. Instead, these techniques—like those of Alcoholics Anonymous—can only arrest it. Part of the reason for this is the fact that the basis for alcoholism is not clearly understood by those attempting to eradicate it.

One hope for curing alcoholism is ongoing basic research into the biochemistry, pharmacology, and physiology of alcoholism. A number of aspects of such efforts are discussed in Ronald Ross Watson's *Diagnosis of Alcohol Abuse* (1989). While the information and answers so far obtained are not yet clear-cut or applicable, it is hoped that the continuation of such efforts will help to provide better insight and solutions to the problem.

Bibliography

Becker, Charles E. "Pharmacotherapy in the Treatment of Alcoholism." In *The Diagnosis and Treatment of Alcoholism*, edited by Jack H. Mendelson and Nancy K. Mello. 2d ed. New York: McGraw-Hill, 1985. This article, with numerous references, in a very useful book aimed at effective treatment of alcoholism, describes the uses and pitfalls of the therapeutic drugs utilized. Topics include management of intoxication and alcohol withdrawal syndrome, postwithdrawal assistance, chronic assistance, and alcoholism and depression.

Bennett, Abram Elting. *Alcoholism and the Brain*. New York: Stratton Intercontinental Medical Book, 1977. Deals with relationships between brain function and alcoholism as a brain disease. Coverage includes the concept of alcoholism as a disease, alcohol actions in the brain, testing for alcoholic brain disease, constructive relationships between psychiatry and other aspects of alcoholism treatment, and rehabilitation methodology.

Cox, W. Miles, ed. *The Treatment and Prevention of Alcohol Problems: A Resource Manual*. Orlando, Fla.: Academic Press, 1987. This edited work contains much information on many of the psychiatric, psychological, and behavioral aspects of alcohol. It is also widely useful in many other related alcoholism issues, including Alcoholics Anonymous, marital therapy, family therapy, and alcoholism prevention.

Eskelson, Cleamond D. "Hereditary Predisposition for Alcoholism." In *Diagnosis of Alcohol Abuse*, edited by Ronald Ross Watson. Boca Raton, Fla.: CRC Press, 1989. This article, in a book full of helpful information, gives considerable useful data on the hereditary aspects of alcoholism, concentrating on alcohol metabolism, animal and human studies, genetic aspects, and genetic markers for the disease. Sixty-five related references are included.

Galanter, Marc, ed. *The Consequences of Alcoholism: Medical, Neuropsychiatric, Economic, Cross-Cultural*. New York: Plenum Press, 1998. An official publication of the American Society of Addiction Medicine and the Research Society on Alcoholism. Examines the physiological effects of alcohol. Includes bibliographical references and an index.

Knott, David H. *Alcohol Problems: Diagnosis and Treatment*. New York: Pergamon Press, 1986. Provides physicians with useful information on diagnosis and treatment of alcoholism. Topics include alcohol use and alcoholism; biochemical factors in alcohol use and abuse; epidemiology, diagnosis, and treatment of the disease; information on special populations affected by alcoholism; and perspectives on its control and prevention.

Leonard, Kenneth E., and Howard T. Blane. *Psychological Theories of Drinking and Alcoholism*. 2d ed. New York: Guilford Press, 1999. This volume in the Guilford Substance Abuse series discusses the psychology behind alcoholism. Includes bibliographical references and an index.

Mecca, Andrew M. *Alcoholism in America: A Modern Perspective*. Belvedere, Calif.: California Health Research Foundation, 1980. This interesting book is useful, entertaining reading, with a wide factual base. It covers the history of alcoholic beverages, the nature of alcoholism, effects of alcoholism on the body, its treatment, community alcoholism prevention, and future perspectives. Included are numerous sources of additional information and a useful glossary.

Rix, Keith J. B., and Elizabeth M. Lumsden Rix. *Alcohol Problems: A Guide for Nurses and Other Health Professionals.* Bristol, England: Wright, 1983. The purpose of this book (with more than two hundred references) is to "provide nurses with information that will contribute to . . . improved education." Contains information on causes of alcoholism, its epidemiology, characteristics of alcohol intoxication and withdrawal, medical treatments, psychosocial aspects, and intervention models and methods.

Watson, Ronald Ross, ed. *Diagnosis of Alcohol Abuse.* Boca Raton, Fla.: CRC Press, 1989. This edited work contains fifteen chapters on various aspects of current alcoholism research. They include basic science issues in biochemistry, genetics enzymology, and nutrition. Other topics covered include diagnosis of alcoholic liver disease, identification of problem drinkers, alcohol testing, and alcoholism screening efforts.

Sanford S. Singer

See also:

Addictive Personality and Behaviors; Codependent Personality; Substance Abuse.

ALZHEIMER'S DISEASE

Type of psychology: Memory; psychopathology
Fields of study: Cognitive processes; organic disorders

Alzheimer's disease is the most common cause of dementia in old age, affecting between 3 and 11 percent of those over sixty-five.

Principal terms

AGNOSIA: an inability to recognize persons or various objects even though the patient sees them clearly

ANOMIA: an inability to remember the names of persons or objects even though the patient sees and recognizes the persons or objects

APHASIA: difficulty in understanding and talking to other people in the absence of hearing impairment

APRAXIA: difficulty in carrying out coordinated voluntary activities (such as dressing, undressing, or brushing one's teeth) in the absence of any muscular weakness

BENIGN SENESCENT FORGETFULNESS: a common source of frustration in old age, associated with memory impairment; unlike dementia, it does not interfere with the individual's social and professional activities

COGNITIVE DEFICIT: an impairment in mental functions, including anomia, agnosia, aphasia, and apraxia; it is usually associated with an impairment in the ability to make rational decisions

DEMENTIA: also called dementing illness; a disease characterized by memory impairment of sufficient severity to interfere with the individual's daily social and professional activities

Causes and Symptoms

Alzheimer's disease is the most common dementing illness in old age. In the United States, it is estimated that its prevalence increases from 3 percent in those aged sixty-five to seventy-four years, to 18.7 percent in those seventy-five to eighty-four years of age, to as much as 47.2 percent of those over the age of eighty-five. While both sexes are about equally affected, there are more women than men with Alzheimer's disease because women tend to live longer. As with other dementing illnesses, the characteristic memory impairment initially affects the recent, rather than the remote, memory and interferes with the patient's daily social and professional activities; the patient's attention span is also significantly reduced.

The disease typically has a slow, insidious onset, and a very slow, gradual progress. Caregivers observing this decline are often unable to agree about when the symptoms began to manifest themselves. The memory deficit is usually accompanied by an impaired ability to make good, rational decisions. One of the most common and earliest problems is an inability to take care of one's financial affairs. In addition to being unable to balance a checkbook, the patient may attempt to pay the same bill several times, while disregarding other financial obligations. Similarly, the patient may be overly generous at times and extremely mean on other occasions.

In Alzheimer's disease, the dementing process is also associated with other evidence of cognitive deficit. When anomia is present, patients often use paraphrases to describe various objects because they have difficulty finding the correct words. For example, they may say "milk pourer" instead of "milk jug." This condition is usually present very early in the disease process, but it is often so slight that it may only be detected by neuropsychological testing. Agnosia develops later and can be quite hazardous. For example, a patient may confuse a knife with a comb. As the disease progresses, a patient may develop aphasia and find it difficult to communicate with other people. Finally, the patient develops apraxia, experiencing difficulty carrying out coordinated activities such as dressing or undressing, even though there is no loss of muscular power. The apraxia may also be responsible for unsteadiness, and the patient may fall repeatedly and may become chairbound or bedfast. Anomia, agnosia, aphasia, and apraxia are sometimes referred to as the "four A's" that accompany the memory deficit seen in Alzheimer's disease.

Alzheimer's disease is progressive, and there is much individual variability in the rate of progress. A number of staging classifications, most of them arbitrary, are available. One of the most practical is the three-stage classification. In stage 1, the memory impairment and degree of cognitive deficit are so slight that patients may still be able to function socially and even professionally, although family members and close associates may have observed strange behavioral patterns. Superficially, the patients may appear "normal," although somewhat eccentric. Although the memory deficit and impaired mental functions are present, patients may use various tricks to mask this deficit. They may ask a partner to keep score of a game they are playing because they have "left their reading glasses at home" or may decline invitations to play card games or socialize altogether. Patients with this disease may also stop engaging in their favorite hobbies and activities. Patients at this stage usually have difficulties balancing their checkbooks. Errors of judgment are not infrequent, although they are initially often attributed by family and friends to age, to eccentricity, or to the patient's having too many things on his or her mind. Patients may buy large quantities of the same item and start hoarding various articles. As time progresses, they may lose their way, and their errors in judgment while driving may result in traffic accidents. One of the main problems in this stage is the inability to learn and retain new information. This mental deficit becomes particularly problematic if the patient's work is being reorganized or if the patient relocates. Agitation, irritability, and anxiety are not uncommon in this stage and probably represent the patient's inability to cope with a loss of control over the environment and a declining mental ability.

In stage 2, the memory impairment, cognitive deficit, and degree of impaired judgment are so great that even a stranger who has never met the patient cannot help but conclude that there is something wrong with the patient's mental func-

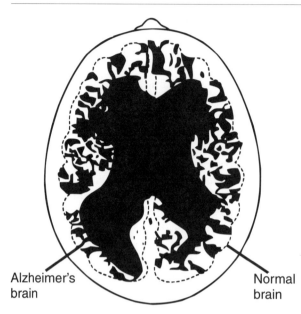

Alzheimer's brain

Normal brain

Alzheimer's disease causes the volume of the brain to shrink substantially. (Hans & Cassidy, Inc.)

tions. In this stage, patients frequently become lost, even in very familiar surroundings, such as in their own houses. They may no longer be able to find their way to the toilet, they may no longer recognize people they know well, and they are unable to take care of their own hygienic needs. They tend to walk aimlessly and wander constantly and are likely to become agitated, irritable, and even aggressive. These symptoms are often pronounced late in the afternoon or early evening and are often referred to as "sundowning syndrome."

In stage 3, in addition to their mental impairment, patients become unsteady on their feet and may sustain repeated falls. Because they have become physically frail, they tend to wander much less and to spend most of their time confined to a chair or bed. They are completely dependent on their caregivers for most activities. Swallowing is often difficult, and feeding through a small tube inserted in the nose (a nasogastric tube) may be required. Patients are at risk of becoming dehydrated and malnourished, and urinary and even fecal incontinence is not uncommon. Mutism gradually sets in, and communication with the patient becomes difficult. Flexion (bending) contractures gradually develop, and the patient slowly adopts the fetal position, with the arms and knees bent. The development of pressure ulcers, or bedsores, is likely. The common cause of death is septicemia (blood poisoning) resulting from a respiratory tract infection, a urinary tract infection, or an infected pressure ulcer.

Alzheimer's disease is characterized by a loss of brain cells, affecting in particular the cerebral cortex. The brain appears smaller in size and atrophic, with the gyri (grooves) much less prominent and the ventricles (cavities inside the brain) enlarged. Multiple deficiencies in the neurotransmitters, chemical substances inside the brain that carry impulses from one cell to another, have been identified with this disease.

At present, there are no positive tests available to make a definitive diagnosis of Alzheimer's disease without examining brain tissue under the microscope. Before such a diagnosis can be considered, several factors should be present. First, the memory impairment should be of sufficient magnitude and consistency to interfere with one's social and professional activities, and it should be accompanied by evidence of cognitive deficit and impaired judgment. These are the main differentiating features between Alzheimer's disease and benign senescent forgetfulness, which is also very common in old age. Although the latter can be quite irritating, it does not significantly interfere with the person's professional and social activities and tends to be selective, with one's forgetting only unimportant and relatively trivial matters. The forgetfulness seen in Alzheimer's disease, on the other hand, is global and does not distinguish between trivial and important matters.

Second, in Alzheimer's disease, the onset of memory impairment is insidious, and the progress is slow. This differentiates it from multiple infarct dementia, which is caused by multiple strokes and which has an abrupt onset and progress marked by bouts of deterioration. Whenever a stroke develops, the patient's condition deteriorates and then stabilizes until the next stroke occurs.

Third, the patient must be alert, not drowsy—one of the main distinctions between Alzheimer's disease and delirium. The latter, in addition to having a sudden onset, is associated with clouding of consciousness, a rambling and incoherent speech, disorganized thinking, hallucinations, and sensory misperceptions.

Finally, as the diagnosis of Alzheimer's disease is still based on a process of exclusion, all other possible causes of impaired mental functions must be ruled out. These causes are numerous and can be conveniently remembered by the mnemonic device DEMENTIA.

The *D* stands for drugs. Older patients are particularly susceptible to the effects of many medications that may impair mental functions. These indications include not only those acting specifically on the brain, such as the sedatives and hypnotics, but also other medications such as those that lower blood pressure. Finally, alcohol is often abused by older people and may significantly interfere with the older person's mental abilities.

The *E* stands for emotional disorders. Depression is very common in old age and may manifest itself with cognitive impairment. Unlike patients with Alzheimer's disease, who except in the very early stages of the disease are not aware of their deficit, those with depression are acutely aware of their problem and often exaggerate it. Often, patients with depression also have a long list of complaints. They lack animation, their appetite is reduced, and they take a diminished interest in their environment and pleasure in their daily activities. Sleep disturbances, in the form of insomnia or increased sleepiness, are common. Although most cases of depression are easily recognized, some may be difficult to diagnose and therefore may require neuropsychological testing to differentiate them from Alzheimer's disease. This differentiation is important, because unlike Alzheimer's disease, depression can be treated, and the outlook is good. Additionally, it is important to emphasize that about 20 percent of patients with Alzheimer's disease have a coexistent depression that often responds to appropriate therapy.

The *M* stands for metabolic disorders. In old age, both overactivity and underactivity of the thyroid gland may be responsible for mental impairment without a patient's exhibiting any of the characteristic clinical features. Dehydration is a common cause of confusion in older patients because their sense of thirst is often reduced. Liver and kidney diseases also may be responsible for impaired mental functions. Similarly, patients with diabetes mellitus are susceptible to a number of metabolic disorders, including an increased or decreased blood sugar level, both of which may cause cognitive impairment. Serum electrolyte disorders also may result in confusional states and can be precipitated by severe vomiting, diarrhea, or the intake of medication. Finally, vitamin B_{12} deficiency may be responsible for impaired mental functions, occasionally without there being any other clinical evidence of this deficiency. Patients who have had a gastrectomy (surgical removal of their stomach) and no vitamin B_{12} replacement are likely to develop B_{12} deficiency a few years after surgery. By this time, however, the patient may have relocated, changed physicians, and probably "forgotten" about the surgery.

The *E* stands for both eyes and ears. For individuals to interact appropriately with others and the environment, they must be aware of the various circumstances surrounding them. If an individual cannot hear properly and guesses at the questions asked, he or she often will not give an appropriate answer and may give the impression of being confused. Hearing impairment is very common among the older population, and often older people choose not to wear a hearing aid because of difficulties manipulating the controls or because of embarrassment. Visual impairment may also interfere with an individual's appropriate interaction with the environment and give the impression of dementia. There are many causes of visual impairment in old age, including glaucoma, cataracts, and macular degeneration (a progressive disorder of the retina).

The *N* stands for neurological disorders; these include other dementias such as multiple infarct dementia and hydrocephalus (increased fluid in the brain).

The *T* stands for both tumors and trauma. A subdural hematoma (a collection of blood inside the skull) may be precipitated by trauma that is usually trivial. The symptoms do not become apparent until a few days or even weeks after the trauma, by which time the patient and caregivers may have forgotten about the physical trauma. Brain tumors may also manifest themselves with impaired mental functions. The computed tomography (CT) scan and magnetic resonance imaging (MRI) are useful tools in diagnosing these conditions.

The *I* stands for infections. Infections, regardless of their location but especially those of the respiratory and urinary tracts, may be associated with confusional states in older people. Unlike younger people, they often do not exhibit a rise in body temperature, thus making the diagnosis of infection difficult. Acquired immunodeficiency syndrome (AIDS) is another cause of dementia that is related to infection; this condition must be suspected when mental functions deteriorate rapidly, especially if the patient has risk factors for AIDS.

The *A* stands for atherosclerosis and includes arteriosclerotic cardiovascular diseases. Older patients who experience myocardial infarction (a "heart attack" caused by a sudden reduction of blood flow to the heart muscle) may not experience any chest pain but may nevertheless develop an acute confusional state. Generalized arteriosclerosis also might be responsible for multiple, small, repeated strokes that can eventually interfere with the patient's cognitive functions.

The accuracy of the clinical diagnosis of Alzheimer's disease can be increased to about 90 percent if a few investigations are conducted. These include a complete blood count, Chem-18 (a series of blood tests to check on the blood levels of many substances and the functioning of the kidneys and liver), thyroid function tests, serum B_{12} measurement, electrocardiogram, and brain imaging tests. Single photon emission computed tomography (SPECT) seems to be a promising test in the diagnosis of Alzheimer's disease and may represent the first step toward being able to make a diagnosis without examining brain tissue microscopically.

Treatment and Therapy

Although the understanding of the pathophysiology of Alzheimer's disease has increased tremendously since it was first described by Alois Alzheimer in the early years of the twentieth century, this understanding has not been translated into effective therapeutic opportunities. A large number of compounds have been and are being tried for the treatment of Alzheimer's disease but, unfortunately, without any significant degree of success. At present, therefore, it is essentially a disease without a cure.

Nevertheless, many things can be done to aid a patient with Alzheimer's disease. It is important to detect the presence of any other disease that may worsen the patient's condition, and unnecessary medications must be avoided for the same reason. Medication may nevertheless be required to control agitation and the sundowning syndrome. Physicians will generally start with the smallest possible dose of medication and then gradually increase it according to the patient's symptoms.

The patient's environment and daily routine should be left as constant as possible, as any change may precipitate or worsen the symptoms and degree of confusion. The patient should be spared the task of having to choose an option among several ones (such as which dress to wear) and to make decisions (such as which activity in which to become involved). Instead, the daily routine should be as structured as possible and yet retain enough flexibility for the patient to withdraw from any activity that is disliked and to join any that is enjoyed.

The patient with Alzheimer's disease should be treated not in isolation but by caregivers and family members, who will also need support and help if they are to cope effectively with their loved one's illness. Social workers and various community agencies can help develop a management program tailored to the individual patient's needs and those of his or her caregivers. A number of community programs are available, and the Alzheimer's Association and support groups are very useful resources. Caregivers and family members should also be given advice concerning financial, legal, and ethical issues, such as obtaining a durable power of attorney and finding out the patient's wishes concerning advance directives prior to incapacitation.

Perspective and Prospects

Alzheimer's disease has been compared to other brain diseases that reduce neurotransmission, how the brain communicates with itself, and the actual number of brain cells. Clinical and experimental drugs have become available that attempt to treat age-related cognitive decline, Alzheimer's disease, and other dementias. By the beginning of the twenty-first century, no panacea had been developed, but research in this area continued to be vigorous and well funded.

Bibliography

American Psychiatric Association. *Practice Guideline for the Treatment of Patients with Alzheimer's Disease and Other Dementias of Late Life.* Washington, D.C.: Author, 1997. May be helpful for individuals seeking information on what to expect in future treatment and assessment for family members.

Hamdy, Ronald C., et al., eds. *Alzheimer's Disease: A Handbook for Caregivers.* 3d ed. St. Louis: Mosby, 1998. Offers practical advice for researchers and caregivers about how to deal with the patient with Alzheimer's disease or another type of dementia. Presents a thorough discussion of the symptoms of these disorders, as compared to normal brain structure and function and the natural effects of aging.

Mace, Nancy L., and Peter V. Rabins. *The Thirty-Six-Hour Day: A Family Guide to Caring for Persons with Alzheimer Disease, Related Dementing Illnesses, and Memory Loss in Later Life.* 3d ed. Baltimore: The Johns Hopkins University Press, 1999. Possibly the best practical and informational guide to the myriad difficulties that caregivers and family members face. Highly regarded within the field.

Scinto, Leonard F. M., and Kirk R. Daffner, eds. *Early Diagnosis of Alzheimer's Disease.* Totowa, N.J.: Humana Press, 2000. An up-to-date work that addresses the genetic aspects of the disease. Includes bibliographical references and an index.

U.S. Congress. Office of Technology Assessment. *Confused Minds, Burdened Families: Finding Help for People with Alzheimer's and Other Dementias.* Washington, D.C.: Government Printing Office, 1990. This official government report describes the current system of services in the United States set up to care for those with Alzheimer's disease and other dementias. Details its many inadequacies and presents an alternative vision of a more efficient system, including recommendations for congressional policy options to make it a reality.

_____. *Losing a Million Minds: Confronting the Tragedy of Alzheimer's Disease and Other Dementias.* Washington, D.C.: Government Printing Office, 1987. Offers a comprehensive assessment of the impact of Alzheimer's disease on the United States, including the psychoeconomic effects of this disease on patients and caregivers, personnel training and quality assurance in public and private programs that serve patients with dementia, and future governmental policies regarding these issues.

Wang, Eugenia, and D. Stephen Snyder, eds. *Handbook of the Aging Brain.* San Diego: Academic Press, 1998. In addition to Alzheimer's disease, examines such topics as normal and abnormal memory, the effects of stress, learning, neuron death, prion diseases, and Parkinson's disease. Includes bibliographical references and an index.

West, Robin L., and Jan D. Sinnott, eds. *Everyday Memory and Aging.* New York:

Springer-Verlag, 1992. This work discusses the methodology of research into the human memory. Focuses on the changes in memory that occur naturally with age, as well as those that are brought about by various forms of dementia in the older individual.

Whitehouse, Peter J., Konrad Maurer, and Jesse F. Ballenger, eds. *Concepts of Alzheimer Disease: Biological, Clinical, and Cultural Perspectives.* Baltimore: The John Hopkins University Press, 2000. Explores the genetic, social, historical, and psychological aspects of Alzheimer's disease and neuroscience in general. Includes bibliographical references and an index.

Ronald C. Hamdy, M.D.
Louis A. Cancellaro, M.D.
Larry Hudgins, M.D.
updated by Paul Moglia

See also:
Brain Disorders; Dementia; Depression; Geriatric Psychiatry; Memory Loss.

Amnesia, Fugue, and Multiple Personality

Type of psychology: Psychopathology
Fields of study: Anxiety disorders; models of abnormality; organic disorders

Amnesia, fugue, and multiple personality form a group of mental disorders that are typically referred to as the dissociative disorders; they are called dissociative because some area of memory is split off, or dissociated, from conscious awareness.

Principal terms

AMNESIA: total or partial memory loss, which is often acute and follows an emotional or physical trauma

BIOGENIC DISORDER: an illness that is attributable primarily to some type of physiological trauma or sickness

DIAGNOSIS: the classification or labeling of a patient's problem within one of a set of recognized categories of abnormal behavior

DISSOCIATIVE DISORDERS: disorders that occur when some psychological function, such as memory, is split off from the rest of the conscious mind

FUGUE STATE: a flight from reality in which the individual leaves his or her present situation, travels to a new location, and establishes a new identity

MULTIPLE PERSONALITY: a rare mental disorder characterized by the development and existence of two or more relatively unique and independent personalities in the same individual

PSYCHOGENIC DISORDER: an illness that is attributable primarily to some psychological conflict or to emotional stress

Causes and Symptoms

Amnesia, fugue, and multiple personality are considered by most mental health professionals to be the three major types of dissociative disorders—disorders in which some important area of memory is split off (dissociated) from the individual's conscious awareness.

Like all the dissociative disorders, amnesia has long fascinated both mental health professionals and the general public. Most professionals define amnesia as the sudden inability to recall important personal information, such as one's name, occupation, or family. Amnesia victims, or amnesiacs, suddenly wonder who they are and why they are in their present circumstances.

In some cases, amnesia is caused by biological factors. A variety of physical traumas, such as a blow to the head, gunshot wound to the brain, stroke, or history of chronic alcoholism, can cause an individual to suffer from impaired memory. When amnesia is caused by such physical problems, the amnesia is said to be biogenic. A person who suffers from biogenic amnesia will typically experience the loss of both personal and general knowledge. For example, a concert pianist with biogenic amnesia not only will lose personal information such as name and family history but also will lose such general information as knowledge of music and the ability to play the piano. If physicians are able to treat the physical causes of biologically based amnesia in a successful manner, the afflicted individual's memory often tends to return slowly—over a period of weeks, months, or even years.

When amnesia is caused by emotional factors, the individual's situation is somewhat different. In these cases, the person is said to have psychogenic amnesia. This person will typically suffer the loss of personal, but not general, information. For example, the concert pianist with psychogenic amnesia may forget such personal information as his or her name and address but will still be able to play difficult pieces of music and recall the complexities of music theory. Such a case of psychogenic amnesia will typically occur when a person is suffering from numerous emotional stressors, such as marital, financial, or career problems, or when the person receives a severe emotional shock, such as the unexpected death of a loved one. The amnesia may thus help the person escape such unpleasant circumstances. Many theorists believe that psychogenic amnesia victims forget in order to avoid the unbearable anxiety that is associated with their problems or traumatic experiences.

A few cases of psychogenic amnesia have continued for the rest of the victim's life. In most cases, however, the afflicted individual will regain his or her memory anywhere from a day to several years after the syndrome's onset; no one knows why many amnesiacs are suddenly able to regain their memory. Psychogenic amnesia will often come and go in a rapid manner.

Like amnesia, a fugue syndrome tends to begin and end abruptly. Fugue (also known as psychogenic fugue) occurs when the afflicted individual takes an unexpected trip or excursion, forgets his or her identity, and assumes a new identity. The term "fugue" is derived from the Latin word *fuga*, meaning flight. This is an appropriate name, since the fugue victim is usually in a state of flight, fleeing some intolerable situation. While amnesiacs may wander about in a confused manner, fugue patients tend to travel in a way that appears both purposeful and deliberate. Fugue patients also tend, unlike amnesiacs, to manufacture a new identity. This new identity allows these individuals greater freedom and an escape from their troubles.

The length of fugue states varies considerably. In most cases, the person travels for little more than a day or two and goes no farther than the next town. A small group of fugue patients, however, will travel hundreds of miles, create new identities, and pursue their new lives for months or even years. During the fugue state, the patient will appear normal to other people. When the person finally "wakes up," he or she will have no memory of what took place during the fugue state. Like amnesia, fugue states seem to occur when a person has numerous troubles or has experienced an unbearable psychological trauma. For this reason fugue states, which are normally quite rare, are more common in wartime or after natural disasters.

While fugue patients travel to a new place to be someone else, individuals with multiple personality disorder stay in one place as they experience the existence of two or more separate personalities. Each personality will have a unique set of habits, tastes, and learned behaviors. Only one personality will dominate the person's thoughts and consciousness at a given time, and the shifts from one personality to the next will be quite abrupt and dramatic. While cases of multiple personality are very rare, this disorder has received considerable attention from the popular media because of its bizarre and fascinating nature.

Most individuals with multiple personality disorder have one primary personality, as well as one or more secondary personalities. The primary personality is the individual who is known to most people. This personality is often quiet, meek, and obedient, while the secondary personalities tend to be more aggressive, irresponsible, and pleasure seeking.

Though it is not entirely clear how an individual comes to have more than one personality, many professionals now believe that this disorder stems from a history of extreme emotional, physical, or sexual abuse during one's childhood. If a small child is severely beaten or molested, he or she may attempt to cope by pretending that the abuse is happening to someone else. The child may even give a name to this "other" person. As the child comes to rely repeatedly on this other person to cope with the abuse, the secondary personality eventually takes on a life of its own.

Treatment and Therapy

Like all psychiatric diagnoses, the dissociative disorders are useful when they help mental health professionals understand the experience of a disturbed individual. If it is known that someone suffers from a particular syndrome, such as amnesia, the knowledge may facilitate the individual's treatment. Diagnostic categories also enable psychologists to place individuals in groups, so that their problems and potential treatment can be studied by research scientists. One way to understand how knowledge of dissociative disorders can help professionals make sense of an individual's problems is to review some of the well-known case studies in this field.

In 1967, Henry Laughlin published the story of a patient named Robert who joined the Army and served for a year during a fugue state. Laughlin reports that Robert was a fifteen-year-old boy who was attending high school in a small New Jersey town. At the onset of his fugue state, Robert was beset by numerous problems. He was unusually large for his age and was frequently teased by peers. He was also engaging in a number of quarrels with his parents and was making poor grades at school. Robert was apparently quite upset by these problems, and he had begun to believe that his current situation was hopeless. One afternoon Robert came home and, with a sense of utter despair, threw his schoolbooks on the front porch.

Robert then remembered nothing more until approximately one year later. At that time, Robert, who was successfully serving under another name in the Army, suddenly recalled his life as a high school student. The last thing he remembered was throwing his books on the front porch. Robert had no idea why he was on an Army base, and he could remember nothing of his military career. His family was eventually contacted, and he was discharged for being underage.

Robert's fugue state was typical in that he had been experiencing considerable stress before the onset of his illness. Like most fugue patients, he temporarily escaped his troubles by creating a new identity in a new locale. Robert was also like most fugue patients in that he regained his memory rapidly and was then unable to recall what had transpired during his travels and military career. Although Robert's fugue state did last for an unusually long time, his case is in many ways a classic example of psychogenic fugue.

A case that is perhaps even more sensational than Robert's is the story of Eve White, a multiple personality patient described by Corbett Thigpen and Hervey Cleckley. Thigpen and Cleckley indicate that Eve White was a young woman who sought medical assistance because of severe headaches and occasional blackouts. This woman was described as "demure, retiring, in some respects almost saintly." Eve White was a devoted mother who worked extremely hard to support and rear a young daughter. Friends and coworkers found Eve White to be quiet, sensitive, and at times a little too serious.

One day as Eve White was describing her problems to her therapist, she was seized by a sudden headache and put both hands to her head. Thigpen and Cleckley report that "after a tense moment of silence, her hands dropped. There was a quick, reckless smile and, in a bright voice that sparkled, she said, 'Hi there, Doc!'" The patient began to talk about Eve White in a casual and carefree manner; she referred to Eve White as "her" and "she." When asked her name, the patient stated, "Oh, I'm Eve Black." As time went on, the therapist began to discover that Eve Black was "a party girl, shrewd, childishly vain, and egocentric." While Eve White was suffering from blackouts, Eve Black would attend parties, flirt with men in bars, and engage in wild spending sprees. Eve Black would then retreat and force Eve White to deal with the consequences of her reckless behavior. Eve White had no awareness of Eve Black. Eve Black was, however, typically conscious of Eve White and her troubles. Eve Black was also able to remember a number of painful childhood memories that Eve White was completely unable to recall. For example, as treatment progressed, it was Eve Black who was able to tell the therapist how Eve White was severely beaten by her parents as a child.

Eventually a third personality emerged from this young woman. This personality, named Jane, was aware of both Eve White and Eve Black. Jane was described as more mature, thoughtful, and balanced than either Eve White or Eve Black. The emergence of Jane may thus have represented an attempt on the part of this patient to integrate aspects of Eve White and Eve Black into one cohesive personality.

As the three personalities became better known, Thigpen and Cleckley eventually published a popular account of them in a book entitled *The Three Faces of Eve* (1957). Eve's case history serves as a clear example of how an individual can develop multiple personalities, each of which can take on a life of his or her own.

Perspective and Prospects

Mental health professionals have known about the existence of dissociative disorders for many years. Sigmund Freud and his followers began to study psychogenic amnesia around the beginning of the twentieth century, and the first widely publicized case of multiple personality was reported by Morton Prince in 1905. Since the time of this early work, both professionals and the general public have been fascinated with the dissociative disorders.

Despite the widespread interest in psychogenic amnesia, psychogenic fugue, and multiple personality, these disorders are actually quite rare. Many experienced psychiatrists and clinical psychologists have never encountered a patient with one of these dissociative disorders in their practice. Because of the extreme rarity of these conditions, the dissociative disorders are not a major mental health problem in the United States.

Many social scientists, however, continue to believe that these disorders merit further study. It is difficult to conduct large-scale research projects on the dissociative disorders, simply because it is so hard to obtain an adequate number of subjects. Carefully conducted case studies, however, will continue to further understanding of the disorders. These case histories may be able to teach some important lessons about human nature. Although most individuals do not experience the dramatic memory problems of amnesia or multiple personality patients, the dissociative experience should not be seen as completely foreign to the ordinary person. Expressions that suggest dissociative reactions are commonly used to describe ordinary individuals. One might say that someone is "running away from his problems," is "not quite herself today," or "has become a different person." All these expressions suggest that the person has somehow disavowed a part of his or her conscious experience or personality style. It is possible that the dissociative disorders of psychogenic amnesia. psychogenic fugue, and multiple personality may thus be nothing more than a very extreme and dramatic exaggeration of a common human experience.

Bibliography

Acocella, Joan Ross. *Creating Hysteria: Women and Multiple Personality Disorder.* San Francisco: Jossey-Bass, 1999. Discusses multiple personality and false memory syndrome among women. Includes bibliographical references and an index.

Alloy, Lauren B., Neil S. Jacobson, and Joan Acocella. *Abnormal Psychology: Current Perspectives.* 8th ed. New York: McGraw-Hill, 1998. This textbook contains an excellent chapter on the dissociative disorders that describes relevant case studies and explains how different psychological theorists view the dissociative diagnoses. The author's discussion of psychogenic amnesia and psychogenic fugue is particularly informative. Clear, easy to read, and understandable by the high school or college student.

Braude, Stephen E. *First Person Plural: Multiple Personality and the Philosophy of Mind.* Rev. ed. Lanham, Md.: Rowman & Littlefield, 1995. Provides in-depth, thought-provoking information about multiple personality.

Cohen, Lewis M., Joan N. Berzoff, and Mark R. Elin, eds. *Dissociative Identity Disorder: Theoretical and Treatment Controversies.* Northvale, N.J.: Jason Aronson, 1995. A study of multiple personality disorder. Includes bibliographical references and an index.

Davison, Gerald C., and John M. Neale. *Abnormal Psychology*. 8th ed. New York: John Wiley & Sons, 2000. Contains a very readable chapter on somatoform and dissociative disorders. The authors give a well-organized overview of the topic and enhance their discussion with a number of lively examples. Recommended for the high school student, college student, or casual reader.

Hacking, Ian. *Rewriting the Soul: Multiple Personality and the Sciences of Memory*. Princeton, N.J.: Princeton University Press, 1995. Th author, a philosopher, uses the concept of multiple personality disorder and its links with child abuse to examine modern morality and politics.

Keyes, Daniel, *The Minds of Billy Milligan*. New York: Random House, 1981. A journalistic account of a young man's multiple personality disorder. Especially helpful to readers who are interested in the relationship between mental illness and the criminal justice system, since the story's protagonist was convicted of raping several women. An interesting discussion of the insanity defense is included.

Sackheim, H., and W. Vingiano. "Dissociative Disorders." In *Adult Psychopathology and Diagnosis*, edited by Samuel M. Turner and Michael Hersen. 3d ed. New York: John Wiley & Sons, 1997. Provides the reader with a scholarly overview of the dissociative disorders. Relevant diagnostic issues are discussed, in conjunction with a thorough review of the major research studies that have been conducted on amnesia, fugue, and multiple personality. Ideal for the student who seeks a detailed and challenging discussion of the dissociative disorders.

Schreiber, Flora Rheta. *Sybil*. New York: Warner Books, 1974. This popular account of a young woman's struggle with multiple personality disorder reads like a well-written novel. The author provides a fascinating description of both the development and treatment of multiple personality. This book will be especially helpful to individuals who are interested in the psychotherapy process.

Walker, Moira, and Jenifer Antony-Black, eds. *Hidden Selves: An Exploration of Multiple Personality*. Philadelphia: Open University Press, 1999. Presents case studies in multiple personality disorder. Includes bibliographical references.

Steven C. Abell

See also:

Abnormality; Anxiety Disorders; Forgetting and Forgetfulness; Identity Crises; Memory Loss; Phobias.

ANALYTICAL PSYCHOTHERAPY

Type of psychology: Psychotherapy
Fields of study: Psychodynamic therapies

Analytical psychotherapy is associated with the theory and techniques of Carl Gustav Jung. Similar to other psychodynamic therapies, it stresses the importance of discovering unconscious material. Unique to this approach is the emphasis on reconciling opposite personality traits that are hidden in the personal and collective unconsciouses.

Principal terms

COLLECTIVE UNCONSCIOUS: memories and emotions of which people are usually unaware but which are shared by all humanity

COMPENSATORY FUNCTION: displaying denied aspects of one's personality; a characteristic of dreams

CONFESSION: the first stage of Jungian psychotherapy, in which the patient relates conflicts in an emotional fashion

EDUCATION: the third stage of Jungian psychotherapy, in which the therapist communicates the danger of one-sided personality development

ELUCIDATION: the second stage of Jungian psychotherapy, in which the patient acts toward the therapist as toward some significant person from the patient's past

METHOD OF ACTIVE IMAGINATION: the process of discovering unconscious material from the patient's artistic productions

METHOD OF AMPLIFICATION: a Jungian technique for dream analysis in which the patient makes multiple associations to the contents of the dream

PERSONAL UNCONSCIOUS: a structure of personality that contains thoughts and emotions that are too anxiety-provoking for conscious awareness

TRANSFERENCE: acting toward the therapist in a similar way as to some significant person from the patient's past

TRANSFORMATION: the fourth stage of Jungian psychotherapy, in which the patient seeks self-discovery through reconciling opposite personality traits

Overview

Analytical psychotherapy is an approach to psychological treatment pioneered by Carl Gustav Jung (1875-1961), a Swiss psychoanalyst. A follower of Sigmund Freud, Jung was trained in the psychoanalytic approach, with its emphasis on the dark, inaccessible material contained in the unconscious mind. Freud was fond of Jung and believed that he was to be the heir to the legacy he had begun. Jung began to disagree with certain aspects of Freud's theory, however, and he and Freud parted ways bitterly in 1914.

Jung's concept of the structure of personality, on which he based his ideas of psychotherapy, was obviously influenced by Freud and the psychoanalytic tradition, but he added his own personal and mystical touches to its concepts. Jung believed that the personality consists of the ego, which is one's conscious mind. It contains the thoughts, feelings, and perceptions of which one is normally aware. Jung also proposed a personal unconscious that contains events and emotions of which people remain unaware because of their anxiety-provoking nature. Memories of traumatic childhood events and conflicts may reside in the personal unconscious. Jung's unique contribution to personality theory is the idea of a collective unconscious. This consists of memories and emotions that are shared by all humanity. Jung believed that certain events and feelings are universal and exert a similar effect on all individuals. An example would be his universal symbol of a shadow, or the evil, primitive nature that resides within everyone. Jung believed that although people are aware of the workings of the conscious ego, it is the unavailable material contained in the personal unconscious and collective unconscious that has the greatest influence on one's behavior.

Jung believed that emotional problems originate from a one-sided development of personality. He believed that this is a natural process and that people must constantly seek a balance of their traits. An example might be a person who becomes overly logical and rational in her behavior and decision making while ignoring her emotional and spontaneous side. Jung believed this one-sided development eventually would lead to emotional difficulty and that one must access the complementary personality forces that reside in the unconscious. Even psychotherapists must be aware that along with their desire to help others, they have complementary darker desires that are destructive to others. Jung believed that emotional problems are a signal that one is becoming unbalanced in one's personality and that this should motivate one to develop more neutral traits.

The process of analytical psychotherapy, as in most psychodynamic approaches, is to make the patient conscious or aware of the material in his or her unconscious mind. Jung believed that if the conscious mind were overly logical and rational, the unconscious mind, to balance it, would be filled with equally illogical and emotional material. To access this material, Jung advocated a free and equal exchange of ideas and information between the analyst and the patient. Jung did not focus on specific techniques as did Freud, but he did believe that the unconscious material would become evident in the context of a strong, trusting therapeutic relationship. Although the patient and analyst have equal status, the analyst serves as a model of an individual who has faced her or his unconscious demons.

Analytic psychotherapy proceeds in four stages. The first stage is that of confession. Jung believed that it is necessary for the patient to tell of his or her conflicts and that this is usually accompanied by an emotional release. Jung did not believe that confession is sufficient to provide a cure for one's ills, however, nor did he believe (unlike Freud) that an intellectual understanding of one's difficulties is adequate. The patient must find a more neutral ground in terms of personality functioning, and this can only be accomplished by facing one's unconscious material.

The second stage of psychotherapy is called elucidation, and it involves becoming aware of one's unconscious transferences. Transference is a process in which a patient transfers emotions about someone else in his or her life onto the therapist; the patient will behave toward the therapist as he or she would toward that other person. It is similar to meeting someone who reminds one of a past relationship; for no apparent reason, one might begin to act toward the new person the same way one did to the previous person. Jung believed that these transferences to the analyst give a clue about unconscious material. A gentle, passive patient might evidence hostile transferences to the therapist, thus giving evidence of considerable rage that is being contained in the unconscious.

The third stage of analytic psychotherapy consists of education. The patient is instructed about the dangers of unequal personality development and is supported in his or her attempts to change. The overly logical business executive may be encouraged to go on a spontaneous vacation with his family with few plans and no fixed destinations. The shy student may be cajoled into joining a debate on emotional campus issues. Jung believed in the value of experiencing the messages of one's unconscious.

The final stage of psychotherapy, and one that is not always necessary, is that of transformation. This goes beyond the superficial encouragements of the previous stages and attempts to get the patient to delve deeply into the unconscious and thereby understand who he or she is. This process of understanding and reconciling one's opposites takes considerable courage and exploration into one's personal and cultural past. It is a quest for one's identity and purpose in life that requires diligent work between the analyst and patient; the result is superior wisdom and a transcendent calm when coping with life's struggles.

Applications

Jung developed several techniques aimed at uncovering material hidden in the unconscious. Like Freud, Jung believed that the content of dreams is indicative of unconscious attitudes. He believed that dreams have a compensatory function; that is, they are reflections of the side of personality that is not displayed during one's conscious, everyday state. The sophisticated librarian may have dreams of being an exotic dancer, according to Jung, as a way of expressing the ignored aspects of personality.

Jung gives an example of the compensatory aspects of dreams when describing the recollections of a dutiful son. The son dreamed that he and his father were leaving home and his father was driving a new automobile. The father began to drive in an erratic fashion. He swerved the car all over the road until he finally succeeded in crashing the car and damaging it very badly. The son was frightened, then became angry and chastised his father for his behavior. Rather than respond, however, his father began to laugh until it became apparent that he was very intoxicated, a condition the son had not previously noticed. Jung interpreted the dream in the context of the son's relationship with his father. The son overly idealized the father while refusing to recognize apparent faults. The dream represented the son's latent anger at his father and his attempt to reduce him in status. Jung indicated to the young man that the dream was a cue from his unconscious that he should evaluate his relationship with his father with a more balanced outlook.

Jung employed the method of amplification for interpreting dreams. This technique involved focusing repeatedly on the contents of the dream and giving multiple associations to them. Jung believed that the dream often is basically what it appears to be. This differs dramatically from Freudian interpretation, which requires the patient to associate dream elements with childhood conflicts.

The amplification method can be applied to a dream reported by a graduate student in clinical psychology. While preparing to defend his dissertation, the final and most anxiety-provoking aspect of receiving the doctorate, the student had a dream about his oral defense. Before presenting the project to his dissertation committee that was to evaluate its worth (and seemingly his own), the student dreamed that he was in the bathroom gathering his resources. He noticed he was wearing a three-piece brown suit; however, none of the pieces matched. They were different shades of brown. Fortunately, the pieces were reversible, so the student attempted to change them so they would all be the same shade. After repeated attempts he was unable to get all three pieces of the suit to be the same shade of brown. He finally gave up in despair and did not appear for his defense. With a little knowledge about the student, an analytical therapist would have an easy time with the meaning of this dream. This was obviously a stressful time in the young man's life, and the dream reflected his denied anxiety. In addition, the student did not like brown suits; one that does not match is even more hideous. It is apparent that he was unhappy and, despite his best attempts to portray confidence, the budding clinician was afraid that he was going to "look stupid." Jung would have encouraged him to face these fears of failure that were hidden in his unconscious.

A final application of analytical psychotherapy stems from Jung's method of active imagination. Jung believed that unconscious messages could come not only from dreams but also from one's artistic productions. He encouraged his patients to produce spontaneous, artistic material. Some patients sketched, while others painted, wrote poetry, or sang songs. He was interested in the symbols that were given during these periods, and he asked his clients to comment on them. Jung believed that considerable material in the unconscious could be discovered during these encounters. He also talked with his patients about the universal meanings of these symbols (as in his idea of the collective unconscious), and they would attempt to relate this material to the patients' cultural pasts.

Many modern therapies, such as art, music, and dance therapy, draw heavily from this idea that one can become aware of unconscious and emotional material through association involving one's artistic productions. These therapists believe, as did Jung, that patients are less defensive during these times of spontaneous work and, therefore, are more likely to discover unconscious material.

Perspective and Prospects

Jung's analytical psychotherapy was a pioneering approach during the very early era of psychological treatment. He conformed to the beliefs of other psychodynamic therapists, such as Sigmund Freud and Alfred Adler, in the importance of discovering unconscious material. The psychoanalysts would be followed by the behavioral school's emphasis on environmental events and the cognitive school's focus on thoughts and perceptions. Psychoanalysis brought a prominence to psychology it had not known previously.

Jung expanded on Freud's beliefs about the unconscious. Rather than focus on instinctual forces, Jung chose to focus on the human being's spiritual side through his idea of the collective unconscious. His mystical beliefs about humankind's spirituality were new to the growing field of psychotherapy and have not been equalled since. Jung also took into account a person's cultural past. He proposed the idea of a universal human relatedness with his idea of common cultural symbols; however, it would be many years before this idea was fully developed.

Analytical psychotherapy is not considered a mainstream approach to psychotherapy, but it does have a small group of devoted followers. Some of Jung's techniques have been adapted into other, more common approaches. Many therapists agree with Jung's de-emphasis on specific techniques in favor of a focus on the establishment of a supportive therapy relationship. Jung moved away from the stereotypical analyst's couch in favor of face-to-face communication between doctor and patient. Many psychotherapists endorse Jung's belief that the analyst and patient should have relatively equal status and input. Jung also reduced the frequency of meeting with his patients to weekly, which is the norm today.

Jung's analytical approach changed the focus of psychotherapy from symptom relief to self-discovery. He was interested not only in patients with major problems but also in those who were dissatisfied with their mundane existences. These people were usually bright, articulate, and occupationally successful.

Jung's most lasting contributions probably have been his insights into the polarity of personality traits. The Myers-Briggs Type Indicator, based on Jungian personality descriptions, is one of the most widely used personality tests in business and industry. Jung also believed that personality changes throughout one's life, and he encouraged a continual evaluation of oneself. The idea of a "midlife crisis," a period when one reevaluates personal and occupational goals, is a product of Jung's theory. He believed that individuals continually should strive to achieve a balance in their personality and behavior.

Bibliography

Campbell, Joseph. *The Hero with a Thousand Faces*. New York: Pantheon Books, 1949. Campbell was a contemporary theorist who developed Jung's ideas of universal symbols and the power of myth. This book discusses Jung's idea of the hero, and Campbell relates this idea to spiritual leaders such as Moses, Jesus, and Muhammad.

Engler, Barbara. *Personality Theories: An Introduction*. 5th ed. Boston: Houghton Mifflin, 1999. Engler's chapter on Jung and his psychotherapy is easy to read and contains a good balance between theory and practical application.

Hall, Calvin S., Gardner Lindzey, and John B. Campbell. *Theories of Personality*. 4th ed. New York: John Wiley & Sons, 1998. This is a classic text in personality theory and application, and it gives a detailed description of Jung's theory. Recommended for the serious student of Jung.

Hall, Calvin S., and Vernon J. Nordby. *A Primer of Jungian Psychology.* New York: New American Library, 1973. This paperback attempts to provide a comprehensive treatment of Jung's ideas. Intended for the beginning student of Jung.

Hannah, Barbara. *Jung: His Life and Work.* New York: Putnam, 1976. An interesting biographical account of Jung by a psychoanalyst who was his friend for more than thirty years. Gives an insight into how his personal beliefs and experiences shaped his theory.

Homans, Peter. *Jung in Context: Modernity and the Making of a Psychology.* 2d ed. Chicago: University of Chicago Press, 1995. A provocative account of the origins, influences, and legacy of Jungian psychology.

McLynn, Frank. *Carl Gustav Jung.* New York: St. Martin's Press, 1997. A lengthy biography of the Austrian psychoanalyst. Includes bibliographical references and an index.

Shamdasani, Sonu. *Cult Fictions: C. G. Jung and the Founding of Analytical Psychology.* New York: Routledge, 1998. An account of the origins of Jungian psychology. Includes bibliographical references and an index.

Stein, Murray. *Practicing Wholeness: Analytical Psychology and Jungian Thought.* New York: Continuum, 1996. Draws on Jung's theory of instincts and archetypes. Concentrates on the clinical practice of psychotherapy.

Brett L. Beck

See also:

Cognitive Behavior Therapy; Cognitive Therapy; Music, Dance, and Theater Therapy; Person-Centered Therapy; Psychoanalysis; Psychotherapy: Goals and Techniques; Psychotherapy: Historical Approaches to Treatment.

ANOREXIA NERVOSA AND BULIMIA NERVOSA

Type of psychology: Psychopathology
Fields of study: Childhood and adolescent disorders

Anorexia and bulimia nervosa are disorders characterized by a distorted body image, an intense fear of becoming obese, and a desperate attempt to lose weight; these disorders most frequently occur in female adolescents, and they present serious health risks.

Principal terms

BEHAVIORAL THERAPY: a treatment that emphasizes the utilization of learning principles—the use of positive reinforcers and negative consequences—in order to change maladaptive behavior

BINGING: a period of excessive eating in which as many as 15,000 calories may be consumed in a few hours

COGNITIVE BEHAVIOR THERAPY: a therapy approach which, in addition to behavioral techniques, uses cognitive methods such as modifying maladaptive personal beliefs and expectations

DISTORTED BODY IMAGE: misperception of one's body size or shape such that one sees oneself as "fat" even though one may be underweight

HYPOTHALAMUS: a brain structure that regulates bodily functions such as hunger, hormonal balance, temperature, and sexual interest

PURGING: a method of weight reduction that most commonly involves the emptying of one's digestive organs through either self-induced vomiting or the use of laxatives

WEIGHT PHOBIA: an intense fear of gaining weight accompanied by an avoidance of eating that increases as weight loss progresses

Causes and Symptoms

Anorexia nervosa and bulimia nervosa are two of several types of eating disorders—ways of managing food and/or weight that are unhealthy. "Anorexia" literally means a "severe loss of appetite," while "nervosa" means "nervousness." Actually, the word "anorexia" is somewhat of a misnomer, given that most people with anorexia nervosa have not lost their appetites. The syndrome of anorexia nervosa consists of four prominent symptoms, according to the American Psychiatric Association. The first symptom is a failure to maintain a normal weight for one's age and height such that one's weight is less than 85 percent of what is considered normal. The weight of most anorectics (persons with anorexia nervosa) is usually much less than 85 percent of their normal weight. For example, a review of treatment studies for anorexia nervosa found that the average anorectic weighed 37 kilograms (82 pounds), 69 percent of normal weight (R. C. Qualls and J. S. Berman, 1988).

The second symptom of anorexia nervosa is an intense fear of gaining weight that increases even as the anorectic continues to lose weight. This second symptom has been labeled weight phobia by some researchers because of the anorectic's anxiety toward food and the desperate attempts she (most documented anorectics have been girls or women) makes to avoid food. The third major symptom of the syndrome is distorted body image. Distorted body image involves the anorectic seeing herself as obese when in reality she is extremely underweight. For example, when an anorectic is asked to view her body in a mirror, she is likely to comment on how fat she looks. The final symptom for women with anorexia nervosa is the absence of at least three menstrual cycles, which is caused by their being severely underweight.

Bulimia nervosa refers to the recurring cycle of binging, a period of excessive overeating, followed by purging, engaging in drastic efforts to lose the weight gained by binging. For the bulimic, binge episodes may consist of consuming up to 15,000 calories, more than five times the recommended daily number, within a few hours. Purging may be accomplished through several means including vomiting (done either by gagging oneself or through the consumption of certain drugs), the use of laxatives, strict dieting, or stringent exercising. In order to meet this first criterion of bulimia, one must engage in the binge-purge cycle at least two times per week for three months.

In addition to the recurrent binging and purging, other symptoms of bulimia nervosa include the feeling that one has no control over one's eating binges and constant concern regarding one's body shape or weight. In contrast to anorectics, who are grossly underweight, bulimics may be normal weight or even slightly obese. That is, the weight-loss effects of a bulimic's purging are often negated by the weight gained during her binging.

There are numerous potential health problems that may occur as a result of anorexia or bulimia. The health problems of anorectics include an abnormally low body temperature and blood pressure, irregular heart functioning, and bone thinning. Of those diagnosed with anorexia, approximately 4 percent die. The health complications of bulimia include the erosion of tooth enamel; sudden mineral depletions, particularly potassium reduction; irregular heart functioning; and a variety of disorders affecting digestive organs. A significantly lower number of people are thought to die from bulimia as compared to anorexia.

When compared to the most common eating disorder, obesity, anorexia and bulimia are rare. Approximately 30 percent of all Americans are reported to be obese. In contrast to the thirty out of one hundred who are obese, about one out of every one thousand Americans will have anorexia during his or her life (L. N. Robins et al., 1984). The incidence of anorexia among adolescent females, however, is about ten times higher than in the general population. In comparison, bulimia is estimated to occur in approximately three out of every one hundred Americans. Again, the incidence of bulimia among adolescent females is believed to be significantly higher.

The proposed causes of anorexia and bulimia can be grouped into the following four categories: biological, sociocultural, familial, and psychological. The notion of biological causes of anorexia and bulimia involves the idea that anorectics and bulimics have specific brain or biochemical disturbances that lead to their inability to maintain a normal weight and/or eating pattern. The most popular biological explanation for the occurrence of anorexia and bulimia is the existence of an abnormal number of certain neurotransmitters. Neurotransmitters are chemical messengers within the brain that transmit nerve impulses between nerve cells. Potential abnormal levels of the neurotransmitters norepinephrine and serotonin have received the most investigation as causes of anorexia and bulimia.

In contrast to biological explanations, sociocultural causes are factors that are thought to exist within a society that lead certain individuals to develop anorexia or bulimia. Joan Brumberg, a historian of anorexia, has outlined the sociocultural forces of the late nineteenth and twentieth centuries that many believe promoted the increased incidence of eating disorders among women (1988). These societal forces included an emphasis on weight reduction, aesthetic self-control, and the regarding of women as sexual objects. The most prominent of these suggested cultural factors is the heightened (some would say obsessive) importance placed on being thin.

Some researchers believe that particular family types cause certain of their members to develop anorexia and bulimia. For example, family investigators believe that a family whose members are too emotionally close to one another may lead one or more family members to strive for independence by refusing to eat, according to Salvador Minuchin, Bernice Rosman, and Lester Baker. Other researchers believe that families whose members are controlling and express an excessive amount of hostility toward one another promote the occurrence of bulimia.

Psychological features make up the final category of causes for anorexia and bulimia. The most prominent of the suggested psychological causes for anorexia and bulimia are those expressed by researchers who take psychoanalytic or cognitive behavioral perspectives. For example, cognitive behavioral theorists emphasize the role of distorted beliefs in the development and continuation of anorexia and bulimia. These distorted beliefs include, "I am only attractive when I weigh a certain number of pounds [well below normal weight]," or "If I eat certain types of food [for example, carbohydrate-rich foods], I will become fat."

Treatment and Therapy

In general, the initial treatment for anorexia occurs within the hospital setting, given the risk of death associated with this disorder. Follow-up therapy for anorexia, as well as the typical treatment for bulimia, takes place on an outpatient basis. Numerous treatments have been used for individuals afflicted by these disorders. These treatments can be broadly grouped into the categories of medical and psychological therapies.

Prior to the 1960's, medical therapies for anorexia included such radical approaches as lobotomies and electroconvulsive therapy (ECT). The performing of a lobotomy involves the surgical removal of prefrontal portions of the brain. Electroconvulsive therapy, commonly known as "shock treatment," involves the introduction of an electrical current into a patient's body through electrodes placed on the patient's head. These treatments were shown to be of no benefit for anorectics. Although a controversial treatment, various types of tube feeding continue to be used when a patient's malnutrition from anorexia poses an imminent risk of death. Tube feeding can be accomplished either intravenously or by inserting a tube via a patient's nasal cavity into the patient's stomach.

Since the 1960's, medications are used more often as the medical treatments of choice for anorexia and bulimia. These medications include such categories of drugs as antidepressants and major tranquilizers. For anorexia, these drugs are thought to increase eating behavior and promote weight gain by correcting imbalances in an individual's neurotransmitters. For bulimia, certain medications are thought to reduce carbohydrate cravings that precede the binge-purge cycle. In addition, antidepressant medication may be prescribed for bulimia because of the depression that often accompanies binging and purging.

Different psychological interventions also have been attempted for anorexia and bulimia. These psychological treatments include individual, family, and group interventions. One type of individual therapy for anorexia is behavioral therapy. In behavioral therapy, weight gain is promoted through the use of positive reinforcers for increases in weight and negative consequences for weight decreases or the absence of weight gain. These positive reinforcers include such things as access to telephone and visitation privileges. Negative consequences for remaining the same weight or weight loss include confinement to bed and denial of all unit privileges. Besides behavioral treatment, other types of individual therapy include cognitive behavioral, Gestalt, hypnosis, and psychoanalytic interventions.

Another common treatment for both anorexia and bulimia is family therapy. The family treatment of an anorectic patient involves the therapist seeking to change the interactions among family members that serve to maintain the self-starvation of the patient. In attempting to correct faulty family interactions, the family therapist might address the overprotectiveness of the patient by her parents or the way that family members manipulate one another's behavior. For the bulimic patient, the family therapist would seek to lower the amount of family conflict or to redirect conflict between the parents away from the bulimic.

Another frequently employed method of treatment for bulimia is group therapy. Group treatment initially involves educating bulimics about their disorder, including its negative health consequences. The group experience provides members with the opportunity to share with fellow bulimics issues regarding their eating problems and to find support from one another in overcoming bulimia. In addition, the therapist or therapists initiate discussions regarding healthy eating and exercise habits as well as specific ways to curb the binge-purge cycle.

A final issue involved in surveying the different interventions for anorexia and bulimia is the effectiveness of these treatments. The effectiveness of treatments for anorexia was addressed by Christopher Qualls and Jeffrey Berman in a 1988 study that grouped treatments reported in one hundred studies according to their type and then analyzed the effectiveness of each. The results of their study indicated that the average anorectic gains approximately 8 kilograms (18 pounds) during the initial phase of treatment and another 5 kilograms (11 pounds) by the time of a follow-up evaluation about four years later. There were only small differences between the various types of treatment for the amount of weight produced during therapy, although behavioral treatments appeared to work faster. Less research has been conducted investigating the effectiveness of different therapies for bulimia. No one therapy for bulimia, however, whether medical or psychological, has shown clear superiority in its effectiveness as compared to other interventions.

Perspective and Prospects

Anorexia is a disorder that can be traced as far back as seven hundred years ago. The disorder was specifically written about in 1874, when Sir William Gull published an article giving the disorder its present name. Bulimia nervosa, as a disorder separate from anorexia, has received meaningful attention only since the late 1970's. There is evidence to suggest that the incidence of both disorders has increased in the last two decades. As previously discussed, the increased emphasis being placed on thinness within current Western societies represents a likely explanation for the increase in eating disorders such as anorexia and bulimia.

Another area within the study of anorexia and bulimia that has begun to receive attention is the prevention of eating disorders. In discussing the prevention of eating disorders, Catherine Shisslak and colleagues have suggested that preventive efforts should be targeted at adolescent females, given that they are at increased risk for developing an eating disorder. These efforts should focus on issues such as the physical as well as emotional and social changes that occur in maturation. Also, information regarding diet and exercise should be provided, and the connection between emotions and eating should be discussed, as should ways to resist the pressure to conform to peers' and societal expectations for one's appearance. It should also be recognized that there are those who oppose preventive efforts, including segments of the media, fashion, and exercise industries.

With evidence of the increasing prevalence of anorexia and bulimia, it is important to learn more regarding the causes and effective treatment methods of these disorders. In these areas, some of the questions that remain to be definitively answered are: Why do certain groups of people have a greater likelihood of developing anorexia and bulimia (notably, white adolescent females) as compared to other groups? Are the underlying causes of anorexia different from those of bulimia? Can a treatment with superior effectiveness be developed for those suffering with anorexia and bulimia? Anorexia and bulimia nervosa remain elusive syndromes for professionals and patients alike. It is hoped that present and future endeavors will answer these and other remaining questions regarding these disorders.

Bibliography

Boskind-White, Marlene, and William C. White, Jr. *Bulimarexia: The Binge/Purge Cycle.* New York: W. W. Norton, 1983. A comprehensible overview of bulimarexia (more commonly referred to as bulimia). Takes a nonpathologizing, empathetic approach in addressing the problems of individuals with bulimia. Filled with illustrative patient histories.

Bruch, Hilde. *The Golden Cage: The Enigma of Anorexia Nervosa.* Cambridge, Mass.: Harvard University Press, 1978. A classic work by a pioneer in the field of eating disorders. Portrays the development of anorexia nervosa as an attempt by a young woman to attain a sense of control and identity. Discusses the etiology and treatment of anorexia from a modified psychoanalytic perspective.

Brumberg, Joan J. *Fasting Girls: The History of Anorexia Nervosa.* Cambridge, Mass.: Harvard University Press, 1988. Outlines the history of anorexia nervosa. Examines the syndrome from multiple perspectives while leaning toward a cultural and feministic perspective. A well-researched and very readable work.

Claude-Pierre, Peggy. *The Secret Language of Eating Disorders: The Revolutionary New Approach to Understanding and Curing Anorexia and Bulimia.* New York: Times Books, 1997. Examines eating disorders and self-esteem in girls and women. Includes bibliographical references and an index.

Garner, David M., and Paul E. Garfinkel, eds. *Handbook of Treatment for Eating Disorders.* 2d ed. New York: Guilford Press, 1997. This is an updated source on the diagnosis, assessment, and treatment of eating disorders, as well as key issues associated with developing eating disorders. Includes bibliographical references and indexes.

Gordon, Richard A. *Eating Disorders: Anatomy of a Social Epidemic.* Oxford, England: Blackwell Publishers, 2000. Examines the social aspects of anorexia nervosa and bulimia nervosa. Includes bibliographical references and an index.

Lask, Bryan, and Rachel Bryant-Waugh, eds. *Anorexia Nervosa and Related Eating Disorders in Childhood and Adolescence.* 2d ed. Hove, East Sussex, England: Psychology Press, 2000. This volume examines, in seventeen parts, the origins and treatment of eating disorders in young people.

Minuchin, Salvador, Bernice L. Rosman, and Lester Baker. *Psychosomatic Families: Anorexia Nervosa in Context.* Cambridge, Mass.: Harvard University Press, 1978. A classic work which outlines the development and treatment of anorexia nervosa from a family systems perspective. Includes a complete description of Salvador Minuchin's famed "family lunch session," in which Minuchin conducts a family assessment and begins treatment of an anorectic patient while eating lunch with the patient and her family.

Mitchell, J. E., and E. D. Eckert. "Scope and Significance of Eating Disorders." *Journal of Consulting and Clinical Psychology* 55 (1987): 37-43. Summarizes relevant research regarding the prevalence, etiology, and treatment of both anorexia and bulimia. The authors' overview of the suggested causes of anorexia and bulimia highlights potential biological factors. Very readable for a scientific piece.

R. Christopher Qualls

See also:
Abnormality: Behavioral Models; Abnormality: Family Models; Abnormality: Sociocultural Models; Cognitive Behavior Therapy; Eating Disorders.

ANTISOCIAL PERSONALITY

Type of psychology: Psychopathology
Fields of study: Aggression; personality disorders; personality theory

Antisocial personality is a personality disorder characterized by chronic criminal and otherwise irresponsible behaviors. Although extensively researched, it is one of the most controversial diagnostic categories, and its causes and treatment remain largely an enigma.

Principal terms

AROUSAL MODIFICATION: the technique of increasing arousal in order to decrease the motivation for antisocial behavior

CONDUCT DISORDER: a disorder, beginning in childhood, in which the rights of others and age-appropriate social norms or rules are repeatedly violated

DYSSOCIAL PSYCHOPATHY: a syndrome in which antisocial behavior results from allegiance to a culturally deviant subgroup

NEUROTIC PSYCHOPATHY: a syndrome in which antisocial behavior is a consequence of psychological conflict and turmoil

PSYCHOPATHIC PERSONALITY: a personality disorder characterized by traits such as guiltlessness, dishonesty, charm, fearlessness, callousness, and egocentricity

SOMATIZATION DISORDER: a condition characterized by multiple physical symptoms lacking any demonstrated medical basis

SUCCESSFUL PSYCHOPATHY: a category consisting of psychopathic personalities who are functioning highly

YERKES-DODSON LAW: the principle that moderate levels of arousal tend to yield optimal performance

Causes and Symptoms

By personality disorder, psychologists mean a disorder in which personality traits are rigid and maladaptive, and produce considerable impairment and distress for the individual. In the case of antisocial personality, these traits are thought to be manifested in criminal and otherwise irresponsible behaviors, which create problems for the individual and, more important, for society—hence the term "antisocial."

Antisocial personalities have a childhood history of conduct disorder—a pattern in which both the rights of others and age-appropriate social norms or rules are repeatedly violated—and continue to exhibit criminal and other irresponsible behaviors in adulthood. The major symptoms of antisocial personality include theft, school truancy, fire setting, vandalism, physical cruelty toward animals and people, financial irresponsibility, repeated lying, reckless driving, sexual promiscuity, and poor parenting. Not surprisingly, a large percentage of incarcerated criminals fulfill the criteria for this disorder.

Many of the symptoms of antisocial personality were identified by the sociologist Lee Robins in her influential work *Deviant Children Grown Up* (1966). Robins found that between 20 and 30 percent of children with conduct disorder develop antisocial personality in adulthood. There is also evidence that a subset of children with hyperactivity or attention-deficit disorder develop antisocial personality in adulthood. Nevertheless, because many of these same children have conduct disorder, it may be conduct disorder, rather than hyperactivity, that is the major determinant of antisocial personality.

In addition to the behaviors mentioned above, antisocial personalities have a number of other psychological and interpersonal difficulties. For example, they have high rates of alcohol and drug abuse, divorce, venereal disease, out-of-wedlock pregnancies, and depression. In addition, individuals with this disorder are more likely than those in the general population to die prematurely from violent crimes and accidents. Antisocial personality is also associated with criminal recidivism: Individuals with this disorder who are released from prison are at high risk for subsequent incarceration.

In the United States, about 3 percent of males and 1 percent of females have antisocial personalities. The reason for this sex difference is unknown; some authors have speculated that females who are predisposed to antisocial personality may be likely to develop somatization disorder, a condition characterized by multiple physical complaints lacking any demonstrated medical basis. Indeed, somatization disorder is found among many of the female relatives of antisocial personalities. Thus, somatization disorder may be an alternative manifestation of antisocial personality that is found primarily among females, although considerably more research will be needed to corroborate this hypothesis. Antisocial personality is also associated with low social class, although the causes of this relationship are unknown.

Many antisocial personalities possess a constellation of personality traits known as the psychopathic personality. In his classic book *The Mask of Sanity* (1941), psychiatrist Hervey Cleckley provided a detailed description of this syndrome. According to Cleckley, psychopathic personalities (or, as they are sometimes called, psychopaths) tend to be superficially charming individuals who are relatively free of anxiety and seem possessed of excellent reason. Nevertheless, they also tend to be guiltless, callous, dishonest, and self-centered persons who rarely learn from their mistakes or take responsibility for their behavior.

Some psychologists believe that psychopathic personality is a more valid category than antisocial personality. According to these researchers, many antisocial personalities lack the traits characteristic of psychopathic personality, and instead exhibit antisocial behavior for a variety of other reasons. For example, some antisocial personalities may fall into a category

POSSIBLE SYMPTOMS OF CONDUCT DISORDERS IN CHILDREN AND ADOLESCENTS

❖ lying
❖ stealing
❖ destroying property
❖ misbehaving sexually
❖ expressing their anger inappropriately
❖ often breaking rules or laws
❖ showing physical and verbal aggressive behavior with other children and/or to adults

known as dyssocial psychopathy, a syndrome in which antisocial behavior results from allegiance to a culturally deviant subgroup. Many gang delinquents or members of organized crime could probably be classified in this group. The behavior of still other antisocial personalities may result from neurotic psychopathy, a syndrome in which antisocial behavior is a consequence of internal psychological conflict and turmoil. Many neurotic psychopaths are probably socially anxious individuals who inhibit their anger for long periods of time and then erupt intermittently but violently.

Conversely, some critics of the antisocial personality diagnosis have argued that many psychopaths do not fulfill the criteria for antisocial personality. Indeed, some psychopaths may function highly in society, and would thus not be detected by the antisocial personality criteria in many cases. Cathy Spatz Widom has found that many persons who possess the traits described by Cleckley can be found outside prisons, and in some cases have socially valued occupations (for example, corporate executive). Further study of these "successful" psychopaths may shed light on factors that allow individuals at risk for antisocial personality to avoid legal and interpersonal problems.

One of the most active areas of research on antisocial personality concerns possible causes of the disorder. Psychologist David Lykken, for example, has theorized that the behavior of many antisocial personalities, particularly those who are psychopaths, can be traced to fearlessness.

Lykken has found that, compared with other individuals with antisocial behavior and with "normals," psychopaths tend to exhibit less sweating of the palms prior to a buzzer that has been repeatedly paired with a painful electric shock. Robert Hare has similarly shown that psychopaths tend to show relatively little palmar sweating during the countdown period prior to a painful electric shock or jarring blast of white noise. Because palmar sweating is often indicative of fear or arousal, the findings of Lykken and Hare can be interpreted to mean that psychopaths are not frightened or aroused by signals of impending punishment. This, in turn, might explain why many psychopaths engage in repeated antisocial behavior: The warning signs that would deter most people from performing such acts have little impact upon the psychopath. The average child or adult is prevented from committing antisocial acts largely by signals that punishment or danger is imminent: a parent or teacher saying "No" as a child reaches for a forbidden piece of candy, the watchful eye of a museum guard as one passes by a valuable painting, a light turning yellow as one approaches a busy intersection. If such signals arouse little or no fear in a person, however, his or her threshold for committing antisocial acts will surely be lowered.

Lykken also constructed a "mental maze" task, in which subjects were required to learn a complex series of lever presses. On each trial, some errors were punished with painful shock, whereas others were not. Lykken found that, compared with other subjects, psychopaths did not make more errors overall, indicating that they can learn certain tasks as well as other individuals. Nevertheless, Lykken found that psychopaths made more punished errors than other individuals, suggesting that they have difficulty learning from punishment. Again, this finding is consistent with the fearlessness hypothesis, because the capacity to benefit from punishment is largely dependent upon the capacity to become frightened of this punishment. Moreover, this finding has important implications; the psychopath's failure to learn from punishment in the laboratory may be a useful model for the antisocial personality's recidivism in the real world.

An alternative hypothesis for the behavior of antisocial personalities is that these individuals have unusually low levels of arousal. According to the Yerkes-Dodson law, moderate levels of arousal are optimal for performance and psychological functioning. Thus, as Herbert Quay and other psychologists have argued, many of the thrill-seeking and dangerous behaviors of antisocial personalities may represent attempts to bring their arousal to higher and thus more optimal levels. George Skrzypek has found that psychopathic delinquents, compared with other delinquents, have a greater preference for complex and novel stimuli. This is consistent with Quay's hypothesis, because such stimuli would be expected to increase arousal. Skrzypek also found that after both groups were placed in sensory isolation, psychopaths' preference for complex and novel stimuli increased more compared with nonpsychopaths.

There is considerable evidence that antisocial personality is influenced by genetic factors. Identical twins (who share all their genes) with antisocial personality are much more likely than are fraternal twins (who share only half their genes on average) to have co-twins with the disorder. Nevertheless, many of the co-twins of identical twins with antisocial personality do not have the disorder, which indicates that environmental factors play an important role in the development of antisocial personality. In addition, adopted children whose natural parents had antisocial personality are more likely to develop the disorder than are adopted children whose natural parents did not. Again, this is consistent with a genetic influence upon antisocial personality.

Nevertheless, several important questions concerning the genetics of antisocial personality remain. First, it is not known what factors are being genetically transmitted. Second, it is not known whether this genetic influence applies to all, or only some, individuals with antisocial personality. For example, this genetic influence might only play a role in individuals with psychopathic personality. Third, it is not known how environmental factors combine or interact with genetic factors to produce antisocial personality. These three questions are likely to occupy researchers for a number of years to come.

Treatment and Therapy

Little is known about the treatment of antisocial personality, except that no clearly effective treatment has been found. A number of therapies have been attempted, including psychoanalysis, behavior therapy, group therapy, and medication, but there is little evidence that any of them have been especially successful. As the symptoms of antisocial personality begin early in life and are easily identifiable, it may be prevention, rather than treatment, that holds the greatest promise for reducing the prevalence of this disorder.

One implication of findings about low arousal is that at least some antisocial personalities might benefit from treatments that boost their arousal levels. For example, antisocial personalities could be encouraged to find occupations (for example, combat soldier) or avocations (for example, skydiving) that might provide outlets for their risk-taking tendencies. Similarly, some researchers have explored the possibility that some antisocial personalities might be helped by stimulant medication. Stanley Schachter and Bibb Latane found that when psychopaths were asked to perform Lykken's mental-maze task while taking adrenaline, a stimulant drug, they were as successful as were nonpsychopaths at learning to avoid punishment. Nevertheless, as these "arousal modification" approaches have not been adequately researched, their potential as treatments for antisocial personality remains speculative.

What happens to antisocial personalities over time? There is evidence that many such individuals "burn out" in middle age: Their antisocial behaviors decrease in frequency and severity in later adulthood. The reasons for this burnout phenomenon are unclear, but it may be a consequence of the decline in activity level and energy seen in most individuals with age.

Perspective and Prospects

Although the term "antisocial personality" did not enjoy widespread currency until the latter half of the twentieth century, individuals with chronic antisocial symptoms have been described by a variety of labels over the years. In 1809, Philippe Pinel discussed a syndrome called *manie sans délire*, or mania without delusion. Such individuals, according to Pinel, are driven by strong instinctual forces but maintain good contact with reality. In 1835, James Pritchard coined the term "moral insanity" to refer to a condition characterized by severe deficits in ethical behavior.

In 1891, German psychiatrist August Koch referred to a group of conditions called "psychopathic inferiorities." In doing so, Koch broadened the concept of the disorder to include a diverse spectrum of abnormalities, not all of which were characterized by moral depravity. Koch's tradition was followed by the great German classifier Kurt Schneider, who in 1923 described a wide variety of psychopathic personalities, each of which was considered to be an exaggeration of a normal personality style. Thus, the German conceptualization was generally inclusive and viewed psychopathic personality as a set of conditions that created problems for the individual, society, or both.

It was authors such as Cleckley and Benjamin Karpman who were largely responsible for shaping contemporary notions of psychopathic personality. These authors emphasized personality traits as the key features of the disorder, and they de-emphasized antisocial and criminal behaviors. This view was reflected in the second edition of the American Psychiatric Association's *Diagnostic and Statistical Manual of Mental Disorders* (DSM-II) in 1968, which focused upon personality traits such as guiltlessness and selfishness as the primary criteria for the disorder.

This personality-based approach, however, came under attack in the 1970's and 1980's for its subjectivity. After all, what one diagnostician might view as a pathological absence of guilt might be viewed by another as a healthy absence of self-criticism. Thus, in 1980, the third edition of the *Diagnostic and Statistical Manual of Mental Disorders* (DSM-III) introduced "antisocial personality disorder," a new diagnosis in which explicit references to personality traits were all but expunged. Instead, the emphasis in DSM-III (as well as in the 1994 fourth edition, DSM-IV) was upon easily agreed-upon transgressions against society. The advantage of this new approach was its objectivity: Clinicians could easily agree upon whether an individual had committed a robbery or driven while intoxicated.

Although advocates of this behavior-based approach contend that their diagnosis identifies a homogeneous group of individuals, many researchers remain convinced that lumping together virtually all chronically antisocial individuals under a single rubric is bound to fail. Nevertheless, advocates of these two approaches agree upon one thing: Their disagreement is more than semantic. Is the smooth confidence artist who bilks others without remorse fundamentally different from the loyal gang member who sacrifices his or her livelihood for the good of the group? The answer to this and related questions will almost certainly have profound implications for psychologists' conceptualizations of antisocial personality, as well as for their approaches to understanding and treating it.

Bibliography

Cleckley, Hervey. *The Mask of Sanity*. St. Louis: C. V. Mosby, 1941. In this classic work, Cleckley delineates the primary features of psychopathic personality in considerable detail and provides a wealth of case history material that vividly illustrates the symptomatology of this disorder. Although many of Cleckley's speculations concerning the causation of this disorder are somewhat outdated, his clinical descriptions remain unparalleled in their depth and richness.

Fishbein, Diana H., ed. *The Science, Treatment, and Prevention of Antisocial Behaviors: Application to the Criminal Justice System*. Kingston, N.J.: Civic Research Institute, 2000. Relates criminal activity to such topics as genetics, brain dysfunction, sexual abuse, addiction, and attention-deficit disorder. Includes bibliographical references and an index.

Hare, Robert D. *Psychopathy: Theory and Research*. New York: John Wiley & Sons, 1970. Perhaps the best overview of early research on the psychopathic personality. Reviews the evidence for a number of models of the causation of this disorder and describes the research literature clearly, thoughtfully, and critically. An excellent primer for the layperson who wishes to learn more about psychopathic and antisocial personalities.

_____. *Without Conscience: The Disturbing World of the Psychopaths Among Us*. New York: Guilford Press, 1999. Discusses antisocial personality disorders. Includes bibliographical references.

Hare, Robert D., and Daisy Schalling, eds. *Psychopathic Behaviour: Approaches to Research*. New York: John Wiley & Sons, 1978. Contains perhaps the finest collection of chapters on research issues relevant to psychopathic and antisocial personalities. Coverage of research on biological models is particularly impressive. Chapters on the history of the psychopathic personality concept and on assessment issues are also highly recommended.

Millon, Theodore, et al., eds. *Psychopathy: Antisocial, Criminal, and Violent Behavior*. New York: Guilford Press, 1998. Discusses antisocial personality disorders. Includes bibliographical references and an index.

Reid, William H., ed. *The Psychopath: A Comprehensive Study of Antisocial Disorders and Behaviors*. New York: Brunner/Mazel, 1978. Another edited volume that contains a number of informative chapters on topics such as the neurological bases of antisocial behavior, psychophysiological findings in psychopaths, and the relation between antisocial personality and substance abuse. Nevertheless, the quality of the book is rather uneven; several chapters are marred by unbridled speculation regarding the psychodynamics of the disorder.

Robins, Lee. *Deviant Children Grown Up*. Baltimore: Williams & Wilkins, 1966. Describes Robins's classic study of the long-term outcome of conduct disordered children and provides a remarkably detailed examination of early risk factors for antisocial personality. Should be required reading for all individuals interested in the development of antisocial and criminal behavior.

Stoff, David M., James Breiling, and Jack D. Maser, eds. *Handbook of Antisocial Behavior*. New York: John Wiley & Sons, 1997. An examination of violence and antisocial personality disorders. Includes bibliographical references and indexes.

Scott O. Lilienfeld

See also:

Addictive Personality and Behaviors; Alcoholism; Attention-Deficit Disorder; Borderline, Histrionic, and Narcissistic Personalities; Juvenile Delinquency; Personality: Psychophysiological Measures; Substance Abuse.

ANXIETY DISORDERS

Type of psychology: Psychopathology; stress
Fields of study: Anxiety disorders; biology of stress

Anxiety is heightened fear or tension that causes psychological and physical distress. The American Psychiatric Association recognizes several types of anxiety disorders, which can be treated with medications or through counseling.

Principal terms

ANXIETY: abnormal fear or tension, which may occur without any obvious trigger
BRAIN IMAGING: any of several techniques used to visualize anatomic regions of the brain, including X rays, magnetic resonance imaging, and positron emission tomography
COMPULSION: a repetitive, stereotyped behavior performed to ward off anxious feelings
GABA/BENZODIAZEPINE RECEPTOR: an area on a nerve cell to which gamma aminobutyric acid (GABA) attaches and that causes inhibition (quieting) of the nerve; benzodiazepine drugs enhance the attachment of GABA to the receptor
OBSESSION: a recurrent, unwelcome, and intrusive thought
PANIC: a sudden episode of intense fearfulness

Causes and Symptoms

Anxiety is a subjective state of fear, apprehension, or tension. In the face of a naturally fearful situation, anxiety is a normal and understandable condition. When anxiety occurs without obvious provocation or is excessive, however, anxiety may be said to be abnormal or pathological (existing in a disease state). Normal anxiety is useful because it provides an alerting signal and improves physical and mental performance. Excessive anxiety results in a deterioration in performance and in emotional and physical discomfort.

There are several forms of pathological anxiety, known collectively as the anxiety disorders. As a group, they constitute the fifth most common medical or psychiatric disorder. In the United States, 14.6 percent of the population will experience anxiety at some point in their lives. More women suffer from anxiety disorders than do men, by a 2:1 ratio.

The anxiety disorders are distinguished from one another by characteristic clusters of symptoms. These disorders include generalized anxiety disorder, panic disorder, obsessive-compulsive disorder, phobias, adjustment disorder with anxious mood, and post-traumatic stress disorder. The first three disorders are characterized by anxious feelings that may occur without any obvious precipitant, while the latter three are closely associated with anxiety-producing events in a person's life.

Generalized anxiety disorder is thought to be a biological form of anxiety disorder in which the individual inherits a habitually high level of tension or

POSSIBLE SYMPTOMS OF GENERALIZED ANXIETY DISORDER

❖ inability to relax
❖ inability to fall asleep or stay asleep
❖ trembling or irritability
❖ twitching or muscle tension
❖ headaches
❖ sweating or hot flashes
❖ feeling lightheaded or out of breath
❖ feeling nauseated
❖ going to the bathroom frequently
❖ feeling tired or unable to concentrate

anxiety that may occur even when no threatening circumstances are present. Generally, these periods of anxiety occur in cycles which may last weeks to years. The prevalence is unknown, but this disorder is not uncommon. The male-to- female ratio is nearly equal.

Evidence suggests that generalized anxiety disorder is related to an abnormality in a common neurotransmitter receptor complex found in many brain neurons. These complexes, the GABA/benzodiazepine receptors, decrease the likelihood that a neuron will transmit an electrochemical signal, resulting in a calming effect on the portion of the brain in which they are found. These receptors exist in large numbers in the cerebral cortex (the outer layer of the brain), the hippocampus (the sea horse-shaped structure inside the temporal lobe), and the amygdala (the almond-shaped gray matter inside the temporal lobe). The hippocampus and amygdala are important parts of the limbic system, which is significantly involved in emotions. Benzodiazepine drugs enhance the efficiency of these receptors and have a calming effect. In contrast, if these receptors are inhibited, feelings of impending doom result.

Panic disorder is found in 1.5 percent of the United States population, and the female-to-male ratio is 2:1. This disorder usually begins during the young adult years. Panic disorder is characterized by recurrent and unexpected attacks of intense fear or panic. Each discrete episode lasts about five to twenty minutes. These episodes are intensely frightening to the individual, who is usually convinced he or she is dying. Because people who suffer from panic attacks are often anxious about having another one (so-called secondary anxiety), they may avoid situations in which they fear an attack may occur, in which help would be unavailable, or in which they would be embarrassed if an attack occurred. This avoidance behavior may cause restricted activity and can lead to agoraphobia, the fear of leaving a safe zone in or around the home. Thus, agoraphobia (literally, "fear of the marketplace") is often secondary to panic disorder.

Panic disorder appears to have a biological basis. In those people with panic disorder, panic attacks can often be induced by sodium lactate infusions, hyperventilation, exercise, or hypocalcemia (low blood calcium). Normal people do not experience panic attacks when these triggers are present. Highly sophisticated scans show abnormal metabolic activity in the right parahippocampal region of the brain of individuals with panic disorder. The parahippocampal region, the area surrounding the hippocampus, is involved in emotions and is connected by fiber tracts to the locus ceruleus, a blue spot in the pons portion of the brain stem that is involved in arousal.

In addition to known biological triggers for panic attacks, emotional or psychological events may also cause an attack. To be diagnosed as having panic disorder, however, a person must experience attacks that arise without any apparent cause. The secondary anxiety and avoidance behavior often seen in these individuals result in difficulties in normal functioning. There is an increased incidence of suicide attempts in people with panic disorder; up to one in five have reported a suicide attempt at some time. The childhoods of people with panic disorder are characterized by an increased incidence of pathological separation anxiety and/or school phobia.

Obsessive-compulsive disorder (OCD) is an uncommon anxiety disorder with an equal male-to-female ratio. It is characterized by obsessions (intrusive, unwelcome thoughts) and compulsions (repetitive, often stereotyped behaviors that are performed to ward off anxiety). The obsessions in OCD are often horrifying to the afflicted person. Common themes concern sex, food, aggression, suicide, bathroom functions, and religion. Compulsive behavior may include checking (such as repeatedly checking to see if the stove is off or the door is locked), cleaning (such as repetitive handwashing or the wearing of gloves to turn a doorknob), or stereotyped behavior (such as dressing by using an exact series of steps that cannot be altered). Frequently, the compulsive behaviors must be repeated many times. Sometimes, there is an exact, almost magical number of times the behavior must be done in order to ward off anxiety. Although people with OCD have some conscious control over their compulsions, they are driven to perform them because intense anxiety results if they fail to do so.

The most common psychological theory for OCD was proposed by Sigmund Freud, who believed that OCD symptoms were a defense against unacceptable unconscious wishes. Genetic and brain imaging studies, however, suggest a biological basis for this disorder. Special brain scans have shown increased metabolism in the front portion of the brain in these patients, and it has been theorized that OCD results from an abnormality in a circuit within the brain (the cortical-striatal-thalamic-cortical circuit). Moreover, OCD is associated with a variety of known neurological diseases, including epilepsy, brain trauma, and certain movement disorders.

Phobias are the most common anxiety disorders. A phobia is an abnormal fear of a particular object or situation. Simple phobias are fears of specific, identifiable triggers such as heights, snakes, flying in an airplane, elevators, or the number thirteen. Social phobia is an exaggerated fear of being in social settings where the phobic person fears he or she will be open to scrutiny by others. This fear may result in phobic avoidance of eating in public, attending church, joining a social club, or participating in other social events. Phobias are more common in men than in women, and they often begin in late childhood or early adolescence.

In classic psychoanalytic theory, phobias were thought to be fears displaced from one object or situation to another. For example, fear of snakes may be a displaced fear of sex because the snake is a phallic symbol. It was thought that this process of displacement took place unconsciously. Many psychologists now believe that phobias are either exaggerations of normal fears or that they develop accidentally, without any symbolic meaning. For example, fear of elephants may arise if a young boy at a zoo is accidentally separated from his parents. At the same time that he realizes he is alone, he notices the elephants. He may then associate elephants with separation from his parents and fear elephants thereafter.

Adjustment disorder with anxious mood is an excessive or maladaptive response to a life event in which the individual experiences anxiety. For example, an individual may become so anxious after losing a job that he or she is unable to eat, sleep, or function and begins to entertain the prospect of suicide. While anxiety is to be expected, this person has excessive anxiety (the inability to eat, sleep, or function) and a maladaptive response (the thought of suicide). The exaggerated response may be attributable to the personality traits of the individual. In this example, a dependent person will be more likely to experience an adjustment disorder than a less dependent person.

Adjustment disorders are very common. In addition to adjustment disorders with anxious mood, people may experience adjustment disorders with depressed mood, mixed emotional features, disturbance of conduct, physical complaints, withdrawal, or inhibition in school or at work. These disorders are considered to be primarily psychological.

Post-traumatic stress disorder (PTSD) is similar to adjustment disorder because it represents a psychological reaction to a significant life event. PTSD only occurs, however, when the precipitating event would be seriously emotionally traumatic to a normal person, such as war, rape, natural disasters such as major earthquakes, or airplane crashes. In PTSD, the individual suffers from flashbacks to the precipitating event and "relives" the experience. These episodes are not simply vivid remembrances of what happened but a transient sensation of actually being in that circumstance. For example, a Vietnam War veteran may literally jump behind bushes when a car backfires.

People who suffer from PTSD usually are anxious and startle easily. They may be depressed and have disturbed sleep and eating patterns. They often lose normal interest in sex, and nightmares are common. These individuals usually try to avoid situations that remind them of their trauma. Relationships with others are often strained, and the patient is generally pessimistic about the future.

In addition to the anxiety disorders described, abnormal anxiety may be caused by a variety of drugs and medical illnesses. Common drug offenders include caffeine, alcohol, stimulants in cold preparations, nicotine, and many illicit drugs, including cocaine and amphetamines. Medical illnesses that may cause anxiety include thyroid disease, heart failure, cardiac arrhythmias, and schizophrenia.

Treatment and Therapy

When an individual has difficulty with anxiety and seeks professional help, the cause of the anxiety must be determined. Before the etiology can be determined, however, the professional must first realize that the patient has an anxiety disorder. People with such disorders often complain primarily of physical symptoms that result from the anxiety. These symptoms may include motor tension (muscle tension, trembling, and fatigue) and autonomic hyperactivity (shortness of breath, palpitations, cold hands, dizziness, gastrointestinal upset, chills, and frequent urination).

When an anxiety disorder is suspected, effective treatment often depends on an accurate diagnosis of the type of anxiety disorder present. A variety of medications can be prescribed for the anxiety disorder. In addition, several types of psychotherapy can be used. For example, patients with panic disorder can be educated about the nature of their illness, reassured that they will not die from it, and taught to ride out a panic attack. This process avoids the development of secondary anxiety, which complicates the panic attack. Phobic patients can be treated with systematic desensitization, in which they are taught relaxation techniques and are given graded exposure to the feared situation so that their fear lessens or disappears.

The origin, diagnosis, and treatment of anxiety disorders can best be portrayed through case examples. Three fictional cases are described below to illustrate typical anxiety disorder patients.

Ms. Smith is a twenty-four-year-old married mother of two young children. She works part-time as a bookkeeper for a construction company. Her health had been good until a month ago, when she began to experience spells of intense fearfulness, a racing heart, tremors of her hands, a dry mouth, and dizziness. The spells would come on suddenly and would last between ten and fifteen minutes. She was convinced that heart disease was causing these episodes and was worried about having a heart attack. As a result, she consulted her family physician.

Physical examination, electrocardiogram, and laboratory studies were all normal. Her physician had initially considered cardiac arrhythmia (abnormal rhythm of the heartbeat) as a cause but diagnosed panic disorder on the basis of Ms. Smith's history and the outcome of the tests. Treatment consisted of medication and comforting explanations of the nonfatal nature of the disorder. Within three weeks, the panic attacks stopped altogether.

This case illustrates many common features of panic disorder. The patient is a young adult female with classic panic attacks striking "out of the blue." Most patients fear that they are having a heart attack or a stroke or that they are going insane. Typically, they present their symptoms to general medical physicians rather than to psychiatrists. Treatment with medication and simple counseling techniques are usually successful.

Mr. Jones is a thirty-five-year-old single man who works as an accountant. He has always been shy and has adopted leisure activities that he can do alone, such as reading, gardening, and coin collecting. As a child, he was bright but withdrawn. His mother described him as "high-strung," "a worrier," and "easily moved to tears." Recently, he has been bothered by muscle achiness, frequent urination, and diarrhea alternating with constipation. He thinks constantly about his health and worries that he has cancer.

Mr. Jones makes frequent visits to his doctor, but no illness is found. His doctor tells him that he worries too much. The patient admits to himself that he is a worrier and has been his whole life. He ruminates about the details of his job, his health, his lack of friends, the state of the economy, and a host of other concerns. His worries make it hard for him to fall asleep at night. Once asleep, however, he sleeps soundly. Finally, Mr. Jones is given a tranquilizer by his physician. He finds that he feels calm, no longer broods over everything, falls asleep easily, and has relief from his physical symptoms. To improve his social functioning, he sees a psychiatrist, who diagnoses a generalized anxiety disorder and an avoidant (shy) personality disorder.

This case illustrates many features of patients with generalized anxiety disorder. These individuals have near-continuous anxiety for weeks or months that is not clearly related to a single life event. In this case, some of the physical manifestations of anxiety are prominent (muscle tension, frequent urination, and diarrhea). Difficulty falling asleep is also common with anxiety. In contrast, patients who are depressed will often have early morning wakening. In this case example, the patient also has a concomitant shy personality that aggravates his condition. Such a patient usually benefits from treatment. Medication may be required for many years, although it may be needed only during active cycles of anxiety. Because some patients attempt to medicate themselves with alcohol, secondary alcoholism is a potential complication.

Ms. Johnson is a forty-two-year-old married homemaker and mother of four children. She works part-time in a fabric store as a salesclerk. She is friendly and outgoing. She has also been very close with her family, especially her mother. Ms. Johnson comes to her family physician because her mother has just had a stroke. Because her mother lives on the other side of the country, Ms. Johnson needs to take an airplane if she is to get to her mother's bedside quickly. Unfortunately, Ms. Johnson has a long-standing fear of flying; even the thought of getting into an airplane terrifies her. She has not personally had a bad experience with flying but remembers reading about a plane crash when she was a teenager. She denies any other unusual fears and otherwise functions well.

Her family physician refers her to a psychologist for systematic desensitization to relieve her phobia for future situations. As a stop-gap measure for the present, however, she is taught a deep-muscle relaxation technique, is shown videotapes designed to reduce fear of flying, and is prescribed a tranquilizer and another drug to reduce the physical manifestations of anxiety (a beta-blocker). This combination of treatments allows her to visit her mother immediately and, eventually, to be able to fly without needing medication.

This case illustrates a typical patient with an isolated phobia. Phobias are probably the most common anxiety disorders. Treatments such as those described above are usually quite helpful.

Perspective and Prospects

Anxiety has been recognized since antiquity and was often attributed to magical or spiritual causes, such as demonic possession. Ancient myths provided explanations for fearful events in people's lives. Pan, a mythological god of mischief, was thought to cause frightening noises in forests, especially at night; the term "panic" is derived from his name. An understanding of the causes of panic and other anxiety disorders has evolved over the years.

Sigmund Freud (1856-1939) distinguished anxiety from fear. He considered fear to be an expected response to a specific, identifiable trigger, whereas anxiety was a similar emotional state without an identifiable trigger. He postulated that anxiety resulted from unconscious, forbidden wishes that conflicted with what the person believed was acceptable. The anxiety that resulted from this mental conflict was called an "anxiety neurosis" and was thought to result in a variety of psychological and physical symptoms. Psychoanalysis was developed to uncover these hidden conflicts and to allow the anxiety to be released.

Freud's theories about anxiety are no longer universally accepted. Many psychiatrists now believe that several anxiety disorders have a biological cause and that they are more neurological diseases than psychological ones. This is primarily true of generalized anxiety disorder, panic disorder, and obsessive-compulsive disorder. It is recognized that anxiety can also be triggered by drugs (legal and illicit) and a variety of medical illnesses.

Psychological causes of anxiety are also recognized. Adjustment disorder with anxious mood, phobias, and post-traumatic stress disorder are all thought to be primarily psychological disorders. Unlike with Freud's conflict theory of anxiety, most modern psychiatrists consider personality factors, life experiences, and views of the world to be the relevant psychological factors in such anxiety disorders. Nonpharmacological therapies are no longer designed to uncover hidden mental conflicts; they provide instead support. Specific therapies include flooding (massive exposure to the feared situation), systematic desensitization (graded exposure), and relaxation techniques.

Bibliography

American Psychiatric Association. *Diagnostic and Statistical Manual of Mental Disorders, Fourth Edition (DSM-IV)*. 4th ed. Washington, D.C.: Author, 1994. This textbook contains the official diagnostic criteria and classification for all the anxiety disorders. Provides useful descriptions, definitions, and prevalence data.

Bellenir, Karen, ed. *Mental Health Disorders Sourcebook: Basic Consumer Health Information About Anxiety Disorders, Depression, and Other Mood Disorders*. 2d ed. Detroit: Omnigraphics, 2000. A volume on mental illness in the health reference series. Includes a bibliography and an index.

Bourne, Edmond J. *The Anxiety and Phobia Workbook*. Oakland, Calif.: New Harbinger, 1995. This is an excellent self-help book for problems related to anxiety. It may also be helpful for family members seeking to understand anxiety better or to support those affected by anxiety.

Craske, Michelle G. *Anxiety Disorders: Psychological Approaches to Theory and Treatment*. Boulder, Colo.: Westview Press, 1999. This volume in the series Perspectives in Clinical Psychology addresses the diagnosis and treatment of anxiety disorders. Includes bibliographical references and an index.

Greist, John H., James W. Jefferson, and Isaac M. Marks. *Anxiety and Its Treatment*. Washington, D.C.: American Psychiatric Press, 1986. A short book written by three psychiatrists with a special interest in the anxiety disorders. Intended for a lay audience, it describes the nature of the anxiety disorders and their treatment.

Kleinknecht, Ronald A. *Mastering Anxiety: The Nature and Treatment of Anxious*

Conditions. New York: Plenum Press, 1991. This book provides a good overview, with statistics and good explanations of the different types of anxiety disorder.

Leaman, Thomas L. *Healing the Anxiety Diseases.* New York: Plenum Press, 1992. A helpful text written by a family physician with an interest in anxiety disorders. Provides a good overview to the subject in nontechnical terms and contains practical advice on dealing with anxiety.

Noyes, Russell, Jr., and Rudolf Hoehn-Saric. *The Anxiety Disorders.* New York: Cambridge University Press, 1998. This comprehensive text covers all the anxiety disorders found in DSM-IV. Includes bibliographical references and an index.

Sheehan, David V. *The Anxiety Disease.* New York: Bantam Books, 1983. A classic book written for the layperson that explains the nature of anxiety, the different types of anxiety disorder, and treatment approaches.

Weekes, Claire. *Hope and Help for Your Nerves.* New York: Hawthorne Books, 1969. A classic text describing the nature of panic disorder. Weekes describes her pioneering approach to the nonpharmacological management of this disorder.

Peter M. Hartmann, M.D.

See also:

Agoraphobia and Panic Disorders; Depression; Grief and Guilt; Hypochondriasis, Conversion, Somatization, and Somatoform Pain; Manic-Depressive Disorder; Midlife Crises; Neurosis; Obsessive-Compulsive Disorder; Paranoia; Phobias; Psychoanalysis; Psychosomatic Disorders; Sexual Dysfunction; Stress; Stress: Coping Strategies.

APHASIAS

Type of psychology: Language
Fields of study: Cognitive processes

Aphasias include a variety of conditions in which a partial or total loss of the ability to understand or produce language-based material occurs; the deficits can be in speech, reading, or writing. Knowledge of aphasias can aid in the localization of brain injuries. An understanding of aphasias is also important because they cause communication problems that require treatment.

Principal terms

EQUIPOTENTIALITY: a theory of cerebral functioning that holds that, although sensory input may be localized, perception involves the whole brain

EXPRESSIVE APHASIA: severe impairment of previously intact language-production abilities as a result of brain injury or cerebral dysfunction

GLOBAL APHASIA: substantial impairments in both language production and language comprehension

INTERACTIONIST THEORY: the idea that perception and behavioral output are based on interactions between basic components; although component processes are localized, there is redundancy in regard to function

LOCALIZATIONIST THEORY: the idea that specific sensory, perceptual, and behavioral processes are controlled by particular cerebral structures and/or areas of the brain

PARAPHASIA: impairment in which articulation is intact but unintended sounds are substituted for others (phonemic paraphasia) or words are substituted (semantic paraphasia)

RECEPTIVE APHASIA: severe impairment of previously intact language-comprehension abilities as a result of brain injury or other cerebral dysfunction

Causes and Symptoms
Nearly all definitions of aphasia agree on the following four points: Aphasia refers to a condition in which a person suffers a loss in the ability to understand or produce language-referenced material; the deficits can be in speech, reading, and/or writing; the impairment is assumed to be caused by cerebral rather than peripheral impairments; and aphasias represent a devastation of a previously manifested ability rather than a developmental failure.

A fifth point, included or implied in most descriptions of aphasias, is that they occur as a result of structural damage or disease processes that directly affect the brain—an organic etiology. This view is taken because functional mental disorders that produce aphasic-like symptoms are best understood in the context of the psychological and environmental events that produce them. Aphasias, however, are best comprehended in relationship to the physical injuries and structural changes that cause their appearance. Furthermore, interventions that would be effective for the treatment of aphasias would have little or no relevance for the amelioration of aphasic-like symptoms that result from functional causes.

Vascular disorders, particularly strokes, are the most frequent cause of aphasia. Other conditions likely to lead to aphasia include traumatic head injuries, brain tumors, infections, toxins, and dementia.

It is left-hemisphere damage that is most commonly associated with aphasia. For most persons, language abilities are localized in the left hemisphere of the brain. Damage to the right side of the brain seldom results in any noticeable effect on language skills. The fact that left-handers sometimes show speech impairments following injury to the right side of the brain has often been taken as evidence that lefthanders are right-brain dominant in regard to language. Research has failed to support this contention. Most left-handers show bilateral or left-hemisphere dominance for language, with no more than 15 percent showing primary control of speech via the right hemisphere.

Aphasias can be divided into three general categories: expressive aphasias, receptive aphasias, and mixed or global aphasias. Most persons with aphasia show a mixture of expressive and receptive symptoms.

Expressive aphasia is often referred to as Broca's aphasia, motor aphasia, nonfluent aphasia, executive aphasia, or verbal aphasia. Expressive aphasia can be considered to subsume subfluent aphasia, anarthric aphasia, expressive dysprosody, kinetic (efferent) motor aphasia, speech apraxia, subcortical motor aphasia (pure word-dumbness), transcortical motor aphasia (dynamic aphasia), conduction (central) aphasia, anomic (amnestic or nominal) aphasia, and agraphia.

Expressive aphasia describes a condition in which language comprehension remains intact but speech—and quite often the ability to write—is impaired. People who suffer from expressive aphasia understand what is being asked of them, and their ability to read is unaffected; they have difficulty, however, communicating their understanding.

When expressive aphasia is extreme, the affected person may be totally unable to speak (aphonia) or may be able to speak only in so distorted a way that he or she becomes incomprehensible. Still, as is the case with all other forms of aphasia, singing and swearing are generally preserved.

Paraphasias are a common form of expressive aphasia. Paraphasia differs from articulation problems, which are also quite prominent. When a person with expressive aphasia has difficulties with articulation, he or she has trouble making recognizable speech sounds. Paraphasia, on the other hand, refers to a condition in which articulation is intact but unintended syllables, words, or phrases are inserted. For example, one patient, in referring to his wife, always said "my dog."

Telegraphic speech, in which speech is reduced to its most elemental aspects, is frequently encountered in expressive aphasia. In telegraphic speech, the meaning is often clear; however, communications are reduced to the bare minimum and consist of simple noun-verb phrases.

Verbal fluency, the capacity to produce uninterrupted phrases and sentences, is typically adversely affected in expressive aphasias. As a result of word-finding difficulties, speech may take on a halting and labored character.

Receptive aphasia is often referred to as Wernicke's aphasia, sensory aphasia, fluent aphasia, or agnosia. Receptive aphasia can be considered to subsume semantic aphasia, jargon aphasia, visual aphasia (pure word-blindness), transcortical sensory aphasia (isolation syndrome), syntactical aphasia, and alexia. In receptive aphasia, speech is generally fluent, with few, if any, articulatory problems; however, deficits in language comprehension are always present.

While fluent, the speech of a person with receptive aphasia is seldom normal. People who have receptive aphasia may insert nonwords—neologisms—into their communications, and in severe cases their communications may contain nothing but jargon speech. For example, one patient, when asked what he had for breakfast, responded, "Eating and food. Got no more heavy come to there. No come good, very good, in morning."

Unlike people who have expressive aphasia, who generally show great distress in regard to their disorder, people who have receptive aphasia may appear oblivious to their disorder. They may produce lengthy nonsensical utterances and then look at the listener as if confused by the listener's lack of comprehension.

Global aphasia describes a condition in which there is a mixture of receptive and expressive deficits. Global aphasia is typically associated with less focalized brain injury. Although comprehension is generally less impaired than production in global aphasia, this disorder does not fit neatly into either the expressive or the receptive category. The prognosis is generally much poorer for persons with global aphasia than for those with purely receptive or expressive deficits.

An appreciation for the nature and extent of aphasias is important because such knowledge can facilitate the identification of disease processes that may be affecting cerebral functioning, can assist in the localization of brain injuries, and can provide information that must be considered in making post-discharge placements. Finally, and perhaps most important, knowledge of aphasias is needed because they cause significant communication deficits that require treatment.

A variety of conditions can lead to aphasic-like symptoms: functional mental disorders, peripheral nervous system damage, peripheral motor impairments, congenital disorders, degenerative disease processes of the brain, cerebral vascular injury, central nervous system toxins, epilepsy, migraine, brain tumors, central nervous system infections, and cerebral trauma. Being able to discriminate between true aphasias (those caused by cerebral complications) and aphasic-like symptoms brought on by other causes can enable the selection of the most effective treatment and improve prognostic prediction. For example, depression, Parkinson's disease, and certain focal lesions can cause persons to appear emotionally unreactive (flat affect) and speak in a manner that lacks expressive intensity and intonation (dysprosody). The treatments of choice for these disorders are substantially different, and some interventions that would be recommended for one disorder would be contraindicated for another. Similarly, knowing that cerebral hemorrhage is most often associated with global aphasia and diffuse tissue damage—whereas cerebral embolisms typically damage areas served by the left middle cerebral artery, resulting in more specific aphasias—has implications in regard to patient monitoring, treatment, and prognosis.

The interrelationships between aphasias and localized brain injuries have important ramifications. Among other implications, knowing the neural basis for language production and processing can facilitate the identification of the best candidate sites for surgical intervention and can provide clues regarding whether a disease process has been arrested or continues to spread. For example, an aphasia that begins with clear articulation and no identifiable deficits in language production would be consistent with conduction aphasia, and it might be assumed that damage to the arcuate fasciculus had occurred. If, over the course of time, the person began to manifest increasing difficulty with speech comprehension but articulation continued to appear intact, it could be inferred that damage was spreading downward and affecting a broader region of the temporal lobe. Such information would have important treatment and prognostic ramifications.

Given the importance of language and the ability to communicate in managing daily affairs, it can be seen that having information concerning the nature and the extent of aphasia is an important consideration that must be taken into account when making postdischarge plans. On the one hand, if the person's deficits are purely expressive in nature, it can be assumed that he or she will more likely be able to manage his or her daily affairs and will be more capable of managing independent placement. On the other hand, persons with receptive aphasia, despite wishes to the contrary, may have to be referred to a more restrictive environment. Not being able to understand the communications of others and perhaps manifesting deficits in safety and judgment require that the person with receptive aphasia be carefully assessed to ascertain the degree to which he or she is competent to manage his or her affairs.

Treatment and Therapy

Aphasias cause significant communication problems that require treatment and amelioration. While there is no doubt that considerable spontaneous recovery takes place in regard to aphasia, research shows that treatment can have a facilitating effect. Furthermore, the earlier treatment is initiated, the more profound its effects.

Under most circumstances, therapy for aphasia is one element of a more comprehensive treatment process. Aphasia seldom occurs in isolation, and, depending on the type of damage, one is likely to see paresis, memory deficits, apraxias, agnosias, and various difficulties related to information processing occurring in conjunction with the aphasia. As a result, the person with aphasia is likely to be treated by an interdisciplinary team. The team will typically consist of one or more physicians, nurses, nursing support personnel, physical therapists, occupational therapists, speech therapists, a rehabilitation psychologist or neuropsychologist, a clinical psychologist, and one or more social workers. Each team member is expected to have an area of expertise and specialization, but the team approach requires that team members work together and, individually and collectively, support each discipline's treatment goals.

The most common treatments for the aphasic person are systematic stimulation, behavioral teaching programs, deblocking, and compensation therapy. Systematic stimulation involves the use of everyday objects and everyday situations to stimulate language production and to facilitate language comprehension. Behavioral teaching programs are similar to systematic stimulation but are more organized, are designed more precisely to take into account known structural damage, and frequently employ behavior modification techniques. Deblocking, a less frequently used therapy, consists of stimulating intact language functions as a vehicle for encouraging rehabilitation of damaged processes. Compensation therapy includes teaching the person alternative communication strategies and utilizing intact abilities to circumvent the functional limitations that result from her or his aphasia.

Perspective and Prospects

The study of aphasias dates back more than four thousand years. An Egyptian papyrus dated between 3000 and 2500 B.C.E. provides a case example of language deficits following traumatic head injury.

The Greeks variously subscribed to hypotheses that mental processes were located in the brain or the heart. Not until the time of the physician Galen (130-201 C.E.) did the brain hypothesis gain full sway. Galen based his arguments on dissection and clinical experience—he spent five years as a physician to the gladiators of the Roman circus, where he was exposed to multiple cases of traumatic head injury.

Over the next thirteen hundred years, little progress was made in relation to an appreciation of cerebral anatomy or physiology. With the anatomical observations of Andreas Vesalius (1514-1564) and the philosophical speculations of René Descartes (1596-1650), however, the stage was set for a new understanding of cerebral functioning.

In the early nineteenth century, phrenology, which postulated that specific areas of the brain controlled particular intellectual and psychological processes, became influential. Although it was subsequently discredited, phrenology provided the foundation for the localizationist position in neuropsychology.

Paul Broca (1824-1880) can be credited with raising the study of cerebral localization of speech to a scientific level. Broca's first case study was "Tan," a patient with apparently intact receptive abilities whose expressive skills had been reduced to uttering the word "tan" and a few colorful oaths. According to Broca, "Tan" was shown in an autopsy to have a lesion of the left anterior lobe of his brain, which caused his speech problems. Subsequently, the syndrome he described became known as Broca's aphasia. Furthermore, the posterior third of the left third frontal convolution of the left hemisphere of the brain became known as Broca's area.

Carl Wernicke (1848-1905) was the next person to make major contributions to the understanding of cerebral organization and language functioning. Wernicke proposed a sequential processing model that held that several areas of the brain affected language development, production, and expression. Following his work, the left first temporal gyrus was named Wernicke's area, and the particular type of receptive aphasia that resulted from damage to this area became known as Wernicke's aphasia.

Over the ensuing years, arguments raged regarding whether the localizationist position was tenable. As a general rule, researchers supporting equipotentiality (sensory input may be localized, but perception involves the whole brain) held sway. By the 1950's, interactionist theory had gained the ascendancy. Interactionist theory holds that basic functions are localized; however, there is redundancy in regard to function. Therefore, damage to a specific area of the brain may or may not cause a deficit in higher-order behaviors, since the damaged functions may be assumed by redundant or parallel backup components.

Recent years have seen notable advances in the understanding and treatment of aphasias. Psychometric instruments founded on modern principles of test construction have become available. Experimental techniques that take into account known aspects of cerebral functioning have been developed. Furthermore, advances in brain imaging have done much to aid in understanding cortical function and the effects of injury as they relate to the development of aphasias.

Bibliography

Brubaker, Susan Howell. *Sourcebook for Aphasia: A Guide to Family Activities and Community Resources.* Detroit: Wayne State University Press, 1982. Brubaker describes activities that relatives of aphasia patients can use to enhance the recovery process. The absence of an introduction to aphasia and minimal guidance regarding which exercises are appropriate for particular symptom presentations are limiting factors in this text.

Collins, Michael. *Diagnosis and Treatment of Global Aphasia.* San Diego: College-Hill Press, 1986. Collins focuses on the practical implications of what is known about global aphasia. The text is somewhat technical, but it is valuable for persons who want to learn more about this disorder.

Ewing, Susan Adair, and Beth Pfalzgraf. *Pathways: Moving Beyond Stroke and Aphasia.* Detroit: Wayne State University Press, 1990. The authors summarize the experiences of six families who attempt to cope with the aftermath of a stroke. Practical and emotional problems that must be confronted by the patient and the family are discussed.

Fitch, James L. *Clinical Applications of Microcomputers in Communication Disorders.* Orlando, Fla.: Academic Press, 1986. Fitch provides an entry-level introduction to the use of computers in audiology and speech pathology. The text lacks an adequate discussion of the use of computers as adaptive devices, but many potential applications are discussed.

Helm-Estabrooks, Nancy, and Audrey L. Holland, eds. *Approaches to the Treatment of Aphasia.* San Diego: Singular Publishing Group, 1998. Presents case studies in the treatment of this disorder. Includes bibliographical references and an index.

Lyon, Jon G. *Coping with Aphasia.* San Diego: Singular Publishing Group, 1998. A popular work on the etiology and diagnosis of aphasia and the rehabilitation of patients. Includes bibliographical references and an index.

Murdoch, B. E. *Acquired Speech and Language Disorders: A Neuroanatomical and Functional Neurological Approach.* London: Chapman and Hall, 1990.

Murdoch provides a comprehensive description of the various types of aphasia and dysarthria. Additionally, the author supplies an extended discussion of agnosia and apraxia. Furthermore, the author elucidates how neurological damage and disease processes affect language production and comprehension.

Sarno, Martha Taylor, ed. *Acquired Aphasia*. 3d ed. San Diego: Academic Press, 1998. Contributions to this volume tend to be technical, but the book contains valuable information concerning neurological and linguistic factors associated with aphasia. The chapters on intelligence, artistry, and social sequelae are unique offerings.

Bruce E. Bailey

See also:

Alzheimer's Disease; Brain Disorders; Dementia; Dyslexia; Learning Disabilities.

ATTENTION-DEFICIT DISORDER

Type of psychology: Psychopathology
Fields of study: Attitudes and behavior; childhood and adolescent disorders

Attention-deficit disorder is one of the most common disorders of childhood and adolescence, but it is also one of the most disturbing and debilitating disorders that a child or adolescent can experience. Research into this disorder has identified its primary causes; however, it remains a difficult disorder to treat effectively.

Principal terms

ETIOLOGY: the factors that are thought to cause or contribute to a particular disorder

IMPULSIVITY: excitability, poor self-control, and inability to delay gratification or to inhibit urges; examples include difficulty waiting, blurting out answers, and interrupting others

INATTENTION: difficulty in sustaining attention, distractibility; examples include poor concentration and distraction by unimportant stimuli, such as a passing vehicle

OVERACTIVITY: excessive levels of vocal or motor activity, such as restlessness, fidgeting, and unnecessary movements

PREVALENCE: the percentage of a population that has a particular disorder at a given time

TREATMENT: the attempt to ameliorate or treat the symptoms of a disorder; treatments can include medication, cognitive-behavioral therapy, and parent training, among others

Causes and Symptoms

Attention-deficit disorder (ADD), also known as attention-deficit/hyperactivity disorder (ADHD) or hyperactivity, is one of the most extensively studied behavior disorders of childhood. It is estimated that there are more than ten thousand individual studies of this disorder, as well as numerous books and other writings. There are a number of reasons why this disorder is of such interest to researchers and clinicians. The two primary reasons are, first, that ADD is a relatively common disorder of childhood, and second, there are numerous problems associated with ADD, including lower levels of intellectual and academic performance and higher levels of aggressive and defiant behavior.

In national and international studies of childhood emotional and behavioral disorders, ADD has been found to be relatively common among children. Although prevalence estimates range from 1 percent to 20 percent, most researchers agree that between 3 percent and 5 percent of children could be diagnosed as having ADD. In order to be diagnosed as having ADD, a child needs to show more than hyperactivity alone. The fourth edition of the *Diagnostic and Statistical Manual of*

Mental Disorders (DSM-IV), which was published by the American Psychiatric Association in 1994, described diagnostic criteria for ADD. A child had to show twelve out of eighteen listed behaviors falling roughly into three categories: inattention (such as having difficulty sustaining attention in play activities or tasks), impulsivity (such as having difficulty waiting one's turn in a game), and hyperactivity (such as difficulty remaining still or seated when asked). Although many of these behaviors are quite common for most children at some point in their lives, the important point to consider is that they must be maladaptive and inconsistent with developmental level. Additionally, it is expected that these behaviors have been present for at least six months.

Boys tend to outnumber girls in the diagnosis of ADD. It is estimated that, of children diagnosed as having ADD, boys outnumber girls six to one. This estimate may be somewhat high, however, since the ratio is reported to be three to one in samples of children who have not been referred for therapy. It may be that boys are disproportionately referred for therapy. ADD boys tend to be more aggressive and antisocial than ADD girls, and therefore boys may be more fre-

POSSIBLE SYMPTOMS OF ADD WITH HYPERACTIVITY (IMPULSIVE) IN CHILDREN
❖ fidgety
❖ leaves seat when should not
❖ runs or climbs inappropriately
❖ talks excessively
❖ difficulty playing quietly
❖ always on the go
❖ blurts out answers
❖ has trouble waiting turns
❖ interrupts

POSSIBLE SYMPTOMS OF ADD WITHOUT HYPERACTIVITY (INATTENTIVE) IN CHILDREN
❖ difficulty following through on instructions
❖ difficulty keeping attention on tasks or play
❖ loses things at school and home
❖ does not listen
❖ fails to give close attention to detail
❖ seems disorganized
❖ trouble with tasks needing long-term effort
❖ forgetful
❖ easily distracted

POSSIBLE SYMPTOMS OF ADD IN ADULTS
❖ a tendency to be easily distracted
❖ hyperactivity, usually in the form of restlessness
❖ mood swings (which very often become the main symptom in adults)
❖ inability to complete things
❖ a hot temper, with low stress tolerance
❖ difficulties getting along with spouses, coworkers, and other significant people in their lives.

quently referred for therapy than girls even when similar levels of ADD behavior occur.

There are a number of additional problems associated with ADD, including the greater likelihood of ADD boys exhibiting aggressive and antisocial behavior. Although many ADD children do not show any associated problems, many ADD children show deficits in both intellectual and behavioral functioning. For example, a number of studies have found that ADD children score an average of seven to fifteen points below normal children on standardized intelligence tests. It may be, however, that this poorer performance reflects poor test-taking skills or inattention during the test rather than actual impairment in intellectual functioning. Additionally, ADD children tend to have difficulty with academic performance and scholastic achievement. It is assumed that this poor academic performance is a result of inattention and impulsiveness in the classrooom. When ADD children are given medication to control their inattention and impulsiveness, their academic productivity has been shown to improve.

ADD children have also been shown to have a high number of associated emotional and behavioral difficulties. As mentioned earlier, ADD boys tend to show higher levels of aggressive and antisocial behavior than ADD girls and normal children. Additionally, it is estimated that 11 percent of ADD children have at least three other psychiatric disorders, 32 percent have at least two other disorders, and 44 percent have at least one other disorder. Many of these problems are related to depression and anxiety, although many ADD children also have severe problems with temper tantrums, stubbornness, and defiant behavior. It is also estimated that up to 50 percent of ADD children have impaired social relations; that is, they do not get along with other children. In general, there are many problems associated with ADD, and this may be part of the reason that researchers have been so intrigued by this disorder.

Researchers must understand a disorder before they can attempt to treat it. There are a variety of theories on the etiology of ADD, but most researchers now believe that there are multiple factors that influence its development. It appears that many children may have a biological predisposition toward ADD; in other words, they may have a greater likelihood of developing ADD as a result of genetic factors. This predisposition is exacerbated by a variety of factors, such as complications during pregnancy, neurological disease, exposure to toxins, family adversity, and inconsistent parental discipline. Although a very popular belief is that food additives or sugar can cause ADD, there has been almost no scientific support for these claims. Since so many factors have been found to be associated with the development of ADD, it is not surprising that numerous treatments have been developed for the amelioration of ADD symptoms. Although numerous treatment methods have been developed and studied, ADD remains a difficult disorder to treat effectively.

Treatment and Therapy

Treatments of ADD can be broken down into roughly two categories: medication; and behavioral or cognitive-behavioral treatment with the individual ADD child, parents, or teachers. It should be noted that traditional psychotherapy and play therapy have not been found to be effective in the treatment of ADD. Stimulant medications have been used in the treatment of ADD since 1937. The most commonly prescribed stimulant medications are methylphenidate (Ritalin), pemoline (Cylert), and dextroamphetamine (Dexedrine). Behavioral improvements caused by stimulant medications include impulse control and improved attending behavior. Overall, approximately 75 percent of ADD children on stimulant medication show behavioral improvement, and 25 percent show either no improvement or decreased behavioral functioning. The findings related to academic performance are mixed. It appears that stimulant medications can help the

ADD child with school productivity and accuracy, but not with overall academic achievement. In addition, although ADD children tend to show improvement while they are on a stimulant medication, there are rarely any long-term benefits to the use of stimulant medications. In general, stimulant medication can be seen as only a short-term management tool.

Antidepressant medications (such as imipramine and desipramine) have also been used with ADD children. These medications are sometimes used when stimulant medication is not appropriate (for example, if the child has motor or vocal tics). Antidepressant medications, however, like stimulant medications, appear to provide only short-term improvement in ADD symptoms. Overall, the use or nonuse of medications in the treatment of ADD should be carefully evaluated by a qualified physician (such as a psychiatrist). If the child is started on medication for ADD, the safety and appropriateness of the medication must be monitored continually throughout its use.

Behavioral and cognitive-behavioral treatments have been used with ADD children themselves, with parents, and with teachers. Most of these techniques attempt to provide the child with a consistent environment in which on-task behavior is rewarded (for example, the teacher praises the child for raising his or her hand and not shouting out an answer), and in which off-task behavior is either ignored or punished (for example, the parent has the child sit alone in a chair near an empty wall, a "time-out chair," after the child impulsively throws a book across the room). In addition, cognitive-behavioral treatments try to teach ADD children to internalize their own self-control by learning to "stop and think" before they act.

One example of a cognitive-behavioral treatment, which was developed by Philip Kendall and Lauren Braswell, is intended to teach the child to learn five "steps" that can be applied to academic tasks as well as social interactions. The five problem-solving steps that children are to repeat to themselves each time they encounter a new situation are the following: Ask "What am I supposed to do?"; ask "What are my choices?"; concentrate and focus in; make a choice; and ask "How did I do?" (If I did well, I can congratulate myself; if I did poorly, I should try to go more slowly next time.) In each therapy session, the child is given twenty plastic chips at the beginning of the session. The child loses a chip each time he or she does not use one of the steps, goes too fast, or gives an incorrect answer. At the end of the session, the child can use the chips to purchase a small prize; chips can also be stored in a "bank" in order to purchase an even larger prize in the following sessions. This treatment approach combines the use of cognitive strategies (the child learns self-instructional steps) and behavioral techniques (the child loses a desired object, a chip, for impulsive behavior).

Overall, behavioral and cognitive-behavioral treatments have been found to be relatively effective in the settings in which they are used and at the time they are being instituted. Like the effects of medication, however, the effects of behavioral and cognitive-behavioral therapies tend not to be long-lasting. There is some evidence to suggest that the combination of medication and behavior therapy can increase the effectiveness of treatment. In the long run, however, no treatment of ADD has been found to be truly effective.

Perspective and Prospects

Children who might now be diagnosed as having ADD have been written about and discussed in scientific publications since the mid-1800's. Attention to ADD began in the United States after an encephalitis epidemic in 1917. Because the damage to the central nervous system caused by the disease led to poor attention, impulsivity, and overactivity in children who survived, researchers began to look for signs of brain injury in other children who had similar behavioral profiles. By the 1950's, researchers began to refer to this disorder as "minimal brain damage," which was then changed to "minimal brain dysfunction" (MBD). By the 1960's, however, the use of the term MBD was severely criticized because of its overinclusiveness and nonspecificity. Researchers began to use terms that more specifically characterized children's problems, such as "hyperkinesis" and "hyperactivity."

The *Diagnostic and Statistical Manual of Mental Disorders* (DSM), published by the American Psychiatric Association, is the primary diagnostic manual used in the United States. In 1968, DSM-II presented the diagnosis of "Hyperkinetic Reaction of Childhood" to characterize children who were overactive and restless. By 1980, when DSM-III was published, researchers had begun to focus on the deficits of attention in these children, so two diagnostic categories were established: "Attention Deficit Disorder with Hyperactivity (ADD with H)" and "Attention Deficit Disorder without Hyperactivity (ADD without H)." After the publication of DSM-III, many researchers argued that there were no empirical data to support the existence of the ADD without H diagnosis. In other words, it was difficult to find any children who were inattentive and impulsive but who were not hyperactive. For this reason, in 1987, when DSM-III-R was published, the only diagnostic category for these children was "Attention-Deficit/Hyperactivity Disorder."

The interest in and commitment to this disorder is likely to continue. Children and adults with ADD, as well as the people around them, have difficult lives to lead. The research community is committed to finding better explanations of the etiology and treatment of this common disorder.

Bibliography

Barkley, Russell A. "Attention-Deficit/Hyperactivity Disorder." In *The Treatment of Childhood Disorders*, edited by Eric J. Mash and Russell A. Barkley. 2d ed. New York: Guilford Press, 1998. This chapter provides a thorough discussion of different treatments for ADD children, including stimulant medication, antidepressant medication, behavior therapy, parent training, teacher training, and cognitive-behavioral therapy. Each treatment modality is discussed in a fair and objective manner, and empirical research is provided to support the conclusions given.

_____. *Attention-Deficit Hyperactivity Disorder: A Handbook for Diagnosis and Treatment*. 2d ed. New York: Guilford Press, 1998. Provides comprehensive discussion of nearly all aspects of ADD, including assessment, diagnosis, and treatment. Also notable for a thorough discussion of ADD in older adolescents and adults. This excellent and comprehensive book is written by one of the leading researchers in the investigation of ADD.

Campbell, Susan B. "The Socialization and Social Development of Hyperactive Children." In *Handbook of Developmental Psychopathology*, edited by Arnold J. Sameroff, Michael Lewis, and Suzanne M. Miller. 2d ed. New York: Plenum Press, 2000. A succinct overview of the social climate surrounding children with ADD. This chapter covers such topics as childrearing practices, sibling conflict, family climate, parental psychopathology, and peer relationships of ADD children.

Horacek, H. Joseph. *Brainstorms: Understanding and Treating the Emotional Storms of Attention Deficit Hyperactivity Disorder from Childhood Through Adulthood*. Northvale, N.J.: Jason Aronson, 1998. Examines the possible neurobiological underpinnings of the emotionally hyperactive and hyperreactive components of ADD and related disorders. Includes bibliographical references and an index.

Kendall, Philip C., and Lauren Braswell. *Cognitive-Behavioral Therapy for Impulsive Children*. 2d ed. New York: Guilford Press, 1993. Presents a comprehensive, step-by-step discussion of a popular cognitive-behavioral treatment for ADD children. The authors provide a thorough rationale for this therapy and provide research data to support the efficacy of the therapy. Practical applications of this therapy are discussed.

Rapport, Mark D. "Attention Deficit Disorder with Hyperactivity." In *Child Behavior Therapy Casebook*, edited by M. Hersen and C. G. Last. New York: Plenum Press, 1988. Presents an in-depth case study of an eight-year-old boy who was referred for treatment of ADD. This chapter provides a thorough discussion of the way in which a child is evaluated and treated for ADD. In this case study, the boy is treated with stimulant medication and behavior therapy techniques. A comprehensive evaluation of the treatment effects is provided, and special attention is given to continuous monitoring of the boy's behavioral and academic performance.

Silver, Larry B., ed. *Attention-Deficit/Hyperactivity Disorder: A Clinical Guide to Diagnosis and Treatment for Health and Mental Health Professionals*. 2d ed. Washington, D.C.: American Psychiatric Press, 1999. Discusses the history of attention disorders, diagnosis, modulating disorders and tic disorders, basic treatment concepts, behavioral management, psychopharmacology, and relevant educational and civil laws. Includes a list of organizations and other resources for further study.

Vicky Phares

See also:

Abnormality; Abnormality: Behavioral Models; Abnormality: Biomedical Models; Child and Adolescent Psychiatry; Cognitive Behavior Therapy; Juvenile Delinquency; Learning Disabilities; Psychoactive Drug Therapy.

AUTISM

Type of psychology: Psychopathology
Fields of study: Childhood and adolescent disorders; interpersonal relations

Autism, a poorly understood, nonschizophrenic psychosocial problem, includes great social unresponsiveness, speech and language impairment, ritualistic play activity, and resistance to change. It causes the parents of autists great grief and disrupts the life of the entire family, although the autist is oblivious to the familial trauma.

Principal terms

AFFECTIVE: behavior resulting from emotions or feelings, rather than from thought
APHASIC: one who has lost the ability to articulate ideas because of brain damage
COGNITIVE: relating to the mental process or faculty by which humans acquire knowledge
ECHOLALIA: an involuntary and parrotlike repetition of words or phrases spoken by others
EPILEPTIC SEIZURE: an attack of epilepsy, characterized by convulsion, motor, sensory, and psychic malfunction
SCHIZOPHRENIA: any of a group of psychotic reactions characterized by withdrawal from reality, with accompanying affective, behavioral, and intellectual disturbances
SEROTONIN: a neurotransmitter produced from the amino acid tryptophan; implicated in a number of psychological disorders
TARDIVE DYSKINESIA: slow, involuntary motor movements, especially of the mouth and tongue, which can become permanent and untreatable

Causes and Symptoms

The modern term "autism" was originated by Leo Kanner in the 1940's. In "Autistic Disturbances of Affective Contact" (1943), he described a group of these children; he viewed them as much more similar to one another than to the schizophrenics, with whom they generally had been associated. Until that time, the classical definition for autism (still seen in some dictionaries) was "a form of childhood schizophrenia characterized by acting out and withdrawal from reality." Kanner believed that these children represented an entirely different clinical psychiatric disorder. He noted four main symptoms associated with the disease: social withdrawal or "extreme autistic aloneness"; either muteness or failure to use spoken language "to convey meaning to others"; an "obsessive desire for maintenance of sameness"; and preoccupation with highly repetitive play habits, producing "severe limitation of spontaneous activity." Kanner also noted that autism—unlike other types of childhood psychoses—began in or near infancy.

Over the years, several attempts have been made to establish precise diagnostic criteria for autism. The criteria given in the American Psychiatric Association's

Diagnostic and Statistical Manual of Mental Disorders (3d ed., 1980, DSM-III) for "Autism Disorder" were onset prior to thirty months of age; pervasive lack of responsiveness to other people; gross deficits in language development; if speech is present, peculiar patterns (such as delayed echolalia and pronoun reversals); bizarre reaction to environmental aspects (resistance to change); and the absence of any symptoms of schizophrenia. These criteria were largely a restatement of Kanner's viewpoint.

Criteria from the fourth edition of the manual, DSM-IV, published in 1994, were qualitative impairment in social interactions, qualitative abnormalities in communication, and restricted repetitive and stereotyped patterns of behavior, interests, and activities. Qualitative impairment in social interactions included marked impairment in the use of multiple nonverbal behaviors; a lack of spontaneous seeking to share enjoyment, interests, or achievements with others; and lack of social or emotional reciprocity. Qualitative abnormalities in communication included delay in or total lack of the development of spoken language not accompanied by an attempt to compensate through alternative modes of communication; stereotyped and repetitive use of language or idiosyncratic language; and lack of varied, spontaneous make-believe play or social imitative play. Restricted repetitive and stereotyped patterns of behavior, interests, and activities included apparently inflexible adherence to specific, nonfunctional routines or rituals; stereotyped and repetitive motor mannerisms such as hand or finger flapping or twisting, and complex whole-body movements; and persistent preoccupation with parts of objects. Delays or abnormal functioning had to be present in at least one of the following areas, with onset prior to age three: social interaction, language as used in social communication, or symbolic or imaginative play.

Although the basic cause of autism is still in dispute, it is believed to be attributable to a fundamental cognitive deficit. The prevalence of autism is generally estimated at between 0.1 and 0.4 percent of the population of the world. Study of the sex distribution shows that it is 2.5 to 4 times as common in males as in females.

Largely because of Kanner's original sample (now known to

POSSIBLE SIGNS OF AUTISM IN AN INFANT OR TODDLER

❖ does not cuddle or respond to affection and touching

❖ does not make eye contact

❖ appears to be unable to communicate

❖ displays persistent failure to develop two-way social relationships in any situation

❖ does not show a preference for parents over other adults

❖ does not develop friendships with other children

❖ has poor language skills; or nonexistent ones

❖ shows unusual, extreme responses to objects— either avoidance or preoccupation

❖ finds moving objects, such as a fan, hold great fascination

❖ may form an unusual attachment to odd objects such as a paper or rubberband

❖ displays repetitive activities of a restrictive range

❖ spins and repeats body movements, such as arm flapping

❖ may repeat television commercials

❖ may indulge in complex bedtime rituals

have been atypical), many people believe that autistic children come from professional families and have the capacity for quite normal intellectual function. Subsequent studies have indicated that this is not so. Rather, autistic children come from families within a wide socioeconomic range, and more than 70 percent of them are mentally retarded, exhibiting quite stable intelligence quotient (IQ) scores over a wide age range.

The behavior that characterizes the autistic personality strongly suggests that the disorder is related to other types of neurologic dysfunction. Identified neurological correlations include soft neurologic signs (such as poor coordination), seizure disorders (such as phenylketonuria), abnormal electroencephalograms, and unusual sleep patterns. This emphasis on neurologic—or organic—explanations for autism is relatively new; autism was previously thought to be an entirely emotional disorder.

The difficulties that autistic children show in social relationships are exhibited in many ways. Most apparent is a child's failure to form social bonds. For example, such youngsters rarely initiate any interactions with other children. Moreover, unlike nonautistic children, they do not seek parental company or run to parents for solace when distressed. Many sources even point to frequent parental statements that an autistic child is not as "cuddly" as normal babies and that autists do not respond to their mothers or to affectionate actions. Autistic children avoid direct eye contact and tend to look through or past other people. In addition, autistic children rarely indulge in any cooperative play activities or strike up close friendships with peers.

Sometimes speech does not develop at all. When speech development does occur, it is very slow and may even disappear again. Another prominent speech pathology in autism is either immediate or delayed repetition of something heard but simply parroted back (such as a television commercial), phenomena called immediate and delayed echolalia, respectively. Yet another problem seen is lack of true language comprehension, shown by the fact that an autistic child's ability to follow instructions is often dependent on situational cues. For example, such a child may understand the request to come and eat dinner only when a parent is eating or sitting at the dinner table.

Behavior denoting resistance to change is often best exemplified by rigid and repetitive play patterns, the interruption of which results in tantrums and even self-injury. Some autistic children also develop very ritualistic preoccupations with an object or a schedule. For example, they may become extremely distressed with events as minor as the rearrangement of furniture in a particular room at home.

Treatment and Therapy

Autistic children can be very frustrating to both parents and siblings, disrupting their lives greatly. Often, autists also cause grief and guilt feelings in parents and may diminish their social standing. According to Mary Van Bourgondien, Gary Mesibov, and Geraldine Dawson, in "Pervasive Developmental Disorders: Autism" (1987), this can be ameliorated by psychodynamic, biological, or behavioral techniques. These authors point out that all psychodynamic therapy views autism as an emotional problem, recommending extensive psychotherapy for the autist and the rest of the family. In contrast, biological methodology applies psychoactive drugs and vitamins. Finally, behavioral therapy uses the axioms of experimental psychology, along with special education techniques that teach and reinforce appropriate behavior.

Some interesting aspects of behavioral techniques are described in *Effective Teaching Methods for Autistic Children* (1974), by Rosalind Oppenheim. For example, it is pointed out that many autists have the speech problems associated with aphasic children and the odd body movements of children with perceptual problems. A suggested technique used successfully by Oppenheim is teaching an autistic child to write and then asking "why" questions, to be answered in writing. This technique is reported to be quite successful at enhancing the "inner intellectual development" of some autists.

One autistic child cited by these authors was a teenager designated as Bill. Initially, Bill was uncommunicative, failed to look at his teacher or school work, and persisted in being uncooperative. Within about five months he was reported as having made substantial improvement in a number of academic areas and in speech. The regimen utilized to cause the improvement was a combination of the use of multiple-choice questions and longer written answers to questions.

A wide discussion of the use of biological intervention can be found in *The Biology of the Autistic Syndrome* (1985), by Mary Coleman and Christopher Gillberg, and in *Autism: Nature, Diagnosis, and Treatment* (1989), edited by Geraldine Dawson. As these authors and others point out, the therapeutic drugs of most frequent choice are anticonvulsants, amphetamines, phenothiazines, Haldol, and megavitamins. Anticonvulsants are utilized to control epileptic seizures because of frequent occurrence of this problem in up to 40 percent of autists. The medications of widest use are those that do not cause hyperactivity, another problem often observed in autistic children. Also used to combat hyperactivity are amphetamines; concurrent with their calming effect, these drugs may make autists more teachable.

Phenothiazines and Haldol are used mostly to reduce the occurrence of aggression and self-injury seen in some autists. It is necessary to use carefully monitored doses of these drugs to prevent the occurrence of epileptic seizures and tardive dyskinesia. Along these lines, the use of large amounts of standard vitamins (megavitamins) has also been attempted, with varying effects.

A major aspect of many drug treatments concerns efforts to alter the serotonin levels in autists, as this neurotransmitter (associated with other psychiatric disorders and elevated in some autists) is thought by many to be related to autism. Such conceptualization has also led to utilization of a drug called fenfluramine, a diet drug that lowers serotonin levels in the general population. Neither consistent results nor clear interrelationships between serotonin level alteration and easing of autistic symptoms have been obtained, however; in some cases, biological intervention has had good results, but successes have been low overall.

Similarly, the psychodynamic approach has had varied success. Regrettably, no widepread and predictable results have been achieved in treating autism with any of the methods tested by the 1980's; the treatment of autistic children remains highly individualized. It has been proposed that this is partly the result of an insufficiency of facilities that provide for special learning and other needs of autists.

Perspective and Prospects

It is widely reported that autistic children, as defined by Kanner in the 1940's, were at first perceived as victims of an affective disorder brought on by their emotionally cold, very intellectual, and compulsive parents. The personality traits of these parents, it was theorized, encouraged such children to withdraw from social contact with them, and then with all other people. This conceptualization fit not only with the data available but also with the highly behavioristic bent of psychiatry and psychology at the time.

In the years that have followed, additional data—as well as conceptual changes in medicine and psychology—have led to the belief that autism, which may actually be a constellation of disorders that exhibit similar symptoms, has a biological basis that may reside in subtle brain and hormone abnormalities. These concepts have been investigated and are leading to definitive changes in the therapy used to treat individual autistic children. Although no general treatment or unifying concept of autism has developed, promising leads include modalities that utilize drugs which alter levels of serotonin and other neurotransmitters, as well as examination of patients by nuclear magnetic resonance and other new techniques useful for studying the brain and the nervous system.

The evolution of educational methodology aimed at helping autists has also been useful, aided by legislation aimed at bringing severely developmentally disabled children into the mainstream. Some cities and states have developed widespread programs for educating autistic people of all ages. Instrumental here has been the development of the National Society for Autistic Children, which has focused some of its efforts on dealing with autistic adolescents and adults.

The fruits of all these efforts are the fact that combined therapy, biological intervention, and educational techniques have helped autistic persons and their families to cope; have decreased behavior problems in autists; have enhanced the scholastic function of a number of these people; and have produced hope for autistic adults, once nearly all institutionalized.

Bibliography

American Psychiatric Association. *Diagnostic and Statistical Manual of Mental Disorders, Fourth Edition (DSM-IV)*. 4th ed. Washington, D.C.: Author, 1994. This manual contains diagnostic criteria and many other useful facts about a wide variety of mental disorders. It provides information useful to the categorization of autism and its comparison with other mental diseases with similar symptoms.

Coleman, Mary, and Christopher Gillberg. *The Biology of the Autistic Syndrome*. New York: Praeger, 1985. Goes into considerable detail at a professional, but readable, level on many aspects of autism. Includes clinical considerations; a review of pertinent literature, disease entities, and treatments within the autistic disorder; and hypotheses concerning its basis. Hundreds of references are included.

Dawson, Geraldine, ed. *Autism: Nature, Diagnosis, and Treatment*. New York: Guilford Press, 1989. Contains a wealth of useful information and many useful references. Seventeen chapters cover a broad range of topics, under the general headings perspectives on the nature of autism, neurobiological issues in autism, and new directions in autism diagnosis and treatment.

Kanner, Leo. "Autistic Disturbances of Affective Contact." *Nervous Child* 2 (1943): 217-250. This landmark article began the modern conceptualization of autism. It describes autistic behavior and differentiates autism from "childhood schizophrenia," as others had previously labeled the disorder. Kanner also identifies the good cognitive potential of autistic children, a belief no longer held.

Schopler, Eric, and Gary B. Mesibov, eds. *Autism in Adolescents and Adults*. New York: Plenum Press, 1983. This edited work distills material presented at a conference attended by national experts in the area. It covers aspects of adult and adolescent autism including perspectives and issues; linguistics; educational, recreational and vocational issues; medical requirements; and familial coping. Covers many issues that are not often described.

Van Bourgondien, Mary E., Gary B. Mesibov, and Geraldine Dawson. "Pervasive Developmental Disorders: Autism." In *The Practical Assessment and Management of Children with Disorders of Development and Learning*, edited by Mark L. Wolraich. Chicago: Year Book Medical Publishers, 1987. Succinctly and clearly describes autism, including its definition, incidence, etiologies and pathophysiologies, assessment and findings, and management. Also included are 133 useful references. Technically written, the article is nevertheless very useful to the beginning reader.

Volkmar, Fred R., ed. *Autism and Pervasive Developmental Disorders*. New York: Cambridge University Press, 1998. A volume in the Cambridge Monographs in Child and Adolescent Psychiatry. Includes bibliographical references and an index.

Waterhouse, Stella. *A Positive Approach to Autism*. Philadelphia: Jessica Kingsley, 2000. Surveys the causes and symptoms of autism, the history of its diagnosis, and its relationship to hyperactivity, attention-deficit disorder, and obsessive-compulsive disorder. The treatments discussed include Secretin, diet, tinted lenses, and auditory integration training.

Sanford S. Singer

See also:

Abnormality: Behavioral Models; Abnormality: Biomedical Models; Abnormality: Family Models; Attention-Deficit Disorder; Brain Disorders; Learning Disabilities; Schizophrenia; Schizophrenia: High-Risk Children.

AVERSION, IMPLOSION, AND SYSTEMATIC DESENSITIZATION THERAPIES

Type of psychology: Psychotherapy
Fields of study: Behavioral therapies

Aversion, implosion, and systematic desensitization therapies are effective therapy techniques based on the principles of Pavlovian conditioning. The latter two are most effective in treating fear and anxiety; aversion therapy is most often used in treating habit disorders such as cigarette smoking or drug abuse.

Principal terms

AVERSION THERAPY: a therapy that involves pairing something negative (such as electric shock) with an undesired behavior (such as drinking alcohol or smoking cigarettes)

COVERT SENSITIZATION: aversion therapy using imagination or "imagery"; for example, having an alcoholic imagine vomiting or becoming sick after sipping a favorite drink

DESENSITIZATION HIERARCHY: a list of feared situations, ordered from the least fear-producing to the most fear-producing, for use in systematic desensitization

EXPOSURE THERAPIES: therapies in which real or imagined exposure to a fear-inducing situation reduces the fear response—for example, systematic desensitization, flooding, and implosion

FLOODING: a therapy in which a phobic person imagines his or her most feared situation until fear decreases; differs from implosion in that it includes only the elements of the situation of which the patient is afraid

IMPLOSION THERAPY: a therapy in which the patient imagines his or her feared situation (plus elements from psychodynamic theory that the therapist thinks are related to the fear) until fear decreases

PAVLOVIAN CONDITIONING: learning in which two stimuli are presented one after the other, and the response to the first changes because of the response to the second stimulus

SYSTEMATIC DESENSITIZATION: an exposure therapy in which the phobic person is gradually presented with a feared object or situation

Overview

Systematic desensitization, implosion, and aversion therapy are all behavior therapy techniques that are based on Pavlovian conditioning. In Pavlovian conditioning, when one stimulus is paired with another, the response to the second stimulus can affect the response to the first. For example, if the presence of a dog is followed by a painful bite, the pain and fear that result from the bite can produce a conditioned response of fear toward dogs. An important process in Pavlovian conditioning is extinction: When the first stimulus is presented a number of times without the second stimulus, the response that became conditioned because of the pairing becomes extinguished. If, after having been bitten by a dog, a person spends time around dogs without being bitten, his or her fear of dogs will gradually disappear. Both systematic desensitization and implosion therapy use extinction to eliminate fear of an object or situation. Aversion therapy uses conditioning to attach a negative response to something pleasant but undesirable (such as cigarettes or alcohol) in order to eliminate a bad habit.

Systematic desensitization, developed and described by Joseph Wolpe in the 1950's, is one of the most well-accepted and effective psychological treatments. It is most successful when used to eliminate phobias, which are fears of specific objects or situations. The goal of systematic desensitization is to put the patient into a relaxed state and gradually present him or her with the feared situation, so that very little anxiety is actually experienced during treatment. The therapist usually presents the feared situation to the patient by having the patient vividly imagine being in the situation. Systematic desensitization starts out with the patient briefly imagining a situation that provokes very little anxiety. This is repeated until no anxiety is produced by the image; then the patient moves on to a slightly more anxiety-provoking image. This continues until the person can imagine his or her most-feared situation with little or no anxiety.

Implosion is similar to systematic desensitization in that a person repeatedly imagines a feared situation until the fear dissipates; however, if systematic desensitization is like lowering inch by inch into a cold pool, implosion is like diving headfirst into the deep end. Unlike systematic desensitization, which proceeds gradually and evokes little discomfort, implosion plunges the patient right into imagining his or her most intensely feared situation. Whereas systematic desensitization uses short image periods, implosion requires a person to keep imagining the feared situation for as long as it takes until the fear begins to decrease. Implosion works best with long sessions of imagining, sometimes two hours or more. As might be expected, implosion works faster than systematic desensitization but is more uncomfortable and is more likely to cause people not to want to try the treatment.

As originally described by Thomas Stampfl, implosion was a mixture of extinction and psychodynamic theory. In addition to imagining the situation that the patient presented as anxiety-provoking, the patient would imagine things the therapist thought were psychodynamic elements related to the anxiety, such as childhood fears or conflict. For example, the therapist might instruct the patient to imagine being rejected by his or her parents. Flooding is very similar to implosion, except that the image is restricted to the specific situations the client describes as fearful and does not include elements the therapist introduces from psychodynamic theory. Flooding is now a more commonly used therapy than implosion.

Both systematic desensitization and flooding can be done through exposure to

Russian physiologist Ivan Pavlov conducted experiments with dogs that lead him to discover several properties regarding the production of behavior. Systematic desensitization, implosion, and aversion therapy are techniques based on Pavlovian conditioning. (©The Nobel Foundation)

the actual situation, as well as through imagining it. For example, a person with a phobia of dogs could approach a real dog rather than merely imagine it. Research has shown that confronting the actual fear situation is more effective than imagining it; however, sometimes there are practical constraints. It would be too expensive, for example, for a person who is afraid of flying to buy an airplane ticket every week to become desensitized to the situation; imagining an airplane trip costs nothing. In practice, treatment usually involves a combination of imagery and actual exposure. The flight phobic might imagine being on an airplane during therapy sessions and between sessions have a homework assignment to drive to an airport and watch planes take off.

Whereas systematic desensitization and flooding try to extinguish a fear response, the goal of aversion therapy is to attach a new, aversive response to a currently positive stimulus. This is usually done to eliminate a bad habit like drinking alcohol, smoking, or overeating. During treatment, the sight, smell, or taste of alcohol, cigarettes, or a favorite food might be followed by electric shock or a nausea-inducing drug. After experiencing a number of these pairings, the person begins to develop a negative response to the previously valued stimulus. Like flooding and systematic desensitization, aversion therapy can be performed either in actuality or through the use of imagery. The use of imagery in this case is called covert sensitization; an example would be an alcoholic who imagines becoming violently ill after sipping his favorite drink.

There are a number of concerns with using aversion therapy. First, there are always ethical concerns about any treatment that involves punishment or severe discomfort. Aversive procedures are preferred only when other effective treatments are not available or if other treatments have failed. A second concern with aversion therapy is its effectiveness. The alcoholic may avoid drinking when he is hooked up to the electric shock or has taken the nausea-producing drug, but aversion therapy may not be effective in stopping him from drinking after treatment, when no punishment will be suffered.

Applications

Systematic desensitization is most useful when applied to reduce fear. The application of systematic desensitization is straightforward. The first step in systematic desensitization is to establish a list of ten to fifteen feared situations (called a desensitization hierarchy), ordered from least to most anxiety-provoking. For example, the hierarchy for a person afraid to fly might start out with making an airplane reservation a month before a scheduled trip and end with actually being in a plane while it is taking off. Creating the desensitization hierarchy is one of the most important parts of treatment and involves finding out what is most important to the phobia: It might be fear of heights, fear of crashing, or fear of being in a closed space with no escape. Two people with the same phobia may have completely different desensitization hierarchies.

When the hierarchy is complete, desensitization can begin. The therapist first gets the patient or client to relax deeply, usually by teaching a specific muscle relaxation technique the patient can practice at home. While the patient is relaxed, the therapist instructs him or her to imagine vividly the item on the hierarchy that provokes the least anxiety. This image is held for only a few seconds, so very little anxiety is felt; then the patient returns to relaxing. This is repeated until no anxiety is felt while imagining the scene; then the person imagines the next situation on the hierarchy. Over the course of a number of sessions, the patient progresses up the hierarchy until he or she can imagine the highest, most fear-provoking scene without feeling any fear. As noted earlier, treatment usually includes between-session homework assignments that involve confronting the fear situation.

Flooding is used in the treatment of similar problems. In this case, the client is immediately immersed in the most fearful situation he can imagine. The person with a fear of flying might be asked immediately to imagine being on a flight over the ocean while the plane is being jostled by severe turbulence. The phobic would continue to imagine this (sometimes for hours) until the anxiety reduces. One interesting and successful application of flooding has been in treating people with compulsive washing rituals. People with obsessive-compulsive disorder will often wash their hands until they are raw or bleeding, or will wash their clothes or clean house many hours a day, fearing unseen contamination and germs. Because of the time and energy this takes, the disorder can severely interfere with a person's life. Treatment involves having the person get his hands dirty by touching garbage or some other feared material (or put on dirty clothes), then not allowing the person to wash. This treatment is technically known as "exposure with response prevention." Because invisible germs are often what is most feared, the treatment also involves having the person imagine germs covering and infecting his skin. In severe cases, the person may need to be prevented from washing for days or even weeks before the anxiety goes away. This is obviously a very uncomfortable treatment for both patient and therapist, but it is one of the few long-lasting treatments for this disorder.

Aversion therapy is used much less frequently than systematic desensitization or flooding, and it is not used when other effective therapies are available. One relatively common application of aversion therapy is rapid smoking. In this technique a cigarette smoker will smoke one cigarette after another in a small, enclosed room until it causes a feeling of nausea. After a few sessions of this, the person begins to anticipate the nausea at the first cigarette, reducing the desire to smoke. Rapid smoking can be effective when used as one component of a treatment program and when there are no medical reasons for the person to avoid this technique.

Although aversion therapy is not used as often as systematic desensitization or flooding, an especially creative application of it, reported by Peter Lang and Barbara Melamed in 1969, illustrates its importance in certain situations. The case involved a nine-month-old infant who was failing to gain weight because he vomited his food ten minutes after every meal. No physical reason for this was found, despite three hospitalizations, many medical tests, and surgery. Several treatments were tried without success prior to beginning aversion therapy. When aversion therapy was begun, the child was in critical condition and was being fed through a nasogastric tube. Therapy involved giving an electric shock to the leg whenever the child was vomiting. Within three days, shocks no longer had to be given. His weight had increased 26 percent by the time he was discharged from the hospital thirteen days after treatment began. One year later, he was still progressing normally. This dramatic case shows that there is a place for aversion therapy in psychology.

Perspective and Prospects

Systematic desensitization, implosion, and aversion therapy were among the first psychotherapies that were developed from principles discovered in the experimental psychology laboratory. During the 1960's, they also were the first therapies to have their effectiveness confirmed in controlled experimental studies. In the 1950's, a patient seeking treatment for a phobia might have received a course of psychoanalysis, potentially stretching hundreds of sessions over several years with questionable effectiveness. By the 1970's, a patient going to a psychologist for the same problem would probably receive systematic desensitization or flooding, treatments with proven effectiveness and lasting only a handful of sessions.

On a broader level, these therapies and the research done on them ushered in a new era of scientific standards for clinical psychology. They led the behavior therapy movement, which continued to develop therapy techniques from research done in experimental psychology and to test the effectiveness of these therapies. This led to an expectation that all therapies should have proven effectiveness. These therapies, then, represent a large step forward for the importance of scientific principles in all areas of clinical psychology and psychiatry.

Although systematic desensitization and flooding are standard and effective treatments, they are not 100 percent effective. Research continues to improve their effectiveness and to reach the percentage of people who do not seem to improve with these therapies. A particularly important area of research is to figure out how best to combine these therapies with drug therapies for fear and anxiety. Regardless of where this research leads, however, systematic desensitization and flooding will remain important therapy techniques in clinical psychology.

Aversion therapy also is important as one of the original scientifically derived and tested treatments, but it has more of a checkered history. One of its initial uses in the 1960's was to "treat" homosexual males by pairing pictures of attractive men with electric shock. It should be noted that this was in an era when society had a much different attitude toward homosexuality, and gay males voluntarily approached psychologists for this treatment. Nevertheless, aversion therapy contributed to an early popular view of behavior therapy as dehumanizing behavior control that took away free will and reduced individual rights. When used thoughtfully and ethically by competent psychologists, aversion therapy has an important role in psychological treatment; however, psychologists will surely continue to debate the ethics and effectiveness of aversion therapy.

Bibliography

Bellack, Alan S., and Michel Hersen. *Behavior Modification: An Introductory Textbook*. Baltimore: Williams & Wilkins, 1977. This book, by two of the leaders in the field of behavior therapy, contains extensive chapters describing research and treatment using systematic desensitization, flooding, implosion, and aversion therapy. Since it is a textbook, it places these treatments in the context of other behavior therapy techniques.

Foa, Edna B., G. S. Steketee, and L. M. Ascher. "Systematic Desensitization." In *Handbook of Behavioral Interventions: A Clinical Guide*, edited by Alan Goldstein and Edna B. Foa. New York: John Wiley & Sons, 1980. This book was written as a "how-to" guide for the psychotherapist; however, the beginner will also find it readable and engaging. It is very well written and is filled with interesting case material and direct transcripts from therapy sessions. This is the best place to experience what systematic desensitization is actually like for the client and the therapist.

Levis, D. J. "Implementing the Techniques of Implosive Therapy." In *Handbook of Behavioral Interventions: A Clinical Guide*, edited by Alan Goldstein and Edna B. Foa. New York: John Wiley & Sons, 1980. This is another chapter from the book described above, and the positive comments above apply to this chapter as well. This book also contains an interesting chapter by Joseph Wolpe on how to gather information to plan treatment and chapters on how to apply exposure therapy to specific disorders such as agoraphobia and obsessive-compulsive disorder.

Martin, Garry, and Joseph Pear. *Behavior Modification—What It Is and How to Do It*. 6th ed. Upper Saddle River, N.J.: Prentice Hall, 1998. Offers readers personal, hands-on experience with the principles of behavior modification and their application to everyday concerns. Includes bibliographical references and an index.

Paul, Gordon L. *Insight vs. Desensitization in Psychotherapy*. Stanford, Calif.: Stanford University Press, 1966. This short book is a classic. It describes an early and very influential study that showed systematic desensitization to be superior to insight-oriented psychotherapy for treating public speaking anxiety. It was one of the first studies to evaluate therapy effectiveness and is a good illustration of how research to test the effect of therapy is done.

Scotti, Joseph R., and Luanna H. Meyer, eds. *Behavioral Intervention: Principles, Models, and Practices*. Baltimore: Paul H. Brookes, 1999. Contains twenty-four chapters written by psychologists, professors, researchers, and program administrators. Offers behavioral intervention strategies designed to resolve behavior problems in children and adults, including those associated with developmental disabilities, emotional disturbances, and chronic psychiatric disorders.

Wolpe, Joseph. *The Practice of Behavior Therapy*. 4th ed. New York: Pergamon Press, 1990. This book describes the practice of behavior therapy in detail, especially systematic desensitization. It includes chapters on aversion therapy and flooding as well as other therapy techniques and illustrates how these techniques can be extended to treat problems other than fear and anxiety.

_____. *Psychotherapy by Reciprocal Inhibition*. Stanford, Calif.: Stanford University Press, 1958. The classic book in which Wolpe introduces and advocates systematic desensitization as an alternative to psychoanalytic treatment developed by Sigmund Freud. Describes the basic principles and practice of systematic desensitization for psychiatrists of the late 1950's, who generally had no knowledge of these techniques.

Scott R. Vrana

See also:

Abnormality: Behavioral Models; Obsessive-Compulsive Disorder; Operant Conditioning Therapies; Phobias.

BED-WETTING

Type of psychology: Developmental psychology
Fields of study: Childhood and adolescent disorders; organic disorders

Bed-wetting, technically known as enuresis, is a disorder characterized by the frequent failure to maintain urinary control by a certain age. It most frequently occurs in young children, although it may continue through adulthood.

Principal terms

ANTIDIURETIC HORMONE (ADH): a naturally occurring hormone within the body, produced by the pituitary gland, that controls urine production

DIURNAL ENURESIS: the presence of enuretic episodes when the individual is awake

NOCTURNAL ENURESIS: the failure to maintain urinary control during sleep

ORGANIC ENURESIS: a type of enuresis caused by identifiable physical problems, such as diabetes

OVERLEARNING: a behavioral principle that involves the enuretic practicing the ability to maintain urinary control under more difficult circumstances than are typically present

PRIMARY ENURESIS: the presence of enuresis in an individual who has never maintained adequate urinary control

SECONDARY ENURESIS: the recurrence of enuresis in an individual who previously has maintained urinary control

Causes and Symptoms

Enuresis is a disorder characterized by an individual's repeated inability to maintain urinary control after having reached an adequate age. Although enuresis may continue into adulthood, it most frequently occurs in young children. For example, at age five, approximately 15 percent of all children are enuretic at night on a once-a-week basis. By age eighteen, however, only about 1 percent of adolescents are enuretic. Among children under the age of eleven, boys are more likely to be enuretic than girls. After age eleven, however, boys and girls have equal rates of enuresis, according to Arthur C. Houts and Hillel Abramson. It should be noted that bed-wetting by children under five years of age and occasional bed-wetting by older children are common and usually not cause for concern.

Because of the many different types of enuresis, several distinctions should be made in discussing the disorder. The first distinction involves the cause. If enuresis is the result of obvious physical causes, such as a urinary tract infection or diabetes, it is referred to as organic enuresis. Although estimates vary, fewer than 5 percent of enuretic cases are thought to be the result of physical causes. The majority of the cases of enuresis are referred to as functional enuresis because no physical cause can be identified. Even though most cases of enuresis are functional types, a medical examination always should be conducted in order to make certain that the enuresis is not the result of a physical problem.

Another important distinction to make in discussing enuresis involves the time at which it occurs. Nocturnal enuresis, bed-wetting, refers to the loss of urinary control when an individual is sleeping. Diurnal enuresis refers to the loss of urinary control during an individual's waking hours. Nocturnal enuresis occurs much more frequently than diurnal enuresis. Diurnal enuresis is more often the result of physiological causes, such as urinary tract infections.

A final useful distinction is that between primary and secondary enuresis. Primary enuretics are individuals who have never demonstrated proper bladder control. Secondary enuretics are individuals who, after a substantial period of urinary control (six months to a year), become enuretic again. Approximately 80 percent of all nocturnal enuretics have never gained proper urinary control. Although professional differences of opinion exist, most researchers believe that the causes of primary and secondary enuresis are usually the same and that children with both types respond equally well to treatment. In order to avoid possible confusion, the remainder of this section will focus on the most common type of enuresis in children: functional primary nocturnal enuresis.

Over the years, numerous explanations have been given for the occurrence of nocturnal enuresis. These various explanations can be grouped into one of three areas: emotional, biological, or learning. An emotional explanation for the occurrence of enuresis involves the idea that the enuretic is suffering from an emotional disorder that causes him or her to lose urinary control. Examples of these proposed emotional disturbances include anxiety disorders, poor impulse control, and passive-aggressive tendencies. Recent research indicates, however, that few enuretic children have emotional problems that cause their enuresis. In fact, among enuretic individuals who do have emotional disturbance, it may be that their enuresis actually causes their emotional problems. In this regard, it is widely accepted that the occurrence of enuresis lowers children's self-esteem as well as increases family conflict.

Biological deficiencies are a second suggested cause of enuresis. Approximately 50 percent of enuretic children have a parent or close family member who has had the disorder. The tendency for enuresis to occur within certain families increases the likelihood that enuresis has a biological cause. There are various biological maladies that have been proposed to cause enuresis, including sleep disorders, small bladder capacity, and a deficiency of antidiuretic hormone.

Danish researcher J. P. Norgaard and his associates investigated the potential physical causes of enuresis. At one time, it was believed by many professionals that enuretics engaged in deeper sleep than nonenuretics. For this reason, they were unable to awaken in response to the sensation of a full bladder. Norgaard's precise measurement of the time that enuretic and nonenuretic individuals spend in different levels of sleep, ranging from light to deep sleep, failed to demonstrate consistent differences between the sleep patterns of these two groups.

The second suggested biological cause, small bladder capacity, has received limited support. The best evidence suggests that while enuretics tend to have small bladder capacities, this factor alone is insufficient to account for their enuresis.

The third suggested biological cause appears to have the most scientific support. This explanation involves the failure of enuretic children to release a sufficient amount of antidiuretic hormone during their sleeping cycle. Antidiuretic hormone (ADH) is secreted by the pituitary gland and is responsible for the control of urine production. Because enuretics do not produce adequate amounts of ADH during sleep, they produce more urine, leading to a greater risk of bed-wetting.

The improper learning of bladder control is the final category of proposed causes of enuresis. This proposition rests on the notion that bladder control is a learned response and that enuretic children have not properly mastered this response. Some support for this proposition comes from the fact that mentally retarded children take longer to control their elimination functions, such as urination and defecation, than intellectually normal children. Enuresis researcher Arthur Houts has proposed that nonenuretic children may be better able to inhibit the contractions of the muscles responsible for urination; that is, while enuretic children may not have impaired muscle reflexes, they may have greater difficulty voluntarily inhibiting these muscles as compared with nonenuretic children.

Treatment and Therapy

Consistent with the large number of suggested causes of enuresis, or bed-wetting, numerous treatments have been attempted. Early "treatments" for enuresis, dating back some three thousand years, included such things as giving the child juniper berries, cypress, and beer, or having the child consume ground hedgehog. Currently, drug and behavioral therapies are the two treatments that have been utilized and studied to the greatest extent.

Among the drug therapies, imipramine was the first drug widely used in the treatment of enuresis. Imipramine has been widely prescribed in the treatment of depression for more than thirty years. In addition to its antidepressant qualities, it was observed early in its usage to stop previously enuretic patients from bed-wetting. Imipramine appears to stop bed-wetting by causing the contraction of the muscles responsible for the release of urine. Based on a review of the scientific literature, Houts and Abramson have concluded that imipramine is effective in treating about half of the children with whom it is used. Unfortunately, once the medication is withdrawn, almost all the successfully treated children return to wetting their beds.

Another medication that has shown promise in the treatment of enuresis is desmopressin (DDAVP). DDAVP is a drug administered internasally that is hypothesized to prevent enuresis by causing the kidneys to concentrate urine, thus preventing its passage into the bladder during sleep. DDAVP is completely effective in about 40 percent of the children for whom it is prescribed; however, the removal of this medication also results in a very high recurrence of bed-wetting.

Another category of enuresis treatment is behavioral therapy. Variations of behavioral therapy have been used with enuretics since the early 1900's. The "urine alarm" is at the center of the behavioral treatment approach; it is a device that typically is attached to the underwear of enuretics prior to their going to bed. When urine comes in contact with the sensors of the device, a loud noise is emitted by the alarm attached to the undershirts or pajama tops of the children. The alarm's sound is utilized in order to awaken the children and the parents at the first emission of urine. It is necessary for parents to be awakened by the alarm because initially the children may have difficulty rousing themselves when the alarm sounds. In order for the children to be sufficiently awakened, it is often necessary to have them wash their faces as a way of increasing alertness. Once the children are awake, they are instructed to void the remainder of their urine. After voiding, the children return to their bedrooms, where parents check the dampness of the bedding and, if it is sufficiently wet, change the bedding. At this point, the children put on dry underwear, reattach the sensors, and return to bed.

During the treatment process, the child and the parents record the child's progress through the use of a chart on which stars are placed when the child has a dry bed. The accumulation of a certain number of stars usually results in the child's earning a reward of his or her choice. The treatment goal is for the enuretic not to wet the bed for fourteen consecutive nights. It typically takes ten to twelve weeks before this goal is met. It is best to instruct all members of the family regarding the purpose and the exact workings of the treatment in order to avoid misunderstandings and potential frustrations during the process. The lack of parental compliance with the treatment procedures is the most frequent reason for therapy failure.

Additional components often are added to the basic behavioral treatment in order to improve therapy effectiveness. Overlearning is one of these additional components; it begins once the previously enuretic child has been dry for fourteen consecutive nights. Based on the child's age, he or she is instructed to drink a certain amount of fluid prior to going to bed. The amount of fluid is gradually increased as the child demonstrates the ability to remain dry during the night. Once the child is able to remain dry after the intake of a maximum amount of fluid (2 ounces plus 1 ounce for every year of the child's age), the procedure is stopped. Overlearning typically reduces the recurrence of bed-wetting by 50 percent as compared with the use of the standard treatment alone.

Urine retention exercises are often another procedure added to the standard behavioral treatment. These exercises involve the child drinking a certain amount of water (for example, 8 ounces) during the daytime and then telling the parents when he or she first feels the need to urinate. At this point, the child is instructed to hold the urine for a specific period of time. Upon successful completion of urine retention, the child is allowed to urinate. Over a period of days, the amount of time the child is asked to wait before urination is increased from three minutes to a maximum of forty-five minutes. The effectiveness of this procedure is based on its ability to increase the child's bladder capacity and to strengthen the muscles responsible for urine release.

Compared with drug therapy, behavior therapy is viewed by the majority of professionals as the most effective treatment for enuresis. In a review study conducted by Houts and Abramson, approximately three out of every four children treated with a behavioral treatment stopped bed-wetting after ten to twelve weeks. In contrast with the high relapse rates of drug treatments, the percentage of children who return to bed-wetting after a behavioral treatment is relatively small. As previously mentioned, this 40 percent relapse can be substantially reduced by the addition of auxiliary treatment components.

Perspective and Prospects

Enuresis is a disorder that has probably existed since the beginning of humankind. In spite of the fact that since the 1960's considerable scientific research has been conducted examining enuresis, many misconceptions continue to exist. For example, many believe that children's bed-wetting is a result of their "laziness" and not wanting to take the time to use the bathroom. This is not the case; most enuretic children desperately want to stop their bed-wetting.

Another misconception is that children will "outgrow" their bed-wetting. In fact, the yearly spontaneous remission rate for enuretic children, a measure of how many children stop wetting their beds without treatment during a year's time, is only about 15 percent. According to Houts and Abramson, on average, it takes more than three years for enuretic children to stop wetting the bed on their own. During this time, the enuretic child may develop poor self-esteem and feelings of failure and isolation.

Misconceptions also continue regarding the effectiveness of different treatments for enuresis. For example, many parents believe if they sufficiently shame or punish their child for bed-wetting that it will cease. This is not an effective approach, and it exerts a negative influence on a child's self-concept. A more humane but also ineffective treatment technique is the restriction of fluids given to the child prior to bedtime. Restricting fluids prior to bedtime is ineffective because the bladder will continue to empty even when fluids are withheld for long periods of time.

One of the reasons for these continued fallacies is the secrecy that often accompanies the disorder. The parents of enuretic children are often unwilling, because of embarrassment, to ask others, including professionals, for assistance in dealing with an enuretic child. When the parents of an enuretic child do seek guidance, they are often given advice that is ineffective in treating the problem. For this reason, better efforts are needed to educate parents and professionals who work with enuretics. In this regard, the basic message that should be delivered to parents is that enuresis is a treatable problem and that they should not be reluctant to take their child to a qualified professional for evaluation and treatment.

Bibliography

Arnold, Samuel J. *No More Bedwetting: How to Help Your Child Stay Dry.* New York: John Wiley & Sons, 1997. Helps parents and other caregivers understand what causes bed-wetting and what can be done about it. Includes bibliographical references and an index.

Azrin, Nathan H., and Victoria A. Besalel. *A Parent's Guide to Bedwetting Control.* New York: Simon & Schuster, 1979. A self-help book written for parents with enuretic children in which Nathan Azrin's "dry-bed training" is described. Azrin's treatment is based on behavioral principles; the specific procedures are discussed in terms that most nonprofessionals will understand.

Houts, Arthur C., and Hillel Abramson. "Assessment and Treatment for Functional Childhood Enuresis and Encopresis: Toward a Partnership Between Health Psychologists and Physicians." In *Child and Adolescent Disorders*, edited by

Sam B. Morgan and Theresa M. Okwumabua. Hillsdale, N.J.: Lawrence Erlbaum, 1990. Summarizes work in the field of enuresis and encopresis, an elimination disorder involving involuntary soiling. Chapter sections include the assessment, causes, and treatment of enuresis. Reviews types and effectiveness of both behavioral and medical treatments.

Houts, Arthur C., and Richard M. Liebert. *Bedwetting: A Guide for Parents and Children.* Springfield, Ill.: Charles C Thomas, 1984. Another self-help book intended for parents that outlines a treatment package for enuresis called the "full spectrum home training" system. This effective treatment approach is described in understandable terms, although the authors advise that the treatment is best conducted under professional supervision.

Maizels, Max, Barbara Keating, and Diane Rosenbaum. *Getting to Dry: How to Help Your Child Overcome Bedwetting.* Boston: Harvard Common Press, 1999. Written by medical professionals and based on the authors' own program. Helps parents end their children's bed-wetting. Includes bibliographical references and an index.

Mills, Joyce C., and Richard J. Crowley. *Sammy the Elephant and Mr. Camel.* New York: Magination Press, 1988. An illustrated book for children that presents a metaphorical story regarding enuresis. Designed to promote the self-esteem of enuretic children and to provide a useful way of discussing bed-wetting with children in a nonthreatening way.

Schaefer, Charles E. *Childhood Encopresis and Enuresis: Causes and Therapy.* New York: Van Nostrand Reinhold, 1979. Provides an overview of the suggested causes and treatment of enuresis and encopresis. Outlines the physiology of bowel and bladder functioning, examines changes in the suggested causes and treatments of the disorder across time, and reviews present treatment procedures. Useful features include diagrams of important material and a glossary of technical terms.

R. Christopher Qualls

See also:

Behavioral Family Therapy; Child and Adolescent Psychiatry; Operant Conditioning Therapies.

BEHAVIORAL ASSESSMENT AND PERSONALITY RATING SCALES

Type of psychology: Personality
Fields of study: Personality assessment

Behavioral assessment and personality rating scales are two methods of examining personality. Both use reports by the person or others of observable behavior rather than making inferences from more subjective sources to determine personality. Both approaches are much more direct than other personality assessment methods.

Principal terms

DISCRIMINATIVE STIMULUS: an event that serves as a cue or a prompt for a response
LEARNING HISTORY: a person's accumulated life experiences, which result in a unique pattern of responding to new situations
RELIABILITY: the extent to which test results are repeatable across different testing sessions
TARGET BEHAVIOR: the specific behavior that is the object of the assessment or intervention
VALIDITY: the extent to which a test actually measures what it is supposed to measure

Overview

Among the various ways of assessing human behavior are behavioral assessment and personality rating scales. These approaches to assessment arose from behavioral research, which offered explanations of human behavior that differed from traditional theories. For example, early behaviorists believed that a person's behavior was the appropriate focus for understanding the person, while other psychologists believed that behavior is only a symbolic representation of an unconscious conflict. Rating scales were developed by psychologists interested in behavioral assessment and in determining the intensity of a behavior experienced by a person. Behavioral assessment and rating scales differ from traditional assessment primarily in the philosophical underpinnings of each.

Traditional assessment approaches describe a person as having a particular trait or characteristic. For example, a person might be described as having an authority conflict or an anxious personality. In contrast, behavioral assessment describes the person's behavior in specific situations. For example, the behavioral assessment might say, "When the person is given an order by a superior, the person argues and makes sarcastic remarks." The behavioral assessment would go on to describe the consequences of arguing and talking back, which could be anything from the superior withdrawing the order to the superior punishing the person who argues.

Contemporary behavioral assessment is concerned with both internal and external events. Marvin Goldfried describes a model of behavioral assessment that includes a systematic analysis of internal and external events. Four classes of variables are assessed in this model: stimulus antecedents, organismic variables, response variables, and consequent variables. Stimulus antecedents refer to the environmental events that precede the occurrence of the target behavior. They are sometimes called discriminative stimuli, and they may be either external or internal. An example of an external event that serves as a stimulus antecedent is drinking a cup of coffee, which serves as a discriminative stimulus for lighting a cigarette. An internal event that might serve as a prompt for an emotional response is thinking about taking a test, which results in a feeling of anxiety. Both internal and external stimulus antecedents can produce behaviors that are experienced as either external (observable) or internal (unobservable).

This model of behavioral assessment includes a thorough description of organismic variables. These variables include anything that is personally relevant and could influence the response to the stimulus antecedents. Both acute and chronic medical conditions which may affect the perception of and/or response to the discriminative stimuli are noted. The influence of the person's genetic makeup is assessed when it seems relevant to the target behavior. Finally, the person's learning history is considered important in understanding the response to the antecedent stimuli. Organismic variables serve as mediators or filters between the stimulus antecedents and the responses.

Response variables are the person's behaviors in response to the stimulus antecedents and filtered through the organismic variables. The response variables are considered to be part of the triple-response system. The triple-response system requires the assessment of behavior in each of three domains: motor, physiological, and cognitive/emotional. Motor behavior refers to the observable actions of the person. Examples of motor behavior include lighting a cigarette, leaving a room, and throwing a temper tantrum. Physiological responses are unobservable behaviors that can be made observable by using specialized instruments. Heart rate is an unobservable physiological response until the person is placed on an instrument that detects and displays it. Cognitive and emotional responses are also unobservable events. The behavioral assessment of these responses requires the person to report his or her own thoughts and feelings in the presence of the stimulus antecedents.

The triple-response system is important from the perspectives of both assessment and treatment. While behaviorists have historically focused on motor behavior, it is well known that people experience physiological changes and cognitive/emotional changes concurrently with the motor behavior in the presence of the stimulus antecedents. As behavioral assessment has become more sophisticated, it has become apparent that the relative importance of the components of the triple-response system varies in different people. Thus, treatment may focus on cognition in one person because it is the most important behavior, and on physiological responses in another.

The final component of this model of behavioral assessment requires a consideration of consequent variables. The events that follow a response are the consequent variables. These variables are important in determining whether the response will be continued or discontinued. The consequences of a response also determine the strength of the response. Any consequence that leads to a reward for the person will strengthen the response it follows. Rewards may include getting something one wants (for example, studying results in a good grade on a test) or ending something that is unpleasant (for example, leaving a situation results in reduced anxiety). Consequences that do not reward the person lead to a weakening of the behavior he or she follows.

The goal of the behavioral assessment is to describe fully the problem behavior and the events that surround it. While earlier approaches tried to limit the assessment to one or two behaviors identified as problems, more recent approaches apply the assessment methodology to clusters of behaviors that may form syndromes or diagnostic categories.

A variety of approaches are used to gather the information that constitutes a behavioral assessment. Naturalistic observation is used to observe the person's behavior in the settings most germane to the behaviors of interest. These settings may include home, school, work, hospital, and others. In self-monitoring, the person observes and records each instance of the behavior of interest. Researchers use role playing and controlled observations to study the behaviors of interest while maintaining more control over the environment than is possible with naturalistic observation. Rating scales are also used to determine the intensity of the behavior under study.

"Personality" is a general term that summarizes the group of behaviors associated with a person's tendency to respond in certain ways. Most behaviorists think that personality is too general a term and that it does not provide much usable information. Nevertheless, personality is assessed in a variety of ways. One approach is to use rating scales. Rating scales assess the intensity of a particular behavior or feeling. The rating may be done by the person being rated (self-rating), by peers, by professionals, or by anyone in a position to observe the behaviors of interest.

In his classic work *Personality and Prediction: Principles of Personality Assessment* (1973), Jerry Wiggins describes one rating scale that provides a multidimensional approach to assessing personality. The semantic differential asks respondents to describe the meaning of a word on each of three scales using dichotomous adjectives to measure the dimensions of evaluation (good versus bad), potency (powerful versus weak), and activity (active versus passive). This particular approach provides information about the intensity and meaning of emotionally laden words or concepts. Other rating scales focus on the intensity to which the concept being rated is experienced.

Applications

Behavioral assessment and personality rating scales have many uses in psychology. There are three major ways of interpreting the data obtained from these assessment procedures. Client-referenced interpretation compares one performance on a task with another performance by the same person on the same task. The simplest example of this is a comparison of pretreatment and post-treatment performance on a task to see if the person improved after the intervention. There is no consideration of how other people do on the task. Criterion-referenced interpretation compares the person's performance to a previously established level of acceptable performance. Finally, norm-referenced interpretations compare an individual's performance with normative data; thus, it is possible to learn how a person compares with all others for whom norms are available. The comparison could be with everyone who has completed the task or taken the test in the normative sample, or with specific age or ethnic groups, genders, or occupational groups. Norm-referenced interpretations can be used to compare an individual with any group for which norms are available. It is up to the psychologist to ensure that the normative group used for comparison is one that is appropriate for the person being evaluated.

Behavioral assessment has been used in industrial and organizational settings. Robert P. Bush and others (1990) describe a procedure for developing a scale to assess the performance of people working in retail sales. They point out the shortage of good information about the performance of people in retail sales and the need for more research in this area. Their article describes the important role the sales force has in the success of the business and the need to measure the behavior of the sales representatives. Richard Reilly and others (1990) describe the use of a behavioral assessment procedure within the context of an assessment center. Assessment centers are established by businesses in order to simulate the tasks associated with different positions. It is assumed that superior performance in the assessment center will translate into superior performance on the job. Reilly and others demonstrated that by incorporating behavioral assessment procedures—checklists—into the assessment center procedures, the validity of the assessment center results was improved.

The clinical use of behavioral assessment procedures is quite extensive and includes both children and adults. Thomas Ollendick and Greta Francis have reviewed the use of behavioral assessment techniques in the assessment and treatment of children with phobias. These authors provide examples of how to obtain information about fears and phobias from children by asking them questions in both direct and indirect ways. A variety of rating scales are reviewed, including the Fear Survey Schedule for Children and and the Children's Manifest Anxiety Scale. The Fear Survey Schedule for Children consists of eighty items pertaining to childhood fears, which the child rates on a scale ranging from "none" to "a lot." Normative data are available for children between the ages of seven and sixteen years. It is possible to obtain information about fear of failure, fear of the unknown, fear of danger and death, and so on. The Children's Manifest Anxiety Scale measures the extent of anxiety the child feels. This scale assesses the child's anxiety in the domains of physiological responsiveness, worry/oversensitivity, and concentration. It is appropriate for children between the ages of six and eighteen years.

Other scales for children, reviewed by Larry D. Evans and Sharon Bradley-

Johnson, assess adaptive behavior. Adaptive behavior is the degree to which a child is able to cope effectively with the environment based upon the child's age. Deficits in adaptive behavior are an important part of the definition of mental retardation. These authors review several measures of adaptive behavior that are completed by teachers, caregivers, or psychologists. Comparisons are made with existing scales assessing adaptive behavior. Rating scales are used to measure various behaviors in adolescents and children. In addition to the behaviors mentioned above, there are rating scales for attention and distractibility, autism, and various psychiatric syndromes.

Randall Morrison describes a variety of rating scales that assess adult psychopathology. These include scales of schizophrenic symptoms that are completed by the psychologist interviewing and observing the person suspected of having schizophrenia. A scale of global adjustment is also reviewed by Morrison. This scale is a 100-point rating scale that is useful with a wide variety of psychiatric patients. It focuses on the extent to which the person has coped effectively with environmental events during the past year. According to Morrison, it has some value in predicting how well a person will cope after treatment, as well as in assessing the effectiveness of the treatment.

There are many rating scales for children, adolescents, and adults. They assess a wide range of behaviors and vary in the degree to which they have been constructed with attention to the standards for test development and the compilation of appropriate norms.

Perspective and Prospects

The history of psychological assessment is replete with examples of attempts to measure the characteristics and traits of people. These traits and characteristics are defined as underlying psychological processes that are pervasive aspects of personality. In fact, they define the personality for many psychologists. Traditional approaches to psychotherapy try to identify the traits in order to develop a therapeutic strategy that will reveal the unconscious conflicts.

Unlike traditional approaches to psychological assessment and psychotherapy, behavioral assessment arose from the need of behavior therapists to describe more completely the events surrounding the problem behavior. The history of behavior therapy is one of defining a target behavior and designing a program to change the behavior. As behavior therapy developed and became more sophisticated, it became apparent that more information was needed to identify the antecedent stimuli, the organismic filters that were operating, which aspect of the triple-response system was relevant, and what the consequences of the target behavior were. In response to that need, behavioral assessment was developed. Initially, behavioral assessment was rather straightforward and did not bother much with the procedures of psychological test construction since the process itself was one of observing behavior rather than making inferences about behavior from test responses. As behavioral assessment has matured, it has become more concerned with meeting the standards of test construction applied to other assessment methods and has become more sophisticated and complex.

Behavioral assessment is used to measure clusters of behaviors and syndromes rather than merely isolated problem behaviors. More attention is paid to the extent to which standards of validity and reliability are met. Psychologists are putting behavioral assessment to the test of demonstrating its worth as an assessment procedure: It must add something to the understanding of the person being assessed in order to justify its use. The challenge is being met, and behavioral assessment continues to provide valuable information about the person being assessed. Information obtained is useful in determining the extent to which certain behaviors are problems. Other information is used in determining the personality of the individual, with all the attendant traits and characteristics.

Bibliography
Bellack, Alan S., Michel Hersen, and Alan E. Kazdin, eds. *International Handbook of Behavior Modification and Therapy*. 2d ed. New York: Perseus, 1990. Provides a good introduction to behavioral assessment.
Bush, Robert P., Alan J. Bush, David J. Ortinau, and Joseph F. Hair, Jr. "Developing a Behavior-Based Scale to Assess Retail Salesperson Performance." *Journal of Retailing* 66, no. 1 (1990): 119-136. A good article describing the development of a rating scale of salesperson performance. An example of the scale content is provided.
Evans, Larry D., and Sharon Bradley-Johnson. "A Review of Recently Developed Measures of Adaptive Behavior." *Psychology in the Schools* 25, no. 3 (1988): 276-287. A thorough review of six rating scales of adaptive behavior. These are compared with older scales that have been in use for a number of years.
Haynes, Stephen N. "The Changing Nature of Behavioral Assessment." In *Behavioral Assessment: A Practical Handbook*, edited by Alan S. Bellack and Michel Hersen. 4th ed. Boston: Allyn & Bacon, 1998. This chapter is a good review of the principles associated with behavioral assessment, which are put in both historical and methodological contexts. The book is a thorough description of behavioral assessment and how it is used in various settings.
Haynes, Stephen N., and William Hayes O'Brien. *Principles and Practice of Behavioral Assessment*. New York: Kluwer Academic/Plenum, 2000. Addresses the basic concepts, applications, and goals of behavioral assessment. Includes bibliographical references and indexes.
Kanfer, Frederick H., and W. Robert Nay. "Behavioral Assessment." In *Contemporary Behavior Therapy: Conceptual and Empirical Foundations*, edited by G. Terence Wilson and Cyril M. Franks. New York: Guilford Press, 1982. A well-written chapter that provides a detailed description of the procedure of behavioral assessment. A fairly advanced description in the context of a presentation of behavior therapy.
Ollendick, Thomas H., and Greta Francis. "Behavioral Assessment and Treatment of Childhood Phobias." *Behavior Modification* 12, no. 2 (1988): 165-204. A very informative review of the normal aspects of fear and the problems associated with abnormal fear. Children's fears and assessment devices for children are the focus of this article.

Phares, E. Jerry, and Timothy J. Trull. *Clinical Psychology: Concepts, Methods, and Profession.* 5th ed. Pacific Grove, Calif.: Brooks/Cole, 1997. Includes a chapter on behavioral assessment within the context of a more comprehensive description of the duties of clinical psychologists.

Reilly, Richard R., Sarah Henry, and James W. Smither. "An Examination of the Effects of Using Behavior Checklists on the Construct Validity of Assessment Center Dimensions." *Personnel Psychology* 43, no. 1 (1990): 71-84. A technical description of a study testing the value of a behavioral assessment procedure in the assessment center.

Segal, Daniel L., and S. Bunny Falk. "Structured Interviews and Rating Scales." In *Behavioral Assessment: A Practical Handbook,* edited by Alan S. Bellack and Michel Hersen. 4th ed. Boston: Allyn & Bacon, 1998. Describes the use of interviews and rating scales in assessing personality. Clearly written; includes examples of both interviews and rating scales, with references.

James T. Trent

See also:

Abnormality: Behavioral Models; Addictive Personality and Behaviors; Antisocial Personality; Behavioral Family Therapy; Borderline, Histrionic, and Narcissistic Personalities; Codependent Personality; Personality: Psychophysiological Measures; Phobias; Projective Personality Traits; Type A Behavior Pattern.

BEHAVIORAL FAMILY THERAPY

Type of psychology: Psychotherapy
Fields of study: Behavioral therapies; group and family therapies

Behavioral family therapy is a type of psychotherapy that applies the principles of learning theory to the treatment of family problems. It is most frequently used to treat parent-child problems, with the parents being taught to apply behavioral techniques in order to correct their children's misbehavior.

Principal terms

CIRCULAR CAUSALITY: the concept that behavior occurs as the result of many factors and circumstances, not as the product of a simple, cause-and-effect relationship

CLASSICAL CONDITIONING: the process by which new behavior becomes more likely to recur because it has been paired with old behavior that has been positively reinforced

CONTINGENCY MANAGEMENT: the providing and removing of positive rewards in accordance with whether the individual being treated engages in the expected behavior

LINEAR CAUSALITY: the concept that a specific action happens as the direct result of the occurrence of another action (simple cause and effect)

OPERANT CONDITIONING: the process by which behavior is made to occur at a faster rate because a specific action is followed by positive reinforcement

POSITIVE REINFORCEMENT: the rewarding consequences that follow a behavior, which increase the rate at which the behavior will recur

RESPONSE COST: negative consequences that follow the commission of an undesired behavior, decreasing the rate at which the misbehavior will recur

Overview

Behavioral family therapy is a type of psychotherapy that is used to treat families in which one or more family members are exhibiting behavior problems. Behavioral therapy was employed originally in the treatment of individual disorders such as phobias (irrational fears). Behavioral family therapy represents an extension of the use of behavioral techniques from the treatment of individual problems to the treatment of family problems. The most common problems treated by behavioral family therapy are parent-child conflicts; however, the principles of this type of therapy have been used to treat other familial difficulties, including marital and sexual problems.

The principles of learning theory underlie the theory and practice of behavioral family therapy. Learning theory was developed through laboratory experimentation largely begun by Ivan Pavlov and Edward L. Thorndike during the early 1900's. Pavlov was a Russian physiologist interested in the digestive processes of dogs. In the process of his experimentation, he discovered several properties regarding the production of behavior which have become embodied in the theory of classical conditioning. Pavlov observed that his dogs began to salivate when he entered their pens because they associated his presence (new behavior) with their being fed (previously reinforced old behavior). From this observation and additional experimentation, Pavlov concluded that a new behavior which is regularly paired with an old behavior acquires the same rewarding or punishing qualities that the old behavior had. That is, new actions become conditioned to produce the same responses as the previously reinforced or punished actions.

Another component of learning theory was discovered by Thorndike. Thorndike observed that actions followed closely by rewards were more likely to recur than those not followed by rewards. Similarly, he observed that actions followed closely by punishment were less likely to recur. Thorndike explained these observations on the basis of the law of effect. The law of effect holds that behavior closely followed by a response will be more or less likely to recur depending on whether the response is reinforcing (rewarding) or punishing. Building on the observations of Thorndike, B. F. Skinner developed the theory of operant conditioning in the 1930's. Operant conditioning is the process by which behavior is made to occur at a faster rate when a specific behavior is followed by positive reinforcement. An example that Skinner used in demonstrating operant conditioning involved placing a rat in a box with different levers. When the rat accidentally pushed a predesignated lever, it was given a food pellet. As predicted by operant conditioning, the rat subsequently increased its pushing of the lever which provided it with food.

The principles of classical and operant conditioning serve to form the foundation of learning theory. Although initially derived from animal experiments, learning theory also was applied to humans. Psychologists who advocated learning theory began to demonstrate that all behavior, whether socially appropriate or inappropriate, occurred because it was either classically or operantly conditioned. John B. Watson, a psychologist of the early twentieth century, illustrated this by producing a fear of rats in an infant named Albert by repeatedly making a loud noise when a rat was presented to Albert. After a number of pairings of the loud noise with the rat, Albert began to show fear when the rat was presented.

In addition to demonstrating how inappropriate behavior was caused, behavioral psychologists began to show how learning theory could be used to treat people with psychological disorders. Joseph Wolpe, a pioneer in the use of behavioral treatment during the 1950's, showed how phobias could be alleviated by using learning principles in a procedure termed systematic desensitization. Systematic desensitization involves three basic steps: teaching the phobic individual how to relax; having the client create a list of images of the feared object (for example, snakes), from least to most feared; and repeatedly exposing the client to the feared object in graduated degrees, from least to most feared images, while the individual is in a relaxed state. This procedure has been shown to be very effective in the treatment of phobias.

Behavioral family therapy makes the same assumptions regarding the causes of both individual and family problems. For example, consider the fictional case of the Williams family, who came to treatment because their seven-year-old son,

John, refused to sleep in his own bed at night. In attempting to explain John's behavior, a behaviorally oriented psychologist would seek to find out what positive reinforcement John was receiving in response to his refusal to stay in his own bed. It may be that when John was younger his parents allowed him to sleep with them, thus reinforcing his behavior by giving him the attention he desired. Now that John

Edward L. Thorndike proposed the law of effect, which holds that behavior closely followed by a response will be more or less likely to recur depending on whether the response is reinforcing (rewarding) or punishing. (Library of Congress)

is seven, however, his parents believe that he needs to sleep in his own bed, but John continues to want to sleep with his parents because he has been reinforced by being allowed to sleep with them for many years. This case provides a clinical example of operant conditioning in that John's behavior, because it was repeatedly followed by positive reinforcement, was resistant to change.

Applications
Behavioral family therapy is a treatment approach that includes the following four steps: problem assessment, family (parent) education, specific treatment design, and treatment goal evaluation. It begins with a thorough assessment of the presenting family problem. This assessment process involves gathering the following information from the family: what circumstances immediately precede the problem behavior; how family members react to the exhibition of the client's problem behavior; how frequently the misbehavior occurs; and how intense the misbehavior is. Behavioral family therapy differs from individual behavior therapy in that all family members are typically involved in the assessment process. As a part of the assessment process, the behavioral family therapist often observes the way in which the family handles the presenting problem. This observation is conducted in order to obtain firsthand information regarding ways the family may be unknowingly reinforcing the problem or otherwise poorly handling the client's misbehavior.

Following the assessment, the behavioral family therapist, with input from family members, establishes treatment goals. These treatment goals should be operationalized; that is, they should be specifically stated in order that they may be easily observed and measured. In the example of John, the boy who refused to sleep in his own bed, an operationalized treatment goal would be as follows: "John will be able to sleep from 9:00 P.M.: to 6:00 A.M.: in his own bed without interrupting his parents during the night."

Once treatment goals have been operationalized, the next stage involves designing an intervention to correct the behavioral problem. The treatment procedure follows from the basic learning principles previously discussed. In cases involving parent-child problems, the behavioral family therapist educates the parents in learning theory principles as they apply to the treatment of behavioral problems. There are three basic learning principles that are explained to the child's parents. First, positive reinforcement should be withdrawn from the unwanted behavior. For example, a parent who meets the demands of a screaming preschooler who throws a temper tantrum in the checkout line of the grocery store because he or she wants a piece of candy is unwittingly reinforcing the child's screaming behavior. "Time-out" is one procedure used to remove the undesired reinforcement from a child's misbehavior. Utilizing time-out involves making a child sit in a corner or other nonreinforcing place for a specified period of time (typically, one minute for each year of the child's age).

Second, appropriate behavior that is incompatible with the undesired behavior should be positively reinforced. In the case of the screaming preschooler, this would involve rewarding him or her for acting correctly. An appropriate reinforcer in this case would be giving the child his or her choice of a candy bar if the child were quiet and cooperative during grocery shopping—behavior inconsistent with a temper tantrum. In order for positive reinforcement to have its maximum benefit, the child should be informed about what is expected of him or her and what reward he or she will receive for fulfilling these responsibilities prior to the beginning of the specific activity (for example, grocery shopping). This process is called contingency management because the promised reward is made contingent upon the child's acting in a prescribed manner. In addition, the positive reinforcement should be given as close to the completion of the appropriate behavior as possible.

Third, aversive consequences should be applied when the problem behavior recurs. That is, when the child engages in the misbehavior, he or she should consistently experience negative costs. In this regard, response cost is a useful technique because it involves taking something away or making the child do something he or she finds unrewarding as a way of making misbehavior cost him or her. For example, the preschooler who has a temper tantrum in the checkout line may have a favorite dessert, which he or she had previously selected while in the store, taken away as the cost for throwing a temper tantrum. As with positive reinforcement, response cost should be applied as quickly as possible following the misbehavior in order for it to produce its maximum effect.

Once the parents receive instruction regarding the principles of behavior therapy, they are actively involved in the process of designing a specific intervention to address their child's behavior problems. The behavioral family therapist relates to the parents as cotherapists with the hope that this approach will increase the parents' involvement in the treatment process. In relating to Mr. and Mrs. Williams as cotherapists, for example, the behavioral family therapist would have the couple design a treatment intervention to correct John's misbehavior. Following the previously described principles, the Williamses might arrive at the following approach: The couple would refuse to give in to John's demands to sleep with them; John would receive a token for each night he slept in his own bed (after earning a certain number of tokens, he could exchange them for toys); and John would be required to go to bed fifteen minutes earlier the following night for each time he asked to sleep with his parents.

Once the intervention has been implemented, the therapist, together with the parents, monitor the results of the treatment. This monitoring process involves assessing the degree to which the established treatment goals are being met. For example, in the Williamses' case, the treatment goal was to reduce the number of times that John attempted to get into bed with his parents. Therapy progress, therefore, would be measured by counting the number of times that John attempted to get into bed with his parents. Careful assessment of an intervention's results is essential in order to determine whether the intervention is accomplishing its goal.

Perspective and Prospects
The development of behavioral family therapy occurred in several stages, starting with the discovery of the principles of learning theory in the animal laboratories of Pavlov and Thorndike. These discoveries were refined by Watson and Skinner

before being applied to the treatment of individual problems, most notably by Wolpe. Gerald Patterson and Richard Stuart, beginning in the late 1960's, were among the first clinicians to apply behavioral techniques, previously utilized with individuals, to the treatment of family problems. While Patterson worked primarily with parent-child problems, Stuart extended behavioral family therapy to the treatment of marital problems.

Given the increasing prevalence of family problems, as seen by the rise in the number of divorces and cases of child abuse, the advent of behavioral family therapy has been welcomed by many therapists who treat families. The findings of a study by William Quinn and Bernard Davidson (1984) revealed the increasing use of this therapy, with more than half of all family therapists reporting the use of behavioral techniques in their family therapy. In spite of its popularity, this type of therapy has not been without its critics. For example, behavioral family therapy's explanations regarding the causes of family problems differ from those given by the advocates of other family therapies. One major difference is that behavioral family therapists are accused of taking a linear (as compared to a circular) view of causality. From a linear perspective, misbehavior occurs because A causes B and B causes C. Those who endorse a circular view of causality, however, assert that this simplistic perspective is inadequate in explaining why misbehavior occurs. Taking a circular perspective involves identifying multiple factors that may be operating at the same time in order to determine the reason for a particular misbehavior. For example, consider John's refusal to sleep in his own bed. From a linear view of causality, John's misbehavior is seen as the result of being reinforced for sleeping with his parents. According to a circular perspective, however, John's behavior may be the result of many factors, all possibly occurring together, such as his parents' marital problems or his genetic predisposition toward insecurity.

Partially in response to this criticism, attempts have been made to integrate behavioral family therapy with other types of family therapy. Another major purpose of integrative efforts is to address the resistance often encountered from families during treatment. Therapeutic resistance is a family's continued attempt to handle the presenting problem in a maladaptive manner in spite of having learned better ways. In the past, behavioral family therapists gave limited attention to dealing with family resistance; however, behavioral family therapy has attempted to improve its ability to handle resistance by incorporating some of the techniques used by other types of family therapy.

In conclusion, numerous research studies have demonstrated that behavioral family therapy is an effective treatment of family problems. One of the major strengths of behavioral family therapy is its willingness to assess objectively its effectiveness in treating family problems. Because of its emphasis on experimentation, behavioral family therapy continues to adapt by modifying its techniques to address the problems of the modern family.

Bibliography
Carr, Alan. *Family Therapy: Concepts, Process, and Practice.* New York: John Wiley & Sons, 2000. Offers a critical evaluation of the major schools of family

therapy and an integrative model for the practice of marital and family therapy.

Clark, Lynn. *The Time-Out Solution*. Chicago: Contemporary Books, 1989. Provides the general reader with an excellent overview of the major techniques used in behavioral family therapy. A good resource for parents or others interested in correcting children's misbehaviors through the use of well-tested methods.

Dangel, Richard F., and Richard A. Polster. *Teaching Child Management Skills*. New York: Pergamon Press, 1988. Although child mental health professionals were the intended audience, this book is written in such a way that most nonprofessionals will readily understand it. Chapters 2 and 3 are the most useful because they outline and well illustrate the basic behavioral techniques used in behavioral family therapy.

Falloon, Ian R. H., ed. *Handbook of Behavioral Family Therapy*. New York: Guilford Press, 1988. Provides a thorough review of the applications of behavioral family therapy; written primarily for persons familiar with behavioral therapy. Six chapters are devoted to general issues in behavioral family therapy; twelve chapters illustrate the use of its principles with families whose members have specific clinical problems.

Goldenberg, Irene, and Herbert Goldenberg. *Family Therapy: An Overview*. 5th ed. Belmont, Calif.: Wadsworth, 2000. Chronicles the history, development, training, research, and interventions of the field of family therapy. Includes case studies with transcripts of actual therapy sessions. Includes bibliographical references and an index.

Gordon, Thomas. *Parent Effectiveness Training*. Rev. ed. New York: Three Rivers Press, 2000. Written primarily for parents interested in successfully handling parent-child interactions. Contains sixteen easily understood chapters that address various topics which primarily relate to improving communication between parents and children as well as handling children's misbehavior.

Horne, Arthur M., et al. *Family Counseling and Therapy*. 3d ed. Itasca, Ill.: F. E. Peacock, 2000. An up-to-date volume on family psychotherapy. Includes bibliographies and indexes.

Robin, Arthur L., and Sharon L. Foster. *Negotiating Parent-Adolescent Conflict: A Behavioral Family Systems Approach*. New York: Guilford Press, 1989. Illustrates the integration of behavioral family therapy with other types of family therapy. Fifteen chapters are nicely divided between assessment and treatment issues. For the person already familiar with the subject.

Simon, Richard, et al., eds. *The Art of Psychotherapy: Case Studies from the Family Therapy Networker*. New York: John Wiley & Sons, 1999. A text that discusses marital and family psychotherapy. Includes case studies.

R. Christopher Qualls

See also:

Abnormality: Behavioral Models; Autism; Bed-Wetting; Child and Adolescent Psychiatry; Cognitive Behavior Therapy; Jealousy; Juvenile Delinquency; Operant Conditioning Therapies; Psychotherapy: Children; Psychotherapy: Goals and Techniques; Sibling Rivalry; Strategic Family Therapy.

BIOFEEDBACK AND RELAXATION

Type of psychology: Stress
Fields of study: Behavioral therapies; coping; stress and illness

Responses to stress by the body have traditionally been thought to be made up of involuntary reactions which are beyond the control of the individual. Some of these responses become maladaptive, and may now be brought under control by using various relaxation techniques and biofeedback.

Principal terms

AUTOGENIC PHRASES: phrases used by the therapist to help the client while relaxing and performing biofeedback (for example, "Your hands feel heavy and warm")

CLASSICAL CONDITIONING: learning that occurs by contiguously pairing two stimuli, whereby the second stimulus comes to yield a response similar to the first; traditionally thought to be successful with involuntary responses mediated by the autonomic nervous system

ELECTROENCEPHALOGRAPHY: measurement of the electrical output of the brain, which may be brought under voluntary control by biofeedback and relaxation

ELECTROMYOGRAPHY: measurement of the electrical output of muscles, which may be brought under voluntary control by biofeedback and relaxation

GALVANIC SKIN RESPONSE (GSR): a measurement of the electrical conductivity of the skin; an operational measure of anxiety which may be brought under voluntary control by biofeedback and relaxation

INSTRUMENTAL CONDITIONING: learning that occurs from reinforcing a response; traditionally thought to be successful with voluntary responses mediated by the skeletal nervous system

THERMAL RESPONSE: a measurement of the amount of blood flow to various areas of the body recorded by heat sensors; may be brought under voluntary control by biofeedback and relaxation

Overview

From the day people are born, and even before that, they are subjected to a variety of stressors from the environment around them. Each one of these exacts a certain toll on their bodies. Some stressors seem to affect individuals differently, while others seem to have a universal effect; in any case, both the mind and the body must mobilize to deal effectively with these factors. The individual is usually able to handle these problems by using various coping strategies to help alleviate the stress. The problem arises when too many stressors are present at one time or when these stressors last too long. The individual must adapt or change his or her coping strategies to return to a normal equilibrium. A coping strategy is a process which takes effort and is learned; the individual must acquire this coping skill as one acquires any skill. It must be practiced.

If the stressors are not dealt with adequately, fatigue and illness may result. In the most serious circumstances, the organism can die. Hans Selye reported on what he termed the general adaptation syndrome (GAS). As stressors affect an organism, a series of neurological and biological responses occur to protect the body. If these responses are prolonged and go unchecked, however, the body will begin to break itself down. In the first phase, the alarm phase, the body mobilizes itself. The adrenal glands enlarge, and release epinephrine (adrenaline) and steroids to cope. After a while, the body adapts and seems to be normal; this is the resistance stage. In fact, the body is not normal. It is very vulnerable to further stress, and, if subjected to additional stressors, it will enter the third stage, exhaustion. The organism can then become extremely sick or die.

It becomes essential for the individual to adopt a successful coping strategy in order to avert this progression of events. Two such techniques will be discussed here. Biofeedback is a procedure whereby the individual is given information about how a variety of body responses are reacting in various circumstances. The individual is generally unaware of these reactions, but biofeedback technology allows the individual to monitor them and eventually bring them under control. Autonomic, visceral responses to stress have traditionally been thought to be involuntary and automatic. Biofeedback is a technique aimed at gaining control over these reactions. Voluntary responses can affect these visceral responses, and this fact complicates the ultimate effectiveness of biofeedback.

Neal E. Miller was one of the early pioneers in the field. His work has been applied to the control of a wide variety of stress-related problems through the use of biofeedback. The control of what have been termed psychosomatic problems has been accomplished using Miller's assumptions. Individuals have learned to control blood pressure, heart rate, muscle spasms, headaches, and myriad other ailments through biofeedback techniques.

Miller believed that these responses to stress can be changed through the use of instrumental conditioning and reinforcement. When a machine makes this information available to a person, the responses can be reinforced (or they can reinforce themselves) when a therapeutic change occurs. The same principle is at work when an experimental rat learns to press a bar for food.

Another coping strategy which can be used to deal with stressors is the adoption of one of a variety of relaxation procedures. As odd as it may sound to some, people must learn to relax in many situations, and this takes practice. Relaxation techniques are often used in conjunction with biofeedback, which sometimes makes it difficult to determine which of the two procedures is responsible for the changes that occur and to what degree they are acting in relationship to each other.

There are several relaxation techniques, and different techniques are successful for different individuals. One of the most widely used techniques is progressive muscle relaxation, proposed by Edmund Jacobson. The individual is instructed to tense a particular muscle group and hold it for several seconds, paying attention to the feelings associated with this state. Then the individual is told to relax the muscle group and is asked to concentrate on the different feelings while the muscle is relaxed. The major muscle groups of the body are put through this procedure. Ultimately, the individual is able to reproduce the relaxed sensations when he or she feels tense.

Rhythmic breathing techniques are also used for relaxation in order to combat stress. The person learns to inhale through the nose to the count of three and exhale through the mouth to the count of five. Between each breath is a count of two. The breathing should be with the stomach as much as possible, as opposed to the chest. Meditation, another relaxation technique that often incorporates rhythmic breathing, may require that the person either visualize an object or repeat a word or phrase with each breath. This prevents the person's mind from wandering to the anxiety-provoking stimuli.

Applications

One of the experiments that pioneered the use of biofeedback in a clinical setting was conducted by Neal Miller using white rats. Miller wanted to demonstrate that the animal was able to learn to increase the blood flow to one ear by dilating the capillaries in the ear. He needed to ensure that the animal was not using a skeletal response ("cheating") to influence this response. For example, a human can accomplish this task by covering the ear with the palm of the hand for a period of time. The question Miller was asking was, could this be done without a skeletal response? Miller administered the drug curare to the rat to incapacitate the skeletal nervous system and kept the animal alive by using an artificial respirator. He attached a sensitive thermometer, which was able to detect slight changes in temperature caused by differential blood flow, to the animal's ear. When a slight increase in temperature was detected, the message was sent to a computer, which delivered an electrical reinforcement to the brain of the subject. This represents the same mechanism which establishes the bar-pressing response in a white rat: operant conditioning. The experiment was successful.

One of the first applications of this experiment to humans came when a woman who had suffered paralysis in an automobile accident was unable even to remain in a sitting position without her blood pressure dropping to dangerous levels. Miller and his staff assembled a biofeedback device which allowed the woman to determine the nature of her blood pressure from moment to moment. No external reinforcement (such as food) was necessary in this case; knowing that the response was therapeutic was reinforcement enough. The woman was able to learn how to raise and lower her blood pressure at will through the use of the biofeedback device. By learning to control her blood pressure (and eventually wean herself off the biofeedback machine), she was able to become more productive and do some tasks on her own.

The concept of biofeedback, then, can be generalized to learning to control any of the visceral responses to accomplish clinically a healthier state. As society's stressors increase, many of the visceral responses can cause clinical problems. Among the most common are headache symptoms: muscular (tension) and vascular (migraine). By using electromyography (EMG) biofeedback, a person can monitor the muscle tension in the forehead and learn to decrease the tension by obtaining constant auditory feedback. By the same token, thermal biofeedback machines can monitor blood flow to the cranial arteries and can teach a person how to reduce the volume of blood to this area and redirect it to the periphery of the body. This often helps other problems associated with migraines such as Raynaud disease, in which the extremities are cold because of lack of blood flow.

The galvanic skin response (GSR) is one of the most common responses used to measure the degree of anxiety and stress. In fact, it is one of the measures in a lie detector, which assumes that when one lies, anxiety increases automatically. The GSR can be brought under control using biofeedback methods. For example, if a pregnant woman is anxious about the upcoming birth, she can receive constant feedback from a GSR biofeedback apparatus and learn to lower the GSR by attending to the machine. As she learns to accomplish this, she can apply these skills on her own and eventually use them during the birth process.

Yet another application of biofeedback in coping with stress has been the use of the technique in controlling brain waves through electroencephalography (EEG) biofeedback. It is thought that the brain's alpha wave (eight to thirteen cycles per second) represents the resting brain. By placing electrodes on the scalp and having a machine monitor the amount of alpha activity from moment to moment, a person can learn to increase alpha production and reduce stress by doing so.

Prior to and during biofeedback training, various relaxation techniques are employed to help with the procedure. This actually leads to an academic problem: Which technique is working and to what degree? The use of Jacobson's progressive muscle relaxation with asthmatic children and adults helped to reduce the frequency and severity of the incidents. One of the common problems that arises from increased stress is insomnia. The use of Jacobson's technique has proved useful in combating this problem in several documented cases. Autogenic phrases are often employed with biofeedback, as well. For muscular disorders, phrases such as "My leg is heavy" can be used. For cardiac problems, a common phrase is "My heartbeat is calm and regular."

Meditation has been shown to produce an increase in alpha-wave activity, as has biofeedback. Practitioners of yoga focus on a phrase or word (a mantra) and exclude everything else. The nervous system shows evidence of reduced stress and arousal. A variety of businesses have used meditation programs for their employees and have realized improved health and productivity from them.

Perspective and Prospects

The ability to gain voluntary control over the autonomic nervous system responses in order to help cope with stressors is a valuable skill. The area of biofeedback has important implications for both the theoretical and clinical sides of the field of psychology. First, it is traditionally thought that classical conditioning deals with the "involuntary" nervous system responses, while instrumental conditioning mediates the "voluntary" skeletal responses. Since biofeedback deals with visceral autonomic nervous system reactions and is basically a form of instrumental conditioning, this traditional dichotomy must be brought into question. Biofeedback, a phenomenon of the second half of the twentieth century, is still in its infancy. Biofeedback techniques ultimately aim at bringing unconscious, previously uncontrolled body responses into conscious awareness in order to bring them under control therapeutically. It is a wonderful example of the interaction of the mind and body and the complicated dilemma of how and when they interact.

Biofeedback therapy invariably uses other therapies, such as relaxation and meditation, along with it in the clinical setting. This naturally raises the question of whether, and to what degree, biofeedback, relaxation, meditation, and their interactions are responsible for changes in the condition of the client. Many experiments are being conducted to determine the answers to these questions, and the results are equivocal. It is also important to know what type of feedback, what type of feedback schedule, and what additional therapies are indicated for various problems.

The control of stress-related disorders without drugs or surgery is obviously a desirable goal, and biofeedback, relaxation, and meditation seem to hold some promise in this field for certain types of cases. The applications seem extensive. Hypertension, insomnia, sexual dysfunction, cardiac arrhythmias, asthma, and gastrointestinal disorders are but a few of the problems which have been tackled so far, with varying degrees of success. The jury is still out concerning the degree of success of biofeedback and relaxation as coping strategies for dealing with stress. The results so far, however, are promising and are spawning much research.

Bibliography

Birbaumer, Niels, and H. D. Kimmel, eds. *Biofeedback and Self-Regulation.* Hillsdale, N.J.: Lawrence Erlbaum, 1979. Reviews the theoretical and clinical issues surrounding biofeedback in particular, as well as relaxation techniques. Clinical examples of headache control, heart rate control, and brain wave control are among the many cases described. Complete indexes, tables, and graphs are included in this excellent book.

D'Zurilla, Thomas J., and Arthur M. Nezu. *Problem-Solving Therapy: A Social Competence Approach to Clinical Intervention.* 2d ed. New York: Springer, 1999. An introduction and guide for therapists and counselors in the mental health professions to the approach as a reliable clinical treatment, health maintenance strategy, and prevention program.

Jacobson, Edmund. *Modern Treatment of Tense Patients.* Springfield, Ill.: Charles C Thomas, 1970. A complete book on the theory and practice of progressive muscle relaxation, including the step-by-step method, instructions, and case studies. Illustrations of each step are included at the end of the book.

_____. *Tension in Medicine.* Springfield, Ill.: Charles C Thomas, 1967. A wonderful description of progressive muscle relaxation, with a variety of case studies illustrating its application and success. Reports from a number of clinicians are included, with clear graphs illustrating the results.

Olton, David S., and Aaron R. Noonberg. *Biofeedback: Clinical Application in Behavioral Medicine.* Englewood Cliffs, N.J.: Prentice-Hall, 1980. An excellent review of the theory behind biofeedback and relaxation, along with numerous chapters on clinical applications of coping with stress-related problems. Precise tables and illustrations are provided.

Robbins, Jim. *A Symphony in the Brain*. New York: Atlantic Monthly Press, 2000. Traces the development of neurofeedback. Offers case studies, scientific explanations, and dramatic personal accounts. Includes bibliographical references and an index.

Soroka, George E. *Twelve Steps to BioFeedback*. Demarest, N.J.: Ariel Starr Productions, 1998. A self-help book that provides ways of promoting relaxation in stressful situations.

Jonathan Kahane

See also:

Cognitive Behavior Therapy; Operant Conditioning Therapies; Psychosomatic Disorders; Stress; Stress: Coping Strategies; Type A Behavior Pattern.

BORDERLINE, HISTRIONIC, AND NARCISSISTIC PERSONALITIES

Type of psychology: Psychopathology
Fields of study: Personality assessment; personality disorders; personality theory

Borderline, histrionic, and narcissistic personalities are three of the major personality disorders in the diagnostic system. The diagnosis of these disorders is highly controversial, and their causes are largely unknown.

Principal terms

ANTISOCIAL PERSONALITY: a personality disorder characterized by a history of chronic criminal and otherwise irresponsible behavior

EGO-SYNTONIC: perceived as acceptable to the person and as consistent with one's self-image

ENTITLEMENT: the expectation of special or unusually favorable treatment by others, which is commonly seen among narcissistic personalities

HETEROGENEITY: differences among individuals given the same diagnosis

OBJECT RELATIONS THEORY: a personality theory that focuses upon the relations among internalized persons and objects and their implications for personality development

PERSONALITY DISORDER: a disorder in which personality traits are rigid and maladaptive and produce considerable impairment or distress for the individual

SCHIZOPHRENIA: a condition characterized by severe abnormalities in thinking processes

SOMATIZATION DISORDER: a condition characterized by multiple physical symptoms lacking any demonstrated medical basis

VALIDITY: the extent to which a psychological test measures what it is intended to measure

Causes and Symptoms

Of all psychiatric disorders, the group of conditions that psychologists call personality disorders is perhaps the most puzzling and controversial. According to most researchers, personality disorders can be viewed as conditions in which personality traits are rigid and maladaptive and cause considerable impairment or distress for the individual. Some of these disorders are notable for the psychological pain that they cause the person afflicted with them. Others, however, are more notable for the psychological pain that they cause others. Borderline, histrionic, and narcissistic personality disorders fall primarily into this latter group. This is not to imply that individuals with these disorders do not suffer: Many such persons experience chronic feelings of depression, emptiness, and anger. Nevertheless, what distinguishes people with these disorders from the majority of other psychiatric patients is the distress that they inflict upon others, especially those close to them.

These three disorders share at least two important features. First, individuals with these disorders tend to view their problems as ego-syntonic—that is, as acceptable and as consistent with their self-image. As a result, such individuals tend to view their difficulties in life as stemming primarily from others' actions, rather than from their own. Second, the behavior of individuals with these disorders tends to be impulsive, unpredictable, and dramatic. Given the similarities among these three disorders, perhaps it is not surprising that they overlap substantially within individuals; a person with one of these disorders is likely to have features of one or both of the other two. Nevertheless, despite their commonalities, these disorders possess a number of important characteristics that differentiate them from one another; these are outlined below.

Individuals with borderline personality share one major feature: instability. More specifically, borderline personality, which is generally found among women, is characterized by instability in sense of self, relationships with others, and mood. In fact, borderline personalities have been described as possessing a kind of "stable instability"—their instability seems an ingrained part of their personality structure.

One of the central features of borderline personality is confusion with regard to identity. Borderline personalities often express concerns such as "I don't really know who I am," and they may be uncertain regarding what types of friends to have, values to hold, or career aspirations to pursue. In many cases, borderline personalities appear to rely heavily upon others to define their identity. Perhaps as a consequence, they often go to great lengths to avoid abandonment and frequently feel "empty" or bored, especially when alone.

Borderline personalities tend to be impulsive individuals who may excessively eat, drink alcohol, spend money, or have sex. In addition, they often explode angrily in response to minor provocations. Suicide attempts, threats, and gestures are common, as is self-mutilating behavior such as wrist-slashing. The relationships of borderline personalities frequently alternate between the extremes of overidealization and devaluation: Friends or lovers are initially worshiped or "placed on a pedestal" but abruptly fall from grace when they are perceived as having erred. Borderline personalities also tend to be moody individuals whose emotions shift radically with little or no warning.

Histrionic personalities who, like borderline personalities, tend be to female, are characterized by excessive emotionality and attention-seeking. Such persons tend to be extremely dramatic and often seem to be playing the part of an actor or actress—hence the term "histrionic." They frequently express their emotions with great intensity; for example, they may cry uncontrollably after a mild rebuff or passionately hug individuals they have just met.

Histrionic personalities tend to enjoy "being in the spotlight" greatly and are often uncomfortable when they are not being showered with adoration or praise. Moreover, they are often sexually seductive individuals who behave flirtatiously and are overconcerned with their dress and appearance. Histrionic personalities are often vain and self-centered individuals who have difficulty postponing gratification. Finally, many histrionic personalities have been described as possessing a style of speech that is vague and impressionistic: For example, they may make frequent use of hyperbolic statements such as "Oh, it was just terrible," or "She is absolutely wonderful."

Finally, narcissistic personalities are characterized by egocentricity, lack of empathy, and oversensitivity to negative evaluation by others. (In contrast with borderline and histrionic personalities, little is known about the sex ratio of this disorder.) Narcissistic personalities often have an inordinate sense of self-importance and may be surprised or indignant when others fail to appreciate their "unique" qualities. In addition, they are often consumed with fantasies of greatness, power, or meeting the perfect romantic partner.

Such individuals commonly possess "entitlements," that is, expectations of unusually favorable treatment by others. For example, they may believe that certain rules or norms, such as having to wait one's turn in line or having to pay taxes, should not apply to them. Narcissistic personalities often appear to have little empathy; for example, they may become enraged when a friend who is very ill cancels a date. In addition, they often seem quite willing to "step on others' toes" to accomplish their goals. Finally, narcissistic personalities often tend to be very envious of other peoples' successes or accomplishments.

Unfortunately, there has been relatively little research done on these three disorders. In part, this lack is probably a result of the fact that these disorders, especially borderline and narcissistic personality disorders, are relatively new additions to the diagnostic nomenclature. In addition, many of the symptoms of these disorders (for example, identity disturbance) are latent constructs that are difficult to measure with adequate reliability—that is, with consistency. Typically, the reliability of a psychiatric diagnosis is indexed by agreement among different observers. By this standard, the reliability of these disorders, as well as that of most personality disorders, is among the lowest of all psychiatric conditions: Two clinicians interviewing the same patient will often disagree on whether that patient has one of these disorders. This is important because reliability sets an upper limit upon validity—the extent to which a measure (in this case, a diagnosis) measures what it is intended to measure. As cited below, the validity of these disorders has been a major bone of contention among researchers.

Of the three disorders, borderline personality has been probably the most extensively researched. One question that has occupied many researchers is whether borderline personality is a single disorder or a group of disorders. Psychologist Harrison Pope and his colleagues found that borderline personality seems to identify a rather heterogeneous group of patients—that is, there appear to be a number of important differences among individuals given a borderline diagnosis. Specifically, Pope found that some patients with borderline personality suffer from depression, whereas others suffer from a variety of personality disorders. Moreover, Pope reported that borderline personalities were difficult to distinguish from other personality-disordered patients with respect to variables such as outcome and family history of psychiatric illness. Similarly, Hagop Akiskal has found that borderline personality overlaps substantially with a variety of psychiatric conditions, especially depression and antisocial personality, and personality disorder characterized by a history of chronic criminal and otherwise irresponsible behavior. Akiskal also reported that a subset of borderline patients appears to suffer from a mild from of schizophrenia, a condition characterized by severe abnormalities in thinking processes.

What are the implications of these findings? Although more research is necessary, it appears that patients given a borderline personality diagnosis do not all suffer from the same major underlying problem. Instead, these patients seem to have a variety of underlying pathologies that are superficially similar to one another. A major challenge for future researchers will be to isolate subgroups of borderline patients who are relatively homogeneous in terms of factors such as family history, outcome, and response to treatment.

If the nature of borderline personality is unclear, the picture is perhaps even fuzzier for histrionic and narcissistic personalities. There has been relatively little research on histrionic personality, although several investigators have found that, like borderline personality, it overlaps substantially with antisocial personality. In addition, there is good evidence that histrionic personalities are at substantially increased risk for somatization disorder, a condition characterized by multiple physical symptoms lacking any demonstrated medical basis. The reasons for this association, however, are unknown.

Similarly, little is known about narcissistic personalities, although it has been reported that such individuals are prone to episodes of depressed mood, especially in middle age. These episodes may occur when these individuals perceive that others no longer admire or idolize them. Some authors, including Christopher Lasch, have argued that narcissistic personality may be increasing in prevalence in Western culture, perhaps as a result of social changes such as an increased emphasis upon individualism, success, and hedonism. Nevertheless, systematic research is not yet available to corroborate this conjecture.

Although the causes of these three disorders are largely unknown, it seems likely that genetic factors play at least some role. Auke Tellegen and his colleagues have found that genetic factors strongly influence traits such as impulsivity, risk-taking, and the propensity to experience negative emotions, all of which are commonly found among individuals with these three disorders. Nevertheless, it also seems clear that environmental factors play an important role. For example, there is some evidence that borderline patients have an elevated rate of physical and sexual abuse in childhood. Although genetic factors cannot be excluded as a mediator of this association, it seems plausible that such abuse might lead predisposed individuals to develop problems such as identity disturbance, chronic anger, and other symptoms common to borderline personalities.

Treatment and Therapy

Almost nothing is known about the treatment of these disorders. There is evidence, however, that a subset of borderline personalities may benefit from medications used to treat depression. This is consistent with the possibility that at least some of these patients have an underlying form of depression. Surprisingly, there have been virtually no systematic studies of the effectiveness of psychotherapy for any of these three conditions, although many individuals with these disorders have undergone psychotherapy for decades.

As noted, these three conditions overlap substantially within individuals. A number of researchers have argued that this overlap calls into question the validity of these conditions, because psychiatric disorders have traditionally been viewed as fairly distinct categories that do not blend into one another extensively. Thus, perhaps the primary challenge for researchers in this area will be to determine whether these three diagnoses actually represent three different conditions or instead represent variants of one underlying disorder.

Perspective and Prospects

The term "borderline personality" has a long and rather checkered history. Initially, this term referred to a condition "on the border" between neurosis and psychosis. Later, however, the term increasingly came to refer to a disorder that is qualitatively distinct from these two broad classes of conditions. In 1968, Roy Grinker and his colleagues delineated several features that they believed distinguished borderlines from other patients, including chronic anger and identity problems.

Another influential approach to borderline (as well as narcissistic) personality has been object relations theory. This theory focuses upon the relations among internalized persons and objects and the implications of these relations for personality development. Otto Kernberg, for example, discusses the "borderline personality organization," a character structure that he believes results from disturbances in the child's psychological internalization of parental images. According to Kernberg, borderline individuals never learn to incorporate good and bad representations of themselves or others simultaneously; consequently, they lack the capacity to view themselves and others as possessing both good and bad attributes.

Unfortunately, the overlap among these different conceptualizations is not as great as might be hoped; in 1978, J. Christopher Perry and Gerald Klerman reported that four commonly used criteria sets for borderline personality differed substantially in the symptoms they assess. The third edition of the *Diagnostic and Statistical Manual of Mental Disorders* (1980, DSM-III) provided researchers with the first standard set of criteria to assess the disorder.

Although the term "histrionic personality" did not formally appear until the advent of DSM-III, the "hysterical personality" has a lengthy history in psychiatry. Indeed, the concept of "hysteria" (literally, "wandering womb") dates back at least four thousand years to Egypt, where it was believed that the disorder was attributable to a displaced uterus. In the late nineteenth century, French neurologist Jean Charcot and, later, his student Sigmund Freud attempted to treat hysterics, many of whom probably had what would today be called histrionic personality, by means of hypnosis. In 1958, psychiatrists Paul Chodoff and Henry Lyons outlined the major features of hysterical personality, including vanity, dramatic behavior, and coquetry. Their conceptualization had a major influence upon subsequent criteria for histrionic personality.

Freud was one of the first major authors to discuss narcissism as a pathological character trait. According to Freud, narcissism resulted from a failure of the child to develop beyond the stage in which sexual impulses are focused upon the self. Thus, according to Freud, narcissistic individuals are psychologically "stuck" at a primitive stage of development characterized by an inability to direct sexual urges toward other individuals. More recently, object relations theorists, such as Heinz Kohut, have argued that narcissistic personality results from profound failures in parental empathy. As a result of these failures, according to Kohut, such individuals remain "stuck" at an early stage of development characterized by self-centeredness, resulting in a never-ending search for the love and admiration they never received.

Bibliography
Cooper, Arnold M., Allen J. Frances, and Michael H. Sacks, eds. *The Personality Disorders and Neuroses*. New York: Basic Books, 1986. This edited volume contains chapters on each major personality disorder as well as a discussion of general theoretical and treatment models for the personality disorders and neuroses. Michael H. Stone's chapter on borderline personality, which contains a good overview of different uses of the term, and Otto Kernberg's chapters on narcissistic and histrionic personalities are particularly recommended.

Goldstein, Eda G. *Borderline Disorders: Clinical Models and Techniques*. New York: Guilford Press, 1990. Goldstein lucidly outlines the major clinical features of borderline personality, discusses its development from a variety of theoretical perspectives, and contrasts the major contemporary psychotherapeutic approaches to the disorder. Appropriate for the reader with some background in psychoanalytic theory.

Heller, Leland Michael. *Life at the Border: Understanding and Recovering from the Borderline Personality Disorder*. Okeechobee, Fla.: Dyslimbia Press, 1999. Explains for laypeople what it is like to live with borderline personality disorder and how to recover.

Lasch, Christopher. *The Culture of Narcissism*. New York: Warner Books, 1979. Lasch outlines the characteristics of "the narcissistic personality of our time," discusses large-scale social changes that he believes are responsible for the increase in narcissism in Western culture, and provides compelling critiques of the awareness movement and other contemporary fads. Although Lasch's tone at times verges on the polemical, his observations are thought-provoking and perceptive.

Roy, Alec, ed. *Hysteria*. New York: John Wiley & Sons, 1982. Contains chapters dealing with a number of important issues relevant to histrionic personality, somatization disorder, and related conditions. The coverage of historical issues and genetic and biological factors is especially thorough. The chapters on multiple personality and the relation of hysteria to hypnosis may also be of interest.

Sadock, Benjamin J., and Virginia A. Sadock, eds. *Kaplan and Sadock's Comprehensive Textbook of Psychiatry*. 7th ed. Baltimore: Lippincott, Williams &

Wilkins, 1999. Provides an overview of key conceptual issues relevant to personality disorders (for example, classification models, genetic and environmental factors, treatment approaches) and clearly discusses the clinical features of each disorder. Provides one of the most succinct summaries of the personality disorders literature.

Santoro, Joseph. *The Angry Heart: Overcoming Borderline and Addictive Disorders*. Oakland, Calif.: New Harbinger, 1997. Provides insights, exercises, information, and motivation that can help a person to overcome borderline and addictive behaviors.

Tyrer, Peter J., ed. *Personality Disorders: Diagnosis, Management, and Course*. 2d ed. Boston: Butterworth Heinemann, 2000. Written for psychologists. Offers a practical approach to personality disorders with a variety of interventions. Includes bibliographical references and an index.

Scott O. Lilienfeld

See also:

Antisocial Personality; Behavioral Assessment and Personality Rating Scales; Depression; Jealousy; Psychoactive Drug Therapy.

BRAIN DISORDERS

Type of psychology: Psychopathology
Fields of study: Organic disorders

Disorders of the brain can interfere with its role in the control of body functions, behavior, learning, and expression, while defects can also threaten life itself.

Principal terms

ANENCEPHALY: a fatal congenital condition in which tissues that should have differentiated to form the brain failed to do so

COMA: a condition of unconsciousness that may or may not be reversible; various degrees of coma are assessed by the presence or absence of reflex responses, such as pupil dilation when a light is shone into the eyes

DEMENTIA: a diseased state in which intellectual ability is ever decreasing; personality changes, decreased interest or ability to care for one's self, and long-term and short-term memory loss can indicate dementia

HYDROCEPHALUS: a painful condition caused by excess cerebrospinal fluid within the spaces of the brain

ISCHEMIA: an inadequate blood flow to a region; may be caused by an incomplete blockage in or constriction of a blood vessel (as may occur with atherosclerosis or a blood clot)

SEIZURE: a misfiring of cortical neurons that alters the patient's level of consciousness; the seizure may or may not involve muscular convulsions

STROKE: a complete loss of blood flow to a region of the brain that is of sudden onset and causes abrupt muscular weakness, usually to one side of the body

Causes and Symptoms

The cerebral cortex acts as a processor for sensory information and as an integrator of memory, interpretation, creativity, intellect, and passion. Disorders of the brain or brain defects can disrupt these processing or integrating functions. Disorders of the brain include such commonly heard terms as stroke, ischemia, dementia, seizure, and coma. Brain disorders may also occur as a result of infection, various tumors, traumas leading to blot clots (hematomas) or lack of oxygen (hypoxia), and cancer. Brain defects include anencephaly, a congenital defect in which a newborn lacks a brain, and hydrocephaly, commonly called "water on the brain."

A stroke is any situation in which the blood supply to a region of the brain is lost. This can occur as a result of a cerebral hemorrhage, during which blood escapes from blood vessels to surround and compress brain tissue; cerebral thrombosis, whereby a clot attached to the wall of a blood vessel restricts the amount of blood flowing to a particular region; or an embolus, a foreign substance which may be a clot that migrates in the bloodstream, often to lodge in a smaller vessel in the brain. The embolus will block blood flow to some area. An embolus can originate from substances other than a blood clot, which is why health care staff often squirt fluid out of a needle before administering a shot or other therapy: to ensure that no air embolus, which could induce a stroke or prove fatal if it enters the brain, is injected.

Transient ischemic attacks (TIAs) are often thought of as small strokes, but, technically, ischemia simply means that oxygen is not reaching the cells within a tissue. Basically, the mechanism is similar to a stroke, in that blood flow to a portion of the brain is compromised. Although blood actually reaches the brain tissue during ischemia, there is not a sufficient flow to ensure that all cells are receiving the oxygen necessary to continue cellular life. This condition is called hypoxia (low oxygen). If hypoxia is sustained over a sufficient period of time, cellular death occurs, causing irreversible brain damage.

The important differences between a stroke and a TIA are the onset and duration of symptoms, as well as the severity of the damage. Persons with atherosclerosis actually have fat deposits along the interior walls of their blood vessels. These people are vulnerable to experiencing multiple TIAs. Many TIAs are small enough to be dismissed and ignored; others are truly inapparent, causing no symptoms. This is unfortunate because TIAs often serve as a warning of an impending full-scale stroke. Action and treatments could be implemented, if medical advice is sought early, to decrease the likelihood of a stroke. Repeated TIAs also contribute to dementia.

Dementia is not the normal path for the elderly, nor is it a sign of aging. Dementia is a sign of neurological chaos and can be caused by diseases such as Alzheimer's disease or acquired immunodeficiency syndrome (AIDS). Although most elderly are not afflicted with dementia, nearly all have a slowing of reaction and response time. This slowing is believed to be associated with chemical changes within nerve cell membranes as aging occurs; slowing of reaction times is not necessarily indicative of the first steps on a path to dementia. In addition, forgetfulness may not be a sign of dementia, since it occurs at all ages. Forgetfulness is such a sign, however, if it is progressive and includes forgetting to dress or forgetting one's name or date of birth.

While it is incorrect to say that dementia is caused by aging, it is correct to say that dementia is age-related. It may first appear in a person any time between the late thirties and the mid-nineties, but it usually begins to appear in the late seventies. Patients with Alzheimer's disease are believed to account for about 20 percent of all cases of dementia. Other diseases cause dementia, including an autosomal-dominant genetic disease called Huntington's disease. Huntington's disease manifests itself with a distinct chorea, or dance, of the body that is neither solicited nor controlled. This genetic disease is particularly cruel in that its symptoms appear in midlife, often after the patient has had offspring and passed on the gene. The disease continues to alter the intellect and personality of the afflicted and progresses to the point of complete debilitation of the body and mind.

A seizure occurs when a collection of neurons misfires, sending nerve impulses that are neither solicited nor controllable. In the everyday use of the term, seizure describes a condition of epilepsy or convulsion. Medically speaking, a seizure is a sign of an underlying problem within the gray matter of the brain; it is the most common neurological disorder. Epilepsy is a term used to describe a condition of repeated seizures, while convulsion is a term generally applied to describe an isolated seizure. A seizure may occur as a consequence of extreme fever or a violent blow to the head. Seizures are also associated with metabolic disorders, such as hypoglycemia (low blood sugar); trauma causing a loss of blood or oxygen to a region, such as in a newborn after a traumatic birth; toxins, as seen in drug abuse or withdrawal; or bacterial or viral encephalitis or meningitis. In addition, about one-third of those persons who survive a gunshot wound to the head will experience seizures afterward. In closed head trauma, which can occur in a sporting or automobile accident, there is a 5 percent chance of post-trauma seizures.

Loss of consciousness can be caused by a violent impact to the head, a lack of oxygen or blood flow to the head, a metabolic imbalance, or the presence of a toxin such as alcohol. Usually, this is a transient event, but it may become a permanent condition. When this happens, a person is said to be in a coma. A comatose person exists in a nonresponsive state and may be assessed for brain death. Brain death is a legally defined term which means that no electrical activity in the brain is seen on an electroencephalogram (EEG). Thus some comatose patients may be determined to be brain-dead, particularly if the condition is deemed irreversible.

Brain defects are not common, but they do occur. One particularly tragic defect is the absence of a brain in a newborn, called anencephaly. Death usually occurs within a few hours of birth. Although anencephaly is rare and generally associated with a genetic factor, there have been cases in population clusters, such as one in the Rio Grande area of south Texas, suggesting that an environmental factor may contribute to these defects.

Another defect that may appear in newborns or in an infant's first months of life is hydrocephalus. Although the descriptive term "water on the brain" is often used, the condition does not involve a collection of water in the cranium; rather, it involves an accumulation of cerebrospinal fluid (CSF). CSF is the fluid that insulates the brain and allows it to "float" under the bony cranial encasement. As the ventricles, or spaces, in the brain fill with CSF, bulging occurs and pressure builds to the point of compressing the surrounding brain tissue. This can be very painful and is fatal if untreated. Hydrocephalus can be caused by an overproduction of CSF or a blockage of the CSF drainage from the ventricles of the brain. The symptoms often include a protrusion or abnormal shape of the cranium. In newborns, the skull bones have not yet sutured (fused) to one another, so the soft bones are pushed apart, causing unusual head shapes. This is a warning sign. Another sign is observed if a newborn's head has a circumference greater than 35.5 centimeters (14 inches); if that is the case, the newborn must be immediately checked for hydrocephalus. Adolescents and adults may also experience hydrocephalus. This can be a response to head trauma, infection, or the overproduction of CSF. The symptoms include lethargy, headache, dullness, blurred vision, nausea, and vomiting.

Treatment and Therapy

TIAs can progress to strokes. In fact, about 30 percent of those diagnosed with TIA will have a major stroke within the subsequent four years. One of the most prevalent causes of TIAs is hypertension. Hypertension is known as the "silent killer" because many persons with this problem ignore the subtle symptoms of fatigue, headache, and general malaise. Hypertension is also known as a good predictor of major strokes if left untreated. Thus, hypertensive persons need to be diagnosed as such in order to control their blood pressure. This allows them to avoid or delay either a major stroke or multiple TIAs. Management for the hypertensive's blood pressure may include taking diuretics and hypotensive drugs (to lower the blood pressure). If taken diligently, these drugs offer longevity and quality of life to the sufferer. Aside from hypertension, TIAs may be induced in some metabolic disorders, which should be corrected if possible, or by constricted blood vessels. Sometimes, surgery on such vessels can stop the ischemic attacks and prevent or delay the onset of a stroke.

Although TIAs lead to strokes, strokes are not necessarily preceded by a TIA. Nearly 90 percent of all major strokes occur without a TIA warning. Sadly, hypertension is the main contributor to this number. Measures can be taken to avoid strokes. This includes maintaining cardiovascular health by exercising, not smoking, and managing hypertension, diabetes mellitus, or other problems that may place stresses on the body's chemical balance.

Dementia is so poorly understood in terms of causes that a rational probe of drug therapy or a cure is nearly impossible. The drugs most often used in dementia treatment, the ergoloid mesylates, are used to manage the symptoms; namely, the confused mind. These drugs, however, do not stop or prevent the unexplained cellular degeneration associated with dementia. It is interesting to note that a tiny subgroup within those persons suffering from Alzheimer's disease have greatly improved in mental status with the drug tacrine. It is unfortunate that all patients are not responsive to this drug—a fact which suggests that Alzheimer's disease is a complex condition.

Seizures are treated pharmacologically according to type. Carbamazepine, phenobarbitol, phenytoin, and valproate are some of the drugs available to treat seizure disorders. Barbiturates may also be used in certain cases. Most of these drugs are highly effective when taken as prescribed, and patient noncompliance is the main cause of drug failure. Sometimes, two drugs are combined in therapy. It should be mentioned that pregnant women with epilepsy are urged to continue taking anti-epilepsy drugs during pregnancy, since a maternal seizure may be more damaging to the fetus than the drug itself.

Some forms of hydrocephalus can be corrected surgically by performing a CSF shunt from the cranium to the peritoneal (abdominal) region, where the fluid can be eliminated from the body as waste. This is not without risk, and the introduction of infection into the brain is a major concern.

Perspective and Prospects

The therapies in use for brain diseases and disorders have been derived from the practical experience of physicians, the laboratory research of scientists, and the hopes of multitudes of doctors, patients, families, and friends. Advances in medical science have done much to improve the lives of those who suffer with seizures, to reduce the risk of strokes to the hypertensive person and those with TIAs, and is making great progress in treating certain kinds of dementia. Yet much remains to be done.

While one can argue that much is known about the human brain, it would be erroneous to argue that the human brain is fully understood. Despite centuries of research, the brain, as it functions in health, remains largely a mystery. Since the healthy brain is yet to be understood, it is not surprising that the medical community struggles to determine what goes wrong in dementia, seizure, or mental illness or to discover drug therapies that can cross the blood-brain barrier. Thus, the human brain is the uncharted frontier in medicine. As technology improves to support researchers and medical practitioners in their pursuits of cures and treatments for brain diseases and disorders, one can only remain hopeful for the future ability to restore health to the damaged human brain.

Bibliography
Bannister, Roger. *Brain and Bannister's Clinical Neurology.* 7th ed. Oxford, England: Oxford University Press, 1992. Several chapters are dedicated to the topics of seizures, dementia, hydrocephalus, and loss of consciousness. Because the writing can be fairly technical, it is best used by someone with a background in human anatomy and physiology.

Cicala, Roger S. *The Brain Disorders Sourcebook.* Chicago: Contemporary, 2000. Describes the normal structure and function of the brain, discusses medical tests for diagnosing brain disorders, and addresses strokes and vascular disease of the brain, brain tumors, and other neurologic diseases, indicating their course, indicated treatment, and likely outcomes.

Clayman, Charles B., ed. *The American Medical Association Family Medical Guide.* 3d rev. ed. New York: Random House, 1994. An excellent reference for the beginner. The scientific accuracy of the text is not compromised by its accessibility.

Parsons, Malcolm. *Colour Atlas of Clinical Neurology.* 2d ed. St. Louis: Mosby Year Book, 1993. An excellent atlas that allows the pictures to tell the story. The color photographs and brief descriptions capture the essence of brain disorders and remind the reader that people are suffering from these maladies.

Reggia, James A., Dennis Glanzman, and Eytan Ruppin, eds. *Disorders of Brain, Behavior, and Cognition: The Neurocomputational Perspective.* New York: Elsevier, 1999. Covers memory disorders, neuropsychology, neurology, and psychiatry. Includes bibliographical references and an index.

Ron, Maria A., and Anthony S. David, eds. *Disorders of Brain and Mind.* New York: Cambridge University Press, 1998. A multidisciplinary overview, with coverage ranging from epilepsy and schizophrenia to basal ganglia disorder and brain lesions. Includes bibliographical references and an index.

Mary C. Fields

See also:

Alzheimer's Disease; Amnesia, Fugue, and Multiple Personality; Aphasias; Dementia; Dyslexia; Electroconvulsive Therapy; Learning Disabilities; Memory Loss.

CHILD ABUSE

Type of psychology: Developmental psychology
Fields of study: Adolescence; infancy and childhood

The experience of physical or psychological abuse in childhood can have a profound, long-term, deleterious effect upon a person's social development and emotional well-being. Child abuse places a youngster at increased risk to develop a variety of psychological problems, including low self-esteem, anxiety and depression, behavior disorders, educational difficulties, and distorted relationships with peers and adults.

Principal terms

NEGLECT: the repeated failure to meet minimal standards for satisfying a child's basic needs for food, clothing, shelter, medical care, and safety

PHYSICAL ABUSE: any nonaccidental injury caused by a parent or a person responsible for a child's care, including fractures, burns, bruises, welts, cuts, and internal injuries

PSYCHOLOGICAL ABUSE: acts by which children are rejected, terrorized, corrupted, isolated, ridiculed, or humiliated; parental behavior fails to meet the child's need for nurturance or penalizes the child for normal behavior

SEXUAL ABUSE: any contact between a child and an adult in which the child is being used for the sexual stimulation of the perpetrator or another person; includes exhibitionism, fondling, rape, and sodomy

Overview

It is difficult to imagine anything more frightening to a child than being rejected, threatened, beaten, or molested by an adult who is supposed to be his or her primary source of nurturance and protection. Yet throughout human history, children have been abandoned, incarcerated, battered, mutilated, and even murdered by their caregivers. Although the problem of child maltreatment is an old one, both the systematic study of child abuse and the legally sanctioned mechanisms for child protection are relatively new and have gained their greatest momentum in the last half of the twentieth century.

In the United States, the Federal Child Abuse Prevention and Treatment Act of 1974 broadly defines child abuse as

> the physical or mental injury, sexual abuse or exploitation, negligent treatment, or maltreatment of a child under the age of eighteen . . . by a person who is responsible for that child's welfare under circumstances which indicate that the child's health or welfare is harmed or threatened thereby.

When applied by legal and mental health professionals in real-world situations, however, the definition of abuse may vary according to the developmental age of the child victim, the frequency or intensity of the behaviors regarded as abusive, the degree of intentionality, and a consideration of extenuating circumstances. In general, however, child abuse includes any act or omission on the part of a parental figure that damages a child's physical or psychological well-being or development that is nonaccidental or the result of a habitual behavioral pattern. A broad spectrum of behaviors are considered to be abusive, ranging from the more easily recognizable physical abuse to the more subtle forms of maltreatment including neglect, sexual abuse, and emotional abuse.

Estimates of the extent of child abuse in the United States have ranged from two hundred thousand to four million cases per year. The most widely accepted incidence figure comes from the National Committee for the Prevention of Child Abuse, which estimates that more than a million children are "severely abused" each year, including more than two thousand abuse-related deaths annually. It is important, when considering the actual magnitude of the problem of child maltreatment, to remember that the estimates given most likely underestimate the true incidence of child abuse, both because of the large number of cases that go unreported and because of the lack of agreement as to precisely which behaviors constitute "abuse" or "neglect." In addition, abusive treatment of children is rarely limited to a single episode, and it frequently occurs within the context of other forms of family violence.

Certain forms of maltreatment seem to appear with greater regularity within certain age groups. Neglect is most often reported for infants and toddlers, with incidence declining with age. Reports of sexual abuse and emotional maltreatment are most common among older school-aged children and adolescents. Physical abuse seems to be reported equally among all age groups; however, children less than five years old and adolescents have the highest rates of actual physical injury.

Although research studies generally conclude that there is no "typical" child abuse case consisting of a typical abused child and a typical abusive parent or family type, there are certain characteristics that occur with greater regularity than others. For example, there is considerable evidence that premature infants, low-birth-weight infants, and children with problems such as hyperactivity, physical handicaps, and mental retardation are at particularly high risk for being abused by their caregivers. Physical abuse and neglect are reported with approximately equal frequency for girls and boys, while sexual abuse against girls is reported four times more frequently than is sexual abuse against boys.

Contrary to the once-held stereotype of abusive parents, only a small proportion (5 to 10 percent) of abusive parents suffer from a severe psychiatric disorder. While female caregivers are the perpetrators in approximately 60 percent of all reported cases of child maltreatment, male caregivers are more likely to inflict actual physical injury, and they are the primary perpetrators in cases of sexual abuse of both male and female children. Although no one abusive personality type has been identified, research has revealed a number of areas of psychological functioning in which abusive parents often differ from nonabusive parents. Abusive parents tend to exhibit low frustration tolerance and express negative emotions (for example, anger or disappointment) inappropriately. They are more socially isolated than are nonabusive parents. Abusive parents also tend to have unrealistic expectations of their children, to misinterpret their children's motivations for misbehaving, to utilize inconsistent and inflexible parenting skills, and to view themselves as inadequate or incompetent as parents.

Research also indicates that marital conflict, unemployment, large and closely spaced families, overcrowded living conditions, and extreme household disorientation are common in abusive homes. Statistics regarding race, education level, and socioeconomic status of abusive families are somewhat controversial in that there exists the possibility of an underreporting bias favoring the white, middle- to upper-class family; however, like several other negative outcomes in childhood (for example, underachievement, criminality, teen pregnancy), child abuse is associated with poverty, underemployment, insufficient education, and the increased experience of unmanageable stress and social isolation that coexists with these sociodemographic variables.

Applications

Abused children are believed to be at much greater risk of developing some form of pathology in childhood or in later life. When considered as a group and compared with nonabused youngsters, abused children exhibit a variety of psychological difficulties and behavioral problems. Yet there is no single emotional or behavioral reaction that is consistently found in all abused children. It is important, when investigating the impact of child abuse, to view the abuse within a developmental perspective. Given a child's different developmental needs and capabilities over the course of his or her development, one might expect that both the psychological experience and the impact of the abuse would be quite different for an infant than if the same maltreatment involved an eight-year-old child or an adolescent. One should also note that the abuse occurs within a particular psychological context, and that the experience of the abuse per se may not be the singular, most powerful predictor of the psychological difficulties found in abused children. Rather, the child's daily exposure to other, more pervasive aspects of the psychological environment associated with an abusive family situation (for example, general environmental deprivation, impoverished parent-child interactions, or chronic family disruption and disorganization) may prove to be more psychologically damaging. Finally, it is important not to view the range of symptoms associated with abused children solely as deficits or pathology. These "symptoms" represent an abused child's best attempt at coping with an extremely stressful family environment given the limited psychological resources and skills he or she has available at that particular time in his or her development.

From the home environment, and from parents in particular, children learn their earliest and perhaps most influential lessons about how to evaluate themselves as valuable, lovable, and competent human beings. They learn about controlling their own actions and about successfully mastering their environment. They learn something about the goodness of their world and how to relate to the people in it. Growing up in an abusive home distorts these early lessons, often resulting in serious interference with the most important dimensions of a child's development: the development of a healthy sense of self, the development of self-control and a sense of mastery, the capacity to form satisfying relationships, and the ability to utilize one's cognitive capacities to solve problems.

In general, research has shown that abused children often suffer from low self-esteem, poor impulse control, aggressive and antisocial behaviors, fearfulness and anxiety, depression, poor relationships with peers and adults, difficulties with school adjustment, delays in cognitive development, lowered academic achievement, and deficits in social and moral judgment. The way in which these difficulties are expressed will vary according to a child's stage of development.

In infancy, the earliest sign of abuse or neglect is an infant's failure to thrive. These infants show growth retardation (weight loss can be so severe as to be life-threatening) with no obvious physical explanation. To the observer, these infants appear to have "given up" on interacting with the outside world. They become passive, socially apathetic, and exhibit little smiling, vocalization, and curiosity. Other abused infants appear to be quite irritable, exhibiting frequent crying, feeding difficulties, and irregular sleep patterns. In either case, the resulting parent-child attachment bond is often inadequate and mutually unsatisfying.

Abused toddlers and preschoolers seem to lack the infectious love of life, fantasy, and play that is characteristic of that stage of development. They are typically anxious, fearful, and hypervigilant. Their emotions are blunted, lacking the range, the spontaneity, and the vivacity typical of a child that age. Abused toddlers' and preschoolers' ability to play, particularly their ability to engage in imaginative play, may be impaired; it is either deficient or preoccupied with themes of aggression. Abused children at this age can either be passive and overcompliant or oppositional, aggressive, and hyperactive.

School-aged children and adolescents exhibit the more recognizable signs of low self-esteem and depression in the form of a self-deprecating attitude and self-destructive behaviors. They are lonely, withdrawn, and joyless. Behaviorally, some act in a compulsive, overcompliant, or pseudomature manner, while others are overly impulsive, oppositional, and aggressive. Problems with school adjustment and achievement are common. With the school-aged child's increased exposure to the larger social environment, deficits in social competence and interpersonal relationships become more apparent. Progressing through adolescence, the manifestations of low self-esteem, depression, and aggressive, acting-out behaviors may become more pronounced in the form of suicide attempts, delinquency, running away, promiscuity, and drug use.

These distortions in self-esteem, impulse control, and interpersonal relationships often persist into adulthood. There has been much concern expressed regarding the possibility of an intergenerational transmission of abuse—of the experience of abuse as a child predisposing a person to becoming an abusive parent. Research indicates that abused children are six times more likely to abuse their own children than the general population.

Perspective and Prospects

Child maltreatment is a complex phenomenon that does not have a simple, discrete cause, nor does it affect each victim in a predictable or consistent manner. Since the "battered child syndrome" gained national attention in the early 1960's, theories attempting to explain child maltreatment have evolved from the simplistic psychiatric model focusing on the abuser as a "bad" parent suffering from some form of mental illness to a view of child abuse as a multidetermined problem, with anyone from any walk of life a potential abuser.

Perhaps the most comprehensive and widely accepted explanation of child abuse is the ecological model. This model views abuse as the final product of a set of interacting factors including child-mediated stressors (for example, temperamental difficulties, or a mental or physical handicap), parental predispositions (for example, history of abuse as a child, emotional immaturity), and situational stresses (for example, marital conflict, insufficient social support, or financial stress) occurring within a cultural context that inadvertently supports the mistreatment of children by its acceptance of corporal punishment and tolerance for violence, and its reluctance to interfere with family autonomy. Utilizing this ecological framework, one can imagine how an abusive situation can develop when, for example, an irritable, emotionally unresponsive infant is cared for by an inexperienced, socially isolated mother in a conflict-filled and financially strained household embedded within a larger cultural context in which the rights and privileges of childhood do not necessarily include freedom from violence.

Knowledge regarding the impact of child abuse has also changed over the years, from a view of maltreated children as almost doomed to develop some form of psychopathology to an acknowledgment that child abuse, like other major childhood stressors, can result in a broad spectrum of adaptive consequences, ranging from psychological health to severe psychiatric disorder. Some children actually do well in their development despite their experience with extreme stress and adversity. For example, while adults who were abused as children are more likely than nonabused individuals to become child abusers, nearly two-thirds of all abused children do not become abusive parents. The important questions to be answered are why and how this is so. Research on "stress-resistant" individuals such as these nonabusers has shifted the focus away from pathology to the identification of factors within the individual (for example, coping strategies) and within the environment (for example, social support) that appear to serve a protective function.

Finally, while the treatment of abused children and their abusive caregivers remains an important goal in the mental health field, a focus on the prevention of child abuse has also gained momentum. Many abused children and their families can be helped with proper treatment; however, the existing need for services far exceeds the mental health resources available. An increased understanding of the factors that protect families against engaging in abusive behaviors has resulted in the creation of successful preventive interventions. These prevention programs seek to reduce the incidence of new cases of child abuse by encouraging the development and strengthening of competencies, resources, and coping strategies that promote psychological well-being and positive development in parents, children, and families.

The problem of child abuse does not occur in isolation. It coexists with other abhorrent problems facing American children such as poverty, lack of guaranteed adequate medical care, insufficient quality day care, and unequal educational resources. Child abuse, like these other problems, can be prevented and eradicated. People have come a long way in terms of their understanding of child maltreatment; yet until the needs of children truly become a national priority, child abuse will continue, brutally and unnecessarily, to rob children of their childhood.

Bibliography

Brassard, Marla R., Robert Germain, and Stuart N. Hart, eds. *Psychological Maltreatment of Children and Youth.* New York: Pergamon Press, 1987. An edited collection of articles that considers emotional maltreatment as the "core" component of all other forms of child abuse. Discusses issues of the definition, dynamics, consequences, and treatment of the psychological abuse of children.

Cicchetti, Dante, and Vicki Carlson, eds. *Child Maltreatment: Theory and Research on the Causes and Consequences of Child Abuse and Neglect.* New York: Cambridge University Press, 1989. Edited chapters by leading experts in the field providing a state-of-the-art evaluation of what is known about the causes and consequences of child maltreatment. Describes the history of child maltreatment and intervention strategies designed to prevent or remediate the negative consequences of abuse.

Clark, Robin E., Judith Freeman Clark, and Chris Adamec. *The Encyclopedia of Child Abuse.* 2d ed. New York: Facts on File, 2000. In encyclopedia form, provides comprehensive information regarding all forms of child maltreatment. Includes discussions of causation, consequences, treatment, and prevention. Entries reflect a range of disciplines including psychology, law, medicine, sociology, economics, history, and education. An extensive bibliography is also included.

Corby, Brian. *Child Abuse.* 2d ed. Philadelphia: Open University Press, 2000. A comprehensive guide to theoretical and practical issues surrounding child abuse. Includes bibliographical references and an index.

Finkelhor, David. *A Sourcebook on Child Sexual Abuse.* Beverly Hills, Calif.: Sage, 1986. Provides a comprehensive overview of the clinical and research knowledge base regarding child sexual abuse, including its causes, consequences, and treatment.

Kim, Henny H. *Child Abuse.* San Diego: Greenhaven Press, 2000. Presents differing views on child abuse. Defines what child abuse is, the seriousness of the problem, and ways to handle and prevent it. Includes bibliographical references and an index.

Straus, Murray Arnold, Richard J. Gelles, and Suzanne K. Steinmetz. *Behind Closed Doors: Violence in the American Family.* Newbury Park, Calif.: Sage, 1981. Reports the results of the first comprehensive national study of violence in the average American family in nontechnical language. The problem of child abuse is discussed within the larger context of other expressions of family violence.

Wolfe, David A. *Child Abuse: Implications for Child Development and Psychopa-*

thology. Newbury Park, Calif.: Sage, 1987. Presents a thorough review of facts and issues regarding the abuse of children, emphasizing topics such as socio-demographic risk factors, variations in family socialization practices, factors associated with healthy versus abusive parent-child relationship, psychological characteristics of the abusive parent, and a developmental perspective on the abused child.

Judith Primavera

See also:

Aggression: Definitions and Theoretical Explanations; Aggression: Reduction and Control; Alcoholism; Antisocial Personality; Behavioral Family Therapy; Divorce and Separation: Children's Issues; Domestic Violence; Juvenile Delinquency; Substance Abuse.

CHILD AND ADOLESCENT PSYCHIATRY

Type of psychology: Developmental psychology; psychotherapy
Fields of study: Adolescence; childhood and adolescent disorders; infancy and childhood

This branch of psychiatry is concerned with the mental and emotional health and development of infants and teenagers.

Principal terms

DEVELOPMENT: the process of progressive change that takes place as one matures from birth to death; development can be gradual, as on a continuum, or ordered, as in distinctly different stages

DISORDER: a persistent or repetitive maladaptive pattern in thinking, behaving, or feeling that necessitates treatment

MENTAL RETARDATION: a condition characterized by a below-average intelligence quotient (IQ) and deficits in adaptive functioning before the age of eighteen years; the degree of retardation ranges from mild to severe

NORMAL: a term of reference that can mean average (as in statistically normal), functional (as in adaptive), or socially appropriate (as in within cultural bounds of acceptability)

Overview

Specialists in child and adolescent psychiatry are responsible for the physical and mental health of the individuals whom they treat. They must be acute observers of individual and family behavior, as well as knowledgeable about how certain nutritional, physical, and situational conditions can present themselves as mental or emotional problems. Particularly with infants, this requires keen knowledge of normal and abnormal development, both mental and physical. Additionally, these specialists must be able to consult with a variety of medical and other professionals—from psychologists, who provide behavioral and diagnostic assessments, to social work professionals and lawyers, when child abuse or neglect enters into the clinical picture.

Practitioners in child or adolescent psychiatry receive extensive training. First, they must complete medical school in order to obtain a doctorate in medicine. Next, they must complete a four-year residency in psychiatry and a two-year specialty residency in child psychiatry. Finally, they must go through licensing and certification procedures in order to practice independently.

This training prepares them to diagnose and treat the wide variety of psychiatric disorders experienced by children and adolescents. Anxiety, attention-deficit/ hyperactivity, autistic, conduct, learning, mental retardation, mood, oppositional-defiant, pervasive developmental, and substance abuse disorders are some of the most well researched disorders in children. Other problems include asthma, bed-wetting or bed-soiling, child abuse and neglect, conflicts related to sexuality, eating disorders, elective mutism, epilepsy, fire-setting and vandalism, identity disorders, personality disorders, school difficulties, schizoid disorders, sleepwalking, sleep terror, stuttering, and tantrums. Disorders such as these are described in detail in the American Psychiatric Association's *Diagnostic and Statistical Manual of Mental Disorders* (4th ed., 1994, DSM-IV).

Applications

Practitioners of child and adolescent psychiatry are generally introduced to their patients via the parents or an intervening medical professional or agency. In most cases, these specialists diagnose disorders through clinical interviews with the patient, the patient's parents, and sometimes even schoolteachers or other observers of relevant problems. Additionally, diagnoses are sometimes confirmed via a patient's response to drugs (such as Ritalin, antidepressants, or lithium carbonate) or via test results from a psychological or behavioral assessment. Some assessments are based on structured, pencil-and-paper tests that measure intelligence or other personal attributes. Others are based on direct observations of the patient and/or family interactions.

Once a diagnosis is made, practitioners provide therapy to the individual child or adolescent and/or to the entire family. Acute or severe problems might be treated in a hospital setting, while chronic or mild problems might be treated on an outpatient basis. Therapies typically selected include medicinal and psychotropic drugs, dietary recommendations, behavioral therapies and parent training, family therapy, play therapy, and individual psychotherapy. In these situations, a good practitioner will try to involve the child in the process of consent to treatment so as to facilitate trust and gain compliance from the child.

Finally, practitioners in this specialty area perform two other important functions. First, in some cases, no disorder is present, and the psychiatrist provides normative information about child and adolescent growth and development. Second, these professionals must provide protection to suspected victims of abuse or neglect. In such cases, the psychiatrist must report these suspicions to the appropriate authorities, initiate referral to social service agencies, and protect the children or adolescents as necessary.

Perspective and Prospects

Work by Sigmund Freud, the Austrian physician and founder of psychoanalysis, marked the birth of this field of study. By focusing his work on the relationship between childhood experiences and adult functioning, Freud was able to foster interest in child development and welfare. Issues such as family relationships; the emotional, physical, and sexual mistreatment of children; and differences in the way that children and adults perceive and experience the world became highlighted through his work and that of those who followed. Finally, in 1959, child psychiatry became a specialty certified by the American Board of Psychiatry and Neurology, adding credibility and importance to this growing field of practice and research.

Today, child and adolescent psychiatry remains in its infancy compared with other specialties. Relationships between childhood and adult disorders continue to be explored through a variety of epidemiological, genetic, psychiatric, and behavioral studies. Prime topics include connections among attention-deficit/hyperactivity, mood, learning, and a broad spectrum of developmental disorders. Similarly, interest in understanding how trauma, neglect, and family influences relate to childhood mood, learning, and substance abuse disorders is also increasing.

Innovative drug and psychotherapeutic strategies are being explored for the disorders described above. The greatest treatment advances should be expected in the development and application of new drug therapies for childhood and adolescent psychiatric disorders. Further, refinement of behavioral assessment and management strategies for both school and home environments are likely to contribute greatly to this progress. Finally, because this specialty faces growing challenges posed by long-term childhood medical disorders, such as cancer, it is likely that interventions will be improved specifically to meet these needs.

Bibliography

American Psychiatric Association. *Diagnostic and Statistical Manual of Mental Disorders, Fourth Edition (DSM-IV)*. 4th ed. Washington, D.C.: Author, 1994. Provides comprehensive descriptions of mental disorders, as well as a glossary of technical terms.

Graham, Philip, Jeremy Turk, and Frank C. Verhulst. *Child Psychiatry: A Developmental Approach*. 3d ed. New York: Oxford University Press, 1999. Discusses normal development, adolescence, psychosocial aspects, abuse, illnesses, and available services. Includes bibliographical references and an index.

Kass, Frederic I., John M. Oldham, and Herbert Pardes, eds. *The Columbia University College of Physicians and Surgeons Complete Home Guide to Mental Health*. New York: Henry Holt, 1995. This popular work addresses mental health issues within the context of the family. Includes an index.

Moshman, David. *Adolescent Psychological Development: Rationality, Morality, and Identity*. Mahwah, N.J.: Lawrence Erlbaum Associates, 1999. Presents a constructivist approach to the development of rationality, morality, and identity in adolescence and early adulthood. Reviews post-Piagetian approaches to adolescent cognition, examining classic theories and current research. Accessible to students with no background in psychology.

Silverman, Wendy K., and Philip D. A. Treffers, eds. *Anxiety Disorders in Children and Adolescents: Research, Assessment and Intervention*. New York: Cambridge University Press, 2000. A volume in the Cambridge Child and Adolescent Psychiatry series that addresses anxiety and its treatment. Includes an index.

Turecki, Stanley, and Leslie Tonner. *The Difficult Child*. 2d rev. ed. New York: Bantam Books, 2000. Provides information on childhood behavior problems. Includes bibliographical references and an index.

Nancy A. Piotrowski

See also:

Addictive Personality and Behaviors; Alcoholism; Anorexia Nervosa and Bulimia Nervosa; Anxiety Disorders; Attention-Deficit Disorder; Autism; Bed-Wetting; Behavioral Family Therapy; Brain Disorders; Child Abuse; Depression; Divorce and Separation: Children's Issues; Domestic Violence; Eating Disorders; Identity Crises; Mental Retardation; Obsessive-Compulsive Disorder; Paranoia; Phobias; Play Therapy; Psychosomatic Disorders; Psychotherapy: Children; Schizophrenia: High-Risk Children; Sleep Apnea Syndromes and Narcolepsy; Strategic Family Therapy; Stress; Teenage Suicide.

CODEPENDENT PERSONALITY

Type of psychology: Psychopathology
Fields of study: Personality theory; substance abuse

The codependent personality is characterized by a lack of a stable self-concept, which manifests itself in a troubled perception of self and disturbed relationships with others. By compulsively taking care of others and denying their own needs, often to the point of serious self-neglect, codependents seek an identity through achieving a favorable image in the eyes of others.

Principal terms

ADDICTION: a progressive, out-of-control pursuit of a substance, object, or relationship that results in life-damaging consequences for the addicted person

COMPULSION: a behavior or thought pattern in which the individual feels driven to engage, normally to ward off anxiety or other uncomfortable feelings

IDENTITY DEVELOPMENT: the process of forming a separate self with distinct thoughts, needs, and feelings that differentiate the self from others

SELF-CONCEPT: the individual's thoughts about the value of the self, particularly in relationship to others; it influences self-esteem, or feelings about the self

SYSTEMS THEORY: the interconnection of individuals in family, work, and community systems so that change in one member in the system necesarily produces change in the other members as well

Overview

At the foundation of the codependent personality is a pervasive lack of identity development. Codependents look to others for thoughts, feelings, and values that would normally come out of a well-developed sense of self. For example, when asked to offer an opinion on the death penalty, a typical codependent reaction would be to wait for the group consensus and offer a "safe" response—one that would be most in keeping with the thoughts of the group. This is often done subconsciously and is in contrast with the healthy reaction of offering an honest personal viewpoint.

In truth, codependents do not withhold their feelings as much as they are unaware of what they feel, because of their incomplete development of a separate self: They cannot reveal what they literally do not know. Since their self-perceptions are composites of the reflections they have received from others, how they present themselves will vary, often markedly, depending on who is with them. Codependents have difficulty recognizing and articulating feelings, and they often hold back their feelings out of fear. Though they may not be aware of their feelings, their feelings do, nevertheless, influence them. Their needs remain unmet in their desire to please others, or at the very least to avoid disapproval. As a result, they accumulate anger and rage for which they have no healthy outlet. Depression is also common, particularly a low-grade, chronic depression that would be relieved if they could focus on their own needs.

Codependents have high, and often unrealistic, expectations for themselves, and they tend to be perfectionists. An exaggerated fear of failure drives them, as does a barely conscious sense of being defective or somehow incomplete as a person. As the result of this poor evaluation of themselves, codependents fear getting close to others because others may judge them as harshly as they judge themselves. To guard against being "found out," they keep emotionally distant, although their behaviors may appear to others as genuinely warm and intimate. In truth, their real selves are closely guarded and available to no one—including themselves.

They often channel this backlog of unmet emotional needs into ad-

POSSIBLE CHARACTERISTICS OF CODEPENDENT PEOPLE

❖ an exaggerated sense of responsibility for the actions of others
❖ a tendency to confuse love and pity, with the tendency to "love" people they can pity and rescue
❖ a tendency to do more than their share, all the time
❖ a tendency to become hurt when people do not recognize their efforts
❖ an unhealthy dependence on relationships; the codependent will do anything to hold on to a relationship to avoid the feeling of abandonment
❖ an extreme need for approval and recognition
❖ a sense of guilt when asserting themselves
❖ a compelling need to control others
❖ lack of trust in self and/or others
❖ fear of being abandoned or alone
❖ difficulty identifying feelings
❖ rigidity/difficulty adjusting to change
❖ problems with intimacy/boundaries
❖ chronic anger
❖ lying/dishonesty
❖ poor communication
❖ difficulty making decisions

dictive or compulsive behaviors. When the pressure builds, codependents may seek diversion in shopping, gambling, work, chemicals, overeating, or other addictions. Instead of experiencing the emotional development that occurs from facing and overcoming interpersonal problems, codependents retreat further from their feelings through the quick "fix" of indulging in addictive behaviors. The effect of their inattention to their needs is cumulative and progressive and interferes with interpersonal relationships. Codependents take care of others, both emotionally and physically, to feel needed as caretakers. Their focus is primarily external, so they pay close attention to how others are feeling and behaving, then adjust how they act to receive the approval they crave.

Since codependents cannot be sure they are interpreting others' wants and needs correctly, their efforts to achieve approval are often unsuccessful. They have unrealistic perceptions of their abilities to control the environment, and when faced with normal limitations, they may frantically increase their efforts in the aim for perfection. As with all their efforts, the goal is self-esteem through external approval. Even when the approval is forthcoming, ironically, the satisfaction is small, because the approval is for a false representation of self. This leaves them feeling that if others really knew them, they would not be accepted. Codependents typically channel this feeling, as they do most other feelings, into more controlling and caretaking behaviors in an attempt to bolster self-esteem.

Because codependents have not developed clear identities, the interdependence between two persons that is characteristic of healthy relationships is not possible. Getting close brings fears of losing what little identity they have. Typically codependents move closer to others to achieve intimacy, then retreat when they fear the closeness will overwhelm them. They fear abandonment as well, so when the emotional distance from others seems too great, they move closer to others and again face their fears of intimacy overwhelming them. This dance between intimacy and distance is ultimately not satisfying and leaves the codependent feeling even more alone.

Codependency originates in settings where individuals feel unwilling or unable to display their true identities. Most typically, codependency occurs in addictive family systems where the family members' needs are secondary to the needs of the addicted individual. Family members cope with and adapt to the addiction in an attempt to stabilize the family system. Individual members' needs are not met if they conflict with the central need of keeping the family in balance and denying the effects of the addiction. Children in these family systems fail to develop separate identities because so much of their energy goes to controlling the environment. The adults in the family also may have failed to develop identities as children, or they may have abandoned their identities as adults under the pressure of keeping the family stable. In other words, codependency can be the result of the failure of normal identity development or of the abandonment of an already developed identity under the pressure of a dysfunctional family system.

Applications

A look at identity development in a healthy family system provides a clear picture of codependency. Theorist Erik Erikson proposed in 1963 that identity formation occurs through the resolution of crises throughout the life cycle. According to Erikson, as the individual masters the tasks of the various stages of development, he or she moves on to the next stage. Failure to work through the tasks of any stage results in incomplete development for the person. In a healthy family that meets a child's basic needs, he or she receives support and guidance to pass through the early stages of identity formation, as outlined by Erikson.

Stage one, trust versus mistrust, occurs from birth through the age of eighteen months; the second stage, autonomy versus shame and doubt, occurs between eighteen months and three years. Stage three, initiative versus guilt, lasts from the age of three to the age of six. Industry versus inferiority, the fourth stage, lasts from the age of six to age eighteen. The emerging identity is built upon the basic sense of trust the child develops in the early years of life. If experience teaches the child that others are not trustworthy, then the child's sense of self will be weak. Therefore, efforts to move through the later developmental stages will be hampered. In short, trust is essential to all the later developmental work.

In a family in which trust is not easily developed, such as in an addictive family system, the children direct most of their energy toward achieving a feeling of relative safety. The children learn to look to others to provide the sense of safety they could not develop internally. As they take care of other family members' needs, the family system remains stable, which provides a type of security, though the children's individual needs are not recognized and met. This external focus is adaptive in the short term, as the children are meeting some of their safety and security needs, but ultimately, mature identity development is thwarted. The more stable and emotionally healthy the parents are, the more likely it is that the child will move successfully through the later developmental stages. With the mastery of the developmental tasks, the child begins to feel like a competent individual in a stable and predictable environment. This emerging identity then forms the core of the self as a distinct individual.

Claudia Black (1981) identified roles that children adopt in alcoholic families in order to get some of their needs met. These roles have been found to be applicable to other dysfunctional family systems as well. The "responsible one," who is often the oldest child, functions as an adult by taking care of many basic needs of the family members, sometimes including the parents. The "adjuster" adapts to whatever the family system needs and avoids calling attention to himself or herself. The "placater" brings comfort and diversion to the family and takes on the responsibility for the family members' emotional stability. A final role is the "acting-out child," who keeps the family focused on his or her problem behaviors and receives punishment, criticism, and predominantly negative attention.

These roles can overlap so that the "responsible one" may alternate his or her overly mature behaviors with periods of acting out that direct the family's attention to the current problem and away from the fact that the whole family system is in trouble. The family can then console itself that without "the problem," it would be fine. The "placater" also might shift roles and take care of physical needs and responsibilities that would be more appropriately handled by the adults in the family. The "acting-out child" does not always act out; she or he can stop delinquent behaviors if they are not needed. The important issue for the development of codependency is not that children put the needs of the family ahead of their own but that they fill these roles to achieve safety emotionally and physically and fail to develop their own individual thoughts, needs, and feelings. Their development gets lost in their efforts to maintain the family balance.

This ability of codependents to adopt roles and cope despite how they feel is a major strength in certain settings, such as in an alcoholic or other unpredictable family setting. The adapting and responding to others becomes a problem when it is not a choice but is the only way that the codependent knows how to react. As adults, their behavioral repertoire is limited, as their response to demands is to adapt and take care of what everyone else needs first.

The picture is not as bleak as it may seem. Basic personality traits for such occupations as teaching, nursing, and counseling include empathy and the ability to "read" others, which are typically highly developed skills for codependents. On the whole, codependents are resourceful people who learned to survive in difficult circumstances by being acutely aware of the needs and viewpoints of others. The focus of treatment for these individuals is not to reconstruct their personalities but to help them expand their range of behavioral and emotional options.

Perspective and Prospects

The term "codependency" originated in the 1970's in the alcohol-treatment field to describe individuals whose lives had become unmanageable because of their relationships with alcoholics. Prior to that time the term used was "co-alcoholic" or "para-alcoholic," which described a cluster of symptoms that the family members of the alcoholic displayed that included depression, anxiety, and interpersonal difficulties. The introduction of the term "codependency" helped to define the cluster of symptoms more clearly so that codependency became a legitimate focus for treatment. Families began receiving treatment targeted at their needs, at times completely independent of the alcoholic's treatment. Research showed that this focus on the family's need resulted in longer-term sobriety for the alcoholic.

In the 1980's, clinicians became aware that while codependency most obviously arose from alcoholic families or relationships, it also occurred where other addictions or serious dysfunctions were present. Thus, the model for understanding codependency began to be applied by professionals to diverse problems such as eating disorders, gambling, and other addictions. Codependency as an issue began to gain the attention of professionals beyond the addictions field and in other treatment disciplines.

Many traditional clinicians and researchers have been slow to accept codependency as a legitimate treatment issue since the theory has not been grounded in the scholarly research considered necessary for establishing new trends in the field. Clinicians who treat clients for codependency issues maintain, however, that it is not necessary to wait for research to verify what has already been shown to be useful in clinical practice. Their position is that when a treatment modality helps people, it is ethical to continue the treatment concurrently with the research that should ultimately validate their work. Treatment for codependency has been multifaceted and is apparently most effective when it includes some combination of individual or group therapy, self-help groups, workshops, and educational resources. Through the various treatment strategies, codependents begin to recognize the positive aspects of their personalities, such as adaptiveness and the ability to intuit what others need. In time they can learn to extend to themselves the same attention and caretaking they previously gave only to others.

A common fear of codependents is that if they stop being "caretakers" of others they will become uncaring individuals. This fear is usually unfounded, since greater intimacy and depth of emotion are possible in relationships in which individuals give to others by choice rather than through the continuing sacrifice of their own needs. Codependent personalities develop out of dysfunctional family, community, or other systems; when left untreated, this situation results in a continued poor self-concept and in disturbed relationships with others. Treatment has apparently been effective in helping codependents make significant changes. Recognition of codependent traits can therefore be a springboard for personal growth and development rather than a cause for despair.

Bibliography

Ackerman, Robert J., ed. *Growing in the Shadow: Children of Alcoholics.* Pompano Beach, Fla.: Health Communications, 1986. A collection of brief essays by leaders in the adult children of alcoholics and codependency recovery movements. Includes an outline of the causes and treatments of codependency as well as crosscultural and family treatment considerations. Valuable to the professional yet readily comprehensible by the lay reader.

Beattie, Melody. *Codependent No More.* New York: Harper/Hazelden, 1987. A comprehensive overview of codependency that is complete with clear examples. A bestseller for many months and probably the most frequently read book in the codependency recovery movement. The majority of the book is devoted to self-help principles for codependents.

Cermak, Timmen L. *Diagnosing and Treating Co-Dependence.* Minneapolis: Johnson Institute Books, 1986. A proposal to have "codependency" declared a diagnostic category by the American Psychiatric Association. Aimed at a professional audience, but may be of interest to the lay reader.

Erikson, Erik H. *Identity, Youth, and Crisis.* New York: W. W. Norton, 1968. Erikson's theory on the development of identity throughout the stages of the life cycle. A highly theoretical, classic work.

Friel, John. *Adult Children: Secrets of Dysfunctional Families.* Deerfield Beach, Fla.: Health Communications, 1988. A comprehensive overview of dysfunctional family systems and their predictable effects on family members. Clearly written, a valuable resource for both general and professional audiences.

Haskell, Robert E. *Adult-Child Research and Experience: Personal and Professional Legacies of a Dysfunctional Co-Dependent Family.* Norwood, N.J.: Ablex, 1993. Focuses on the adult children of alcoholics and the psychology of alcoholism and codependency. Includes bibliographical references and indexes.

Rice, John Steadman. *A Disease of One's Own: Psychotherapy, Addiction, and the Emergence of Co-Dependency.* New Brunswick, N.J.: Transaction, 1996. Examines the phenomenon of codependency from a sociological perspective, not as a disease but as a belief system that offers a way of talking about the self and social relationships. Includes bibliographical references and an index.

Schaef, Anne Wilson. *Co-Dependence: Misunderstood-Mistreated.* San Francisco: Harper & Row, 1986. An integration of the principles of the chemical dependency and mental health fields. Covers the history and development of the concept of codependence. Mostly written for a general audience; some chapters are directed toward professionals.

Linda E. Meashey

See also:

Addictive Personality and Behaviors; Alcoholism; Behavioral Assessment and Personality Rating Scales; Behavioral Family Therapy; Identity Crises; Substance Abuse.

COGNITIVE BEHAVIOR THERAPY

Type of psychology: Psychotherapy
Fields of study: Behavioral therapies

A number of approaches to therapy fall within the scope of cognitive behavior therapy. These approaches all share a theoretical perspective that assumes that internal cognitive processes, called thinking or cognition, affect behavior; that this cognitive activity may be monitored; and that desired behavior change may be effected through cognitive change.

Principal terms

BEHAVIOR THERAPY: a branch of psychotherapy narrowly conceived as the application of classical and operant conditioning to the alteration of clinical problems, but more broadly conceived as applied experimental psychology in a clinical context

COGNITION: private or internal processes such as imagery, symbolic representation of external events, and the verbal coding of experience

COGNITIVE RESTRUCTURING: any behavior therapy procedure that attempts to alter the manner in which clients think about life so that they change their overt behavior and emotions

COGNITIVE THERAPY: a therapeutic approach developed by Aaron T. Beck, the goal of which is for patients to discover for themselves the irrationality of their thoughts

DEPRESSION: strong feelings of sadness, dejection, and often apathy that last more than two weeks and pervade a person's thoughts

Overview

The cognitive behavior therapies are not a single therapeutic approach, but rather a loosely organized collection of therapeutic approaches that share a similar set of assumptions. At their core, cognitive behavior therapies share three fundamental propositions: Cognitive activity affects behavior; cognitive activity may be monitored and altered; and desired behavior change may be effected through cognitive change.

The first of the three fundamental propositions of cognitive behavior therapy suggests that it is not the external situation which determines feelings and behavior, but rather the person's view or perception of that external situation that determines feelings and behavior. For example, if one has failed the first examination of a course, one could appraise it as a temporary setback to be overcome or as a horrible loss. While the situation remains the same, the thinking about that situation is radically different in the two examples cited. Each of these views will lead to significantly different emotions and behaviors.

The third cognitive behavioral assumption suggests that desired behavior change may be effected through cognitive change. Thus, while cognitive behavior theorists do not reject the notion that rewards and punishment (reinforcement contingencies) can alter behavior, they are likely to emphasize that there are alternative methods for behavior change, one in particular being cognitive change. Many approaches to therapy fall within the scope of cognitive behavior therapy as it is defined above. While these approaches share the theoretical assumptions described above, a review of the major therapeutic procedures subsumed under the heading of cognitive behavior therapy reveals a diverse amalgam of principles and procedures, representing a variety of theoretical and philosophical perspectives.

Rational-emotive therapy, developed by psychologist Albert Ellis, is regarded by many as one of the premier examples of the cognitive behavioral approach; it was introduced in the early 1960's. Ellis proposed that many people are made unhappy by their faulty, irrational beliefs, which influence the way they interpret events. The therapist will interact with the patient or client, attempting to direct the patient to more positive and realistic views. Cognitive therapy, pioneered by Aaron T. Beck, has been applied to such problems as depression and stress. For stress reduction, ideas and thoughts that are producing stress in the patient will be questioned; the therapist will get the patient to examine the validity of these thoughts; thought processes can then be restructured so the situations seem less stressful. Cognitive therapy has been found to be quite effective in treating depression, as compared with other therapeutic methods. Beck held that depression is caused by certain types of negative thoughts, such as devaluing the self or viewing the future in a consistently pessimistic way.

Rational behavior therapy, developed by psychiatrist Maxie Maultsby, is a close relative of Ellis's rational-emotive therapy. In this approach, Maultsby combines several approaches to include rational-emotive therapy, neuropsychology, classical and operant conditioning, and psychosomatic research; however, Maultsby was primarily influenced by his association with Ellis. In this approach, Maultsby attempts to couch his theory of emotional disturbance in terms of neuropsychophysiology and learning theory. Rational behavior therapy assumes that repeated pairings of a perception with evaluative thoughts lead to rational or irrational emotive and behavioral reactions. Maultsby suggests that self-talk, which originates in the left hemisphere of the brain, triggers corresponding right-hemisphere emotional equivalents. Thus, in order to maintain a state of psychological health, individuals must practice rational self-talk that will, in turn, cause the right brain to convert left-brain language into appropriate emotional and behavioral reactions.

Rational behavior therapy techniques are quite similar to those of rational-emotive therapy. Both therapies stress the importance of monitoring one's thoughts in order to become aware of the elements of the emotional disturbance. In addition, Maultsby advocates the use of rational-emotive imagery, behavioral practice, and relaxation methods in order to minimize emotional distress.

Self-instructional training was developed by psychologist Donald Meichenbaum in the early 1970's. In contrast to Ellis and Beck, whose prior training was in psychoanalysis, Meichenbaum's roots are in behaviorism and the behavioral therapies. Thus Meichenbaum's approach is heavily couched in behavioral terminology and procedures. Meichenbaum's work stems from his earlier research in training schizophrenic patients to emit "healthy speech." By chance, Meichenbaum observed that patients who engaged in spontaneous self-instruction were less distracted and demonstrated superior task performance on a variety of tasks. As a result, Meichenbaum emphasizes the critical role of "self-instructions"—simple instructions such as, "Relax. . . . Just attend to the task"—and their noticeable effect on subsequent behavior.

Meichenbaum developed self-instructional training to treat the deficits in self-instructions manifested in impulsive children. The ultimate goal of this program was to decrease impulsive behavior. The way to accomplish this goal, as hypothesized by Meichenbaum, was to train impulsive children to generate verbal self-commands, to respond to their verbal self-commands, and to encourage the children to self-reinforce their behavior appropriately.

The specific procedures employed in self-instructional training involve having the child observe a model performing a task. While the model is performing the task, he or she is talking aloud. The child then performs the same task while the model gives verbal instructions. Subsequently, the child performs the task while instructing himself or herself aloud, then while whispering the instructions. Finally, the child performs the task covertly. The self-instructions employed in the program included questions about the nature and demands of the task, answers to these questions in the form of cognitive rehearsal, self-instructions in the form of self-guidance while performing the task, and self-reinforcement. Meichenbaum and his associates have found that this self-instructional training program significantly improves the task performance of impulsive children across a number of measures.

Systematic rational restructuring is a cognitive behavioral procedure developed by psychologist Marvin Goldfried in the mid-1970's. This procedure is a variation on Ellis's rational-emotive therapy; however, it is more clearly structured than Ellis's method. In systematic rational restructuring, Goldfried suggests that early social learning experiences teach individuals to label situations in different ways. Further, Goldfried suggests that emotional reactions may be understood as responses to the way individuals label situations, as opposed to responses to the situations themselves. The goal of systematic rational restructuring is to train clients to perceive situational cues more accurately.

The process of systematic rational restructuring is similar to systematic desensitization, in which a subject is to imagine fearful scenes in a graduated order from the least fear-provoking to the more fear-provoking scenes. In systematic rational restructuring, the client is asked to imagine a hierarchy of anxiety-eliciting situations. At each step, the client is instructed to identify irrational thoughts associated with the specific situation, to dispute them, and to reevaluate the situation more rationally. In addition, clients are instructed to practice rational restructuring in specific real-life situations.

Stress inoculation training incorporates several of the specific therapies already described in this section. This procedure was developed by psychologist Donald

Meichenbaum. Stress inoculation training is analogous to being inoculated against disease. That is, it prepares clients to deal with stress-inducing events by teaching them to use coping skills at low levels of the stressful situation, and then gradually to cope with more and more stressful situations. Stress inoculation training involves three phases: conceptualization, skill acquisition and rehearsal, and application and follow-through.

In the conceptualization phase of stress inoculation training, clients are given an adaptive way of viewing and understanding their negative reactions to stressful events. In the skills-acquisition and rehearsal phase, clients learn coping skills appropriate to the type of stress they are experiencing. With interpersonal anxiety, the client might develop skills that would make the feared situation less threatening (for example, learning to initiate and maintain conversations). The client might also learn deep muscle relaxation to lessen tension. In the case of anger, clients learn to view potential provocations as problems that require a solution rather than as threats that require an attack. Clients are also taught to rehearse alternative strategies for solving the problem at hand.

The application and follow-through phase of stress inoculation training involves the clients practicing and applying the coping skills. Initially, clients are exposed to low levels of stressful situations in imagery. They practice applying their coping skills to handle the stressful events, and they overtly role-play dealing with stressful events. Next, the client is given homework assignments that involve gradual exposure to actual stressful events in his or her everyday life. Stress inoculation training has been effectively applied to many types of problems. It has been used to help people cope with anger, anxiety, fear, pain, and health-related problems (for example, cancer and hypertension). It appears to be suitable for all age levels.

Problem-solving therapy, as developed by psychologists Thomas D'Zurilla and Marvin Goldfried, is also considered one of the cognitive behavioral approaches. In essence, problem-solving therapy is the application of problem-solving theory and research to the domain of personal and emotional problems. Indeed, the authors see the ability to solve problems as the necessary and sufficient condition for emotional and behavioral stability. Problem solving is, in one way or another, a part of all psychotherapies.

Applications
Cognitive behavior therapists have taught general problem-solving skills to clients with two specific aims: to alleviate the particular personal problems for which clients have sought therapy, and to provide clients with a general coping strategy for personal problems.

The actual steps of problem solving that a client is taught to carry out systematically are as follows. First, it is necessary to define the dilemma as a problem to be solved. Next, a goal must be selected which reflects the ultimate outcome the client desires. The client then generates a list of many different possible solutions, without evaluating their potential merit (a kind of brainstorming). Now the client evaluates the pros and cons of each alternative in terms of the probability that it will meet the goal selected and its practicality, which involves considering the potential consequences to oneself and to others of each solution. The alternative solutions are ranked in terms of desirability and practicality, and the highest one is selected. Next, the client tries to implement the solution chosen. Finally, the client evaluates the therapy, assessing whether the solution alleviated the problem and met the goal, and, if not, what went wrong—in other words, which of the steps in problem solving needs to be redone.

Problem-solving therapies have been used to treat a variety of target behaviors with a wide range of clients. Examples include peer relationship difficulties among children and adolescents, examination and interpersonal anxiety among college students, relapse following a program to reduce smoking, harmony among family members, and the ability of chronic psychiatric patients to cope with interpersonal problems.

Self-control therapy for depression, developed by psychologist Lynn Rehm, is an approach to treating depression which combines the self-regulatory notions of behavior therapy and the cognitive focus of the cognitive behavioral approaches. Essentially, Rehm believes that depressed people show deficits in one or some combination of the following areas: monitoring (selectively attending to negative events), self-evaluation (setting unrealistically high goals), and self-reinforcement (emitting high rates of self-punishment and low rates of self-reward). These three components are further broken down into a total of six functional areas.

According to Rehm, the varied symptom picture in clinically depressed clients is a function of different subsets of these deficits. Over the course of therapy with a client, each of the six self-control deficits is described, with emphasis on how a particular deficit is causally related to depression, and on what can be done to remedy the deficit. A variety of clinical strategies are employed to teach clients self-control skills, including group discussion, overt and covert reinforcement, behavioral assignments, self-monitoring, and modeling.

Structural psychotherapy is a cognitive behavioral approach that derives from the work of two Italian mental health professionals, psychiatrist Vittorio Guidano and psychologist Gianni Liotti. These authors are strongly persuaded by cognitive psychology, social learning theory, evolutionary epistemology, psychodynamic theory, and cognitive therapy. Guidano and Liotti suggest that for an understanding of the full complexity of an emotional disorder and subsequent development of an adequate model of psychotherapy, an appreciation of the development and the active role of an individual's knowledge of self and the world is critical. In short, in order to understand a patient, one must understand the structure of that person's world.

Guidano and Liotti's therapeutic process utilizes the empirical problem-solving approach of the scientist. Indeed, the authors suggest that therapists should assist clients in disengaging themselves from certain ingrained beliefs and judgments, and in considering them as hypotheses and theories subject to disproof, confirmation, and logical challenge. A variety of behavioral experiments and cognitive techniques are utilized to assist the patient in assessing and critically evaluating his or her beliefs.

As can be seen, the area of cognitive behavior therapy involves a wide collection of therapeutic approaches and techniques. The approaches described here are but a representative sample of possible cognitive behavioral approaches. Also included within this domain are anxiety management training, which comes from the work of psychologist Richard Suinn. and personal science, from the work of psychologist Michael Mahoney.

The cognitive behavioral approaches are derived from a variety of perspectives, including cognitive theory, classical and operant conditioning approaches, problem-solving theory, and developmental theory. All these approaches share the perspective that internal cognitive processes, called thinking or cognition, affect behavior, and that behavior change may be effected through cognitive change.

These approaches have several other similarities. One is that all the approaches see therapy as time-limited. This is in sharp distinction to the traditional psychoanalytic therapies, which are generally open-ended. The cognitive behavior therapies attempt to effect change rapidly, often with specific, preset lengths of therapeutic contact. Another similarity among the cognitive behavior therapies is that their target of change is also limited. For example, in the treatment of depression, the target of change is the symptoms of depression. Thus, in the cognitive behavioral approaches to treatment, one sees a time-limited focus and a limited target of change.

Perspective and Prospects

Cognitive behavior therapy evolved from two lines of clinical and research activity: First, it derives from the work of the early cognitive therapists (Albert Ellis and Aaron Beck); second, it was strongly influenced by the careful empirical work of the early behaviorists.

Within the domain of behaviorism, cognitive processes were not always seen as a legitimate focus of attention. That is, in behavior therapy, there has always been a strong commitment to an applied science of clinical treatment. In the behavior therapy of the 1950's and 1960's, this emphasis on scientific methods and procedures meant that behavior therapists focused on events that were directly observable and measurable. Within this framework, behavior was seen as a function of external stimuli which determined or were reliably associated with observable responses. Also during this period, there was a deliberate avoidance of such "nebulous" concepts as thoughts, cognitions, or images. It was believed that these processes were by their very nature vague, and one could never be confident that one was reliably observing or measuring these processes.

It is important to note that by following scientific principles, researchers developed major new treatment approaches which in many ways revolutionized clinical practice (among them are systematic desensitization and the use of a token economy). Yet during the 1960's, several developments within behavior therapy had emphasized the limitations of a strict conditioning model to understanding human behavior.

In 1969, psychologist Albert Bandura published his influential volume *Principles of Behavior Modification*. In this volume, Bandura emphasized the role of internal or cognitive factors in the causation and maintenance of behavior. Following from the dissatisfaction of the radical behavioral approaches to understanding complex human behavior and the publication of Bandura's 1969 volume, behavior therapists began actively to seek and study the role of cognitive processes in human behavior.

Bibliography

Basco, Monica Ramirez, and A. John Rush. *Cognitive-Behavioral Therapy for Bipolar Disorder*. Foreword by Robert M. Post. New York: Guilford Press, 1996. Presents useful cognitive-behavioral techniques for managing bipolar disorder. Describes the benefits of using an integrated approach to treating the disorder and discusses its diagnosis, course, and characteristics.

D'Zurilla, Thomas J., and Arthur M. Nezu. *Problem-Solving Therapy: A Social Competence Approach to Clinical Intervention*. 2d ed. New York: Springer, 1999. An introduction and guide for therapists and counselors in the mental health professions to the approach as a reliable clinical treatment, health maintenance strategy, and prevention program.

_____. "Social Problem-Solving in Adults." In *Advances in Cognitive-Behavioral Research and Therapy*, edited by Philip C. Kendall. Vol. 1. New York: Academic Press, 1982. An excellent summary of problem-solving therapy. As indicated by its title, the Kendall book in which this article appears also contains other informative articles dealing with cognitive behavior therapy.

Goldfried, Marvin R. "The Use of Relaxation and Cognitive Relabeling as Coping Skills." In *Behavioral Self-Management: Strategies, Techniques, and Outcomes*, edited by Richard B. Stuart. New York: Brunner/Mazel, 1977. A description of systematic rational restructuring by Marvin Goldfried, who developed the technique; reveals its similarities to and differences from rational-emotive therapy.

Hayes, Steven C., Kirk D. Strosahl, and Kelly G. Wilson. *Acceptance and Commitment Therapy: An Experiential Approach to Behavior Change*. New York: Guilford Press, 1999. Provides a theory of psychopathology and a practical treatment model. The authors show how interventions based on metaphor, paradox, and experiential exercises can help clients make contact with thoughts, feelings, memories, and physical sensations that have been feared and avoided. Features detailed clinical guidelines and case examples demonstrating the approach in action.

Maultsby, Maxie C., Jr. *Rational Behavior Therapy*. Englewood Cliffs, N.J.: Prentice-Hall, 1984. An excellent summary of rational behavior therapy, as developed by Maultsby; discusses self-talk and its emotional and behavioral consequences.

Meichenbaum, Donald. *Cognitive Behavior Modification*. New York: Plenum Press, 1977. A well-written introduction to Meichenbaum's approaches, with clear examples of the applications of self-instructional training to impulsive children and schizophrenic patients.

_____. *Stress Inoculation Training*. New York: Pergamon Press, 1985. This short training manual presents a clear, useful overview of stress inoculation training, along with a detailed account of the empirical research completed in testing the approach.

Sperry, Len. *Cognitive Behavior Therapy of DSM-IV Personality Disorders: Highly Effective Interventions for the Most Common Disorders*. Philadelphia: Brunner/Mazel, 1999. Provides specific treatment strategies for avoidant, borderline, dependent, narcissistic, histrionic, and obsessive-compulsive personality disorders. Includes bibliographical references and an index.

Donald G. Beal

See also:

Analytical Psychotherapy; Cognitive Therapy; Person-Centered Therapy; Psychotherapy: Goals and Techniques; Psychotherapy: Historical Approaches to Treatment.

COGNITIVE THERAPY

Type of psychology: Psychotherapy
Fields of study: Cognitive therapies

Cognitive therapy holds that emotional disorders are largely determined by cognition or thinking, that cognitive activity can take the form of language or images, and that emotional disorders can be treated by helping patients modify their cognitive distortions. Treatment programs based on this model have been highly successful with depression, panic disorder, generalized anxiety disorder, and other emotional problems.

Principal terms

ARBITRARY INFERENCE: the process of drawing a conclusion from an experience where there is no evidence to support such a conclusion

AUTOMATIC THOUGHTS: thoughts experienced by individuals of which they are dimly aware and that seem believable, but that can be highly unrealistic and maladaptive

COGNITIVE SPECIFICITY HYPOTHESIS: the idea that each of the emotional disorders is characterized by its own patterns of thinking or cognitive distortions

COGNITIVE TRIAD: seen as the core of depression; consists of a negative view of the self, one's experiences, and the future

SCHEMATA: fundamental beliefs people hold about themselves or the world; these beliefs appear to be the rules by which one lives

SELECTIVE ABSTRACTION: focusing on something taken out of context and conceptualizing the experience on the basis of this particular element

Overview

Cognitive therapy, originally developed by Aaron T. Beck, is based on the view that cognition (the process of acquiring knowledge and forming beliefs) is a primary determinant of mood and behavior. Beck developed his theory while treating depressed patients. He noticed that these patients tended to distort whatever happened to them in the direction of self-blame and catastrophes. Thus, an event interpreted by a normal person as irritating and inconvenient (for example, the malfunctioning of an automobile) would be interpreted by the depressed patient as another example of the utter hopelessness of life. Beck's central point is that depressives draw illogical conclusions and come to evaluate negatively themselves, their immediate world, and their future. They see only personal failings, present misfortunes, and overwhelming difficulties ahead. It is from these cognitions that all the other symptoms of depression derive.

It was from Beck's early work with depressed patients that cognitive therapy was developed. Shortly thereafter, the concepts and procedures were applied to other psychological problems, with notable success.

Two concepts of particular relevance to cognitive therapy are the concepts of automatic thoughts and schemata (schemata is the plural of schema). Automatic thoughts are thoughts that appear to be going on all the time. These thoughts are quite brief—only the essential words in a sentence seem to occur, as in a tele-graphic style. Further, they seem to be autonomous, in that the person made no effort to initiate them, and they seem plausible or reasonable to the person (although they may seem far-fetched to somebody else). Thus, as a depressed person is giving a talk to a group of business colleagues, he or she will have a variety of thoughts. There will be thoughts about the content of the material. There is also a second stream of thoughts occurring. In this second channel, the person may experience such thoughts as: "This is a waste of time," or "They think I'm dumb." These are automatic thoughts.

Beck has suggested that although automatic thoughts are occurring all the time, the person is likely to overlook these thoughts when asked what he or she is thinking. Thus, it is necessary to train the person to attend to these automatic thoughts. Beck pointed out that when people are depressed, these automatic thoughts are filled with negative thoughts of the self, the world, and the future. Further, these automatic thoughts are quite distorted, and finally, when these thoughts are carefully examined and modified to be more in keeping with reality, the depression subsides.

The concept of schemata, or core beliefs, becomes critical in understanding why some people are prone to having emotional difficulties and others are not. The schema appears to be the root from which the automatic thoughts derive. Beck suggests that people develop a propensity to think crookedly as a result of early life experiences. He theorizes that in early life, an individual forms concepts—realistic as well as unrealis-tic—from experiences. Of particular importance are individuals' attitudes toward themselves, their environment, and their future. These deeply held core beliefs about oneself are seen by Beck as critical in the causation of emotional disorders. According to cognitive theory, the reason these early beliefs are so critical is that once they are formed, the person has a tendency to distort or view subsequent experiences to be consistent with these core beliefs. Thus, an individual who, as a child, was subjected to severe, unprovoked punishment from a disturbed parent may conclude "I am weak" or "I am inferior." Once this conclusion has been formulated, it would appear to be strongly reinforced over years and years of experiences at the hands of the parent. Thus, when this individual becomes an adult, he or she tends to interpret even normal frustrations as more proof of the original belief: "See, I really am inferior." Examples of these negative schemata or core beliefs are: "I am weak," "I am inferior," "I am unlovable," and "I cannot do anything right." People holding such core beliefs about themselves would differ strongly in their views of a frustrating experience from those people who hold a core belief such as "I am capable."

Another major contribution of cognitive therapy is Beck's cognitive specificity hypothesis. Specifically, Beck has suggested that each of the emotional disorders is characterized by its own patterns of thinking. In the case of depression, the thought content is concerned with ideas of personal deficiency, impossible envi-ronmental demands and obstacles, and nihilistic expectations. For example, a depressed patient might interpret a frustrating situation, such as a malfunctioning automobile, as evidence of his or her own inadequacy: "If I were really competent, I would have anticipated this problem and been able to avoid it." Additionally, the depressed patient might react to the malfunctioning automobile with: "This is too much, I cannot take it anymore." To the depressed patient, this would simply be another example of the utter hopelessness of life.

While the cognitive content of depression emphasizes the negative view of the self, the world, and the future, anxiety disorders are characterized by fears of physical and psychological danger. The anxious patient's thoughts are filled with themes of danger. These people anticipate detrimental occurrences to themselves, their family, their property, their status, and other intangibles that they value.

In phobias, as in anxiety, there is the cognitive theme of danger; however, the "danger" is confined to definable situations. As long as phobic sufferers are able to avoid these situations, then they do not feel threatened and may be relatively calm. The cognitive content of panic disorder is characterized by a catastrophic interpretation of bodily or mental experiences. Thus, patients with panic disorder are prone to regard any unexplained symptom or sensation as a sign of some impending catastrophe. As a result, their cognitive processing system focuses their attention on bodily or psychological experience. For example, one patient saw discomfort in the chest as evidence of an impending heart attack.

The cognitive feature of the paranoid reaction is the misinterpretation of experience in terms of mistreatment, abuse, or persecution. The cognitive theme of the conversion disorder (a disorder characterized by physical complaints such as paralysis or blindness, where no underlying physical basis can be determined) is the conviction that one has a physical disorder. As a result of this belief, the patient experiences sensory and/or motor abnormalities that are consistent with the patient's faulty conception of organic pathology.

Applications

The goal of cognitive therapy is to assist the patient to evaluate his or her thought processes carefully, to identify cognitive errors, and to substitute more adaptive, realistic cognitions. This goal is accomplished by therapists helping patients to see their thinking about themselves (or their situation) as similar to the activity of a scientist—that they are engaged in the activity of developing hypotheses (or theories) about their world. Like a scientist, the patient needs to "test" his or her theory carefully. Thus, patients who have concluded that they are "worthless" people would be encouraged to test their "theories" rigorously to determine if this is indeed accurate. Further, in the event that the theories are not accurate, patients would be encouraged to change their theories to make them more consistent with reality (what they find in their experience).

A slightly different intervention developed by Beck and his colleagues is to help the patient identify common cognitive distortions. Beck originally identified four cognitive distortions frequently found in emotional disorders: arbitrary inference, selective abstraction, overgeneralization, and magnification or minimization. These were later expanded to ten or more by Beck's colleagues and students.

Arbitrary inference is defined as the process of drawing a conclusion from a situation, event, or experience when there is no evidence to support the conclusion or when the conclusion is contrary to the evidence. For example, a depressed patient on a shopping trip had the thought, "The salesclerk thinks I am a nobody." The patient then felt sad. On being questioned by the psychologist, the patient realized that there was no factual basis for this thought. Selective abstraction refers to the process of focusing on a detail taken out of context, ignoring other, more salient features of the situation, and conceptualizing the whole experience on the basis of this element. For example, a patient was praised by friends about the patient's child-care activities. Through an oversight, however, the patient failed to have her child vaccinated during the appropriate week. Her immediate thought was, "I am a failure as a mother." This idea became paramount despite all the other evidence of her competence.

Overgeneralization refers to patients' patterns of drawing a general conclusion about their ability, their performance, or their worth on the basis of a single incident. For example, a student regards his poor performance on the first examination of the semester as final proof that he "will never make it in college." Magnification and minimization refer to gross errors in evaluation. For example, a person, believing that he has completely ruined his car (magnification) when he sees that there is a slight scratch on the rear fender, regards himself as "good for nothing." In contrast, minimization refers to minimizing one's achievements, protesting that these achievements do not mean anything. For example, a highly successful businesswoman who was depressed concluded that her many prior successes "were nothing . . . simply luck." Using the cognitive distortions, people are taught to examine their thoughts, to identify any distortions, and then to modify their thoughts in order to eliminate the distortions.

In terms of the therapeutic process, the focus is initially on the automatic thoughts of patients. Once patients are relatively adept at identifying and modifying their maladaptive automatic thoughts, the therapy begins to focus on the maladaptive underlying beliefs or schemata. As previously noted, these beliefs are fundamental beliefs that people hold about themselves. These beliefs are not as easy to identify as the automatic thoughts. Rather, they are identified in an inferential process. Common patterns are observed; for example, the person may seem to be operating by the rule: "If I am not the best [parent, spouse, employee], then I am a failure," or "If I am not loved by my spouse or mate, then I am worthless." As in the case of the earlier cognitive work with automatic thoughts, these beliefs are carefully evaluated for their adaptability or rationality. Maladaptive beliefs are then modified to more adaptive, realistic beliefs.

A variety of techniques have been developed by cognitive therapists for modifying maladaptive cognitions. One example of these techniques is self-monitoring. This involves the patient's keeping a careful hour-by-hour record of his or her activities, associated moods, or other pertinent phenomena. One useful variant is to have the patient record his or her mood on a simple zero-to-one-hundred scale, where zero represents the worst he or she has ever felt and one hundred represents the best. In addition, the patient can record the degree of mastery or pleasure associated with each recorded activity.

A number of hypotheses can be tested using self-monitoring, such as: "It does not do any good for me to get out of bed," "I am always miserable; it never lets up," and "My schedule is too full for me to accomplish what I must." By simply checking the self-monitoring log, one can easily determine if one's miserable mood ever ceases. A careful examination of the completed record is a far better basis for judging such hypotheses than is the patient's memory of recent events, because his or her recollections are almost always tainted by the depression.

As therapy progresses and patients begin to experience more elevated moods, the focus of treatment becomes more cognitive. Patients are instructed to observe and record automatic thoughts, perhaps at a specific time each evening, as well as recording when they become aware of increased dysphoria. Typically, the thoughts are negative self-referents ("I am worthless"; "I will never amount to anything"), and initially, the therapist points out their unreasonable and self-defeating nature. With practice, patients learn "distancing," that is, dealing with such thoughts objectively and evaluating them rather than blindly accepting them. Homework assignments can facilitate distancing: The patient records an automatic thought, and next to it he or she writes down a thought that counters the automatic thought, as the therapist might have done. According to Beck, certain basic themes soon emerge, such as being abandoned, as well as stylistic patterns of thinking, such as overgeneralization. The themes reflect the aforementioned rules, and the ultimate goal of therapy is to assist the patient to modify them.

Finally, cognitive therapy has been applied to a variety of psychological disorders with striking success. For example, studies from seven independent centers have compared the efficacy of cognitive therapy with antidepressant medication, a treatment of established efficacy. Comparisons of cognitive therapy to drugs have found cognitive therapy to be superior or equal to antidepressant medication. Further, follow-up studies indicate that cognitive therapy has greater long-term effects than drug therapy. Of special significance is the evidence of greater sustained improvement over time with cognitive therapy.

Cognitive therapy has been successfully applied to panic disorder, resulting in practically complete reduction of panic attacks after twelve to sixteen weeks of treatment. Additionally, cognitive therapy has been successfully applied to generalized anxiety disorder, eating disorders, and inpatient depression.

Perspective and Prospects

Cognitive theory and cognitive therapy originated in Aaron T. Beck's observation and treatment of depressed patients. Originally trained in psychoanalysis, Beck observed that his patients experienced specific types of thoughts, of which they were only dimly aware, that they did not report during their free associations. Beck noticed that these thoughts were frequently followed by an unpleasant effect. Further, he noted that as the patients examined and modified their thoughts, their mood began to improve.

At the time of the emergence of the cognitive model, the treatment world was dominated primarily by the psychoanalytic model (with its heavy emphasis on the unconscious processes) and to a lesser extent by the behavioral model (with its emphasis on the behavioral processes, to the exclusion of thought). The psycho-analytic model was under attack, primarily because of a lack of careful empirical support. In contrast, behavior therapists were actively demonstrating the efficacy of their approaches in carefully designed studies. Beck and his students began to develop and test cognitive procedures systematically, and they have developed an impressive body of research support for the approach.

Bibliography

Beck, Aaron T. *Cognitive Therapy and the Emotional Disorders.* New York: International Universities Press, 1976. An easy-to-read book that presents a general overview of the cognitive model and illustrates the cognitive model of different psychological disorders.

Beck, Aaron T., and Gary Emery. *Anxiety Disorders and Phobias: A Cognitive Perspective.* New York: Basic Books, 1985. Presents the cognitive theory and model of anxiety disorders, as well as the clinical techniques used with anxious patients.

Beck, Aaron T., A. J. Rush, B. F. Shaw, and Gary Emery. *Cognitive Therapy of Depression.* New York: Guilford Press, 1979. Presents the cognitive theory of depression and actual techniques used with depressed patients. Both makes a theoretical contribution and serves as a clinical handbook on depression.

Bieber, Irving. *Cognitive Psychoanalysis.* New York: Jason Aronson, 1995. Examines cognition and self-perception. Includes a bibliography and an index.

Bucci, Wilma. *Psychoanalysis and Cognitive Science: A Multiple Code Theory.* New York: Guilford Press, 1997. Proposes a new model of psychological organization that integrates psychoanalytic theory with the investigation of mental processes. Based in cognitive science.

Dowd, E. Thomas. *Cognitive Hypnotherapy.* Northvale, N.J.: Jason Aronson, 2000. This volume in the series New Directions in Cognitive-Behavior Therapy addresses the therapeutic use of hypnotism. Includes bibliographical references and an index.

Leahy, Robert L. *Cognitive Therapy: Basic Principles and Applications.* Northvale, N.J.: Jason Aronson, 1996. Describes Beck's model of depression, anxiety, anger, and relationship conflict, showing how each is handled through cognitive therapy. Includes bibliographical references and an index.

McCullough, James P., Jr. *Treatment for Chronic Depression: Cognitive Behavioral Analysis System of Psychotherapy (CBASP).* New York: Guilford Press, 2000. Discusses the diagnosis of and therapy for depressive disorder. Includes bibliographical references and an index.

McMullin, Rian E. *The New Handbook of Cognitive Therapy Techniques.* Rev. ed. New York: W. W. Norton, 2000. A manual discussing cognitive therapies. Includes bibliographical references and an index.

Donald G. Beal

See also:

Agoraphobia and Panic Disorders; Analytical Psychotherapy; Anxiety Disorders; Cognitive Behavior Therapy; Depression; Person-Centered Therapy; Psychotherapy: Goals and Techniques; Psychotherapy: Historical Approaches to Treatment.

COMMUNITY PSYCHOLOGY

Type of psychology: Social psychology
Fields of study: Attitudes and behavior; social perception and cognition

Community psychology is dedicated to the development of a knowledge base that can be used to implement and evaluate culturally congruent human-services programs. Community psychology is associated with the community mental health movement, and community psychologists have a particular interest in research and services that focus on prevention.

Principal terms

ACTION-ORIENTED RESEARCH: the study of real-world problems using ecologically valid methods; findings should be translated into a policy context and recommendations implemented

CULTURALLY CONGRUENT SERVICES: interventions that take into account the history, aspirations, belief systems, and environmental circumstances of the service recipient

EPIDEMIOLOGY: the study of the rates and distributions of disorders as these data pertain to causes and prevention

INCIDENCE: the number of new cases of a disorder that occur in a given population over a specific time period

PERSON-ENVIRONMENT FIT: a concept related to the fact that adaptation requires compatibility between an individual's behavior and the demands of the environmental setting

PRIMARY PREVENTION: interventions designed to eradicate the causes of disorders and/or the development of interventions that can be initiated before pathology develops

SECONDARY PREVENTION: interventions designed to reduce the prevalence of disorders by means of early identification and timely intervention

TERTIARY PREVENTION: interventions in which the underlying disorder is not directly treated or eliminated; instead, the focus is on mitigating the consequences of the disorder

Overview

Community psychology is founded on the following precepts: an emphasis on the competence of persons and communities; an appreciation of personal and cultural diversity; an orientation that promotes prevention; a preference for organizational, community-level and/or systems-level intervention; and a belief in the need for an ecologically valid data base with which to determine the appropriateness and value of human-service interventions.

Community psychology emphasizes social, environmental, and cultural factors as significant elements influencing the development and expression of behaviors commonly identified as signs of maladjustment. Community psychology demands a respect for human diversity—people have a right to be different. Requiring that people fit into a particular mold or conform to a particular standard increases the probability that some people will be considered failures or maladjusted individuals. Instead of focusing on how to motivate "deviant" people to adjust, the community psychologist attempts to increase behavioral options, expand cultural and environmental choices, redistribute resources, and foster the acceptance of variability.

From a community psychology perspective, it is not the weakness of the individual that causes psychopathology but a lack of person-environment fit. The concept of person-environment fit is founded in ecology. Ecology posits that each organism is in constant interaction with all aspects of its environment, including all things animate and inanimate. From the ecological perspective, it is the unique interaction of species and the environmental milieu that dictates survival. In relation to people, ecology requires not only an appreciation for the ambient environment but also social, psychological, personal, and cultural factors that interact and influence an individual's adjustment and survival.

Community psychologists use their knowledge of ecological principles to create culturally congruent interventions that maximize service effectiveness. To develop services that are culturally congruent requires an appreciation for the history, aspirations, belief systems, and environmental circumstances of the community or group with which one is to work. Knowing that it is interactions and the fit between persons and environments that are of primary importance, community psychologists work to promote changes at a systems level rather than only working to change the individual. Community psychologists know, however, that even systems-level changes will be of little value—and will perhaps even lead to harm—if they are not personally and culturally relevant to the persons they are designed to help.

There is considerable diversity in the training and orientation of community psychologists. Still, as a general rule, community psychologists can be expected to have knowledge and expertise in the following areas: program development, resource utilization, community organization, consultation, community mental health programming, preventive interventions, program evaluation, grant writing, needs assessment, advocacy, crisis intervention, direct service delivery, manpower training, systems analysis, and the political ramifications of social change. Community psychologists use their knowledge of the preceding areas as they work within the framework of one of the following models: clinical/community, community/clinical, community activist, academic/research, prevention, social ecology, evaluation/policy analysis, or consultation.

Psychologists trained in the clinical/community model have expertise in individual assessment and psychotherapy. They are likely to work within community mental health centers or other human-services programs as direct service providers. They differ from traditionally trained clinical psychologists in having an orientation that is directed toward crisis intervention, public health, and prevention.

The community/clinical model leads to a primary emphasis of working with community groups to enable the development, implementation, and administration of human-services initiatives. This model is very similar to the community-activist model; persons with a community/clinical orientation, however, are more likely to work within the system than outside it.

Persons following the community-activist model draw on their training in psychology to enable them to confront social injustice and misallocation of resources. These individuals are versed in grassroots community organization, the realities of social confrontation, and advocacy.

The academic/research model of community psychology is founded on the principles of action-oriented research. Here the researcher is directed to work on real-world problems using ecologically valid methods. Furthermore, action-oriented research requires that recommendations that follow from the researcher's findings be implemented.

Psychologists who advocate the prevention model use epidemiological data— information concerning the rates and distribution of disorders—to enable the development of programs designed to prevent mental health problems. Primary prevention programs—undertakings that attempt to keep problems from form-ing—are the preferred initiatives.

Persons trained in the social-ecology model participate in the development of research and interventions based on an ecological perspective. Here an apprecia-tion of the complexities and the myriad interactions of communities and social organizations is paramount.

The evaluation/policy-analysis model requires that adherents be versed in pro-gram evaluation methods—techniques related to the assessment of the quality, efficiency, and effectiveness of service initiatives. This model dictates that infor-mation obtained from program evaluation be fed back into the system in the form of policy recommendations.

The consultation model provides a framework for the dissemination of knowl-edge. To be an effective consultant, the community psychologist must be cognizant of various consultation methods. Furthermore, she or he must have specialized expertise founded in one of the preceding models.

Regardless of the model followed, community psychology demands a commit-ment to the community, group, or individual served. The job of the community psychologist is to foster competence and independence. The ideal client, whether the client is an individual or a community, is the client who no longer needs the psychologist.

Applications

Community psychology has played a major role in sensitizing human-services professionals to the need for services oriented toward prevention. Many of the assumptions and principles of prevention are taken from the field of public health medicine. Public health officials know that disease cannot be eradicated by treat-ment alone. Furthermore, the significant gains in life expectancy that have oc-curred over the last one hundred years are not primarily the result of wonder drugs, transplants, or other marvels of modern medicine. Instead, improved sanitation, immunizations, and access to an adequate food supply have been the key factors in conquering diseases and increasing the human life span.

In order to design and implement effective prevention-oriented programs, one must have an understanding of epidemiology, incidence, and prevalence. Epidemiology is the study of the rates and distributions of disorders as these data pertain to causes and prevention. Incidence is the number of new cases of a disorder that occur in a given population in a specific period. Prevalence is either the total number of cases of a disorder in a given population at a specific point in time or the average number of cases during a specific period. By combining information concerning epidemiology, incidence, and prevalence, it is possible to arrive at insights into the causes of a disorder, likely methods of transmission, prognosis, and intervention methods that may prove fruitful.

Community psychologists identify prevention activities as falling into one of three classifications: primary prevention, secondary prevention, and tertiary prevention. Although some have argued that only primary prevention activities should be recognized as prevention, all three classifications have a place.

In tertiary prevention, the underlying disorder is not directly treated or eliminated; instead, tertiary prevention focuses on mitigating the consequences of a disorder. Tertiary prevention has no effect on incidence rates and little or no effect on prevalence rates. Reducing the stigma associated with the label "mental illness," increasing the self-help skills of persons who have mental retardation, promoting the independence of persons with chronic mental disorders, and developing programs to provide cognitive retraining for persons who have suffered head injuries are examples of tertiary-prevention activities.

An example of a tertiary-prevention program is the community lodge program developed by George Fairweather, which has come to be known as the Fairweather Lodge Program. The program was begun as an attempt to solve a problem that arose in an experiment in giving psychiatric patients the power to direct their treatment by means of self-governing groups. Although it was quite effective, the program suffered because many of its gains did not carry over after patients were discharged. The community lodge program was developed to deal with this problem. During their hospital stays, patients were encouraged to form small support groups. Prior to discharge, members of these support groups would be introduced to the lodge concept. The lodge concept called for former patients to live together, pool their resources, and work as a team in a lodge-owned enterprise. This program, which began in the early 1960's, has been replicated on numerous occasions. Data show that patients discharged to a community lodge are more likely to maintain gainful employment and are less likely to be readmitted to the hospital than are patients discharged to a traditional community mental health program.

Secondary prevention has its basis in the belief that prevalence rates can be reduced if disorders are identified and treated as early as possible. Diversion programs for youths who manifest predelinquent behavior, acute care for persons with mental disorders, employee assistance programs, and psychological screenings for schoolchildren are examples of secondary prevention.

An example of a secondary-prevention program is the Primary Mental Health Project (PMHP) developed by Emory Cowen in the late 1950's. The PMHP was founded on the basis of the idea that maladjustment in early school grades is associated with the development of behavioral and emotional problems later in life. The program was designed to provide early detection so that interventions could be introduced before significant dysfunction had an opportunity to develop. Furthermore, consultation and competency building—rather than traditional therapeutic techniques—were viewed as the most effective interventions. Although the PMHP has not had a demonstrated effect in reducing later psychiatric disorders, the program has been shown to have other beneficial effects.

Primary prevention is aimed at the eradication of the causes of disorders and/or the development of interventions that can be initiated before pathology develops. Primary prevention results in a lowering of both incidence and prevalence rates. Psychological services for disaster victims, genetic screening, parenting classes, reducing exposure to toxins, immunization for rubella, and maternal nutrition programs are examples of primary-prevention activities. Another example of primary prevention is community education programs designed to teach safe sex and/or to reduce the sharing of contaminated needles. To the extent that these programs reduce the spread of acquired immunodeficiency syndrome (AIDS), they will also decrease the incidence of AIDS dementia complex.

Community psychologists are involved in many service activities besides prevention-oriented enterprises. These initiatives include the training and utilization of paraprofessionals, the promotion of self-help groups and natural helping networks, advocacy, community consultation, program evaluation, the planning and implementation of new human-services programs, crisis intervention, and mental health education.

Perspective and Prospects

Community psychology had its origins in the 1960's, a time of radical ideas, antiestablishment attitudes, and a belief in the perfectibility of humankind. In 1965 in Swampscott, Massachusetts, a meeting was called to ascertain how psychology could most effectively contribute to the emerging community mental health movement.

A transformation in treatment focus was taking place at the time of the Swampscott meeting. This change had been provided with a blueprint for its development in a report by the Joint Commission on Mental Illness and Health written in 1961. The Joint Commission report, *Action for Mental Health,* called for a shift from treating psychiatric patients in large state mental hospitals to the provision of care through outpatient community mental health clinics and smaller inpatient units located in general hospitals. Additionally, the report included the following recommendations: increasing support for research, developing "aftercare," providing partial hospitalization and rehabilitation services, and expanding mental health education to ensure that the public became more aware of mental disorders and to reduce the stigmatization associated with mental illness.

On February 5, 1963, President John F. Kennedy became the first president of the United States to address Congress regarding the needs of the mentally ill and the mentally retarded. President Kennedy called for a "bold new approach" that would include funding for prevention; expanding the knowledge base regarding causes of disorders and treatment alternatives; and creating a new type of treatment facility that, independent of the ability to pay, would provide high-quality comprehensive care in the local community—the creation of community mental health centers.

In October of 1963, President Kennedy signed into law the Community Mental Health Centers Act. The law required that programs funded through the act provide five essential services: inpatient care, outpatient treatment, emergency services, partial hospitalization, and consultation and education.

Although the initial purpose for convening the Swampscott meeting had been to determine how psychology could contribute to the staffing needs of community mental health centers, the conferees took a broader perspective and chose to view the community mental health movement as addressing a limited aspect of a larger set of social problems. As a consequence, the meeting failed to address adequately the training needs of psychologists who would be working in the new community mental health centers; intead, the most significant result of the meeting was the birth of community psychology.

In the ensuing years, community psychology and community psychology training programs have varied in the degree to which they involve the educational needs of psychologists employed by community mental health centers. Still, there is no doubt that the research and service initiatives that community psychologists have developed in regard to crisis intervention, consulation, prevention, empowerment, the use of paraprofessionals, program planning, resource development, and program evaluation serve as valuable models and contribute to the successful operation of community mental health programs and a variety of other human-services activities.

Bibliography

Bloom, Bernard L. *Community Mental Health: A General Introduction.* 2d ed. Monterey, Calif.: Brooks/Cole, 1984. Although Bloom focuses primarily on community mental health, he provides much information that is relevant to community psychology. The discussion of direct service interventions is something that most books on community psychology lack.

Caplan, Gerald. *Principles of Preventive Psychiatry.* New York: Basic Books, 1964. Caplan was a key figure in directing attention to the need to be informed concerning biological, psychological, and sociocultural factors as they influence psychopathology. Furthermore, Caplan's call for an emphasis on primary prevention antedated the origin of community psychology.

Felner, Robert David, et al., eds. *Preventive Psychology: Theory, Research, and Practice.* New York: Pergamon Press, 1983. While its origins may be in community psychology, preventive psychology is presented as a broader enterprise. This volume attempts to provide an integrating framework for preventive psychology with the goal of stimulating applications.

Heller, Kenneth, et al. *Psychology and Community Change: Challenges of the Future.* 2d ed. Homewood, Ill.: Dorsey Press, 1984. Describes how knowledge of groups, organizations, and communities can be applied in addressing social problems. Ecological approaches and prevention-oriented interventions are the primary substance of the text.

Levine, Murray, and David V. Perkins. *Principles of Community Psychology: Perspectives and Applications.* 2d ed. New York: Oxford University Press, 1997. The authors provide an extended discussion of social problems, the conceptual foundations of community psychology, and the application of community-psychology principles to promote effective change. Substantial portions of the text are devoted to labeling theory and the effects of crises.

Mann, Philip A. *Community Psychology: Concepts and Applications.* New York: Free Press, 1978. The origins of community psychology and the relevance of the concept of community are described. Additionally, the assumptions and implications of four models are detailed: the mental health model, organizational model, social-action model, and ecological model.

Nietzel, Michael T., et al. *Behavioral Approaches to Community Psychology.* New York: Pergamon Press, 1977. The authors describe how behavior-modification techniques can be used to solve community problems. Behavior modification is presented as providing both a means to initiate change and a method for evaluating the results.

Rappaport, Julian. *Community Psychology: Values, Research, and Action.* New York: Holt, Rinehart and Winston, 1977. Rappaport provides a comprehensive survey of the paradigms, principles, and practice of community psychology. The book focuses attention on the social roots of pathology and the need for systems-level interventions that are culturally congruent.

Scileppi, John A., Elizabeth Lee Teed, and Robin Diller Torres. *Community Psychology: A Common Sense Approach to Mental Health.* Upper Saddle River, N.J.: Prentice Hall, 2000. Combines theory, research, and applications. Presents major principles, strategies and ethical guidelines, and both classical and current research. Includes bibliographical references and indexes.

Bruce E. Bailey

See also:

Abnormality: Sociocultural Models; Juvenile Delinquency; Mental Health Practitioners.

COUPLES THERAPY

Type of psychology: Psychotherapy
Fields of study: Group and family therapies

Relationship distress represents one of the most common reasons that individuals seek psychological help in the United States. As a result, there is an increasing demand for treatment services which are both effective in altering destructive marital interactions and efficient in the use of the therapist's and client's time.

Principal terms

CROSS-COMPLAINING LOOP: an interactional sequence wherein both individuals describe areas of dissatisfaction within the relationship yet fail to attend to the issue raised by their partner

DOMESTIC VIOLENCE: physical, emotional, psychological, or sexual abuse perpetrated by a family member toward another family member; typically the abuse follows a repetitive, predictable pattern

OPERANT CONDITIONING: a type of learning in which behaviors are altered primarily by the consequences that follow them (reinforcement or punishment)

PREVENTION PROGRAMS: intervention strategies designed to reduce or eliminate difficulties in the future by providing training in specific skills

PROSOCIAL BEHAVIOR: activities or behaviors performed by an individual which are intended to benefit others or society

PSYCHOPHYSIOLOGICAL: referring to the interaction between the psyche (mind) and the physiology (such as the regulatory processes of the nervous system) of an organism

VALIDATION LOOP: an interactional sequence in which one partner expresses dissatisfaction and the other partner expresses either agreement or support

Overview

Traditionally, marriage vows have represented pledges of mutual love and enduring commitment. Since the 1960's, however, marital relationships have changed dramatically. In fact, while more than 90 percent of the United States population will marry at least once in their lifetime, it is anticipated that approximately 50 percent of first marriages and 60 percent of second marriages will end in divorce. Moreover, while the average first marriage in the United States will last only five to seven years, second marriages typically endure only for five years. It appears that a repetitive pattern of marriage, distress, and divorce has become commonplace. Such a cycle often results in considerable pain and psychological turmoil for the couple, their family, and their friends. These statistics dramatically indicate the need for effective ways to help couples examine and reapproach their relationships before deciding whether to terminate them.

Research has found evidence that links divorce and relationship distress to a wide variety of emotional disorders in spouses and their children. Depressive syndromes are evident in approximately half of female spouses and nearly 15 percent of male partners in dysfunctional marriages. Almost half of all first admissions to state hospitals in the United States have relationship stress as a major factor. Evidence further reveals that suicide often follows marital discord, separation, and divorce. In fact, divorce and marital separation represent two of the most common yet significant stressors in adult life.

Partners who seek couples therapy or counseling frequently have problems in two areas: communication and conflict resolution. These are the two major difficulties that most often lead to divorce. It has been shown that communication skills differentiate satisfied and dissatisfied couples more powerfully than any other factor. Indeed, communication difficulties are the most frequently cited complaint among partners reporting relationship distress.

Psychologist John M. Gottman, in his books *Marital Interaction: Experimental Investigations* (1979) and *A Couple's Guide to Communication* (Gottman et al., 1976), and various other researchers have highlighted the importance of communication problems within distressed relationships. Many characteristic differences between distressed and satisfied couples have been noted. Partners in distressed couples often misperceive "well-intended" statements from their partners, whereas satisfied couples are more likely to rate well-intended messages as positive; distressed partners also engage in fewer rewarding exchanges and more frequent punishing interactions than nondistressed couples. A partner in a distressed relationship is more immediately reactive to perceived negative communication exhibited by his or her partner. There is generally a greater emphasis on negative communication strategies between distressed partners.

Distressed couples appear to be generally unskilled at generating positive change in their relationship. Gottman also reported that distressed couples are often ineffectual in their attempts to resolve conflicts. Whereas nondistressed couples employ "validation loops" during problem-solving exercises (one partner states the conflict and the other partner expresses agreement or support), distressed couples typically enter into repetitive, cross-complaining loops. Moreover, as one spouse initiates aversive control tactics, the other spouse will typically reciprocate with similar behavior.

Couples therapy attempts to alleviate distress, resolve conflicts, improve daily functioning, and prevent problems via an intensive focus on the couple as a unit and on each partner as an individual. Couples therapists are faced with a variety of choices regarding treatment format and therapeutic approach. Individual therapy focuses treatment on only one of the partners. Although generally discouraged by most practitioners, individual treatment of one partner can provide greater opportunities for the client to focus more on his or her own thoughts, feelings, problems, and behaviors. Clients may feel less hesitant in sharing some details they would not want a spouse to hear, and individual treatment may encourage the client to take greater personal responsibility for problems and successes. In general, these advantages are outweighed by the difficulties encountered when treating "relationship problems" without both partners being present. In particular, interpersonal interactions are complex phenomena that need to be evaluated and treated with both partners present.

Concurrent therapy involves both partners being seen in treatment separately, either by the same therapist or by two separate but collaborating therapists. Advantages of the concurrent format include greater individual attention and opportunities to develop strategies to improve relationship skills by teaching each partner those techniques separately. Concurrent treatment, however, does not allow the therapist(s) to evaluate and treat the nature of the interpersonal difficulties with both partners simultaneously present in the same room.

Conjoint format, on the other hand, involves both partners simultaneously in the therapy session. Conjoint treatment tends to be widely used and generally recommended because it focuses intensively on the quality of the relationship, promotes dialogue between the couple, and can attend to the needs and goals of each partner as well as the needs and goals of the couple. The history of conjoint marital therapy begins, ironically, with Sigmund Freud's failures in this area. He believed firmly that it was counterproductive and dangerous for a therapist ever to treat more than one member of the same family. In fact, after attempting to provide services simultaneously to a husband and wife, Freud (in 1912) concluded that he was at a complete loss in terms of understanding how to treat relationship problems within a couple. He also added that he had little faith in individual therapy for them.

As currently practiced, conjoint treatment is designed to focus intensively on the relationship in order to effect specific therapeutic change for that particular couple. Interventions can be "tailor-made" for the couple seeking treatment, regardless of the nature of the problem the couple describes (such as sexual relations, child rearing, household responsibilities). Moreover, couples are constantly engaged in a direct dialogue with each other, which can foster improved understanding and resolution or conflict. As compared with other approaches, conjoint marital therapy can focus on each of the specific needs and goals of the individual couple.

Group couples treatment programs have received increased attention and have shown very good to excellent treatment success. Advantages of group treatment for couples include opportunities for direct assessment and intervention of the relationship within a setting which promotes greater opportunity for feedback and suggestions from other couples experiencing similar difficulties. In fact, group therapy may promote positive expectations through witnessing improvements among other couples as well as fostering a sense of cohesiveness among couples within the group. In the group format, each partner has the opportunity to develop improved communication and conflict resolution appraoches by learning relationship skills via interaction with the therapist(s), his or her spouse, and other group members. In addition, the cost of individual, concurrent, and conjoint therapy, in terms of time as well as dollars, has prompted several researchers and clinicians to recommend group couples therapy.

Applications

There are numerous approaches to the treatment of relationship problems currently practiced in the United States. Psychodynamic therapy focuses attention on the unconscious needs and issues raised during an individual's childhood. Phenomenological therapists focus on the here-and-now experiences of being in a relationship and have developed a variety of creative therapeutic techniques. Systems therapists view interpersonal problems as being maintained by the nature of the relationship structure, patterns of communication, and family roles and rules.

Behavioral marital therapy, however, is the most thoroughly investigated approach within the couples therapy field. Starting from a focus on operant conditioning, behavioral marital therapy includes a wide range of assessment and treatment strategies. The underlying assumption that best differentiates behavioral treatments for distressed couples from other approaches is that the two partners are viewed as ineffectual in their attempts to satisfy each other. Thus, the goal of therapy is to improve relationship satisfaction by creating a supportive environment in which the skills can be acquired. Behavioral marital therapy incorporates strategies designed to improve daily interactions, communication patterns, and problem-solving abilities, and to examine and modify unreasonable expectations and faulty thinking styles.

Psychologists Philip and Marcy Bornstein, in their book *Marital Therapy: A Behavioral-Communications Approach* (1986), described a sequential five-step procedure in the treatment of relationship dysfunction. These steps include intake interviewing, behavioral exchange strategies, communication skills acquisition, training in problem solving, and maintenance and generalization of treatment gains.

Intake interviewing is designed to accomplish three primary goals: development of a working relationship with the therapist, collection of assessment information, and implementation of initial therapeutic regimens. Because spouses entering treatment have often spent months, if not years, in conflict and distress, the intake procedure attempts to provide a unique opportunity to impact and assess the couple's relationship immediately. Since distressed couples often devote a considerable amount of time thinking about and engaging in discordant interpersonal interactions with each other, it naturally follows that they will attempt to engage in unpleasant interactions during initial sessions. Information about current difficulties and concerns is clearly valuable, but improved communication skills and positive interactions appear to be of even greater merit early in treatment. Thus, couples are discouraged from engaging in cross-complaining loops and are encouraged to develop skills and implement homework procedures designed to enhance the relationship.

Building a positive working relationship between partners is viewed as essential in couples treatment programs. During training in behavioral exchange strategies, couples are aided in specifying and pinpointing behaviors that tend to promote increased harmony in their relationship. Couples engage in contracting and compromise activities in order to disrupt the downward spiral of their distressed relationship.

Training in communication skills focuses on teaching and practicing the basics of communication (such as respect, understanding, and sensitivity), positive principles of communication (timeliness, marital manners, specification, and "mind reading"), improving nonverbal behaviors, and learning "molecular" verbal behaviors (such as assertiveness and constructive agreement). Improved communication styles are fostered via a direct, active approach designed to identify, reinforce, and rehearse desirable patterns of interactions. Clients are generally provided with specific instructions and "practice periods" during sessions in which partners are encouraged to begin improving their interactional styles. It is common that these sessions are audiotaped or videotaped to give couples specific feedback regarding their communication styles.

Training in problem solving is intended to teach clients to negotiate and resolve conflicts in a mutually beneficial manner. Conflict resolution training focuses on teaching, practicing, and experiencing effective problem-solving approaches. Couples receive specific instruction on systematic problem-solving approaches and are given homework assignments designed to improve problem-solving skills. Because the value of couples therapy lies in the improvement, maintenance, and use of positive interaction styles over time and across situations, treatment often aims to promote constructive procedures after the termination of active treatment. Thus, people are taught that it is generally easier to change oneself than one's partner, that positive interaction styles may be forgotten or unlearned if these strategies are not regularly practiced, and that new positive interactions can continue to develop in a variety of settings even as treatment ends.

To highlight further the utility and effectiveness of behavioral-communications relationship therapy, Philip Bornstein, Laurie Wilson, and Gregory L. Wilson (1988) conducted an empirical investigation comparing conjoint behavioral-communications therapy and group behavioral-communications therapy to a waiting-list control group (the waiting-list control group included couples who were asked to wait two months prior to beginning treatment). Fifteen distressed couples were randomly assigned to experimental conditions and offered eight sessions of couples therapy. At the conclusion of treatment (as well as six months later), the couples in active treatment revealed significant alleviation of relationship distress. The conjoint and group couples revealed similar levels of improvement in communication skills, problem-solving abilities, and general relationship satisfaction. The waiting-list couples, on the other hand, revealed no improvement while they waited for treatment, indicating that relationship distress does not tend to improve simply as the result of the passage of time.

Another line of couples research has focused on the utility of premarital intervention, or distress and divorce prevention programs. Unlike treatment programs, prevention programs intervene prior to the development of relationship distress. Prevention efforts are focused on the future and typically involve the training of specific skills which are viewed as useful in preventing relationship distress. Three major approaches to premarital intervention include the Minnesota Couples Communication Program, Bernard Guerney's relationship enhancement approach, and the Premarital Relationship Enhancement Program. Research is generally supportive of the effectiveness of these programs in helping partners learn useful skills which translate into improved relationships for at least three to eight years following the program. In addition, some evidence indicates that the alarming divorce rate in the United States can be decreased if partners participate in prevention programs prior to marriage; prevention programs that emphasize communication and conflict-resolution skills seem most advantageous.

There has also been considerable interest in the utility of couples-based treatment for various psychological disorders, including depression, anxiety disorders, and alcoholism. For example, the rationale for couples intervention as a viable treatment for depressed clients rests on the assumption that marital dysfunction is either causative or related to the maintenance of the depressed state. Whereas more than 50 percent of married couples seeking relationship therapy have at least one spouse who is depressed, and nearly 50 percent of women seeking depression treatment report marital discord, it appears that depression and marital dysfunction are not necessarily distinct problems. Thus, a primary advantage of marital therapy strategies in the resolution of depression is the simultaneous emphasis and demonstrated effectiveness of such interventions in reducing relationship discord as well as depression.

Perspective and Prospects

Since 1970, researchers and clinicians have witnessed large increases in the numbers of couples seeking treatment from therapists. As the demand for couples treatment has increased, more time and effort has been devoted to improving treatment methods. The behavioral approach has been shown to be highly effective in reducing relationship distress and preventing divorce; however, several investigations have demonstrated that cognitive components such as causal attributions and expectations are strongly related to satisfaction in the relationship. Moreover, it has been argued that dysfunctional cognitions may interfere with both the establishment and maintenance of positive behavior change. Evidence has prompted several researchers and practitioners alike to advocate a more systematic inclusion of strategies of cognitive behavior therapy within the behavioral marital therapy framework. Specifically, it is possible that the combination of cognitive and behavioral approaches will demonstrate increased utility if the two treatments are presented together in a singular, integrated treatment intervention. Such treatment would afford couples the opportunity to benefit from either one or both of the complementary approaches, depending on their own unique needs, at any time during the course of treatment. Moreover, such an integration of cognitive and behavioral tactics would parallel effective approaches already employed with depressed and anxious clients.

Interpersonal relationships are a highly complex yet important area of study and investigation. The decision to marry (or at least to commit to a serious intimate relationship) is clearly one of the most significant choices people make in their lives. Unfortunately, it is rare to find school curricula that offer any assistance, training, or education to help young people understand interpersonal relationships or make the decision to marry. Fortunately, advances in couples therapy have led to increased knowledge about interpersonal relationships and methods for improving relationship satisfaction. These advances have been documented in the scientific literature, and they extend to the treatment of cohabitating partners, premarital couples, remarried partners, gay or lesbian couples, separating or divorced couples, and stepfamilies. Moreover, couples-based treatment programs have shown effectiveness in the treatment of depression, anxiety disorders, domestic violence, sexual dysfunction, and a host of other problems.

Bibliography

Beck, Aaron T. *Love Is Never Enough.* New York: Harper & Row, 1988. This text presents a review of cognitive therapy and includes many suggestions for couples wishing to improve their relationship. Through clinical examples and dialogues with couples in treatment, Beck highlights some of the key strategies for avoiding difficulties associated with misperceptions and miscommunication.

Bornstein, Philip H., and Marcy T. Bornstein. *Marital Therapy: A Behavioral-Communications Approach.* New York: Pergamon Press, 1986. Highlights some of the key research findings that differentiate distressed and satisfied partners in the areas of communication and conflict resolution. Also presents a clinical guide for counselors and therapists who work with couples to alleviate relationship dysfunction.

Gottman, John M. *The Marriage Clinic: A Scientifically-Based Marital Therapy.* New York: W. W. Norton, 1999. Presents a complete marital therapy program based on Gottman's research on marital success and failure. Includes bibliographical references and an index.

_____, et al. *A Couple's Guide to Communication.* Champaign, Ill.: Research Press, 1990. A very useful guidebook for couples wishing to improve their communication and conflict-resolution skills. Suggestions for practicing improved interactions and increasing daily happiness are included.

Gurman, A. S., and D. P. Kniskern. *Handbook of Family Therapy.* Vol. 2. New York: Brunner/Mazel, 1991. A significant resource on the various models of treatment for couples and families. Presents a historical overview of marital and family therapy, describes various models and conceptualizations of treatment, and highlights special topics such as sex therapy and divorce interventions.

Jacobson, Neil S., and A. S. Gurman. *Clinical Handbook of Marital Therapy.* New York: Guilford Press, 1986. Provides an overview and numerous clinical sections on the major models of relationship therapy and treatment suggestions for selected psychiatric disorders. Designed for clinicians and researchers alike, this edited text presents the views of most of the major figures in marital therapy.

Jacobson, Neil S., and Gayla Margolin. *Marital Therapy: Strategies Based on Social Learning and Behavior Exchange Principles.* New York: Brunner/Mazel, 1979. Presents a description of social learning theory and the methods typically employed in behavioral marital therapy. A landmark book in terms of the history of marital therapy which still offers much candid clinical insight into the most effective methods for alleviating relationship distress.

Kadis, Leslie B., and Ruth McClendon, eds. *Concise Guide to Marital and Family Therapy.* Washington, D.C.: American Psychiatric Press, 1998. Presents both theoretical and practical cornerstones of relationship therapy, focusing on therapy with families and couples.

Gregory L. Wilson

See also:

Behavioral Family Therapy; Cognitive Behavior Therapy; Depression; Divorce and Separation: Adult Issues; Domestic Violence; Group Therapy; Midlife Crises; Psychotherapy: Effectiveness; Psychotherapy: Goals and Techniques; Strategic Family Therapy.

DEMENTIA

Type of psychology: Memory; psychopathology
Fields of study: Cognitive processes; organic disorders

Dementia is a generally irreversible decline in intellectual ability resulting from a variety of causes. It differs from mental retardation, in which the affected person never reaches an expected level of mental growth.

Principal terms

BASAL GANGLIA: a collection of nerve cells deep inside the brain, below the cortex, that controls muscle tone and automatic actions such as walking

CORTICAL DEMENTIA: dementia resulting from damage to the brain cortex, the outer layer of the brain that contains the bodies of the nerve cells

DELIRIUM: an acute condition characterized by confusion, a fluctuating level of consciousness, and visual, auditory, and even tactile hallucinations; often caused by acute disease, such as infection or intoxication

HYDROCEPHALUS: a condition resulting from the accumulation of fluid inside the brain in cavities known as ventricles; as fluid accumulates, it exerts pressure on the neighboring brain cells, which may be destroyed

SUBCORTICAL DEMENTIA: dementia resulting from damage to the area of the brain below the cortex; this area contains nerve fibers that connect various parts of the brain with one another and with the basal ganglia

VASCULAR DEMENTIA: dementia caused by repeated strokes, resulting in interference with the blood supply to parts of the brain

Causes and Symptoms

Dementia affects millions of people in the United States and is a major cause of disability in old age. Its prevalence increases with age. Dementia is characterized by a permanent memory deficit affecting recent memory in particular and of sufficient severity to interfere with the patient's ability to take part in professional and social activities. Although the aging process is associated with a gradual loss of brain cells, dementia is not part of the aging process. It also is not synonymous with benign senescent forgetfulness, which is very common in old age and affects recent memory. Although the latter is a source of frustration, it does not significantly interfere with the individual's professional and social activities because it tends to affect only trivial matters (or what the individual considers trivial). Furthermore, patients with benign forgetfulness usually can remember what was forgotten by utilizing a number of subterfuges, such as writing lists or notes to themselves and leaving them in conspicuous places. Individuals with benign forgetfulness also are acutely aware of their memory deficit, while those with dementia—except in the early stages of the disease—have no insight into their memory deficit and often blame others for their problems.

In addition to the memory deficit interfering with the patient's daily activities, patients with dementia have evidence of impaired abstract thinking, impaired judgment, or other disturbances of higher cortical functions such as aphasia (the inability to use or comprehend language), apraxia (the inability to execute complex, coordinated movements), or agnosia (the inability to recognize familiar objects).

Dementia may result from damage to the cerebral cortex (the outer layer of the brain), as in Alzheimer's disease, or from damage to the subcortical structures (the structures below the cortex), such as white matter, the thalamus, or the basal ganglia. Although memory is impaired in both cortical and subcortical dementias, the associated features are different. In cortical dementias, for example, cognitive functions such as the ability to understand speech and to talk and the ability to perform mathematical calculations are severely impaired. In subcortical dementias, on the other hand, there is evidence of disturbances of arousal, motivation, and mood, in addition to a significant slowing of cognition and of information processing.

Alzheimer's disease, the most common cause of presenile dementia, is characterized by progressive disorientation, memory loss, speech disturbances, and personality disorders. Pick's disease is another cortical dementia, but unlike Alzheimer's disease, it is rare, tends to affect younger patients, and is more common in women. In the early stages of Pick's disease, changes in personality, disinhibition, inappropriate social and sexual conduct, and lack of foresight may be evident—features that are not common in Alzheimer's disease. Patients also may become euphoric or apathetic. Poverty of speech is often present and gradually progresses to mutism, although speech comprehension is usually spared. Pick's disease is characterized by cortical atrophy localized to the frontal and temporal lobes.

Vascular dementia is a common cause of dementia in patients over the age of sixty-five. It is caused by interference with the blood flow to the brain. Although the overall prevalence of vascular dementia is decreasing, there are some geographical variations, with the prevalence being higher in countries with a high incidence of cardiovascular and cerebrovascular diseases, such as Finland and Japan. About 20 percent of patients with dementia have both Alzheimer's disease and vascular dementia. Several types of vascular dementia have been identified.

Multiple infarct dementia (MID) is the most common type of vascular dementia. As its name implies, it is the result of multiple, discrete cerebral infarcts (strokes) that have destroyed enough brain tissue to interfere with the patient's higher mental functions. The onset of MID is usually sudden and is associated with neurological deficit, such as the paralysis or weakness of an arm or leg or the inability to speak. The disease characteristically progresses in steps: With each stroke experienced, the patient's condition suddenly deteriorates and then stabilizes or even improves slightly until another stroke occurs. In about 20 percent of patients with MID, however, the disease displays an insidious onset and causes gradual deterioration. Most patients also show evidence of arteriosclerosis and other factors predisposing them to the development of strokes, such as hypertension, cigarette smoking, high blood cholesterol, diabetes mellitus, narrowing of one or both carotid arteries, or

Possible Symptoms of Multiple Infarct Dementia

❖ wandering or getting lost in familiar surroundings
❖ moving with rapid, shuffling steps
❖ loss of bladder or bowel control
❖ laughing or crying inappropriately
❖ difficulty following instructions
❖ problems handling money

cardiac disorders, especially atrial fibrillation (an irregular heartbeat). Somatic complaints, mood changes, depression, and nocturnal confusion tend to be more common in vascular dementias, although there is relative preservation of the patient's personality. In such cases, magnetic resonance imaging (MRI) or a computed tomography (CT) scan of the brain often shows evidence of multiple strokes.

Strokes are not always associated with clinical evidence of neurological deficits, since the stroke may affect a "silent" area of the brain or may be so small that its immediate impact is not noticeable. Nevertheless, when several of these small strokes have occurred, the resulting loss of brain tissue may interfere with the patient's cognitive functions. This is, in fact, the basis of the lacunar dementias. The infarcted tissue is absorbed into the rest of the brain, leaving a small cavity or lacuna. Brain-imaging techniques and especially MRI are useful in detecting these lacunae.

A number of neurological disorders are associated with dementia. The combination of dementia, urinary incontinence, and muscle rigidity causing difficulties in walking should raise the suspicion of hydrocephalus. In this condition, fluid accumulates inside the ventricles (cavities within the brain) and results in increased pressure on the brain cells. A CT scan demonstrates enlargement of the ventricles. Although some patients may respond well to surgical shunting of the cerebrospinal fluid, it is often difficult to identify those who will benefit from surgery. Postoperative complications are significant and include strokes and subdural hematomas.

Dementia has been linked to Parkinson's disease, a chronic, progressive neurological disorder that usually manifests itself in middle or late life. It has an insidious onset and a very slow progression rate. Although intellectual deterioration is not part of the classical features of Parkinson's disease, dementia is being recognized as a late manifestation of the disease, with as many as one-third of the patients eventually being afflicted. The dementing process also has an insidious onset and slow progression rate. Some of the medication used to treat Parkinson's disease also may induce confusion, particularly in older patients.

Subdural hematomas (collections of blood inside the brain) may lead to mental impairment and are usually precipitated by trauma to the head. Usually, the trauma is slight and the patient neither loses consciousness nor experiences any immediate significant effects. A few days or even weeks later, however, the patient may develop evidence of mental impairment. By that time, the patient and caregivers may have forgotten about the slight trauma that the patient had experienced. A subdural hematoma should be suspected in the presence of a fairly sudden onset and progressing course. Headaches are common. A CT scan can reveal the presence of a hematoma. The surgical removal of the hematoma is usually associated with a good prognosis if the surgery is done in a timely manner, before irreversible brain damage occurs.

Brain tumors may lead to dementia, particularly if they are slow growing. Most tumors of this type can be diagnosed by CT scanning or MRI. Occasionally, cancer may induce dementia through an inflammation of the brain.

Many chronic infections affecting the brain can lead to dementia; they include conditions that, when treated, may reverse or prevent the progression of dementia, such as syphilis, tuberculosis, slow viruses, and some fungal and protozoal infections. Human immunodeficiency virus (HIV) infection is also a cause of dementia, and it may be suspected if the rate of progress is rapid and the patient has risk factors for the development of HIV infection. Although the dementia is part of the acquired immunodeficiency syndrome (AIDS) complex, it may occasionally be the first manifestation of the disease.

It is often difficult to differentiate depression from dementia. Nevertheless, sudden onset—especially if preceded by an emotional event, the presence of sleep disturbances, and a history of previous psychiatric illness—is suggestive of depression. The level of mental functioning of patients with depression is often inconsistent. They may, for example, be able to give clear accounts of topics that are of personal interest to them but be very vague about, and at times may not even attempt to answer, questions on topics that are of no interest to them. Variability in performance during testing is suggestive of depression, especially if it improves with positive reinforcement.

For physicians, an important aspect of diagnosing patients with dementia is detecting potentially reversible causes which may be responsible for the impaired mental functions. A detailed history followed by a meticulous and thorough clinical examination and a few selected laboratory tests are usually sufficient to reach a diagnosis. Various investigators have estimated that reversible causes of dementia can be identified in 10 percent to 20 percent of patients with dementia. Recommended investigations include brain imaging (CT scanning or MRI), a complete blood count, and tests of erythrocyte sedimentation rate, blood glucose, serum electrolytes, serum calcium, liver function, thyroid function, and serum B_{12} and folate. Some investigators also recommend routine testing for syphilis. Other tests, such as those for the detection of HIV infection, cerebrospinal fluid examination, neuropsychological testing, drug and toxin screen, serum copper and ceruloplasmin analysis, carotid and cerebral angiography, and electroencephalography, are performed when appropriate.

Treatment and Therapy

It is of paramount importance for health care providers to adopt a positive attitude when managing patients with dementia. Although at present little can be done to treat and reverse dementia, it is important to identify the cause of the dementia. In some cases, it may be possible to prevent the disease from progressing. For example, if the dementia is the result of hypertension, adequate control of this condition may prevent further brain damage. Moreover, the prevalence of vascular dementia is decreasing in countries where efforts to reduce cardiovascular and cerebrovascular diseases have been successful. Similarly, if the dementia is the result of repeated emboli (blood clots reaching the brain) complicating atrial fibrillation, then anticoagulants or aspirin may be recommended.

Even after a diagnosis of dementia is made, it is important for the physician to detect the presence of other conditions that may worsen the patient's mental functions, such as the inadvertent intake of medications that may induce confusion and mental impairment. Medications with this potential are numerous and include not only those that act on the brain, such as sedatives and hypnotics, but also hypotensive agents (especially if given in large doses), diuretics, and antibiotics. Whenever the condition of a patient with dementia deteriorates, the physician meticulously reviews all the medications that the patient is taking, both medical prescriptions and medications that may have been purchased over the counter. Even if innocuous, some over-the-counter preparations may interact with other medications that the patient is taking and lead to a worsening of mental functions. Inquiries are also made into the patient's alcohol intake. The brain of an older person is much more sensitive to the effects of alcohol than that of a younger person, and some medications may interact with the alcohol to impair the patient's cognitive functions further.

Many other disease states also may worsen the patient's mental functions. For example, patients with diabetes mellitus are susceptible to developing a variety of metabolic abnormalities including a low or high blood glucose level, both of which may be associated with confusional states. Similarly, dehydration and acid-base or electrolyte disorders, which may result from prolonged vomiting or diarrhea, may also precipitate confusional states. Infections, particularly respiratory and urinary tract infections, often worsen the patient's cognitive deficit. Finally, patients with dementia may experience myocardial infarctions (heart attacks) that are not associated with any chest pain but that may manifest themselves with confusion.

The casual observer of the dementing process is often overwhelmed with concern for the patient, but it is the family that truly suffers. The patients themselves experience no physical pain or distress, and except in the very early stages of the disease, they are oblivious to their plight as a result of their loss of insight. Health care professionals therefore are alert to the stress imposed on the caregivers who must deal with loved ones with dementia. Adequate support from agencies available in the community is essential.

When a diagnosis of dementia is made, the physician discusses a number of ethical, financial, and legal issues with the family, and also the patient if it is believed that he or she can understand the implications of this discussion. Families are encouraged to make a list of all the patient's assets, including insurance policies, and to discuss this information with an attorney in order to protect the patient's and the family's assets. If the patient is still competent, it is recommended that he or she select a trusted person to have durable power of attorney. Unlike the regular power of attorney, the former does not become invalidated when the patient becomes mentally incompetent and continues to be in effect regardless of the degree of mental impairment of the person who executed it. Because durable power of attorney cannot be easily reversed once the person is incompetent, great care should be taken when selecting a person, and the specific powers granted should be clearly specified. It is also important for the patient to make his or her desires known concerning advance directives and the use of life-support systems.

Courts may appoint a guardian or conservator to have charge and custody of the patient's property (including real estate and money) when no responsible family members or friends are willing or available to serve as guardian. Courts supervise the actions of the guardian, who is expected to report all the patient's income and expenditures to the court once a year. The court may also charge the guardian to ensure that the patient is adequately housed, fed, and clothed and receiving appropriate medical care.

Perspective and Prospects

Dementia is a very serious and common condition, especially among the older population. Dementia permanently robs patients of their minds and prevents them from functioning adequately in their environment by impairing memory and interfering with the ability to make rational decisions. It therefore deprives patients of their dignity and independence.

Because dementia is mostly irreversible, cannot be adequately treated at present, and is associated with a fairly long survival period, it has a significant impact not only on the patient's life but also on the patient's family and caregivers and on society in general. The expense of long-term care for patients with dementia, whether at home or in institutions, is staggering. Every effort, therefore, is made to reach an accurate diagnosis and especially to detect any other condition that may worsen the patient's underlying dementia. Finally, health care professionals do not treat the patient in isolation but also concern themselves with the impact of the illness on the patient's caregivers and family.

Much progress has been made in defining dementia and determining its cause. Terms such as "senile dementia" are no longer in use, and even the use of the term "dementia" to diagnose a patient's condition is frowned upon because there are so many types of dementia. The recognition of the type of dementia affecting a particular patient is important because of its practical implications, both for the patient and for research into the prevention, management, and treatment of dementia. The prevalence of vascular dementia, for example, is decreasing in many countries where the prevention of cardiovascular diseases such as hypertension and arteriosclerosis has been successful.

Unfortunately, there is little that can be done to cure dementia and no effective means to regenerate nerve cells. Researchers, however, are feverishly trying to identify factors that control the growth and regeneration of nerve cells. Although no single medication is expected to be of benefit to all types of dementia, it is hoped that effective therapy for many dementias will be developed.

Bibliography

Hamdy, Ronald C., et al., eds. *Alzheimer's Disease: A Handbook for Caregivers.* 3d ed. St. Louis: Mosby, 1998. A comprehensive discussion of the symptoms and characteristic features of Alzheimer's disease and other dementias. Abnormal brain structure and function in these patients are discussed, and the normal effects of aging are reviewed. Gives caregivers practical advice concerning the encouragement of patients with dementia.

Hoffman, Stephanie B., and Constance A. Platt. *Comforting the Confused: Strategies for Managing Dementia.* 2d ed. New York: Springer, 2000. Describes the effects of aging and dementia on the ability to communicate and explains strategies that can maximize communication. Appropriate for geriatric psychologists and other caregivers.

Howe, M. L., M. J. Stones, and C. J. Brainerd, eds. *Cognitive and Behavioral Performance Factors in Atypical Aging.* New York: Springer-Verlag, 1990. A review of the factors controlling behavior, test performance, and brain function in both young and older patients.

Kovach, Christine, ed. *Late Stage Dementia Care: A Basic Guide.* Washington, D.C.: Taylor & Francis, 1997. Provides information on assessment and treatment management for individuals experiencing dementia. A valuable source for caregivers and family members of those affected.

Terry, Robert D., ed. *Aging and the Brain.* New York: Raven Press, 1988. A review of the application of concepts in neurobiology and technology in the study of brain structure and function in normal elderly people and those with different types of dementia.

U.S. Congress. Office of Technology Assessment. *Confused Minds, Burdened Families: Finding Help for People with Alzheimer's and Other Dementias.* Washington, D.C.: Government Printing Office, 1990. A report from the Office of Technology Assessment analyzing the problems of locating and arranging services for people with dementia in the United States. Also presents a framework for an effective system to provide appropriate services and discusses congressional policy options for establishing such a system.

_____. *Losing a Million Minds: Confronting the Tragedy of Alzheimer's Disease and Other Dementias.* Washington, D.C.: Government Printing Office, 1987. A comprehensive report from the Office of Technology Assessment reviewing the nature and psychological, sociological, and economic implications of dementia in the United States. The various programs and services available are reviewed, and recommendations concerning future policies are made. The issues of personnel training and quality assurance are also addressed.

West, Robin L., and Jan D. Sinnott, eds. *Everyday Memory and Aging.* New York: Springer-Verlag, 1992. A review of issues relating to memory research and methodology, especially as they apply to aging.

Whitehouse, Peter J., Konrad Maurer, and Jesse F. Ballenger, eds. *Concepts of Alzheimer Disease: Biological, Clinical, and Cultural Perspectives.* Baltimore: The Johns Hopkins University Press, 2000. Explores the genetic, social, historical, and psychological aspects of Alzheimer's disease and neuroscience in general. Includes bibliographical references and an index.

Ronald C. Hamdy, M.D.
Louis A. Cancellaro, M.D.
Larry Hudgins, M.D.

See also:

Alzheimer's Disease; Amnesia, Fugue, and Multiple Personality; Brain Disorders; Geriatric Psychiatry; Memory Loss.

DEPRESSION

Type of psychology: Psychopathology
Fields of study: Depression

Depression is the single most common psychiatric disorder, caused by biological and/or psychological factors; approximately 15 percent of cases result in suicide.

Principal terms

BIPOLAR DISORDER: a mood disorder characterized by one or more manic and major depressive episodes occurring simultaneously or in cycles

CYCLOTHYMIA: a mood disorder characterized as a less intense form of bipolar disorder

DYSTHYMIA: a mood disorder characterized as a less intense form of depressive disorder

ELECTROCONVULSIVE THERAPY: the use of electric shocks to induce seizure in depressed patients as a form of treatment

MAJOR DEPRESSIVE DISORDER: a pattern of major depressive episodes that form an identified psychiatric disorder

MAJOR DEPRESSIVE EPISODE: a syndrome of symptoms characterized by depressed mood; required for the diagnosis of some mood disorders

MANIC EPISODE: a syndrome of symptoms characterized by elevated, expansive, or irritable mood; required for the diagnosis of some mood disorders

SEASONAL AFFECTIVE DISORDER: a mood disorder associated with the winter season, when the amount of daylight hours is reduced

Causes and Symptoms

The term "depression" is used to describe a fleeting mood, an outward physical appearance of sadness, or a diagnosable clinical disorder. It is estimated that 13 million Americans suffer from a clinically diagnosed depression, a mood disorder that often affects personal, vocational, social, and health functioning. The *Diagnostic and Statistical Manual of Mental Disorders* (4th ed., 1994, DSM-IV) of the American Psychiatric Association delineates a number of mood disorders that subsume the various types of clinical depression.

A major depressive episode is a syndrome of symptoms, present during a two-week period and representing a change from previous functioning. The symptoms include at least five of the following: depressed or irritable mood, diminished interest in previously pleasurable activities, significant weight loss or weight gain, insomnia or hypersomnia, physical excitation or slowness, loss of energy, feelings of worthlessness or guilt, indecisiveness or a diminished ability to concentrate, and recurrent thoughts of death. The clinical depression cannot be initiated or maintained by another illness or condition, and it cannot be a normal reaction to the death of a loved one (some symptoms of depression are a normal part of the grief reaction).

Many of the psychosocial stressors associated with old age, such as the deaths of loved ones and chronic illnesses, are common causes of clinical depression. (PhotoDisc)

In major depressive disorder, the patient experiences a major depressive episode and does not have a history of mania or hypomania. Major depressive disorder is often first recognized in the patient's late twenties, while a major depressive episode can occur at any age, including infancy. Women are twice as likely to suffer from the disorder than are men.

There are several potential causes of major depressive disorder. Genetic studies suggest a familial link with higher rates of clinical depression in first-degree relatives. There also appears to be a relationship between clinical depression and levels of the brain's neurochemicals, specifically serotonin and norepinephrine. It is important to keep in mind, however, that 20 to 30 percent of adults will experience depression in their lifetime. Common causes of clinical depression include psychosocial stressors, such as the death of a loved one or the loss of a job, or any of a number of personal stressors; it is unclear why some people respond to a specific psychosocial stressor with a clinical depression and others do not. Finally, certain prescription medications have been noted to cause clinical depression. These drugs include muscle relaxants, heart medications, hypertensive medications, ulcer medications, oral contraceptives, and steroids. Thus there are many causes of clinical depression, and no single cause is sufficient to explain all clinical depressions.

Another category of depressive disorder are bipolar disorders, which affect approximately 1 to 2 percent of the population. Bipolar I disorder is characterized by one or more manic episodes along with persisting symptoms of depression. A manic episode is defined as a distinct period of abnormally and persistently elevated, expansive, or irritable mood. Three of the following symptoms must occur during the period of mood disturbance: inflated self-esteem, decreased need for sleep, unusual talkativeness or pressure to keep talking, racing thoughts, distractibility, excessive goal-oriented activities (especially in work, school, or social areas), and reckless activities with a high potential for negative consequences (such as buying sprees or risky business ventures). For a diagnosis of bipolar disorder, the symptoms must be sufficiently severe to cause impairment in functioning and/or concern regarding the person's danger to himself/herself or to others, must not be superimposed on another psychotic disorder, and must not be initiated or maintained by another illness or condition. Bipolar II disorder is characterized by a history of a major depressive episode and current symptoms of mania.

Patients with bipolar disorder will display cycles in which they experience a manic episode followed by a short episode of a major depressive episode, or vice versa. These cycles are often separated by a period of normal mood. Occasionally, two or more cycles can occur in a year without a period of remission between them, in what is referred to as rapid cycling. The two mood disorders can also occur simultaneously in a single episode. Bipolar disorder is often first recognized in adolescence or in the patient's early twenties; it is not unusual, however, for the initial recognition to occur later in life. Bipolar disorder is equally common in both males and females.

Genetic patterns are strongly involved in bipolar disorder. Brain chemicals (particularly dopamine, acetylcholine, GABA, and serotonin), hormones, drug reactions, and life stressors have all been linked to its development. Of particular interest are findings which suggest that, for some patients with bipolar disorder, changes in the seasons affect the frequency and severity of the disorder. These meteorological effects, while not well understood, have been observed in relation to other disorders of mood.

Cyclothymia is another cyclic mood disorder related to depression; it has a reported lifetime prevalence of approximately 1 to 2 percent. This chronic mood disorder is characterized by manic symptoms without marked social or occupational impairment ("hypomanic" episodes) and symptoms of major depressive episode that do not meet the clinical criteria (less than five of the nine symptoms described above). These symptoms must be present for at least two years, and if the patient has periods without symptoms, these periods cannot be longer than two months. Cyclothymia cannot be superimposed on another psychotic disorder and cannot be initiated or maintained by another illness or condition. This mood disorder has its onset in adolescence and early adulthood and is equally common in men and women. It is a particularly persistent and chronic disorder with an identified familial pattern.

Dysthymia is another chronic mood disorder affecting approximately 2 to 4 percent of the population. Dysthymia is characterized by at least a two-year history of depressed mood and at least two of the following symptoms: poor appetite, insomnia or hypersomnia, low energy or fatigue, low self-esteem, poor concentration or decision making, or feelings of hopelessness. There cannot be evidence of a major depressive episode during the first two years of the dysthymia or a history of manic episodes or hypomanic episodes. The patient cannot be without the symptoms for more than two months at a time, the disorder cannot be superimposed on another psychotic disorder, and it cannot be initiated or maintained by another illness or condition. Dysthymia appears to begin at an earlier age, as young as childhood, with symptoms typically evident by young adulthood. Dysthymia is more common in adult females, equally common in both sexes of children, and with a greater prevalence in families. The causes of dysthymia are believed to be similar to those listed for major depressive disorder.

Treatment and Therapy
Crucial to the choice of treatment for clinical depression is determining the variant of depression being experienced. Each of the diagnostic categories has associated treatment approaches that are more effective for a particular diagnosis. Multiple assessment techniques are available to the health care professional to determine the type of clinical depression. The most valid and reliable is the clinical interview. The health care provider may conduct either an informal interview or a structured, formal clinical interview assessing the symptoms that would confirm the diagnosis of clinical depression. If the patient meets the criteria set forth in the DSM-IV, then the patient is considered for depression treatments. Patients who meet many but not all diagnostic criteria are sometimes diagnosed with a "subclinical" depression. These patients might also be considered appropriate for the treatment of depression, at the discretion of their health care providers.

Another assessment technique is the "paper-and-pencil" measure, or depression questionnaire. A variety of questionnaires have proven useful in confirming the diagnosis of clinical depression. Questionnaires such as the Beck Depression Inventory, Hamilton Depression Rating Scale, Zung Self-Rating Depression Scale, and the Center for Epidemiologic Studies Depression Scale are used to identify persons with clinical depression and to document changes with treatment. This technique is often used as an adjunct to the clinical interview and rarely stands alone as the definitive assessment approach to diagnosing clinical depression.

Laboratory tests, most notably the dexamethasone suppression test, have also been used in the diagnosis of depression. The dexamethasone suppression test involves injecting a steroid (dexamethasone) into the patient and measuring the production levels of another steroid (cortisol) in response. Studies have demonstrated, however, that certain severely depressed patients do not reveal the suppression of cortisol production that would be expected following the administration of dexamethasone. The test has also failed to identify some patients who were depressed and has mistakenly identified others as depressed. Research continues to determine the efficacy of other laboratory measures of brain activity to include computed tomography (CT) scanning, positron emission tomography (PET) scanning, and magnetic resonance imaging (MRI). At this time, laboratory tests are not a reliable diagnostic strategy for depression.

Once a clinical depression (or a subclinical depression) is identified, there are at least four general classes of treatment options available. These options are dependent on the subtype and severity of the depression and include psychopharmacology (drug therapy), individual and group psychotherapy, light therapy, family therapy, electroconvulsive therapy (ECT), and other less traditional treatments. These treatment options can be provided to the patient as part of an outpatient program or, in certain severe cases of clinical depression in which the person is a danger to himself/herself or others, as part of a hospitalization.

Clinical depression often affects the patient physically, emotionally, and socially. Therefore, prior to beginning any treatment with a clinically depressed individual, the health care provider will attempt to develop an open and communicative relationship with the patient. This relationship will allow the health care provider to provide patient education on the illness and to solicit the collaboration of the patient in treatment. Supportiveness, understanding, and collaboration are all necessary components of any treatment approach.

Three primary types of medications are used in the treatment of clinical depression: cyclic antidepressants, monoamine oxidase inhibitors (MAOIs), and lithium salts. These medications are considered equally effective in decreasing the symptoms of depression, which begin to resolve in three to four weeks after initiating treatment. The health care professional will select an antidepressant based on side effects, dosing convenience (once daily versus three times a day), and cost.

The cyclic antidepressants are the largest class of antidepressant medications. As the name implies, the chemical makeup of the medication contains chemical rings, or "cycles." There are unicyclic (buproprion and fluoxetine, or Prozac), bicyclic (sertraline and trazodone), tricyclic (amitriptyline, desipramine, and nortriptyline), and tetracyclic (maprotiline) antidepressants. These antidepressants function to either block the reuptake of neurotransmitters by the neurons, allowing more of the neurotransmitter to be available at a receptor site, or increase the amount of neurotransmitter produced. The side effects associated with the cyclic antidepressants—dry mouth, blurred vision, constipation, urinary difficulties, palpitations, and sleep disturbance—vary and can be quite problematic. Some of these antidepressants have deadly toxic effects at high levels, so they are not prescribed to patients who are at risk of suicide.

Monoamine oxidase inhibitors (MAOIs) (isocarboxazid, phenelzine, and tranylcypromine) are the second class of antidepressants. They function by slowing the production of the enzyme monoamine oxidase. This enzyme is responsible for breaking down the neurotransmitters norepinephrine and serotonin, which are believed to be responsible for depression. By slowing the decomposition of these transmitters, more of them are available to the receptors for a longer period of time. Restlessness, dizziness, weight gain, insomnia, and sexual dysfunction are common side effects of the MAOIs. MAOIs are most notable because of the dangerous adverse reaction (severely high blood pressure) that can occur if the patient consumes large quantities of foods high in tyramine (such as aged cheeses, fermented sausages, red wine, foods with a heavy yeast content, and pickled fish). Because of this potentially dangerous reaction, MAOIs are not usually the first choice of medication and are more commonly reserved for depressed patients who do not respond to the cyclic antidepressants.

A third class of medication used in the treatment of depressive disorders consists of the mood stabilizers, the most notable being lithium carbonate, which is used primarily for bipolar disorder. Lithium is a chemical salt that is believed to effect mood stabilization by influencing the production, storage, release, and reuptake of certain neurotransmitters. It is particularly useful in stabilizing and preventing manic episodes and preventing depressive episodes in patients with bipolar disorder.

Another drug occasionally used in the treatment of depression is alprazolam, a muscle relaxant benzodiazepine commonly used in the treatment of anxiety. Alprazolam is believed to affect the nervous system by decreasing the sensitivity of neuronal receptors believed to be involved in depression. While this may in fact occur, the more likely explanation for its positive effect for some patients is that it reduces the anxiety or irritability often coexisting with depression in certain patients.

Psychotherapy refers to a number of different treatment techniques used to deal with the psychosocial contributors and consequences of clinical depression. Psychotherapy is a common supplement to drug therapy. In psychotherapy, the patients develop knowledge and insight into the causes and treatment for their clinical depression. In cognitive psychotherapy, cure comes from assisting patients in modifying maladaptive, irrational, or automatic beliefs that can lead to clinical depression. In behavioral psychotherapy, patients modify their environment such that social or personal rewards are more forthcoming. This process might involve being more assertive, reducing isolation by becoming more socially active, increasing physical activities or exercise, or learning relaxation techniques. Research on the effectiveness of these and other psychotherapy techniques indicates that psychotherapy is as effective as certain antidepressants for many patients and, in combination with certain medications, is more effective than either treatment alone.

Electroconvulsive (or "shock") therapy is the single most effective treatment for severe and persistent depression. If the clinically depressed patient fails to respond to medications or psychotherapy and the depression is life-threatening, electroconvulsive therapy is considered. It is also considered if the patient cannot physically tolerate antidepressants, as with elders who have other medical conditions. This therapy involves inducing a seizure in the patient by administering an electrical current to specific parts of the brain. The therapy is quite sophisticated and safe, involving little risk to the patient. Patients undergo six to twelve treatments over a two-day to five-day period. Some temporary memory impairment is a common side effect of this treatment.

A variant of clinical depression is known as seasonal affective disorder. Patients with this illness demonstrate a pattern of clinical depression during the winter, when there is a reduction in the amount of daylight hours. For these patients, phototherapy has proven effective. Phototherapy, or light therapy, involves exposing patients to bright light (greater than or equal to 2,500 lux) for two hours daily during the depression episode. The manner in which this treatment approach modifies the depression is unclear and awaits further research.

Psychosurgery, the final treatment option, is quite rare. It refers to surgical removal or destruction of certain portions of the brain believed to be responsible for causing severe depression. Psychosurgery is used only after all treatment options have failed and the clinical depression is life-threatening. Approximately 50 percent of patients who undergo psychosurgery benefit from the procedure.

Perspective and Prospects

Depression, or the more historical term "melancholy," has had a history predating modern medicine. Writings from the time of the ancient Greek physician Hippocrates refer to patients with a symptom complex similar to the present-day definition of clinical depression.

Major depressive episodes and the various subtypes of depression are the leading psychiatric diagnoses treated by health care professionals. Prevalence rates from large-scale studies of depression suggest that approximately 1 in 20 adults will meet the criteria for a major depressive episode at some point in their lives; 1 in 100 for bipolar disorder; 1 in 33 for dysthymia; and 1 in 100 for cyclothymia.

The rates of clinical depression have increased since the early twentieth century, while the age of onset of clinical depression has decreased. Women appear to be at least twice as likely as men to suffer from clinical depression, and people who are happily married have a lower risk for clinical depression than those who are separated, divorced, or dissatisfied in their marital relationship. These data, along with recurrence rates of 50 to 70 percent, indicate the importance of this psychiatric disorder.

While most psychiatric disorders are nonfatal, clinical depression can lead to death. Of the approximately 30,000 suicide deaths per year in the United States, 40 to 80 percent are believed to be related to depression. Approximately 15 percent of patients with major depressive disorder will die by suicide. There are, however, other costs of clinical depression. In the United States, billions of dollars are spent on clinical depression, divided among the following areas: treatment, suicide, and absenteeism (the largest). Clinical depression obviously has a significant economic impact on a society.

The future of clinical depression lies in early identification and treatment. Identification will involve two areas. The first is improving the social awareness of mental health issues to include clinical depression. By eliminating the negative social stigma associated with mental illness and mental health treatment, there will be an increased level of the reporting of depression symptoms and thereby an improved opportunity for early intervention, preventing the progression of the disorder to the point of suicide. The second approach to identification involves the development of reliable assessment strategies for clinical depression. Data suggest that the majority of those who commit suicide see a physician within thirty days of the suicide. The field will continue to strive to identify biological markers and other methods to predict and/or identify clinical depression more accurately. Treatment advances will focus on further development of pharmacological strategies and drugs with more specific actions and fewer side effects. Adjuncts to traditional drug therapies need continued development and refinement to maximize the success of integrated treatments.

Bibliography
American Psychiatric Association. *Diagnostic and Statistical Manual of Mental Disorders, Fourth Edition (DSM-IV).* 4th ed. Washington, D.C.: Author, 1994. This reference book lists the clinical criteria for psychiatric disorders, including the mood disorders that incorporate the depressions.

Bellenir, Karen, ed. *Mental Health Disorders Sourcebook: Basic Consumer Health Information About Anxiety Disorders, Depression, and Other Mood Disorders.* 2d ed. Detroit: Omnigraphics, 2000. A volume on mental illness in the health reference series. Includes a bibliography and an index.

Beutler, Larry E., John F. Clarkin, and Bruce Bongar. *Guidelines for the Systematic Treatment of the Depressed Patient.* New York: Oxford University Press, 2000. Presents general guidelines and optimal ones requiring training and monitoring. Includes bibliographical references and an index.

DePaulo, J. Raymond, Jr., and Keith R. Ablow. *How to Cope with Depression: A Complete Guide for You and Your Family.* New York: McGraw-Hill, 1989. Written for patients diagnosed with depression and for their families and friends. The authors use case histories of patients seen at The Johns Hopkins University Hospital to highlight their clinical information. Includes a nice section on bipolar (manic-depressive) disorder.

Greist, John H., and James W. Jefferson. *Depression and Its Treatment.* Rev. ed. Washington, D.C.: American Psychiatric Press, 1992. A patient's guide to depression. The authors describe mood disorders and the identification of depression, and they review the various treatments that are available. The appendices offer a listing of national organizations concerned with depression and an excellent reading list.

McCullough, James P., Jr. *Treatment for Chronic Depression: Cognitive Behavioral Analysis System of Psychotherapy (CBASP).* New York: Guilford Press, 2000. Discusses the diagnosis of and therapy for depressive disorder. Includes bibliographical references and an index.

Matson, Johnny L. *Treating Depression in Children and Adolescents.* New York: Pergamon Press, 1989. This book, written by one of the leaders in the scientific study of depression, presents a guide to the evaluation and treatment of depression in children and adolescents. The author describes the assessment and treatment approaches that are unique for this nonadult population.

Roesch, Roberta. *The Encyclopedia of Depression.* New York: Facts on File, 1991. This volume was written for both a lay and a professional audience. Covers all aspects of depression, including bereavement, grief, and mourning. The appendices include references, self-help groups, national associations, and institutes.

Stoppard, Janet M. *Understanding Depression: Feminist Social Constructionist Approaches.* New York: Routledge, 2000. A volume in the Women and Psychology series. Provides an in-depth critical examination of mainstream approaches to understanding and treating depression from a feminist perspective. Includes bibliographical references and indexes.

Weissman, Myrna M., John C. Markowitz, and Gerald L. Klerman. *Comprehensive Guide to Interpersonal Psychotherapy.* New York: Basic Books, 2000. This text in basic behavorial science discusses depression and other mental disorders, interpersonal relations, and methods of psychotherapy. A bibliography and an index are provided.

Oliver Oyama
updated by Nancy A. Piotrowski

See also:

Anxiety Disorders; Child and Adolescent Psychiatry; Dementia; Eating Disorders; Electroconvulsive Therapy; Geriatric Psychiatry; Grief and Guilt; Hypochondriasis, Conversion, Somatization, and Somatoform Pain; Manic-Depressive Disorder; Midlife Crises; Obsessive-Compulsive Disorder; Paranoia; Phobias; Psychoanalysis; Psychosomatic Disorders; Stress; Suicide.

DIAGNOSIS AND CLASSIFICATION

Type of psychology: Psychopathology
Fields of study: Personality assessment; schizophrenia; stress and illness

The standard system of diagnosis and classification of psychological and emotional disorders utilizes the DSM-IV, the fourth edition of the Diagnostic and Statistical Manual of Mental Disorders *of the American Psychiatric Association. Mental health workers in the United States use this system of communication for insurance purposes, treatment recommendations, and overall assessment and research.*

Principal terms

CLUSTER ANALYSIS: analysis that involves the grouping of variables that explain the same event

CRITERIA: specific behavioral, cognitive, emotional, social, or physical components of disorders that must be met in order to render a diagnosis

FACTOR ANALYSIS: the statistical procedure of determining the key factors that describe a given event

MENTAL DISORDERS: a pattern of clinically significant behavioral or psychological problems associated with distress, disability, or increased risk of suffering pain, death, or loss of freedom.

NEUROLOGICAL PROBLEMS: problems that are the result of brain or central-nervous-system damage

SUICIDAL IDEATION: thoughts and ideas that revolve around the act of suicide

VALIDITY: a statistical value that tells the degree to which a test measures what it is intended to measure; the test is usually compared to external criteria

Overview

Nearly all mental health workers in the United States employ the same system for making psychological and psychiatric diagnoses. This system, which was established by the American Psychiatric Association, is called the *Diagnostic and Statistical Manual of Mental Disorders* (4th ed., 1994, DSM-IV). This manual was coordinated with an international diagnostic system that was established by the World Health Organization and published in the *Manual of the International Statistical Classification of Diseases, Injuries, and Causes of Death* (10th ed., 1992). This coordination of diagnoses permits researchers to investigate whether some disorders are more prevalent in certain areas and whether some disorders are virtually nonexistent in certain countries or ethnic groups.

DSM-IV is a multiaxial classification system; that is, a patient is diagnosed on a series of relevant axes that examine various aspects of the patient's functioning. This classification system consists of five axes. Axis 1 requires the diagnostician to indicate the major disorder of the patient. This refers to the set of symptoms that best describes the patient's problems. There are sixteen categories of disorders listed under axis 1. There is one category that is not attributed to mental disorders but for which people may seek help, such as marital problems, parent-child problems, and academic or vocational problems. Generally, however, axis 1 reflects serious disorders that require treatment, such as anxiety disorders, sexual disorders, mood disorders, substance-abuse disorders, schizophrenia, dissociative disorders, delirium, dementia, and amnesiac disorders, and disorders first evidenced in infancy, childhood, and adolescence (excluding mental retardation). In order for a person to be diagnosed under axis 1, the patient must exhibit a required number of symptoms for specific periods of time. The presence of a minimum number of symptoms or criteria for each disorder ensures that all diagnosticians rate the same disorder in the same way.

Axis 2 includes personality disorders and mental retardation. Personality disorders refer to long-standing maladaptive behaviors that lead to difficulty in social or occupational functioning. Often, individuals who suffer from personality disorders exhibit behavior that makes it difficult for them to function effectively under ordinary circumstances. When such persons tend to resist treatment, their pattern of adjustment tends to become progressively worse.

Axis 3 requires the clinician to indicate any physical disorders that the patient may have or conditions that may be relevant to the management or treatment of the case, such as neurological problems or diabetes or any physical condition that could affect the patient's treatment.

Axis 4 refers to the severity of any psychosocial or environmental stress that might affect the diagnosis, treatment, or prognosis. The clinician is asked to list these stresses. Examples of stress are marital separation, the loss of a job, or the the death of a spouse or a child. With children or adolescents, psychosocial stressors take on a different perspective. For example, stress might involve the divorce of parents, an arrest by the police, sexual or physical abuse, or the death of a parent. The death of both parents or the development of a life-threatening illness such as leukemia also would be considered major stress for children and adolescents.

Axis 5 is called "Global Assessment of Functioning" (GAF). This axis allows the clinician to indicate an overall judgment of the patient's psychological, social, and occupational functioning during the past year. The GAF scale is viewed as a hypothetical scale of mental health and illness. It ranges from 0 to 100. A zero indicates that the rater did not have enough information to make a judgment. A ranking at the end of the scale near the value of 1 reflects the presence of a serious psychological disorder as a result of which the person is dangerous either to himself or herself or to others. The high end of the scale reflects the absence of symptoms or the presence of very minimal symptoms; in other words, it indicates a person who is functioning well in daily life.

This classification system is a noticeable improvement over those of previous diagnostic manuals. The format of five axes allows clinicians to describe more accurately the symptoms and syndromes the patient is expressing. It also allows the clinician to indicate several diagnoses for the same patient if they happen to coexist. For example, while the patient may be principally exhibiting a depressed mode, he or she may also be experiencing a personality disorder. This system allows for a broader perspective on the patient's functioning, since multiple diagnoses may be made.

Characteristically, the clinician will assess the patient on all five axes. These are all viewed as the important clinical axes. The last two, however, are often used for research purposes. These axes, which provide for background information on the patient, are useful as a means of collecting information about situations and stresses that may contribute to and sustain some disorders. They also provide clinicians with a way to index progress or deterioration during treatment.

Users of this system have indicated its advantages and disadvantages. Those who see its advantages point out that such a system is important in facilitating communication between professional persons. They also note that it is useful for statistical purposes, since it tracks the incidence of disorders nationally and internationally. Such a system can contribute to the planning for a patient's treatment if what the patient is experiencing is known. In addition, using specific diagnostic criteria that match a clear list of symptoms with a client's behavior increases the accuracy and reliability of the diagnosis.

Critics of the system point out that this is basically a medical approach to classification and diagnosis rather than a psychological approach. They point out that the medical model that looks for symptoms leading to treatment may not be accurate or applicable to psychological disorders. Many emotional problems show the same symptoms but emerge from different causes, often requiring very different forms of treatment.

A second criticism involves the question of the reliability and validity of the diagnosis. Reliability refers to whether clinicians viewing the same patient would arrive at the same diagnosis. While the reliability of this system is substantially better than the reliability of systems described in prior manuals, there is still some question about the reliability of the diagnosis when judging axis 2. Finally, some criticize this system for providing no explanations for why the disorders exist. The system simply lists symptoms and behaviors without attempting to explain the cause or the reasons for their existence. These critics believe that the system is much too descriptive, providing little explanation for the existence of the disorder itself. Others see this as a prime strength, however, as it allows for these problems to be investigated from a variety of different theoretical perspectives.

Applications

Since it was first devised in 1952, the *Diagnostic and Statistical Manual of Mental Disorders* has become an important part of the diagnostic process for most mental health workers. This is partly because almost all insurance companies require the diagnosis of a patient's illness before payment is made for services, and the DSM-IV system has been widely accepted. The following example will illustrate the way in which clinicians translate a case study into the multiaxial system.

This is the case of a twenty-five-year-old male who came to the clinic complaining about depression, sadness, suicidal thoughts, and a general sense of hopelessness. He was born and reared in a large city on the East Coast. His mother was a caring, affectionate woman who nurtured her four children, but his father was a chronic alcoholic who verbally and physically abused his wife and children. The patient, the oldest boy in the family, was made to feel responsible for everything that went wrong.

At age seventeen, he left home and moved to California, where he had hoped the stress of life would be diminished. He found himself drinking heavily, using drugs excessively, and slowly drifting into a life of homelessness. He tried several times to obtain a job but was refused because of his disheveled appearance. In his wandering, he met a girl who shared his life of alcohol and drugs. This relationship, while superficial, was the only meaningful adult relationship that the patient had. They had traveled together for several years when, without much explanation, his girlfriend committed suicide. At this time, the patient's depression and despair became more severe, and his alcohol problems increased significantly. Two weeks after this event, he was admitted to a mental health clinic for attempting to slash his wrists after being arrested for alcohol intoxication. The mental health worker who conducted the initial interview produced the following diagnoses.

On axis 1, the clinician diagnosed "Major Depressive Disorder, single episode, severe, without psychotic features," "Alcohol Intoxication," and "Alcohol Dependence." The clinician observed some significant symptoms lasting more than two weeks that are characteristic of major depression, even when the client was not intoxicated: a depressed mood most of the day nearly every day; a marked diminished interest in any activities during the day; a significant weight loss and decrease in appetite; feelings of worthlessness and guilt, particularly over the death of the girlfriend; and recurrent thoughts of death, as well as a suicide attempt. Since this patient also had alcohol problems for more than a year (consisting of tolerance of alcohol, withdrawal when he stopped drinking, and an inability to quit despite a strong desire to quit), he was also diagnosed on axis 1 with alcohol dependence. The diagnosis of alcohol intoxication characterized his presentation when he arrived at the treatment unit. No diagnosis was made on axis 2 or on axis 3. On axis 4, the clinician found "Psychological Stressors." The death of the man's girlfriend by suicide was judged to be a significant stressor.

On axis 5, the current "Global Assessment of Functioning" was rated 10 because of the persistent danger of the patient committing suicide. The clinician was also asked to estimate the highest global assessment of functioning during the past year. Prior to the suicide attempt of his girlfriend, the patient was judged to be functioning at 50. This reflected the fact that there was suicidal ideation and that it was difficult for this young man to find and keep a job for any long period of time.

This illustrates the manner in which clinicians report information after taking a thorough history and often doing considerable psychological testing to determine the assets and liabilities of the patient's functioning at the moment.

Perspective and Prospects
Prior to 1952, there was no systematic procedure for establishing diagnosis and classification. Clinics and hospitals devised systems that were unique to their own

settings and often to their own communities. It was difficult for professionals to communicate with one another when a patient went from one setting to another or from one therapist to another.

It was not until 1952 that the American Psychiatric Association published its first manual, the *Diagnostic and Statistical Manual of Mental Disorders*, which attempted to define all the known psychological and psychiatric disorders. It encouraged all mental health workers to use the same terminology and the same description of disorders so that statistical data could be accumulated on the incidence of mental health disorders in various communities and states. That early manual achieved the purpose of standardizing diagnostic terms, but it had shortcomings; for example, it had no section for children or adolescents. The manual assumed that only adult disorders were diagnosable. Additionally, the manual made assumptions about the origins of disorders on the basis of only one theory: psychoanalytic theory. Since most psychiatrists at that time were psychoanalytically oriented, the manual reflected their theoretical bias in its description of some of the major disorders.

In 1968, the second revision of the *Diagnostic and Statistical Manual of Mental Disorders*, DSM-II, was published. In this version, many disorders that had been omitted from the first volume were added. A new section—"Behavior Disorders of Childhood and Adolescence," which listed six disorders—was added. While this was a notable improvement on the prior volume, it certainly did not reflect a comprehensive understanding of disorders in children or adolescents.

In 1980, the third version of the diagnostic manual, DSM-III, was published; a complete revision was made. This manual was more complete than the previous one; it added many more disorders that were not present in the previous volume and omitted those disorders that were duplicated or extremely rare. This volume also altered its theoretical perspective by attempting to describe behaviors rather than to explain them. No theoretical assumptions were made regarding the cause of the disorders. The clinician was to match the list of symptoms with the disorder. This volume used more precise language, increased its coverage, and introduced the multiaxial classification system that was described above. It also made a significant attempt to coordinate the manual with the International Classification of Diseases, a system adopted by the World Health Assembly of the World Health Organization, thus allowing statistical comparisons to be made between different countries and different parts of the world.

In 1980, the third, revised edition was published. It built upon the strengths of DSM-III by being somewhat more dimensional, not discussing disorders just as categories, but also in terms of severity. It also incorporated research findings derived from the categories listed in DSM-III and advanced a wide variety of disorders in terms of making them more specifically defined. Another prime improvement in DSM-III-R was that the text avoided labeling people and instead labeled disorders. So, rather than discussing "schizophrenics" or "alcoholics," the text referred to individuals with schizophrenia or individuals with alcohol dependence.

The publication of DSM-IV in 1994, however, marked a significant advance.

The emphasis of severity within diagnostic categories received much more attention. A section was also added defining criteria sets for further study, consisting of disorders that are not yet in the classification, but need to be researched further. These include conditions such as passive-aggressive personality disorder, depressive personality disorder, postconcussional disorder, premenstrual dysphoric disorder, and mild neurocognitive disorder. Additionally, several new axes were proposed to describe better psychological defenses and specific functioning in relationships and social and occupational roles. DSM-IV also has a special section on cultural issues (Appendix I). This provides an outline of cultural issues to be noticed in assessment and treatment in diverse ethnic and cultural settings. Additionally, a variety of culture-bound syndromes are described. These are syndromes that appear only in certain cultures.

As the diagnostic field advances, clinical psychology is taking more of a role in the establishment of the diagnosis and classification of psychological disorders. This perspective is based on a psychological rather than a medical model. Its starting point is the assumption that measured behavior determines the description of a syndrome. Such measured characteristics are obtained by means of rating scales or tests. Using a statistical procedure called cluster analysis or factor analysis, one reduces the largest number of variables into the smallest number of categories that are distinctly different from one another. These categories are viewed as different diagnostic states. This procedure increases the reliability of the measurement and the validity of the diagnosis. It also allows for the establishment of a direct relationship between the diagnosis of the clinician and the data from which that diagnosis is obtained. The American Psychological Association has discussed ways of proceeding with the establishment of such a system of classification. As such, it is likely that collaborative efforts between psychologists and psychiatrists will continue to improve the DSM system.

Bibliography

American Psychiatric Association. *Diagnostic and Statistical Manual of Mental Disorders, Fourth Edition (DSM-IV)*. 4th ed. Washington, D.C.: Author, 1994. This manual summarizes all the psychological and psychiatric disorders and gives the criteria for each classification. Almost all mental health workers are familiar with this volume and use it when diagnoses must be made for insurance companies.

Frances, Allen, M.D., and Ruth Ross. *DSM-IV Case Studies: A Clinical Guide to Differential Diagnosis*. Washington, D.C.: American Psychiatric Press, 1996. Case studies illustrating the diagnostic descriptions found in DSM-IV, and the process of differentiating one diagnosis from another. For psychiatrists and students.

Spitzer, Robert L., Michael B. First, Janet B. Williams, Miriam Gibbon, and Andrew E. Skodol. *DSM-IV Casebook: A Learning Companion to the Diagnostic and Statistical Manual of Mental Disorders*. 4th ed. Washington, D.C.: American Psychiatric Press, 1994. This excellent paperback provides many case histories, with accompanying diagnoses according to the DSM-IV. The book, which also includes mental disorders of children and adolescents, discusses fascinating historical cases that were treated by such great therapists as Sigmund Freud, Emil Kraepelin, and Alois Alzheimer. In addition, presents a number of cases from Africa, India, Polynesia, and Russia.

World Health Organization. *Manual of the International Statistical Classification of Diseases, Injuries, and Causes of Death.* 10th ed. Geneva, Switzerland: Author, 1992. An internationally recognized diagnostic system established under the auspices of the United Nations. It allows the diagnostician to record and compare disorders from around the world. The mental health section permits nations to compare the incidence of specific psychological disorders in different countries.

Gerald Sperrazzo
updated by Nancy A. Piotrowski

See also:

Abnormality: Behavioral Models; Abnormality: Biomedical Models; Abnormality: Psychodynamic Models; Anxiety Disorders; Depression; Manic-Depressive Disorder; Schizophrenia.

DIVORCE AND SEPARATION
Adult Issues

Type of psychology: Developmental psychology
Fields of study: Adulthood; coping; interpersonal relations

Divorce results in serious psychological and economic consequences for parents and children; adults must confront feelings of anger, loss, and alienation. They need to create new lives, with different social and economic realities, and must often approach relationships with their children in new ways.

Principal terms

CUSTODIAL PARENT: the parent with physical custody—the parent with whom the child normally lives

DIVORCE MEDIATION: mediation of the terms of divorce by a mental health professional or a team composed of such a professional and an attorney

INVOLUNTARY CHILD-ABSENCE SYNDROME: a pattern of depression and anger shown by fathers who are out of touch with their children

JOINT LEGAL CUSTODY: an arrangement in which each parent has the right to provide input on major decisions affecting the child but only one has physical custody

JOINT PHYSICAL CUSTODY: an arrangement in which each parent has significant time living with the child, who usually moves between homes; the time with each parent does not have to be exactly equal

NONCUSTODIAL PARENT: the parent who has only visitation rights to see the child and the obligation to pay child support

SOLE CUSTODY: all rights to make decisions, to have physical custody of a child, and to receive support on the behalf of the child; the noncustodial parent may get visitation rights and owes support

Overview

Once it was believed that traumatic events, such as earthquakes or divorce, would cause shock followed by quick and complete recovery. Studies of people exposed to natural disasters, however, have shown that recovery is a process with acute followed by chronic stages. The sequence is called post-traumatic stress disorder (PTSD). The acute stage is marked by denial, defensive reactions, and passivity. Cognitive integration, realism, and active adjustment mark the chronic stage. Reactions to divorce follow this pattern. Divorce is not one event, but a continuum beginning in an unhappy marriage and continuing for many years. Divorce is a catalyst for change, but many factors influence which choices will be available. Rage is almost inevitable, and it can serve as a defense against depression. Divorce is the only major interpersonal crisis with a high probability of violence.

Judith Wallerstein and Sandra Blakeslee in 1989 proposed a stage model for divorce in their book *Second Chances*. Their three stages are an acute stage, a transitional stage, and a stage of renewed stability. Escalating unhappiness ends with the divorce decision and ejection of one parent from the home. In the acute stage, divorce unleashes primitive impulses, sometimes including violence, often in front of the children. People act in odd ways, and parental affairs frighten children.

Women are almost twice as likely to have initiated the divorce, are more likely to believe it is justified, and adjust better initially. Many experience euphoria at escaping and defensively deny real problems, anxieties, inadequate skills, and the chaos in their homes. Women first tend to be more independent, and men more likely to attempt reconciliation. More women feel that they control the divorce; men feel controlled by their external situations.

During the transitional stage, the divorced persons make efforts to solve problems and develop new lifestyles through trial and error. Families are unstable; there are new lovers and friends. In the renewed stability stage, cognitive restructuring that reflects postdivorce reality occurs, allowing major changes in parenting, social, and occupational behaviors. Self-esteem often drops. The differences in adjustment favoring women decrease. Ten years after divorce, almost half of women and about one-third of men remain very angry and feel exploited and rejected.

Adjustment during this stage depends on the resources available compared with the needs that must be met. Women tend to have more social resources, but men tend to have more financial resources. Women who are divorced by their early thirties are often energized, and 70 percent remarry. Assertive women tend to do well; maintaining a low-conflict relationship with the former husband predicts physical and emotional health.

According to Wallerstein and Blakeslee's research, women have a difficult job maintaining both parenting and economic support. Child support is a constant source of tension and conflict. Women in their late thirties and older are often immobilized by anger, depression, and helplessness. Many work hard at low-paying jobs and gain little; many women believe that eligible men are too hard to find and give up. Few older women studied by Wallerstein and Blakeslee explored new second chances. They involved themselves in clubs, friends, and churches but remained lonely and missed their marriage roles. They tended to become dependent on their children, and they had more physical complaints.

Many men who are divorced in their twenties stop maturing; most fail in second marriages. Of those studied by Wallerstein and Blakeslee, half had no stable careers five years after the divorce. Fewer than a third paid full child support, and most saw their children rarely, if at all. Most of their social contacts were with dates or male friends. Most took the blame for their failed marriages; older men more than older women had regrets, accepted responsibility, and did not remarry. Having visitation rights was experienced as being far inferior to watching their children grow up day by day, and many men had little life except their work.

More than half of divorced fathers eventually lose close contact with their children. When a custodial parent uses the children against the noncustodial parent, the children may become hostile toward the "out" parent. The majority of divorced fathers show the involuntary child-absence syndrome characterized by depression, anxiety, physical symptoms, and anger.

Joint physical custody, usually simply called joint custody, means that both parents share significant time with the children. This solves some problems but produces new ones. Most states reduce child-support payments with joint custody, although some of a parent's costs continue even when the child is with the other parent. Joint custody requires the continuation of stressful adjustments. More joint physical custody fathers stay involved with their children, pay more support, and talk with the mothers, yet the communication is too often hostile, and some fathers do become violent. Joint legal custody means that both parents can share important decisions. The child lives with one parent, and the other has visitation rights. Joint legal custody can ease a father's feelings of powerlessness about his children. This is beneficial both emotionally and economically, because fathers will be more likely to stop disapproving of the divorce and more likely to pay child support. More joint legal custody fathers continue parenting; they also start fewer court battles.

Many adults, especially women, ultimately grow in competence and self-esteem after a divorce. People with histories of talent, marketable skills, and social networks do best; the person filing the divorce petition is more likely to be happy and more social. The most consistent winners are well-established men in their thirties and forties. All the men in Wallerstein and Blakeslee's studies who initiated divorce had another, usually younger, woman waiting. The best predictor of good adjustment was a successful second marriage. These men knew they wanted, and found, women they believed to be less critical, sexier, or more responsive. Once remarried, they developed community ties and more friendships than unmarried men. Many did well as parents of a new set of children.

Lenore Weitzman has critiqued joint custody and no-fault divorce as impoverishing mothers. Many women experience a sharp drop in their standard of living immediately after divorce, but do better with a few years. Unmarried mothers with custody have, on average, about half the earnings of single-father households. The average child-support payments made (by those men who do pay) represent about half the cost of rearing each child. Fewer than half of divorced women receive full payments. Fathers are unlikely to pay for college, and most focus on legal duties—not on the children's needs.

Remarriage often improves a divorced woman's economic condition, and it may increase the happiness and economic status of a single parent of either sex. Remarriages tend to be fragile, however, and the divorce rates higher. The failure of a second marriage produces more trauma than a first failure. Fathers who marry mothers with children encounter financial burdens. Unless parents bringing children to a remarriage make a special effort to create a significant legitimate role for a stepparent, the stepparent often feels like an outsider.

Applications
Research on the effects of divorce shows that the effects are often harmful and may last a lifetime. Sometimes they may even last over generations; the children of

divorce who witnessed physical abuse at home are much more likely to be abusive or to be abused. Problems are created that need to be addressed by family therapy and other interventions.

Stage models of divorce adjustment have important implications for family therapy. Clinicians must evaluate the amount of time elapsed since the beginning of the divorce process when judging the appropriateness of a divorcing or divorced client's reactions. Because early reactions to divorce are so different from long-term reactions, therapists should be careful about assuming that a happy client will continue doing well. Women surveyed soon after divorce may have good emotional health, unless they are victims of violence, despite problems with social support and finances. This good adjustment, however, can gradually deteriorate in the face of unpleasant realities.

Single-parent families make the poorest transition; they are more vulnerable, and have few economic and social resources. Women's self-esteem drops as stress and fear of being alone continue. Men may cope with feelings of helplessness by having distorted and abnormally negative perceptions of their former wives. The need for counseling services may be even greater after a divorce than before or during the divorce. Fifty-five percent of divorced adults and 60 percent of adults divorced after a second marriage seek counseling. There is no significant difference between male and female readiness to seek professional help.

Father dropout is infrequent for fathers who have joint custody (and who were involved with the children before the separation), but joint custody is not a magic solution to the problems of the children or parents of divorce. High levels of conflict between former spouses correlate with poor adjustment of parents and children. Since the legal adversary system often promotes conflict, more use should be made of nonadversary procedures such as mediation of disputes to reduce continuing conflict between parents. Mediators help resolve disputes by acting as referees and information sources. The variables that determine whether mediation will be successful must be explored. When divorcing parents are each uncritically supported by an attorney of their own sex, a voluntary settlement is less likely. Interventions with divorcing families and their children need to address distorted attributions and perceptions that result from a flawed cognitive restructuring process as well as personal and environmental factors.

There needs to be greater understanding about the psychological issues that underlie the inadequate parenting provided by noncustodial parents, mainly fathers. The quality of parenting by a father before divorce does not accurately predict postdivorce parenting. The present system of forcing fathers to pay support without receiving some compensating right or benefit has resulted in withdrawn fathers. Visitation needs to be designed to meet the needs of both children and fathers or it fails in its essential purpose. The legal system's response to the feminization of poverty—using more force to make men pay more—motivates more fathers to contest custody and creates lasting bad feelings. Even those fathers who do pay support rarely pay for college once the court order expires. The children of divorce underachieve relative to their parents and their peers from intact homes.

Divorce makes women feel powerless because of the financial and emotional costs of rearing children. It makes men feel powerless because they face the loss of power in their relationships with their children. Moreover, many men face the prospect of having a large part of their salary support not only their children but also the woman who has made it difficult to continue to be a parent. Custodial mothers need more money; noncustodial fathers need easier and more rewarding access to their children. Children need to be in real relationships with both parents.

Research on divorce and its effects suggests many changes that could be made in how divorce is handled and in how families can best approach life after divorce. Among the things that are needed are reasonable support orders, with strict enforcement as well as a sharing of parental power. Moderately priced and high-quality day care services are needed; more mental health professionals are needed to work in mediation, family services, and private practice to help divorced parents reduce conflict and avoid focusing on blame and power.

About 12 percent of parents become or remain friends after divorce. An additional 38 percent manage to cooperate by considering the child or children first instead of attempting to win a power struggle with the other parent. Few "friends after divorce" remain friends after one partner enters a new stable relationship, but they usually continue to cooperate. New female partners are more likely to be threatened by a former spouse and create problems in the coparenting arrangement. The new partners in the process should be recognized and involved. Further study is needed on how to encourage cooperation between former spouses to create healthier "binuclear" families for the estimated one in three children who will grow up with stepparents.

Perspective and Prospects

Longitudinal research on the process of divorce is a relatively recent area of psychology. The historical impetus was the adoption by all states of some form of no-fault divorce, beginning in California in 1970. No-fault divorce contributed to a great increase in divorces—to a level of one divorce for every two marriages, a rate double that of most countries. The explosion in the number of people undergoing divorce made their experiences a desirable area for large-scale research. Divorce research has origins in sociology, social psychology, clinical psychology, and developmental psychology. The results have been surprising and disturbing, with implications for cognitive psychology, stress theory, and personality theories.

The traditional view of divorce was that it was a one-time traumatic event with a few aftereffects. Both the public and psychologists believed that ties between the parents of children should be cut to allow stepfathers to replace former husbands more easily. It is now known that the effects of separation and divorce act much like other severe traumas and produce a prolonged post-traumatic stress disorder. Stage models of divorce, and Wallerstein and others' research results, have shown that recovery is often very slow, if indeed it occurs at all. Children have a continued need for close contacts with biological fathers, and fathers suffer from the loss of parenting experiences. Clinical problems persist in a very large percentage of the divorced, and these problems relate to the lack of critical resources.

Psychologists once thought that human development ended after adolescence. Now it is known that people continue to grow and change throughout their lives. Maturation can be stunted by the absence of healthy family structures; full social maturation of men requires parenting experiences. Theories of child development are mainly based on observations of intact two-parent families. Finally, the psychology of personality variables and cognitive learning may be altered by recent research on the long-term effects of divorce. Perceptions of the locus of control in the divorced person shifts as real power to control events changes. Cognitive restructuring in stressful situations may be adaptive and protective, but the tendency of divorced men to devalue their former mates severely can be mean-spirited and harmful. Understanding the cognitive mechanisms operating in this behavior will help in coping with severe stress.

The implications of divorce are important and pervasive. About 15 million children are growing up in single-parent homes, and 10 million in homes with a stepparent. Predictions from early research are that about a third of them will be seriously disturbed, depressed, poorly motivated, or easily defeated by rejections and losses. Large numbers of older divorced women are living alone in poverty. Millions of young men remain fixated at an immature level of development, preoccupied with dating and working but disconnected from future generations.

Bibliography

Gray, J. D., and R. C. Silver. "Opposite Sides of the Same Coin: Former Spouses' Divergent Perspectives in Coping with Their Divorce." *Journal of Personality and Social Psychology* 59, no. 6 (1990): 1180-1191. Canadians rated their former spouses; both agreed that the former wife was more likely to have wanted the divorce. Both saw the other as more desirous of a reconciliation, and the men devalued their former partners to an extent not found in most normal groups of people. Gray and Silver interpret these results in terms of cognitive mechanisms for coping with severe chronic stresses.

Hetherington, E. Mavis, ed. *Coping with Divorce, Single Parenting, and Remarriage: A Risk and Resiliency Perspective.* Mahwah, N.J.: Lawrence Erlbaum Associates, 1999. Studies of families headed by single or repartnered parents. Includes bibliographical references and indexes.

Knox, David. *Choices in Relationships: An Introduction to Marriage and the Family.* 2d ed. St. Paul, Minn.: West, 1988. An excellent source for information about the American family, from its formation through dating and marriage to separation, divorce, and postdivorce adjustment. There is a wealth of statistical information as well as comprehensive reviews of psychological research on the effects of separation, divorce, custody arrangements, and remarriage.

Pam, Alvin, and Judith Pearson. *Splitting Up: Enmeshment and Estrangement in the Process of Divorce.* New York: Guilford Press, 1998. Examines the emotional process of divorce. Explores why marriages fail, the reactions of both partners, the psychodynamics of jealousy, the possibility of reconciliation, and the impact on children. Presents case studies and includes bibliographical references and an index.

Stark, Elizabeth. "Friends Through It All." *Psychology Today* 20 (May, 1986): 54-60. A study of the long-term adjustment of couples who stayed in contact because of either shared parenting or personal reasons. Stark finds that many divorced people develop positive and mutually satisfying relationships but that these often become more distant when one former spouse develops a new romantic involvement. Stark identifies several factors that predict a positive continuing relationship.

Wallerstein, Judith S., and Sandra Blakeslee. *Second Chances: Men, Women, and Children a Decade After Divorce.* New York: Ticknor & Fields, 1989. A very important source of information about the long-term effects of separation, divorce, and remarriage. Wallerstein followed a sample of sixty couples and their 131 children for more than fifteen years and produced comprehensive data on changes within the individuals' lives. She identifies factors related to doing well and poorly for both adults and the children of divorce.

Weitzman, Lenore J. *The Divorce Revolution.* New York: Free Press, 1985. The author makes a strong case that changes in divorce laws have caused the feminization of poverty. The work is not without methodological flaws, and the author is a determined advocate of her thesis that no-fault divorce and joint or father custody harm women; however, there is much important information here about an escalating social problem.

Leland C. Swenson

See also:

Couples Therapy; Depression; Divorce and Separation: Children's Issues; Midlife Crises; Stress.

DIVORCE AND SEPARATION
Children's Issues

Type of psychology: Developmental psychology
Fields of study: Adolescence; coping; infancy and childhood; psychodynamic and
neoanalytic models

*Research on divorce and separation has provided insight into how this event affects
family life and child development. Understanding the consequences of divorce-related issues for children has permitted the refinement of methods to prevent or
relieve the emotional distress associated with family breakup.*

Principal terms

CUSTODIAL PARENT: as decided by the court, the parent with whom a child lives
after a divorce

DISPLACEMENT COMMUNICATION: a method of indirect communication that uses an
object or fictional character to represent the action and thoughts of the person
to whom one is talking

EGO DEFENSE MECHANISMS: unconscious and irrational ways in which people
distort reality in order to reduce anxiety

EGOCENTRIC THINKING: an intellectual tendency to attribute the cause of events to
oneself

ENMESHMENT: an excessively close relationship between parent and child in which
adult concerns and needs are communicated and in which overdependence on
the child is apparent

REGRESSION: an ego defense mechanism that a person uses to return to an earlier
stage of development when experiencing stress

STAGE THEORY OF DEVELOPMENT: the belief that development moves through a set
sequence of stages; the quality of behavior at each stage is unique but is
dependent upon movement through earlier stages

Overview

Separation and divorce terminate the social and legal contract of marriage and
result in the breakup of a family. Divorce can represent the end of emotional
suffering and an escape from an abusive environment, and it can provide the
potential for personal growth. Conversely, the adult experience of divorce and
separation can be devastating. Strong feelings of loss, anxiety, and damage to
self-esteem often accompany divorce. Anger, depression, and guilt are also commonly reported. Divorced men are more likely than married men to experience
psychiatric problems, serious accidents, and poor health; divorced women frequently experience depression and economic impoverishment.

The trouble that children have in adjusting to divorce has long been acknowledged. Between 30 and 50 percent of children of divorced parents experience

long-lasting problems related to the divorce. Primary symptoms include anger and aggressive behavior, sadness, low self-esteem, depression, and impaired academic performance. Children of divorced parents are also more likely to experience trouble with intimate relationships in adulthood.

Contemporary mental health workers no longer view divorce as a discrete event, but as a process. Neil Kalter takes this view in his book *Growing Up with Divorce: Helping Your Child Avoid Immediate and Later Emotional Problems* (1989). He describes divorce as a three-stage process: the immediate-crisis stage, the short-term aftermath stage, and the long-range period. The help children will require hinges upon which stage the divorce is in, their level of emotional and intellectual development, and their gender.

During the immediate-crisis stage, parents are often enraged. Wounded pride and self-esteem provoke responses ranging from verbal insult to physical violence. Frequently during this initial stage, little regard for the children is apparent, and children react with shock and disbelief. They are frightened, surprised, and saddened by the news that their parents are divorcing. They see that their parents are often short-tempered and occasionally show extreme anger. Conversely, they may see a parent crying, oversleeping, and anxious. During this stage, parents are often inattentive to the needs of their children. When parents show these behaviors, it creates stress for children. There are additional sources of stress for children as well. The rupture of a safe and predictable home environment and the loss of father-presence troubles them. If the parent with whom a child is living is having emotional trouble, enmeshment can represent another source of stress. Enmeshment refers to an excessively close and overdependent relationship between a parent and a child.

As parents and children move into the short-term aftermath stage, the realities of the divorce are better understood. Issues of economic support, custody, and visitation schedules become routine, and with effort, life becomes more predictable. Warfare between parents, however, often proceeds. Children are frequently enlisted as allies, weapons, and messengers in this battle. It is also possible for parents to develop an enmeshed relationship with a child during this stage. Sometimes parents do this unconsciously in an attempt to ward off feelings of loneliness and rejection. The children are counted on for adultlike emotional support as well as help with childrearing and household chores.

Another source of stress to children is the sense that they have lost their parents. The noncustodial parent is often absent in both the psychological and the physical sense. By this time, most children have little or no contact with the noncustodial parent. Since this is likely to be their father, children often lose access to the father-child relationship. This is unfortunate, because the father represents a model of masculine behavior that is important for both genders. The children may also see their mother less frequently. She may be working longer hours, engaging in acquiring additional training, or investing more time in her social life. Dating on the part of the single parent represents a particularly salient source of stress for children, especially older elementary school children and adolescents. Young children fear abandonment, while older children harbor competitive feelings and resentment toward their parents' dating partners. Older children must also face the reality of their parents' sexuality.

Between two and three years after the divorce, the long-range period begins. A major source of stress for children during this period occurs when parents continue to show open anger toward each other. This happens primarily because one parent is having trouble accepting the divorce. This parent may feel a desperate need for emotional support and entertain a fantasy of reuniting with the former spouse. Alternatively, one parent may feel the need to heap punishment on the other for deciding upon the divorce. This particular source of stress has been found to increase the likelihood that children will develop severe emotional and/or behavioral disorders. Serious—and, if necessary, legal—efforts to put an end to warring between parents must now be made. A second important source of stress to children during the long-range period is remarriage.

The remarriage of a parent is stressful to children of all ages, with the possible exception of infants. Children often view a stepparent as a rival for the time and love of the custodial parent. Younger children may fear abandonment. Loyalty conflicts between the stepparent and the noncustodial parent may exist. Children often become angry because the fantasy that their parents may reunite is shattered. Finally, children frequently become furious when a stepparent takes on the role of a parent. This is particularly true if the stepparent assigns chores and takes on a disciplinary role too quickly. The situation will be especially stressful if new siblings are brought to the marriage, thereby increasing feelings of competition for the time and affection of the custodial parent.

Divorce presents children with myriad external stressors. Older children, because of their expanding intellectual abilities, often create debilitating internal stressors for themselves as well.

Applications

Knowledge gained through study of the divorce process can be used to help children adapt. Examining some of the issues involved in helping children between three and five years of age adjust to divorce will help to illustrate this point. One must understand, however, that reactions to divorce are largely tied to the developmental level of the child.

During the immediate-crisis stage, stressors for preschool children include unpredictable daily routines, warfare between parents, distraught parents, and loss of the father-child relationship. During the short-term aftermath stage, key stressors are fighting between parents, enmeshed relationships, and the loss of the father-child relationship. Stressors in the long-range period include parental warfare, relocations, a distant father-child relationship, and remarriage.

A common symptom indicating a reaction of preschool children to stress is called regression. Regression is an ego defense mechanism. Ego defense mechanisms are ways in which people distort reality in order to reduce stress; regression is evident when a child returns to an earlier stage of development. Regression in sleeping patterns, eating habits, motor achievements, language, toilet training, and emotional independence all signal trouble. For example, a child who was consistently using the toilet may begin to soil and wet himself or herself again. Children may also show a failure to develop psychologically; for example, a child of four may continue to panic when her mother leaves her sight.

In addition to regression, preschool children display the ego defenses of displacement and denial. Displacement is apparent when children show their anger at parents indirectly by becoming uncooperative or by fighting more frequently with other children. Denial is apparent when they simply do not admit that the divorce has taken place, or deny the divorce in fantasy. Preschool children also show a phenomenon known as emotional resonance. They resonate to the anger of their parents, and this results in diffuse feelings of distress. If warring between parents is not controlled, it produces chronic fear and a reluctance to engage in new activities and begin new social relationships.

An intellectual characteristic of preschool children is their tendency to have trouble separating fact from fantasy. They also show egocentric thinking—the tendency to attribute the cause of events to themselves. Consequently, they can create their own stress. For example, they are likely to blame themselves for the divorce, believing that their father left because they were bad. Leaving a child at a day care center may lead her to fear that she is being abandoned because she is no longer loved. In a similar way, relocations and remarriage can spawn egocentric fantasies. Once such fantasies are developed, children believe them.

Preschool children have a more advanced striving for independence from their mothers than younger children. The absence of a father will hamper this progress. Both genders are expanding their social worlds; however, their sense of social and emotional independence is still shaky. They need a safe home-base in order to consolidate their independence. Since children are attempting to establish their independence from their mothers, their fathers provide a good alternative relationship. Further, boys need access to their fathers to nurture their emerging sense of masculine identity. Girls look to their fathers for acceptance of their feminine identity. In males, long-term father absence may produce a reluctance to interact with other boys; in females, it increases the probability of an enmeshed relationship with their mothers. Further, as children become more psychologically distant from their father, they may become angry at being forced to visit him. In addition, they may misunderstand why they must visit. For example, they may believe they are forced to visit because their mother does not care about them or does not want them around. This can produce symptoms of displaced anger, sadness, and withdrawal.

The thrust in helping these children cope is to reduce or eliminate their stress. Several steps are recommended in order to reduce external stress. Efforts should be made to ensure that the child's daily schedule is routine and predictable. Anger between parents should be reduced or eliminated. Professional help should be obtained for a distraught parent. Finally, establishing an effective coparenting relationship is critically important. In this way, the child's divorce environment can be brought in line with his or her needs. Children between the ages of three and five need a predictable, safe, and tranquil environment. Although alleviating sources of external stress is enormously helpful, the stress that children create themselves must also be addressed.

Research shows that discussing the divorce with preschool children before it occurs is helpful. The content of the discussion should be concrete and make clear what the divorce will mean. For example, the child should be told which parent will be moving out, where this parent will be living, and when he or she will see the noncustodial parent. Any changes in daily routine should also be explained. Reasons for the divorce should be explained in age-appropriate terms. The child's role in the divorce should be made clear, and it should be explained that divorce is adult business and that the child had no part in the decision. It should be emphasized that the divorce does not mean that parents will stop loving the child or will love the child any less.

If stress is minimized and the divorce has been clearly explained, chances are much better that post-divorce adjustment will go smoothly. It is, however, still possible, and perhaps likely, that the child will display divorce-related symptoms. If signals of distress occur, they are probably a result of egocentric fantasies. A technique known as displacement communication has been found to be an extremely effective way to reduce or eliminate sources of internal stress; Kalter's book provides several excellent examples of how to apply this approach.

Perspective and Prospects

The study of divorce as it affects family life and child development has long been of concern to psychology. Many works on the subject began to appear in the 1970's, reflecting an increased need for knowledge that corresponded to a rising divorce rate (the rate of divorce tripled between 1960 and 1980). In 1977, the *Journal of Divorce* was founded as a vehicle for the publication of data relating to divorce. This journal publishes interdisciplinary findings on all aspects of divorce—from clinical practice to theory and research. It will be important to persist in accumulating data on divorce-related effects on child development, since projections indicate that divorce rates are expected to continue increasing.

Beginning in the late 1970's, systematic studies of how divorce affects child development began to appear. During this time, the emphasis in research shifted from describing case studies and reporting descriptive statistics to refining existing knowledge of how children perceive and react to divorce. The focus was on understanding specific divorce-related effects on psychological development, and the way in which long-range effects are mediated as a function of developmental level and family relations became a popular area of research. Further, significant gains have been made in understanding how to mediate in the divorce process in order to minimize negative consequences on children.

Contemporary understanding of how divorce affects child development may be viewed as growing out of Erik Erikson's theory of personality development and Jean Piaget's theory of intellectual development. Although some disagreement exists in the details of their perspectives, in general, agreements outweigh disagreements. Both are stage theorists who adhere to the notion that development is not a continuous process. This means that characteristics of personality and intelligence differ in quality as a function of age. These characteristics are so different that they are better described as new features of the person—features that did not exist before. As stage theorists, Erikson and Piaget adhere to the notion that development unfolds in an invariant sequence of stages. Consequently, success at earlier stages in development is viewed as crucial for success at later stages. Both theorists agree that achievements of emotional and intellectual development depend on biological maturity; that is, biological maturity is necessary to permit a child to benefit, or suffer, from experience. Both theorists would predict that the impact of divorce on a child will depend on the child's developmental level and gender and on the types of experiences to which he or she is exposed.

Data gathered since the 1960's on how divorce affects children lend validity to these perspectives. The notion that development occurs in a stagelike manner and unfolds in an invariant sequence has generally been supported. The notion that early success or failure affects later development has become clear. The tenet that experience interacts with biological maturity to determine outcome has also found strong support in the divorce literature. Furthermore, the stress-related symptoms that children display in attempting to cope with divorce clearly support Erikson's notions about the function of ego defense mechanisms.

Bibliography

Emery, Robert E. *Marriage, Divorce, and Children's Adjustment.* 2d ed. Thousand Oaks, Calif.: Sage Publications, 1999. Reviews and integrates the existing research and clinical work on divorce and its impact on children's adjustment. Includes bibliographical references and an index.

Garrity, Carla, Mitchell A. Baris, Karen Bruenig, and Janet R. Johnston, eds. *Through the Eyes of Children: Healing Stories for Children of Divorce.* New York: Simon & Schuster, 1997. A tool for parents and professionals who work with children struggling with family breakup.

Hetherington, E. Mavis, M. Cox, and R. Cox. "The Aftermath of Divorce." In *Mother-Child, Father-Child Relationships*, edited by Joseph H. Stevens, Jr., and Marilyn Mathews. Washington, D.C.: National Association for the Education of Young Children, 1978. This chapter represents pioneering work that documents how divorce affects children. Reactions of children to the news of divorce and to its aftermath are vividly described.

Johnston, Janet R., and Linda E. Campbell. *Impasses of Divorce: The Dynamics and Resolution of Family Conflict.* New York: Free Press, 1988. The authors' project focused on helping parents mediate differences in hostile divorce situations. Issues sustaining conflict and preventing the development of a coparenting relationship are discussed, and methods to achieve a resolution are presented. An excellent source for family counselors.

Johnston, Janet R., and Vivienne Roseby. *In the Name of the Child: A Developmental Approach to Understanding and Helping Children of Conflicted and Violent Divorce.* New York: Free Press, 1997. A detailed examination of the immediate and longer-term effects of high-conflict divorce on children. Includes bibliographical references and an index.

Kalter, Neil. *Growing Up with Divorce: Helping Your Child Avoid Immediate and Later Emotional Problems.* New York: Free Press, 1989. Presents comprehensive advice on the emotional pitfalls of divorce, warning signs of distress, and methods of preventing and alleviating distress in children from infancy through adolescence. Provides a chapter on communicating with children that parents will find very useful.

Wallerstein, Judith S., and Sandra Blakeslee. *Second Chances: Men, Women, and Children a Decade After Divorce*. New York: Ticknor & Fields, 1989. This is a follow-up of Wallerstein's original study, cited below. Wallerstein's work presents data on the long-term effects of divorce on both parents and children, and for this reason it is extremely valuable. Useful for those who are anticipating divorce, attempting to cope with divorce, or interested in the long-term consequences of divorce.

Wallerstein, Judith S., and Joan Berlin Kelly. *Surviving the Breakup: How Parents and Children Cope with Divorce*. New York: Basic Books, 1980. The results of a five-year study investigating how parents and children adjust to divorce. The authors present data on how parents reacted to divorce and how these parental reactions affected their children's adjustment. They also report how children interpreted and reacted to the divorce and how their views solidified or changed over the period of the study.

Alan J. Beauchamp

See also:

Behavioral Family Therapy; Child and Adolescent Psychiatry; Depression; Divorce and Separation: Adult Issues; Psychotherapy: Children; Strategic Family Therapy.

DOMESTIC VIOLENCE

Type of psychology: Psychopathology
Fields of study: Adolescence; adulthood; aggression; infancy and childhood; interpersonal relations

Domestic violence is assaultive behavior intended to punish, dominate, or control another in an intimate family relationship. Physicians are often best able to identify situations of domestic violence and assist victims to implement preventive interventions.

Principal terms

CYCLE OF VIOLENCE: a repeating pattern of violence characterized by increasing tension, culminating in violent action, and followed by remorse

FAMILY VIOLENCE: violence against an intimate partner, typically to assert domination, control actions, or punish, which occurs as a pattern of behavior, not as a single, isolated act; also called battering, marital violence, domestic violence, relationship violence, child abuse, or elder abuse

FUNNELING: an interviewing technique for assessing violence in a patient's relationship, beginning with broad questions of relationship conflict and gradually narrowing to focus on specific violent actions

HANDS-OFF VIOLENCE: indirect attacks meant to terrorize or control a victim; may include property or pet destruction, threats, intimidating behavior, verbal abuse, stalking, and monitoring

HANDS-ON VIOLENCE: direct attacks upon the victim's body, including physical and sexual violence; comprises a continuum of acts ranging from seemingly minor to obviously severe

LETHALITY: the potential, given the particular dynamics of violence in a relationship, for one or both partners to be killed

SAFETY PLANNING: the development of a specific set of actions and strategies to enable a victim either to avoid violence altogether or, once violence has begun, to escape and minimize damage and injury

Causes and Symptoms

Domestic or family violence is the intentional use of violence against an intimate partner. The purpose of the violence is to assert domination, to control the victim's actions, or to punish the victim for some actions. Family violence generally occurs as a pattern of behavior over time rather than as a single, isolated act.

Forms of family violence include child physical abuse, child sexual abuse, spousal or partner abuse, and elder abuse. These forms of violence are related, in that they occur within the context of the family unit. Therefore, the victims and perpetrators know one another, are related to one another, may live together, and may love one another. These various forms of violence also differ insofar as victims may be children, adults, or frail, elderly adults. The needs of victims differ with age and independence, but there are also many similarities between the different types of violence. One such similarity is the relationship between the offender and the victim. Specifically, victims of abuse are always less powerful than abusers. Power includes the ability to exert physical and psychological control over situations. For example, a child abuser has the ability to lock a child in a bathroom or to abandon him or her in a remote area in order to control access to authorities. A spouse abuser has the ability to physically injure a spouse, disconnect the phone, and keep the victim from leaving for help. An elder abuser can exert similar control. Such differences in power between victims and offenders are seen as a primary cause of abuse; that is, people batter others because they can.

Families that are violent are often isolated. The members usually keep to themselves and have few or no friends or relatives with whom they are involved, even if they live in a city. This social isolation prevents victims from seeking help from others and allows the abuser to establish rules for the relationship without answering to anyone for these actions. Abuse continues and worsens because the violence occurs in private, with few consequences for the abuser.

Victims of all forms of family violence share common experiences. In addition to physical violence, victims are also attacked psychologically, being told they are worthless and responsible for the abuse that they receive. Because they are socially isolated, victims do not have an opportunity to take social roles where they can experience success, recognition, or love. As a result, victims often have low self-esteem and truly believe that they cause the violence. Without the experience of being worthwhile, victims often become severely depressed and anxious, and they experience more stress-related illnesses such as headaches, fatigue, or gastro-intestinal problems.

Child and partner abuse are linked in several ways. About half of the men who batter their wives also batter their children. Further, women who are battered are more likely to abuse their children than are nonbattered women. Even if a child of a spouse-abusing father is not battered, living in a violent home and observing the father's violence has negative effects. Such children often experience low self-esteem, aggression toward other children, and school problems. Moreover, abused children are more likely to commit violent offenses as adults. Children, especially males, who have observed violence between parents are at increased risk of assaulting their partners as adults. Adult sexual offenders have an increased likelihood of having been sexually abused as children. Yet, while these and other problems are reported more frequently by adults who were abused as children than by adults who were not, many former victims do not become violent. The most common outcomes of childhood abuse in adults are emotional problems. Although much less is known about the relationship between child abuse and future elder abuse, many elder abusers did suffer abuse as children. While most people who have been abused do not themselves become abusers, this intergenerational effect remains a cause for concern.

In its various forms, family violence is a public health epidemic in the United States. Once thought to be rare, family violence occurs with high frequency in the general population. Although exact figures are lacking and domestic violence tends to be underreported, it is estimated that each year 1.9 million children are physically abused; 250,000 children are sexually molested; 1.6 million women are assaulted by their male partners; and between 500,000 and 2.5 million elders are abused. Rates of violence directed toward unmarried heterosexual women, married heterosexual women, and members of homosexual male and female couples tend to be similar. No one is immune: Victims come from all social classes, races, and religions. Partner violence directed toward heterosexual men, however, is rare and usually occurs in relationships in which the man hits first.

Because family violence is so pervasive, physicians encounter many victims. One out of every three to five women visiting emergency rooms is seeking medical care for injuries related to partner violence. In primary care clinics, including family medicine, internal medicine, and obstetrics and gynecology, one out of every four female patients reports violence in the past year, and two out of five report violence at some time in their lives. It is therefore reasonable to expect all physicians and other health care professionals working in primary care and emergency rooms to provide services for victims of family violence.

Family violence typically consists of a pattern of behavior occurring over time and involving both hands-on and hands-off violence. Hands-on violence consists of direct attacks against the victim's body. Such acts range from pushing, shoving, and restraining to slapping, punching, kicking, clubbing, choking, burning, stabbing, or shooting. Hands-on violence also includes sexual assault, ranging from forced fondling of breasts, buttocks, and genitals; to forced touching of the abuser; to forced intercourse with the abuser or with other people.

Hands-off violence includes physical violence that is not directed at the victim's body but is intended to display destructive power and assert domination and control. Examples include breaking through windows or locked doors, punching holes through walls, smashing objects, destroying personal property, and harming or killing pet animals. The victim is often blamed for this destruction and forced to clean up the mess. Hands-off violence also includes psychological control, coercion, and terror. This includes name calling, threats of violence or abandonment, gestures suggesting the possibility of violence, monitoring of the victim's whereabouts, controlling of resources (such as money, transportation, and property), forced viewing of pornography, sexual exposure, or threatening to contest child custody. These psychological tactics may occur simultaneously with physical assaults or may occur separately. Whatever the pattern of psychological and physical tactics, abusers exert extreme control over their partners.

Neglect—the failure of one person to provide for the basic needs of another dependent person—is another form of hands-off abuse. Neglect may involve failure to provide food, clothing, health care, and shelter. Children, older adults, and developmentally delayed or physically handicapped people are particularly vulnerable to neglect.

Family violence differs in two respects from violence directed at strangers. First, the offender and victim are related and may love each other, live together, share property, have children, and share friends and relatives. Hence, unlike victims of stranger violence, victims of family violence cannot quickly or easily sever ties with or avoid seeing their assailants. Second, family violence often increases slowly in intensity, progressing until victims feel immobilized, unworthy, and responsible for the violence that is directed toward them. Victims may also feel substantial and well-grounded fear about leaving their abusers or seeking legal help, because they have been threatened or assaulted in the past and may encounter significant difficulty obtaining help to escape. In the case of children, the frail and elderly, or people with disabilities, dependency upon the caregiver and cognitive limitations make escape from an abuser difficult. Remaining in the relationship increases the risk of continued victimization. Understanding this unique context of the violent family can help physicians and other health care providers understand why battered victims often have difficulty admitting abuse or leaving the abuser.

Family violence follows a characteristic cycle. This cycle of violence begins with escalating tension and anger in the abuser. Victims describe a feeling of "walking on eggs." Next comes an outburst of violence. Outbursts of violence sometimes coincide with episodes of alcohol and drug abuse. Following the outburst, the abuser may feel remorse and expect forgiveness. The abuser often demands reconciliation, including sexual interaction. After a period of calm, the abuser again becomes increasingly tense and angry. This cycle generally repeats, with violence becoming increasingly severe. In partner abuse, victims are at greatest risk when there is a transition in the relationship such as pregnancy, divorce, or separation. In the case of elder abuse, risk increases as the elder becomes increasingly dependent on the primary caregiver, who may be inexperienced or unwilling to provide needed assistance. Without active intervention, the abuser rarely stops spontaneously and often becomes more violent.

Treatment and Therapy

Physicians play an important role in stopping family violence by first identifying people who are victims of violence, then taking steps to intervene and help. Physicians use different techniques with each age group because children, adults, and older adults each have special needs and varying abilities to help themselves. This section will first consider the physician's role with children and then will examine the physician's role with adults and older adults.

Because children do not usually tell a physician directly if they are being abused physically or sexually, physicians use several strategies to identify child and adolescent victims. Physicians screen for abuse during regular checkups by asking children if anyone has hurt them, touched them in private places, or scared them. To accomplish this screening with five-year-old patients having a routine checkup, physicians may teach their young patients about private areas of the body; let them know that they can tell a parent, teacher, or doctor if anyone ever touches them in private places; and ask the patients if anyone has ever touched them in a way that they did not like. For fifteen-year-old patients, physicians may screen potential victims by providing information on sexual abuse and date rape, then ask the patients if they have ever experienced either.

A second strategy that physicians use to identify children who are victims of family violence is to remain alert for general signs of distress that may indicate a child or youth lives in a violent situation. General signs of distress in children, which may be caused by family violence or by other stressors, include depression, anxiety, low self-esteem, hyperactivity, disruptive behaviors, aggressiveness toward other children, and lack of friends.

In addition to general signs of distress, there are certain specific signs and symptoms of physical and sexual abuse in children which indicate that the child has probably been exposed to violence. For example, bruises that look like a handprint, belt mark, or rope burn would indicate abuse. X rays can show a history of broken bones that are suspicious. Intentional burns from hot water, fire, or cigarettes often have a characteristic pattern. Sexually transmitted diseases in the genital, anal, or oral cavity of a child who is aged fourteen or under would suggest sexual abuse.

A physician observing specific signs of abuse or violence in a child, or even suspecting physical or sexual abuse, has an ethical and legal obligation to provide this information to state child protective services. Every state has laws that require physicians to report suspected child abuse. Physicians do not need to find proof of abuse before filing a report. In fact, the physician should never attempt to prove abuse or interview the child in detail because this can interfere with interviews conducted by experts in law, psychology, and the medicine of child abuse. When children are in immediate danger, they may be hospitalized so that they may receive a thorough medical and psychological evaluation while also being removed from the dangerous situation. In addition to filing a report, the physician records all observations in the child's medical chart. This record includes anything that the child or parents said, drawings or photographs of the injury, the physician's professional opinion regarding exposure to violence, and a description of the child abuse report.

The physician's final step is to offer support to the child's family. Families of child victims often have multiple problems, including violence between adults, drug and alcohol abuse, economic problems, and social isolation. Appropriate interventions for promoting safety include foster care for children, court-ordered counseling for one or both parents, and in-home education in parenting skills. The physician's goal, however, is to maintain a nonjudgmental manner while encouraging parental involvement.

Physicians also play a key role in helping victims of partner violence. Like children and adolescents, adult victims will usually not disclose violence. Therefore physicians should screen for partner violence and ask about partner violence whenever they notice specific signs of abuse or general signs of distress. Physicians screen for current and past violence during routine patient visits, such as during initial appointments; school, athletic, and work physicals; premarital exams; obstetrical visits; and regular checkups. General signs of distress include depression, anxiety disorders, low self-esteem, suicidal ideation, drug and alcohol abuse, stress illnesses (headache, stomach problems, chronic pain), or patient comments about a partner being jealous, angry, controlling, or irritable. Specific signs of violence include physical injury consistent with assault, including those requiring emergency treatment.

When a victim reports partner violence, there are five steps that a physician can take to help. Communicating belief and support is the first step. Sometimes abuse is extreme and patient reports may seem incredible. The physician validates the victim's experience by expressing belief in the story and exonerating the patient of blame. The physician can begin this process by making eye contact and telling the victim, "You have a right to be safe and respected" and "No one should be treated this way."

The second step is helping the patient assess danger. This is done by asking about types and severity of violent acts, duration and frequency of violence, and injuries received. Specific factors that seem to increase the risk of death in violent relationships include the abuser's use of drugs and alcohol, threats to kill the victim, and the victim's suicidal ideation or attempts. Finally, the physician should ask if the victim feels safe returning home. With this information, the physician can help the patient assess lethal potential and begin to make appropriate safety plans.

The third step is helping the patient identify resources and make a safety plan. The physician begins this process by simply expressing concern for the victim's safety and providing information about local resources such as mandatory arrest laws, legal advocacy services, and shelters. For patients planning to return to an abusive relationship, the physician should encourage a detailed safety plan by helping the patient identify safe havens with family members, friends, or a shelter; assess escape routes from the residence; make specific plans for dangerous situations or when violence recurs; and gather copies of important papers, money, and extra clothing in a safe place in or out of the home in the event of a quick exit. Before the patient leaves, the physician should give the patient a follow-up appointment within two weeks. This provides the victim with a specific, known resource. Follow-up visits should continue until the victim has developed other supportive resources.

The physician's final step is documentation in the patient's medical chart. This written note includes the victim's report of violence, the physician's own observations of injuries and behavior, assessment of danger, safety planning, and follow-up. This record can be helpful in the event of criminal or civil action taken by the victim against the offender. The medical chart, and all communications with the patient, is kept strictly confidential. Confronting the offender about the abuse can place the victim at risk of further, more severe violence. Improper disclosure can also result in loss of the patient's trust, precluding further opportunities for help.

There are several things that a physician should never do when working with a patient-victim. The physician should not encourage a patient to leave a violent relationship as a first or primary choice. Leaving an abuser is the most dangerous time for victims and should be attempted only with adequate planning and resources. The physician should not recommend couples counseling. Couples counseling endangers victims by raising the victim's expectation that issues can be discussed safely. The abuser often batters the victim after disclosure of sensitive information. Finally, the physician should not overlook violence if the violence appears to be "minor." Seemingly minor acts of aggression can be highly injurious.

Physicians also play an important role in helping adults who are older, developmentally delayed, or physically disabled. People in all three groups experience a high rate of family violence. Each group presents unique challenges for the physician. One common element among all three groups is that the victims may be somewhat dependent upon other adults to meet their basic needs. Because of this dependence, abuse may sometimes take the form of failing to provide basic needs such as adequate food or medical care. In many states, adults who are developmentally delayed are covered by mandatory child abuse reporting laws.

The signs and symptoms of the abuse of elders are similar to the other forms of family violence. These include physical injuries consistent with assault, signs of distress, and neglect, including self-neglect. Elder abuse victims are often reluctant to reveal abuse because of fear of retaliation, abandonment, or institutionalization. Therefore, a key to intervention is coordinating with appropriate social service and allied health agencies to support an elder adequately, either at home or in a care center. Such agencies include aging councils, visiting nurses, home health aids, and respite or adult day care centers. Counseling and assistance for caregivers is also an important part of intervention.

Many states require physicians to report suspected elder abuse. Because many elder abuse victims are mentally competent, however, it is important that they be made part of the decision-making and reporting process. Such collaboration puts needed control in the elder's hands and therefore facilitates healing. Many other aspects of intervention described for partner abuse apply to working with elders, including providing emotional support, assessing danger, safety planning, and documentation.

In addition to helping the victims of acute, ongoing family violence, physicians have an important role to play in helping survivors of past family violence. People who have survived family violence may continue to experience negative effects similar to those experienced by acute victims. Physicians can identify survivors of family violence by screening for past violence during routine exams. A careful history can determine whether the patient has been suffering medical or psychological problems related to the violence. Finally, the physician should identify local resources for the patient, including a mutual help group and a therapist.

Physicians can also help prevent family violence. One avenue of prevention is through education of patients by discussing partner violence with patients at key life transitions, such as during adolescence when youths begin dating, prior to marriage, during pregnancy, and during divorce or separation. A second avenue of prevention is making medical clinic waiting rooms and examination rooms into education centers by displaying educational posters and providing pamphlets.

Perspective and Prospects
Despite its frequency, family violence has not always been viewed as a problem. In the 1800's, it was legal in the United States for a man to beat his wife, or for parents to use brutal physical punishment with children. Although the formation of the New York Society for the Prevention of Cruelty to Children in 1874 signaled rising concern about child maltreatment, the extent of the problem was underestimated. As recently as 1960, family violence was viewed as a rare, aberrant

phenomenon and women who were victims of violence were often seen as partially responsible because of "masochistic tendencies." Several factors combined to turn the tide during the next thirty years. Medical research published in the early 1960's began documenting the severity of the problem of child abuse. By 1968, every state in the United States had passed a law requiring that physicians report suspected child abuse, and many states established child protective services to investigate and protect vulnerable children.

Progress in the battle against partner violence was slower. The battered women's movement brought new attention and a feminist understanding to the widespread and serious nature of partner violence. This growing awareness provided the impetus, during the 1970's and 1980's, for reform in the criminal justice system, scientific research, continued growth of women's shelters, and the development of treatment programs for offenders.

The medical profession's response to partner abuse followed these changes. In 1986, Surgeon General C. Everett Koop declared family violence to be a public health problem and called upon physicians to learn to identify and intervene with victims. In 1992, the American Medical Association (AMA) echoed the Surgeon General and stated that physicians have an ethical obligation to identify and assist victims of partner violence, and it established standards and protocols for identifying and helping victims of family violence. Because partner and elder abuse have been recognized only recently by the medical community, many physicians are just beginning to learn about their essential role.

Family violence has at various times been considered as a social problem, a legal problem, a political problem, and a medical problem. Because of this shifting understanding and because of the grassroots political origins of the child and partner violence movements, some may question why physicians should be involved. There are three compelling reasons.

First, there is a medical need: Family violence is one of the most common causes of injury, illness, and death for women and children. Victims seeking treatment for acute injuries make up a sizable portion of emergency room visits. Even in outpatient clinics, women report high rates of recent and ongoing violence and injury from partners. In addition to physical injuries, many victims experience stress-related medical problems for which they seek medical care. Among obstetrical patients who are battered, there is a risk of injury to both the woman and her unborn child. Hence, physicians working in clinics and emergency rooms will see many people who are victims.

Second, physicians have a stake in breaking the cycle of violence because they are interested in injury prevention and health promotion. When a physician treats a child or adult victim for physical or psychological injury but does not identify root causes, the victim will return to a dangerous situation. Prevention of future injury requires proper diagnosis of root causes, rather than mere treatment of symptoms.

Third, physicians have a stake in treatment of partner violence because it is a professional and ethical obligation. Two principles of medical ethics apply. First, a physician's actions should benefit the patient. Physicians can benefit patients who are suffering the effects of family violence only if they correctly recognize the root cause and intervene in a sensitive and professional manner. Physicians should also "do no harm." A physician who fails to recognize and treat partner violence will harm the patient by providing inappropriate advice and treatment.

Bibliography

Barnett, Ola W., Cindy-Lou Miller-Perrin, and Robert D. Perrin. *Family Violence Across the Lifespan: An Introduction.* Thousand Oaks, Calif.: Sage Publications, 1997. Provides information about the different ways that domestic violence, and the warning signs associated with it, may be recognized at various stages in the life spans of individuals and families.

Bass, Ellen, and Laura Davis. *The Courage to Heal: A Guide for Women Survivors of Child Sexual Abuse.* 3d rev. and updated ed. New York: HarperPerennial, 1994. A practical guide to understanding child sexual abuse for female survivors. Informative, but not intended as a substitute for professional therapy.

Island, David, and Patrick Letellier. *Men Who Beat the Men Who Love Them.* New York: Haworth Press, 1991. The first published book that tackles the issue of gay male partner violence. The authors write in a lively, straightforward manner that is easy to understand. Proposes novel ways of thinking about partner violence.

Jones, Ann, and Susan Schechter. *When Love Goes Wrong: What to Do When You Can't Do Anything Right.* New York: HarperCollins, 1992. Contains practical and useful information for women caught in controlling and abusive relationships, such as how to leave an abusive relationship.

Pagelow, Mildred. *Family Violence.* New York: Praeger, 1984. One of the most comprehensive texts on family violence available. Though an academic text, it is easy to read and provides a balanced discussion of the major definitions, issues, and controversies in the field of family violence.

Straus, Murray A., Richard J. Gelles, and Suzanne K. Steinmetz. *Behind Closed Doors: Violence in the American Family.* Garden City, N.Y.: Anchor Press/ Doubleday, 1980. A report of the first national survey on violence in the American family. Though many statistics are presented, they are explained in layperson's terms.

Wexler, David B. *Domestic Violence 2000: An Integrated Skills Program for Men.* New York: W. W. Norton, 2000. A program for preventing further violence by engaging abusive men in their own education and healing. Includes bibliographical references and an index.

Wilson, K. J. *When Violence Begins at Home: A Comprehensive Guide to Understanding and Ending Domestic Abuse.* Alameda, Calif.: Hunter House, 1997. The author reflects on her work against domestic violence after surviving an abusive relationship herself. Addresses behavioral patterns, the role of alcohol and drugs, leaving abusive relationships, and legislation on domestic violence. A manual for counselors, legal professionals, and victims of abuse.

Wolfe, David A., Christine Wekerle, and Katreena Scott. *Alternatives to Violence: Empowering Youth to Develop Healthy Relationships.* Thousand Oaks, Calif.:

Sage Publications, 1997. Offers information about how to recognize problems related to the development of violence in relationships, as well as strategies to help adolescents develop healthy relationship habits.

L. Kevin Hamberger
Bruce Ambuel

See also:

Abnormality: Family Models; Addictive Personality and Behaviors; Alcoholism; Antisocial Personality; Borderline, Histrionic, and Narcissistic Personalities; Child Abuse; Child and Adolescent Psychiatry; Codependent Personality; Depression; Divorce and Separation: Adult Issues; Divorce and Separation: Children's Issues; Geriatric Psychiatry; Jealousy; Substance Abuse.

DOWN SYNDROME

Type of psychology: Developmental psychology; psychopathology
Fields of study: Cognitive processes; organic disorders

Down syndrome is a congenital abnormality characterized by moderate to severe mental retardation and a distinctive physical appearance caused by a chromosomal aberration, the result of either an error during embryonic cell division or the inheritance of defective chromosomal material.

Principal terms

CHROMOSOMES: small, threadlike bodies containing the genes that are microscopically visible during cell division

GAMETES: the egg and sperm cells that unite to form the fertilized egg (zygote) in reproduction

GENE: a segment of the DNA strand containing instructions for the production of a protein

HOMOLOGOUS CHROMOSOMES: chromosome pairs of the same size and centromere position that possess genes for the same traits; one homologous chromosome is inherited from the father and the other from the mother

MEIOSIS: the type of cell division that produces the cells of reproduction, which contain one-half of the chromosome number found in the original cell before division

MITOSIS: the type of cell division that occurs in nonsex cells, which conserves chromosome number by equal allocation to each of the newly formed cells

TRANSLOCATION: an aberration in chromosome structure resulting from the attachment of chromosomal material to a nonhomologous chromosome

Causes and Symptoms

Down syndrome is an example of a genetic disorder, that is, a disorder arising from an abnormality in an individual's genetic material. Down syndrome results from an incorrect transfer of genetic material in the formation of cells. It is also termed trisomy 21 because it most commonly results from the presence of an extra copy of the smallest human chromosome, chromosome 21. Actually, it is not the entire extra chromosome 21 that is responsible, but rather a small segment of the long arm of this chromosome. Only two other trisomies occur with any significant frequency: trisomy 13 (Patau's syndrome) and trisomy 18 (Edwards's syndrome). Both of these disorders are accompanied by multiple severe malformations, resulting in death within a few months of birth. Most incidences of Down syndrome are a consequence of a nondisjunction during meiosis. In about 75 percent of these cases, the extra chromosome is present in the egg. About 1 percent of Down syndrome cases occur after the fertilization of normal gametes from a mitosis nondisjunction, producing a mosaic in which some of the embryo's cells are normal and some exhibit trisomy. The degree of mosaicism and its location will determine the physiological consequences of the nondisjunction. Although mosaic individuals range from apparent normality to completely affected, typically the disorder is less severe.

In about 4 percent of all Down syndrome cases, the individual possesses not an entire third copy of chromosome 21 but rather extra chromosome 21 material, which has been incorporated via a translocation into a nonhomologous chromosome. In translocation, pieces of arms are swapped between two nonrelated chromosomes, forming "hybrid" chromosomes. The most common translocation associated with Down syndrome is that between the long arm (Down gene area) of chromosome 21 and an end of chromosome 14. The individual in whom the

Many agencies offer social and emotional support for people with Down syndrome and their families. (National Library of Medicine)

translocation has occurred shows no evidence of the aberration, since the normal complement of genetic material is still present, only at different chromosomal locations. The difficulty arises when this individual forms gametes. A mother who possesses the 21/14 translocation, for example, has one normal 21, one normal 14, and the hybrid chromosomes. She is a genetic carrier for the disorder, because she can pass it on to her offspring even though she is clinically normal. This mother could produce three types of viable gametes: one containing the normal 14 and 21; one containing both translocations, which would result in clinical normality; and one containing the normal 21 and the translocated 14 having the long arm of 21. If each gamete were fertilized by normal sperm, two apparently normal embryos and one partial trisomy 21 Down syndrome embryo would result. Down syndrome that results from the passing on of translocations is termed familial Down syndrome and is an inherited disorder.

The presence of an extra copy of the long arm of chromosome 21 causes defects in many tissues and organs. One major effect of Down syndrome is mental retardation. The intelligence quotients (IQs) of affected individuals are typically in the range of 40-50. The IQ varies with age, being higher in childhood than in adolescence or adult life. The disorder is often accompanied by physical traits such as short stature, stubby fingers and toes, protruding tongue, and an unusual pattern of hand creases. Perhaps the most recognized physical feature is the distinctive slanting of the eyes, caused by a vertical fold (epicanthal fold) of skin near the nasal bridge which pulls and tilts the eyes slightly toward the nostrils. For normal Caucasians, the eye runs parallel to the skin fold below the eyebrow; for Asians, this skin fold covers a major portion of the upper eyelid. In contrast, the epicanthal fold in trisomy 21 does not cover a major part of the upper eyelid.

It should be noted that not all defects associated with Down syndrome are found in every affected individual. About 40 percent of Down syndrome patients have congenital heart defects, while about 10 percent have intestinal blockages. Affected individuals are prone to respiratory infections and contract leukemia at a rate twenty times that of the general population. Although Down syndrome children develop the same types of leukemia in the same proportions as other children, the survival rate of the two groups is markedly different. While the survival rate for non-Down syndrome patients after ten years is about 30 percent, survival beyond five years is negligible in Down syndrome patients. It appears that the extra copy of chromosome 21 not only increases the risk of contracting the cancer but also exerts a decisive influence on the disease's outcome. Reproductively, males are sterile while some females are fertile. Although many Down syndrome infants die in the first year of life, the mean life expectancy is about thirty years. This reduced life expectancy results from defects in the immune system, causing a high susceptibility to infectious disease. Most older Down syndrome individuals develop an Alzheimer's-like condition, and less than 3 percent live beyond fifty years of age.

Treatment and Therapy

Trisomy 21 is one of the most common human chromosomal aberrations, occurring in about 0.5 percent of all conceptions and in one out of every seven hundred to eight hundred live births. About 15 percent of the patients institutionalized for mental deficiency suffer from Down syndrome.

Even before the chromosomal basis for the disorder was determined, the frequency of Down syndrome births was correlated with increased maternal age. For mothers at age twenty, the incidence of Down syndrome is about 0.05 percent, which increases to 0.9 percent by age thirty-five and 3 percent for age forty-five. Studies comparing the chromosomes of the affected offspring with both parents have shown that the nondisjunction event is maternal about 75 percent of the time. This maternal age effect is thought to result from the different manner in which the male and female gametes are produced.

Gamete production in the male is a continual, lifelong process, while it is a one-time event in females. Formation of the female's gametes begins early in embryonic life, somewhere between the eighth and twentieth weeks. During this time, cells in the developing ovary divide rapidly by mitosis, forming cells called primary oocytes. These cells then begin meiosis by pairing up the homologues. The process is interrupted at this point, and the cells are held in a state of suspended animation until needed in reproduction, when they are triggered to complete their division and form eggs. It appears that the frequency of nondisjunction events increases with the length of the storage period. Studies have demonstrated that cells in a state of meiosis are particularly sensitive to environmental influences such as viruses, X rays, and cytotoxic chemicals. It is possible that environmental influences may play a role in nondisjunction events. Up to age thirty-two, males contribute an extra chromosome 21 as often as do females. Beyond this age, there is a rapid increase in nondisjunctional eggs, while the number of nondisjunctional sperm remains constant. Where the maternal age effect is minimal, mosaicism may be an important source of the trisomy. An apparently normal mother who possesses undetected mosaicism can produce trisomy offspring if gametes with an extra chromosome are produced. In some instances, characteristics such as abnormal fingerprint patterns have been observed in the mothers and their Down syndrome offspring.

Techniques such as amniocentesis, chorionic villus sampling, and alpha-fetoprotein screening are available for prenatal diagnosis of Down syndrome in fetuses. Amniocentesis, the most widely used technique for prenatal diagnosis, is generally performed between the fourteenth and sixteenth weeks of pregnancy. In this technique, about one ounce of fluid is removed from the amniotic cavity surrounding the fetus by a needle inserted through the mother's abdomen. Although some testing can be done directly on the fluid (such as the assay for spina bifida), more information is obtained from the cells shed from the fetus that accompany the fluid. The mixture obtained in the amniocentesis is spun in a centrifuge to separate the fluid from the fetal cells. Unfortunately, the chromosome analysis for Down syndrome cannot be conducted directly on the amount of cellular material obtained. Although the majority of the cells collected are nonviable, some will grow in culture. These cells are allowed to grow and multiply in culture for two to four weeks, and then the chromosomes undergo karyotyping, which will detect both trisomy 21 and translocational aberration.

In karyotyping, the chromosomes are spread on a microscope slide, stained, and photographed. Each type of chromosome gives a unique, observable banding pattern when stained which allows it to be identified. The chromosomes are then cut out of the photograph and arranged in homologous pairs, in numerical order. Trisomy 21 is easily observed, since three copies of chromosome 21 are present, while the translocation shows up as an abnormal banding pattern. Termination of the pregnancy in the wake of an unfavorable amniocentesis diagnosis is complicated, because the fetus at this point is usually about eighteen to twenty weeks old, and elective abortions are normally performed between the sixth and twelfth weeks of pregnancy. Earlier sampling of the amniotic fluid is not possible because of the small amount of fluid present.

An alternate testing procedure called chorionic villus sampling became available in the mid-1980's. In this procedure, a chromosomal analysis is conducted on a piece of placental tissue that is obtained either vaginally or through the abdomen during the eighth to eleventh week of pregnancy. The advantages of this procedure are that it can be done much earlier in the pregnancy and that enough tissue can be collected to conduct the chromosome analysis immediately, without the cell culture step. Consequently, diagnosis can be completed during the first trimester of the pregnancy, making therapeutic abortion an option for the parents. Chorionic villus sampling does have some negative aspects. One disadvantage is the slightly higher incidence of test-induced miscarriage as compared to amniocentesis—around 1 percent (versus less than 0.5 percent). Also, because tissue of both the mother and the fetus are obtained in the sampling process, they must be carefully separated, complicating the analysis. Occasionally, chromosomal abnormalities are observed in the tested tissue that are not present in the fetus itself.

Prenatal maternal alpha-fetoprotein testing has also been used to diagnose Down syndrome. Abnormal levels of a substance called maternal alpha-fetoprotein are often associated with chromosomal disorders. Several research studies have described a high correlation between low levels of maternal alpha-fetoprotein and the occurrence of trisomy 21 in the fetus. By correlating alpha-fetoprotein levels, the age of the mother, and specific female hormone levels, between 60 percent and 80 percent of fetuses with Down syndrome can be detected. Although techniques allow Down syndrome to be detected readily in a fetus, there is no effective intrauterine therapy available to correct the abnormality.

The care of a Down syndrome child presents many challenges for the family unit. Until the 1970's, most of these children spent their lives in institutions. With the increased support services available, however, it is now common for such children to remain in the family environment. Although many Down syndrome children have happy dispositions, a significant number have behavioral problems that can consume the energies of the parents, to the detriment of the other children. Rearing a Down syndrome child often places a large financial burden on the family: Such children are, for example, susceptible to illness; they also have special educational needs. Since Down syndrome children are often conceived late in the parents' reproductive period, the parents may not be able to continue to care for these children throughout their offspring's adult years. This is problematic because many Down syndrome individuals do not possess sufficient mental skills to earn a living or to manage their affairs without supervision.

All women in their mid-thirties have an increased risk of producing a Down syndrome infant. Since the resultant trisomy 21 is not of a hereditary nature, the abnormality can be detected only by the prenatal screening, which is recommended for all pregnancies of women older than age thirty-four.

For parents who have produced a Down syndrome child, genetic counseling can be beneficial in determining their risk factor for future pregnancies. The genetic counselor determines the specific chromosomal aberration that occurred utilizing chromosome studies of the parents and affected child, along with additional information provided by the family history. If the cause was nondisjunction and the mother is young, the recurrence risk is much less than 1 percent; for mothers over the age of thirty-four, it is about 5 percent. If the cause was translocational, the Down syndrome is hereditary and risk is much greater—statistically, a one-in-three chance. In addition, there is a one-in-three chance that clinically normal offspring will be carriers of the syndrome, producing it in the next generation. For couples who come from families having a history of spontaneous abortions, which often result from lethal chromosomal aberrations and/or incidence of Down syndrome, it is suggested that they undergo chromosomal screening to detect the presence of a Down syndrome translocation.

Perspective and Prospects

English physician John L. H. Down is credited with the first clinical description of Down syndrome, in 1886. Since the distinctive epicanthic fold gave Down children an appearance that John Down associated with Asians, he termed the condition "mongolism"—an unfortunate term showing a certain racism on Down's part, since it implies that those affected with the condition are throwbacks to a more "primitive" racial group. Today, the inappropriate term has been replaced with the term "Down syndrome."

A French physician, Jérôme Lejeune, suspected that Down syndrome had a genetic basis and began to study the condition in 1953. A comparison of the fingerprints and palm prints of affected individuals with those of unaffected individuals showed a high frequency of abnormalities in the prints of those with Down syndrome. These prints are developed very early in development and serve as a record of events that take place early in embryogenesis. The extent of the changes in print patterns led Lejeune to the conclusion that the condition was not a result of the action of one or two genes but rather of many genes or even an entire chromosome. Upon microscopic examination, he observed that Down syndrome children possess forty-seven chromosomes instead of the forty-six chromosomes found in normal children. In 1959, Lejeune published his findings, showing that Down syndrome is caused by the presence of an extra chromosome which was later identified as an extra copy of chromosome 21. This first observation of a human chromosomal abnormality marked a turning point in the study of human genetics. It demonstrated that genetic defects not only were caused by mutations of single genes but also could be associated with changes in chromosome number. Although the presence of an extra chromosome allows varying degrees of development to occur, most of these abnormalities result in fetal death, with only a few resulting in live birth. Down syndrome is unusual in that the affected individual often survives into adulthood.

Bibliography

Blatt, Robin J. R. *Prenatal Tests*. New York: Vintage Books, 1988. Discusses tests available for prenatal screening, their benefits, the risk factors of the tests, and how to decide whether to have prenatal testing.

Cunningham, Cliff. *Understanding Down Syndrome: An Introduction for Parents*. Cambridge, Mass.: Brookline Books, 1996. Helps parents and beginning practitioners understand the characteristics of the condition, covers treatment methods, and gives advice on caring for young children, adolescents, and older people. Stresses the importance of professional guidance and how to obtain it.

Hassold, Terry J., and David Patterson, eds. *Down Syndrome: A Promising Future, Together*. New York: Wiley-Liss, 1999. A comprehensive, up-to-date look at life with Down syndrome. Addresses medical, developmental, educational, and vocational issues. Designed for parents and professionals.

Pueschel, Siegfried. *A Parent's Guide to Down Syndrome*. Baltimore: Paul H. Brookes, 1990. An informative guide highlighting the important developmental stages in the life of a child with Down syndrome.

Rondal, Jean A., et al., eds. *Down's Syndrome: Psychological, Psychobiological, and Socioeducational Perspectives*. San Diego: Singular, 1996. An academic text on issues surrounding Down syndrome. Includes references and an index.

Selikowitz, Mark. *Down Syndrome: The Facts*. New York: Oxford University Press, 1997. A concise but thorough guide to Down syndrome. Offers advice on how to raise a child with the disease, cope with prejudice, and maintain the child's health.

Shaw, Michael, ed. *Everything You Need to Know About Diseases*. Springhouse, Pa.: Springhouse Press, 1996. This well-illustrated consumer reference, compiled by more than one hundred doctors and medical experts, describes five hundred illnesses and conditions, their causes, symptoms, diagnosis, treatment, and prevention. A valuable reference book for everyone interested in health and disease. Of particular interest is chapter 21, "Genetic Disorders."

Tingey, Carol, ed. *Down Syndrome: A Resource Handbook*. Boston: Little, Brown, 1988. A practical resource for rearing a Down syndrome child, including guidelines on daily life, developmental expectations, and health and medical needs.

Arlene R. Courtney

See also:

Child and Adolescent Psychiatry; Learning Disabilities; Mental Retardation.

DYSLEXIA

Type of psychology: Language
Fields of study: Childhood and adolescent disorders

Dyslexia is often defined as severe reading disability in children of otherwise average or above-average intelligence; it is thought to be caused by neuropsychological problems. Dyslexia frustrates afflicted children, damages their self-image, produces grave maladjustment in many cases, and decreases their adult contributions to society.

Principal terms

AUDITORY DYSLEXIA: the inability to perceive individual sounds associated with written language (for example, certain vowels or consonants)

BRAIN DYSFUNCTION: disordered or impaired brain function resulting from damage too minor to be observed by existing biomedical technology

DYSGRAPHIA: the inability to write legibly, resulting from badly impaired hand-eye coordination

IMPRINTING: a method of training a dyslexic person to overcome reading problems by use of often-repeated, exaggerated language drills

KINESTHETIC: related to the sensation of body position, presence, or movement, resulting mostly from the stimulation of sensory nerves in muscles, tendons, and joints

PHONOLOGY: the science of speech sounds, especially phonetics and phonemics

VISUAL DYSLEXIA: the lack of ability to translate observed written or printed language into meaningful terms

Causes and Symptoms

The ability to read quickly and well is essential for success in modern industrialized societies. Several researchers, including Robert E. Valett, have pointed out that an individual must acquire considerable basic cognitive and perceptual-linguistic skills in order to learn to read. First, it is necessary to learn to focus one's attention, to concentrate, to follow directions, and to understand the language spoken in daily life. Next, it is essential to develop the following: auditory and visual memory with sequencing ability; word-decoding skills; a facility for structural-contextual language analysis; the ability to interpret the written language; a useful vocabulary that expands as needed; and speed in scanning and interpreting written language. Valett has noted that these skills are taught in all good developmental reading programs.

Yet 20 to 25 percent of the population of the United States and many other industrialized societies, people who otherwise possess at least average intelligence, cannot develop good reading skills. Many such people are viewed as suffering from a neurological disorder called dyslexia, a term that was first introduced by a German ophthalmologist, Rudolph Berlin, more than one hundred years ago.

Berlin meant it to designate all those individuals who possessed an average or above-average performance intelligence quotient (IQ) but who could not read adequately because of an inability to process language symbols.

Others reported children who could see perfectly well but who acted as if they were blind to the written language. For example, they could see a bird flying but were unable to identify the word "bird" written in a sentence. In essence, though the problem has been redefined many times over the ensuing years, the modern definition of dyslexia is still fairly close to Berlin's definition.

Two basic explanations have evolved for dyslexia. Many physicians propose that it is caused by either brain damage or brain dysfunction. Evolution of the problem is attributed to accident, to disease, or to faults in body chemistry. Diagnosis is made by the use of electroencephalograms (EEGs), computed tomography (CT) scans, and other related technology. After such evaluation, medication is often used to diminish hyperactivity and nervousness, and a group of physical training procedures called patterning are used as tools to counter the neurological defects.

In contrast, many special educators and other related researchers believe that the problem is one of dormant, immature, or undeveloped learning centers in the brain. The proponents of this concept encourage the correction of dyslexic problems by emphasized teaching of specific reading skills to appropriate individuals. While such experts also agree that use of appropriate medication can be of value, they lend most of their efforts to curing the problem by a process called imprinting, which essentially trains the dyslexic patient through use of often-repeated, exaggerated language drills.

Another interesting point of view is the idea that dyslexia may at least partly be the fault of the written languages of the Western world. Rudolph F. Wagner has pointed out that children in Japan exhibit an incidence of dyslexia that is less than 1 percent. One explanation for this, say Wagner and others, is that the languages of the Western world require reading from left to right. This characteristic is absent in Japanese—possibly, they suggest, making it easier to learn.

A number of experts, among them Dale R. Jordan, recognize three types of dyslexia. The most common type—and the one most often identified as dyslexia—is visual dyslexia: the lack of ability to translate observed written or printed language into meaningful terms. The major difficulty here is that the afflicted people see certain letters backward or upside down. The result is that, to them, a written sentence is a jumble of letters whose accurate translation may require five times as much time as would be needed by an unafflicted person.

The other two problems viewed as dyslexia are auditory dyslexia and dysgraphia. Auditory dyslexia is the inability to perceive individual sounds of spoken language. Despite having normal hearing, auditory dyslexics are deaf to the differences between certain vowel or consonant sounds; what they cannot hear, they cannot write. Dysgraphia is the inability to write legibly. The basis for this problem is a lack of the hand-eye coordination required to write legibly.

Usually, a child who suffers from visual dyslexia also exhibits elements of auditory dyslexia. This complicates the issue of teaching such a student, because only one type of dyslexic symptom can be treated at a time. Also, dyslexia appears to be a sex-linked disorder; three to four times as many boys have it as do girls. In all cases, early diagnosis and treatment of dyslexia are essential to its eventual correction. For example, if treatment begins before the third grade, there is an 80 percent probability that dyslexia can be corrected. When dyslexia remains undiscovered until the fifth grade, this probability is halved. If treatment does not begin until the seventh grade, the probability of successful treatment is only 3 to 5 percent.

Preliminary identification of the dyslexic child often can be made from symptoms that include poor written schoolwork, easy distractibility, clumsiness, poor coordination and spatial orientation, confused writing and/or spelling, and poor left-right orientation. Because nondyslexic children can also show many of these symptoms, the second step of such identification is the use of written tests designed to pick out dyslexic children. These include the Peabody Individual Achievement Test, the Halstead-Reitan Neuropsychological Test Battery, and the SOYBAR Criterion Tests. Many more personalized tests are also available.

Treatment and Therapy

Once conclusive identification of a dyslexic child has been made, it becomes possible to begin a corrective treatment program. Most such programs are carried out by special-education teachers in school resource rooms, in special classes limited to children with reading disabilities, and in schools that specialize in treating the disorder.

One often-cited method is that of Grace Fernald, which utilizes kinesthetic imprinting, based on a combination of "language experience" and tactile stimulation. In this popular method, a given child learns to read as follows. First, the child relates a spontaneous story to the teacher, who transcribes it. Next, each word unknown to the child is written down by the teacher, and the child traces its letters over and over until he or she can write that word without using the model. Each word learned becomes part of the child's word file. A large number of stories are handled this way. Many variants of the method are in use. Though it is quite slow, many anecdotal reports praise its results. (Despite this, Donald K. Routh pointed out in 1987 that the method had never been subjected to a rigorous, controlled study of its efficacy.)

A second common method utilized by special educators is the Orton-Gillingham-Stillman method, developed in a collaboration by teachers Anna Gillingham and Essie Stillman and the pediatric neurologist Samuel T. Orton. The method evolved from Orton's conceptualization of language as developing from a sequence of processes in the nervous system that end in unilateral control by the left cerebral hemisphere. He proposed that dyslexia arises from conflicts, which need to be corrected, between this hemisphere and the right cerebral hemisphere, usually involved in the handling of nonverbal, pictorial, and spatial stimuli.

Consequently, the method used is multisensory and kinesthetic, like Fernald's; however, it begins with the teaching of individual letters and phonemes, and progresses to dealing with syllables, words, and sentences. Children taught by this method are drilled systematically to imprint a mastery of phonics and the sounding out of unknown written words. They are encouraged to learn how the elements of written language look, how they sound, how it feels to pronounce them, and how it feels to write them down. Donald Routh has pointed out that the Orton-Gillingham-Stillman method is equally laborious as that of Fernald. It is widely used and appreciated, however, and believed to work well.

Another method that merits brief discussion is the use of therapeutic drugs in the treatment of dyslexia. Most physicians and educators propose the use of these drugs as a useful adjunct to the training of dyslexic children who are easily distracted and restless or who have low morale because of embarrassment resulting from peer pressure. The drugs used most often are the amphetamine Dexedrine and methylphenidate (Ritalin).

These stimulants, taken in appropriate doses, lengthen the time period during which some dyslexic children function well in the classroom and also produce feelings of self-confidence. Side effects of overdose, however, include lost appetite, nausea, nervousness, and sleeplessness. Furthermore, there is the potential problem of drug abuse. Despite this, numerous sources (including both Valett and Jordan) indicate that stimulant benefits far outweigh any possible risks when the drugs are utilized carefully and under close medical supervision. Other, less dependable therapies sometimes attempted include special diets and the use of vitamins and minerals.

One other important aspect of the treatment of dyslexia is good parental emotional support, which helps children cope with their problems and with peer pressure. Useful aspects of this support include a positive attitude toward the afflicted child; appropriate home help for the child that complements efforts undertaken at school; encouragement and praise for achievements, without recrimination when repeated mistakes are made; and good interaction with special-education teachers assigned to a child.

Perspective and Prospects

The identification of dyslexia more than one hundred years ago, which resulted from the endeavors of the German physician Rudolph Berlin and of W. A. Morgan, in England, launched efforts to find a cure for this unfortunate disorder. In 1917, the Scottish eye surgeon James Hinshelwood published a book on dyslexia, which he viewed as being a hereditary problem, and the phenomenon became better known to physicians. Attempts at educating dyslexics, as recommended by Hinshelwood and other physicians, were highly individualized until the endeavors of Orton and coworkers and of Fernald led to more standardized and soon widely used methods.

Furthermore, with the development of a more complete understanding of the brain and its many functions, better counseling facilities, and the conceptualization and actualization of both parent-child and parent-counselor interactions, the prognosis for successful dyslexic training has improved significantly. Also, a number of extensive studies of dyslexic children have been carried out and have identified dyslexia as a complex syndrome composed of numerous associated behavioral dysfunctions related to visual-motor brain immaturity. These include poor memory for details, easy distractibility, poor motor skills, letter and word reversal, and the inability to distinguish between important elements of the spoken language.

A particularly extensive and useful study was carried out by Edith Klasen and described in her book *The Syndrome of Specific Dyslexia: With Special Considera-tion of Its Physiological, Psychological, Testpsychological, and Social Correlates* (1972). The Klasen study identified the role of psychoanalytical interventions in the treatment of some dyslexic subjects, and it pointed out that environmental and socioeconomic factors contribute relatively little to occurrence of dyslexia but affect the outcomes of its treatment.

It is the endeavors of special education that have made the greatest inroads into treatment of dyslexia. Further advances in the area will undoubtedly be made, as the science of the mind grows and diversifies and as the contributions of the psychologist, physician, physiologist, and special educator mesh together more effectively.

Bibliography
Jordan, Dale R. *Overcoming Dyslexia in Children, Adolescents, and Adults.* 2d ed. Austin, Tex.: Pro-ed, 1996. Reviews the history and current knowledge of dyslexia and learning disabilities. Includes sources of instructional materials, organizations, and diagnostic checklists.
Klasen, Edith. *The Syndrome of Specific Dyslexia: With Special Consideration of Its Physiological, Psychological, Testpsychological, and Social Correlates.* Baltimore: University Park Press, 1972. Klasen's classic study of five hundred dyslexic students—containing 153 references—provides much useful informa-tion. Covers many aspects of dyslexia etiology, associated speech disorders, related organic-sensory and neuropsychological symptoms, psychopathology, therapy, psychological test results, socioeconomic and family backgrounds, intersibling relationships, and parental attitudes.
Klein, Raymond M., and Patricia A. McMullen, eds. *Converging Methods for Understanding Reading and Dyslexia.* Cambridge, Mass.: MIT Press, 1999. An interdisciplinary look at the acquisition, loss, and remediation of normal read-ing processes. Includes bibliographical references and an index.
Lundberg, Ingvar, Finn Egil Tønnessen, and Ingolv Austad, eds. *Dyslexia: Ad-vances in Theory and Practice.* Boston: Kluwer Academic, 1999. A balanced view of recent research on reading disability. Includes bibliographical refer-ences and indexes.
Routh, Donald K. "Disorders of Learning." In *The Practical Assessment and Management of Children with Disorders of Development and Learning*, edited by Mark L. Wolraich. Chicago: Year Book Medical Publishers, 1987. Succinctly summarizes many salient facts about learning disorders, including their etiol-ogy, their assessment, their management, and their outcome. The interested reader will also find many useful references to more detailed works.
Snowling, Margaret J. *Dyslexia: A Cognitive Developmental Perspective.* New York: Basil Blackwell, 1987. Covers many aspects of dyslexia, including its identification, associated cognitive defects, the basis for development of lan-

guage skills, and the importance of phonology. Also contains many references.

Turner, Martin. *Psychological Assessment of Dyslexia*. San Diego: Singular Publishing Group, 1997. Focuses on the diagnosis of dyslexia with a combination of psychometric techniques and experimental cognitive psychology. Includes bibliographical references and an index.

Wagner, Rudolf F. *Dyslexia and Your Child: A Guide for Teachers and Parents*. Rev. ed. New York: Harper & Row, 1979. A clear, useful, and simply written book "for teachers and parents concerned with children . . . referred to as dyslexic." Includes careful exposition of dyslexic symptoms, commentary on the problem, ways to treat dyslexia and associated problems, other useful topics, an appendix of recommended reading, and a glossary.

Sanford S. Singer

See also:

Attention-Deficit Disorder; Brain Disorders; Child and Adolescent Psychiatry; Learning Disabilities.

EATING DISORDERS

Type of psychology: Psychopathology
Fields of study: Childhood and adolescent disorders

A set of emotional disorders centering on body image that lead to misuse of food in a variety of ways—through overeating, overeating and purging, or undereating—that severely threaten the physical and mental well-being of the individual.

Principal terms

AMENORRHEA: the cessation of menstruation
ANOREXIA NERVOSA: a disorder characterized by the phobic avoidance of eating, the relentless pursuit of thinness, and fear of gaining weight
ARRHYTHMIA: irregularity or loss of rhythm, especially of the heartbeat
BULIMIA: a disorder characterized by binge eating followed by self-induced vomiting
ELECTROLYTES: ionized salts in blood, tissue fluid, and cells, including salts of potassium, sodium, and chloride

Causes and Symptoms

The presence of an eating disorder in a patient is defined by an abnormal mental and physical relationship between body image and eating. While obesity is considered an eating disorder, the most prominent conditions are anorexia nervosa and bulimia nervosa. Anorexia nervosa (the word "anorexia" comes from the Greek for "loss of appetite") is an illness characterized by the relentless pursuit of thinness and fear of gaining weight. Bulimia nervosa (the word "bulimia" comes from the Greek for "ox appetite") refers to binge eating followed by self-induced vomiting. These conditions are related in intimate, yet ill-defined ways.

Anorexia nervosa affects more women than men by the overwhelming ratio of nineteen to one. It most often begins in adolescence and is more common among the upper and middle classes of the Western world. According to most studies, its incidence increased severalfold from the 1970's to the 1990's. Prevalence figures vary from 0.5 to 0.8 cases per one hundred adolescent girls. A familiar pattern of anorexia nervosa is often present, and studies indicate that 16 percent of the mothers and 23 percent of the fathers of anorectic patients had a history of significantly low adolescent weight or weight phobia.

The criteria for anorexia nervosa include intense fear of becoming obese, which does not diminish with the progression of weight loss; disturbance of body image, or feeling "fat" even when emaciated; refusal to maintain body weight over a minimal weight for age and height; the loss of 25 percent of original body weight or being 25 percent below expected weight based on standard growth charts; and no known physical illness that would account for the weight loss. Anorexia nervosa is also classified into primary and secondary forms. The primary condition is the distinct constellation of behaviors described above. In secondary anorexia nervosa, the weight loss results from another emotional or organic disorder.

The most prominent symptom of anorexia nervosa is a phobic avoidance of eating that goes beyond any reasonable level of dieting in the presence of striking thinness. Attending this symptom is the characteristic distorted body image and faulty perceptions of hunger and satiety, as well as a pervasive sense of inadequacy.

The distortion of body image renders patients unable to evaluate their body weight accurately, so that they react to weight loss by intensifying their desire for thinness. Patients characteristically describe themselves as "fat" and "gross" even when totally emaciated. The degree of disturbance in body image is a useful prognostic index. Faulty perception of inner, visceral sensations, such as hunger and satiety, extends also to emotional states. The problem of nonrecognition of feelings is usually intensified with starvation.

Other cognitive distortions are also common in anorectic patients. Dichotomous reasoning—the assessment of self or others—is either idealized or degraded. Personalization of situations and a tendency to overgeneralize are common. Anorectics display an extraordinary amount of energy, directed to exercise and schoolwork in the face of starvation, but may curtail or avoid social relationships. Crying spells and complaints of depression are common findings and may persist in some anorectic patients even after weight is gained.

Sleep disturbances have also been reported in anorectics. Obsessive and/or compulsive behaviors, usually developing after the onset of the eating symptoms, abound with anorexia. Obsession with cleanliness and house cleaning, frequent handwashing, compulsive studying habits, and ritualistic behaviors are common.

As expected, the most striking compulsions involve food and eating. Anorectics' intense involvement with food belies their apparent lack of interest in it. The term "anorexia" is, in fact, a misnomer because lack of appetite is rare until late in the illness. Anorectics often carry large quantities of sweets in their purses and hide candies or cookies in various places. They frequently collect recipes and engage in elaborate meal preparation for others. Anorectics' behavior also includes refusal to eat with their families and in public places. When unable to reduce food intake openly, they may resort to such subterfuge as hiding food or disposing of it in toilets. If the restriction of food intake does not suffice for losing weight, the patient may resort to vomiting, usually at night and in secret. Self-induced vomiting then becomes associated with bulimia. Some patients also abuse laxatives and diuretics.

Commonly reported physical symptoms include constipation, abdominal pain, and cold intolerance. With severe weight loss, feelings of weakness and lethargy replace the drive to exercise. Amenorrhea (cessation of menstruation) occurs in virtually all cases, although it is not essential for a diagnosis of anorexia. Weight loss generally precedes the loss of the menstrual cycle. Other physical symptoms reveal the effects of starvation. Potassium depletion is the most frequent serious problem occurring with both anorexia and bulimia. Gastrointestinal disturbances are common, and death may occur from either infection or electrolyte imbalance.

Bulimia usually occurs between the ages of twelve and forty, with greatest frequency between the ages of fifteen and thirty. Unlike anorectics, bulimics usually are of normal weight, although some have a history of anorexia or obesity.

Like anorectics, however, they are not satisfied by normal food intake. The characteristic symptom of bulimia is episodic, uncontrollable binge eating followed by vomiting or purging. The binge eating, usually preceded by a period of dieting lasting a few months or more, occurs when patients are alone at home and lasts about one hour. In the early stages of the illness, patients may need to stimulate their throat with a finger or spoon to induce vomiting, but later they can vomit at will. At times, abrasions and bruises on the back of the hand are produced during vomiting. The binge-purge cycle is usually followed by sadness, self-deprecation, and regret. Bulimic patients have troubled interpersonal relationships, poor self-concept, a high level of anxiety and depression, and poor impulse control. Alcohol and drug abuse are not uncommon with bulimia, in contrast to their infrequency with anorexia.

From the medical perspective, bulimia is nearly as damaging to its practitioners as anorexia. Dental problems, including discoloration and erosion of tooth enamel and irritation of gums by highly acidic gastric juice, are frequent. Electrolyte imbalance, such as metabolic alkalosis or hypokalemia (low potassium levels) caused by the self-induced vomiting, is a constant threat. Parotid gland enlargement, esophageal lacerations, and acute gastric dilatation may occur. Cardiac irregularities may also result. The chronic use of emetics such as ipecac to induce vomiting after eating may result in cardiomyopathy (disease of the middle layer of the walls of the heart, the myocardium), occasionally with a fatal outcome. While their menstrual periods are irregular, these patients are seldom amenorrheic.

Another eating disorder, obesity, is the most prevalent nutritional disorder of the Western world. Using the most commonly accepted definition of obesity—a body weight greater than 20 percent above an individual's normal or desirable weight— approximately 35 percent of adults in the United States were considered obese at the end of the 1990's. This figure represents twice the proportion of the population that was obese in 1900. More sedentary lifestyles strongly contributed to this increase. Although the problem affects both sexes, obesity is found in a larger portion of women than men. In the forty- to forty-nine-year-old age group, 40 percent of women, while only 30 percent of men, were found to meet the criterion for obesity. Prevalence of obesity increases with both age and lower socioeconomic status.

While results of both animal and human studies suggest that obesity is genetically influenced to some degree, most human obesity is reflective of numerous influences and conditions. Evidence indicates that the relationship between caloric intake and adipose tissue is not as straightforward as had been assumed. In the light of this evidence, the failure to lose unwanted pounds and the failure to maintain hard-won weight loss experienced by many dieters seem much more understandable. Frequently, obese individuals are viewed pejoratively by others and by themselves. They are seen as having insufficient willpower and self-discipline. It is incorrectly assumed that it is no more difficult for most obese individuals to lose fat by decreasing caloric intake than it is for individuals in a normal weight range and that it is just as easy for the obese to maintain normal weight as it is for those who have never been obese.

Treatment and Therapy

The management of anorectic patients, in either hospital or outpatient settings, may include individual psychotherapy, family therapy, behavior modification, and pharmacotherapy. Many anorectic patients are quite physically ill when they first consult a physician, and medical evaluation and management in a hospital may be necessary at this stage. A gastroenterologist or other medical specialist familiar with this condition may be required to evaluate electrolyte disturbance, emaciation, hypothermia, skin problems, hair loss, sensitivity to cold, fatigue, and cardiac arrhythmias. Starvation may cause cognitive and psychological disturbances that limit the patient's cooperation with treatment.

Indications for hospitalization are weight loss exceeding 30 percent of ideal body weight or the presence of serious medical complications. Most clinicians continue the hospitalization until 80 percent to 85 percent of the ideal body weight is reached. The hospitalization makes possible hyperalimentation (intravenous infusion of nutrients) when medically necessary. Furthermore, individual and family psychiatric evaluations can be performed and a therapeutic alliance established more rapidly with the patient hospitalized.

Most programs utilize behavior modification during the course of hospitalization, making increased privileges such as physical and social activities and visiting contingent on weight gain. A medically safe rate of weight gain is approximately one-quarter of a pound a day. Patients are weighed daily, after the bladder is emptied, and daily fluid intake and output are recorded. Patients with bulimic characteristics may be required to stay in the room two hours after each meal without access to the bathroom to prevent vomiting. Some behavior modification programs emphasize formal contracting, negative contingencies, the practice of avoidance behavior, relaxation techniques, role-playing, and systematic desensitization.

The goal of dynamic psychotherapy is to achieve patient autonomy and independence. The female anorectic patient often uses her body as a battleground for the separation or individuation struggle with her mother. The cognitive therapeutic approach begins with helping the patient to articulate beliefs, change her view of herself as the center of the universe, and render her expectations of the consequences of food intake less catastrophic. The therapist acknowledges the patient's beliefs as genuine, particularly the belief that her self-worth is dependent on achieving and maintaining a low weight. Through a gradual modification of self-assessment, the deficits in the patient's self-esteem are remedied. The therapist also challenges the cultural values surrounding body shape and addresses behavioral and family issues such as setting weight goals and living conditions.

The behavioral management of bulimia includes an examination of the patient's thinking and behavior toward eating and life challenges in general. The patient is made fully aware of the extent of her binging by being asked to keep a daily record of her eating and vomiting practices. A contract is then established with the patient to help her restrict her eating to three or four planned meals per day. The second stage of treatment emphasizes self-control in eating as well as in other areas of the patient's life. In the final stage of treatment, the patient is assisted in maintaining her new, more constructive eating behaviors.

Almost all clinicians work intensively with the family of anorectic patients, particularly in the initial stage of treatment. Family treatment begins with the current family structure and later addresses the early family functioning that can influence family dynamics dramatically. Multigenerational sources of conflict are also examined.

Family therapy with bulimics explores the sources of family conflicts and helps the family to resolve them. Particular attention is directed toward gender roles in the family, as well as the anxiety of the parents in allowing their children autonomy and self-sufficiency. The roots of impulsive and depressive behaviors and the role of parental satisfaction with the patients' lives and circumstances are often explored and addressed.

In the treatment of obesity, the use of a reduced-calorie diet regimen alone does not appear to be an effective treatment approach for many patients, and it is believed that clinicians may do more harm than good by prescribing it. In addition to the high number of therapeutic failures and possible exacerbation of the problem, negative emotional responses are common side effects. Depression, anxiety, irritability, and preoccupation with food appear to be associated with dieting. Such responses have been found to occur in as many as half of the general obese population while on weight-loss diets and are seen with even greater frequency in the severely obese. Some researchers conclude that some cases are better off with no treatment. Their reasoning is based not only on the ineffectiveness of past treatments and the evidence of biological bases for differences in body size but also on the fact that mild to moderate obesity does not appear to put women (or men) at significant health risk. Moreover, an increase in the incidence of serious eating disorders in women has accompanied the increasingly stringent cultural standards of thinness for women. Given the present level of knowledge, it may be that some individuals would benefit most by adjusting to a weight that is higher than the culturally determined ideal.

When an individual of twenty-five to thirty-four years of age is more than 100 percent above normal weight level, however, there is a twelvefold increase in mortality, and the need for treatment is clear. Although much of the increased risk is related to the effects of extreme overweight on other diseases (such as diabetes, hypertension, and arthritis), these risks can decrease with weight loss. Conservative treatments have had very poor success rates with this group, both in achieving weight reduction and in maintaining any reductions accomplished. Inpatient starvation therapy has had some success in reducing weight in the severely obese but is a disruptive, expensive, and risky procedure requiring very careful medical monitoring to avoid fatality. Furthermore, for those patients who successfully reduce their weight by this method, only about half will maintain the reduction.

Severe obesity seems to be treated most effectively by surgical measures, which include wiring the jaws to make oral intake nearly impossible, reducing the size of the stomach by suturing methods, or short-circuiting a portion of the intestine so as to reduce the area available for uptake of nutrients. None of these methods, however, are without risk.

Perspective and Prospects

The apparent increase in the incidence of anorexia and bulimia in the 1980's and the interest that they have generated both within the scientific community and among the general public have created the impression that these are new diseases. Although scientific writings on the two disorders were uncommon before the early 1960's, eating disorders are by no means recent developments.

Many early accounts of what might have been the condition of anorexia nervosa exist. The clearest and most-detailed account is probably the treatise by Richard Morton, a London physician, in his *Phthisiologica: Or, A Treatise of Consumptions* (1964), first published in Latin. In the book, he described several conditions of consumption, devoting one section to the condition of "nervous consumption" in which the emaciation occurred without any remarkable fever, cough, or shortness of breath. He believed the illness to be the result of violent "passions of the mind," the intemperate drinking of alcohol, and an "unwholesome air." He then described two cases, an eighteen-year-old woman who subsequently died following a "fainting fit" and a sixteen-year-old boy who made a partial recovery.

The term "anorexia nervosa" was first used by Sir William Gull (1816-1890), a physician at Guy's Hospital in London, in a paper published in 1874 in which he described the case histories of four women, including one for whom the illness was fatal. He had first mentioned the illness, briefly calling it "apepsia hysterica," in a lengthy address on diagnosis in medicine that he delivered in Oxford, England, in 1868. By 1874, however, he believed that the term "anorexia" would be more correct, and he preferred the more general term "nervosa," since the disease occurs in males as well as females. As part of the clinical picture of the illness, he emphasized the presence of amenorrhea, constipation, bradycardia, loss of appetite, emaciation, and in some cases low body temperature, edema in the legs, and cyanotic peripheries. He commented particularly on the remarkable restlessness and "mental perversity" of the patients and was convinced that the loss of appetite was central in origin. He found the illness to occur mainly in young females between the ages of sixteen and twenty-three.

Ernest Charles Laseque (1816-1883), a professor of clinical medicine in Paris, published an article in 1873 in which he reported on eight patients. He found the illness to occur mostly in young women between the ages of fifteen and twenty, with the onset precipitated by some emotional upset. He also described the occurrence of diminished food intake, constipation, increased activity, amenorrhea, and the patient's contentment with her condition despite the entreaties and threats of family members.

Despite these promising beginnings, the concept of anorexia nervosa was not clearly established until modern times. The main reason for the conceptual confusion was the overgeneralized interpretation of the nature of the patient's refusal to eat. A second source of confusion was the erroneous view that severe emaciation was a frequent, if not primary, feature of hypopituitarism, a condition first described in 1914. That anorexia nervosa was not related to hypopituitarism was finally clarified by researchers in 1949, but the overgeneralized interpretation of the nature of the food refusal persisted into the early 1960's.

If anorexia is taken to mean a loss of the desire to eat, then there is no doubt that the term "anorexia nervosa" is a misnomer. Anorectic patients refuse to eat not because they have no appetite, but because they are afraid to eat; the food refusal or aversion to eating is the result of an implacable and distorted attitude toward weight, shape, and fatness. The idea that this characteristic attitude is the primary feature of the disorder was not clearly formulated until the early 1960's. Once the concept took hold, the illness of anorexia nervosa became distinguishable from other illnesses that led to similar malnutrition. Thus, for example, a person with hysteria may refuse to eat because of a genuine loss of appetite but does demonstrate the characteristic pursuit of thinness. In the 1980's, there was a revival of the idea that the eating disorders are merely variants of an affective illness.

After occurrences of vomiting and binge eating in a context of anorexia nervosa were described, other investigators proposed two subgroups of anorectic patients: the restrictors and the vomiters. This idea was taken further in 1980 by researchers who divided anorexia nervosa into the restrictor and the bulimic subgroups. The occurrence of binge eating in the context of obesity was described as early as 1959, and in 1970, one investigator described the condition as the "stuffing syndrome." Meanwhile, in 1977, several researchers in Japan proposed that *kibarashigui* (binge eating with an orgiastic quality) be delineated as a separate syndrome from anorexia nervosa. The confusion produced by using a symptom (bulimia) to describe a syndrome (also bulimia) is considerable, and in the English-speaking world the terms "bulimarexia," "dietary chaos syndrome," and "abnormal normal weight control syndrome" have been proposed for the binge-eating syndrome in patients with a normal or near-normal weight.

In 1980, the American Psychiatric Association (APA) distinguished bulimia as a syndrome from anorexia nervosa, and in 1987, the APA replaced the term with "bulimia nervosa." Doubts still persisted, however, regarding the identification of the eating disorders. On the one hand, the boundary between the disorders and "normal" dieting behavior seems blurred. On the other hand, the eating disorders are sometimes considered to be variants of other psychiatric illnesses, previously schizophrenia, obsessive-compulsive disorder, and in the 1980's, the mood disorders. A discussion of the eating disorders is necessary if researchers are to agree on definitions so that the disorders are distinguishable from a major depression or from each other.

Bibliography

Abraham, Suzanne A., and Derek Llewellyn-Jones. *Eating Disorders*. 4th ed. New York: Oxford University Press, 1997. Considers why eating disorders occur and then looks at each in turn, describing the behaviors, diagnosis, and treatments available.

Brownell, Kelly D., and Christopher G. Fairburn, eds. *Eating Disorders and Obesity: A Comprehensive Handbook*. New York: Guilford Press, 1995. This text addresses all eating disorders, particularly obesity. Includes references and an index.

Bruch, Hilde. *Eating Disorders: Obesity, Anorexia Nervosa, and the Person Within*.

New York: Basic Books, 1973. Intended for the general audience, this classic work provides useful information on eating disorders, their detection, and treatment alternatives. Contains a bibliography.

Claude-Pierre, Peggy. *The Secret Language of Eating Disorders: The Revolutionary New Approach to Understanding and Curing Anorexia and Bulimia.* New York: Times Books, 1997. Examines eating disorders and self-esteem in girls and women. Includes bibliographical references and an index.

Field, Howard L., and Barbara B. Domangue, eds. *Eating Disorders Throughout the Life Span.* New York: Praeger, 1987. This collection of essays, intended for the layperson as well as the professional, offers insight into eating disorders of infancy and childhood, adolescent and adult eating disorders, and eating disturbances in the elderly. Includes a bibliography.

Garner, David M., and Paul E. Garfinkel, eds. *Handbook of Treatment for Eating Disorders.* 2d ed. New York: Guilford Press, 1997. This is an updated source on the diagnosis, assessment, and treatment of eating disorders, as well as key issues associated with how eating disorders develop.

Gordon, Richard A. *Eating Disorders: Anatomy of a Social Epidemic.* Oxford, England: Blackwell Publishers, 2000. Examines the social aspects of anorexia nervosa and bulimia nervosa. Includes bibliographical references and an index.

Hsu, L. K. George. *Eating Disorders.* New York: Guilford Press, 1990. The work provides a summary of the knowledge about the eating disorders of anorexia and bulimia, a historical development of the concepts, their clinical features, methods of diagnostic evaluation, and various treatment options.

Lask, Bryan, and Rachel Bryant-Waugh, eds. *Anorexia Nervosa and Related Eating Disorders in Childhood and Adolescence.* 2d ed. Hove, East Sussex, England: Psychology Press, 2000. This volume examines, in seventeen parts, the origins and treatment of eating disorders in young people.

Lemberg, Raymond, and Leigh Cohn, eds. *Eating Disorders: A Reference Sourcebook.* Rev. ed. Phoenix, Ariz.: Oryx Press, 1999. Discusses symptoms, causes, and physiological, medical, and sociocultural issues. Includes bibliographical references and an index.

Genevieve Slomski

See also:

Addictive Personality and Disorders; Anorexia Nervosa and Bulimia Nervosa; Anxiety; Child and Adolescent Psychiatry; Depression; Obsessive-Compulsive Disorder; Stress.

ELECTROCONVULSIVE THERAPY

Type of psychology: Psychotherapy
Fields of study: Biological treatments

Electroconvulsive therapy (ECT), or "shock" therapy, is the controlled application of an electric current to the brain to induce a seizure. This treatment is used primarily for severe and debilitating mental disorders, such as major depression. It is a controversial treatment that has both proponents and opponents.

Principal terms

ANTEROGRADE AMNESIA: the inability to remember new material

GRAND MAL SEIZURE: a seizure characterized by intense stiffening of the body followed by sharp, jerky movements and unconsciousness

MANIA: a mental disorder marked by extreme hyperactivity, agitation, racing thoughts, and distractibility

PSYCHOTROPIC MEDICATION: medication that is used in the treatment of mental disorders

RETROGRADE AMNESIA: the inability to remember things from the past

SCHIZOPHRENIA: a mental disorder marked by disorganized and odd thinking, hearing or seeing things that are not there, and flattened or blunt affect

SOMATIC THERAPY: a treatment for a mental disorder that involves a physical component, such as medications or ECT

Overview

Electroconvulsive therapy (ECT), sometimes known as shock therapy, is a somatic, or physical, form of therapy that is used for some individuals who suffer from severe mental disorders. It involves the direct application of an electric current to the brain. Typically, this current lasts for up to one second at a rate of 140 to 170 volts. The purpose of this electrical charge is to induce a grand mal seizure that will usually last for thirty to sixty seconds. The seizure that is induced is similar to those experienced in some types of epilepsy. It is through this grand mal seizure that ECT has its beneficial effect in reducing the symptoms of the patient.

The use of electrical charges as a medical treatment has been reported for centuries. As early as 47 C.E., Scribonius Largus used an electric eel to treat headaches. During the sixteenth century, Ethiopians were reported to have used electric catfish to expel evil spirits from the bodies of the mentally ill. Direct electric charges for the treatment of nervous complaints was also reported during the eighteenth century in Europe.

The modern application of electric current for the treatment of individuals with mental disorders began in 1938. It was at this time that two Italians, Ungo Cerletti, a psychiatrist, and Lucino Bini, a neuropathologist, invented the first ECT machine for use on humans. Cerletti and Bini first used their newly developed ECT machine to induce convulsions for the treatment of schizophrenic patients, and they reported that the treatment was a success.

ECT was introduced into the United States in 1940, at which time it quickly became the major somatic treatment for all severely disturbed individuals, regardless of mental disorder. By the mid-1950's, its use began to decline rapidly for several reasons, including the introduction of psychotropic medications, increasing demands for civil rights for the mentally ill, and concerns about potential adverse effects of ECT. Subsequently, however, a growing body of research has indicated that ECT is an effective treatment for some severe mental disorders. This research has led to a gradual increase in the acceptance of its use, particularly in the treatment of severely depressed individuals.

When ECT was first used for the treatment of mental disorders, the patient would be strapped to a table and, without any medications or other medical safeguards, would be administered the electrical current and sent into a convulsion. During this convulsion, the patient would thrash around on the table, often being left with broken limbs and other physical complications. In its current use, prior to administration of the ECT, the patient is given a muscle relaxant, which completely immobilizes the body, and anesthesia, which makes the patient completely unconscious. The result of these safeguards has been a much safer treatment of the patient.

The theoretical basis of the original use of ECT had to do with the observation that schizophrenia and epilepsy rarely occur together, suggesting that the two are mutually exclusive. Based on this observation, it was hypothesized that, if a seizure could be induced in a schizophrenic, the schizophrenic symptoms could be eliminated. Physicians had tried previously to induce such seizures by means of injections of insulin, camphor, and other chemicals, but these approaches proved to be too dangerous for the patients.

Although this early theory of the mechanics of ECT has been refuted, there still is little knowledge of how and why ECT actually works. The only fact that has been firmly established is that it is the seizure that ECT induces that creates any positive changes in the patient's symptoms. There is no clear-cut explanation, however, of how the seizure creates the changes. Several theories have been developed to explain the process, most of which center on ECT's effect on neurotransmitters.

Neurotransmitters are chemicals that are used in the brain to transmit messages from one cell to another. One well-accepted theory holds that abnormalities in the level and utilization of certain neurotransmitters lead to the development of mental disorders such as depression, schizophrenia, and mania. Consequently, it is thought that ECT, through the creation of a seizure, somehow affects the level and utilization of some of these neurotransmitters, and that it is this process that reduces the patient's symptoms of mental disorder. While research to investigate how ECT works continues, it is important to remember that, as with all somatic treatments, ECT does not cure the disorder; it provides only temporary relief from the symptoms.

Despite its reported effectiveness, ECT remains a controversial treatment for mental disorders. Opponents point to potential adverse effects that ECT can cause, particularly the possibility of permanent brain damage resulting from the induced seizure. These opponents, who highlight the negative effects that ECT can have on a patient's memory, prefer the use of alternative treatment methods. The public media have served to exacerbate negative perceptions of ECT by depicting it as an inhumane treatment that is used only to control and punish malcontents, not to help the severely disturbed. There is perhaps no better example of the media's distorted depiction of ECT than that found in the film *One Flew over the Cuckoo's Nest* (1975), in which ECT was used as a brutal method to control and manage the main character. As a result of these misunderstandings and distorted perceptions, ECT is often not used when it might be helpful.

Applications
It has been estimated that each year 60,000 to 100,000 people in the United States receive electroconvulsive therapy. This form of treatment has been used to treat a veriety of mental disorders, including severe major depression, schizophrenia, and mania. Several surveys have indicated that more than three-fourths of individuals who receive ECT have been diagnosed as suffering from severe major depression. The second-largest group of individuals receiving ECT consists of those who have been diagnosed as schizophrenic. While there is substantial evidence that ECT is effective in the treatment of severe major depression, the evidence supporting the use of ECT to treat other disorders is not as strong.

Generally speaking, ECT is not seen as a treatment of choice. That is, it will most likely not be the first treatment given to someone suffering from a severe mental disorder. Instead, it is typically viewed as the treatment of last resort and is used primarily to treat individuals who do not respond to any other treatments. For example, a typical course of treatment for an individual suffering from debilitating severe major depression would be first to try talking therapy and to use one of the many antidepressant medications. For most people, it takes two to four weeks to respond to such medications. If the patient does not respond to the medication, another antidepressant medication may be tried. If, after several trials of medication, the patient still does not respond and continues to be severely depressed, ECT might be considered a viable option.

There are few individuals for whom ECT might be considered the treatment of choice. These individuals include those who are in a life-threatening situation, such as those who show symptoms of severe anorexia or strong suicidal tendencies, or those for whom medications would be damaging. ECT might be used to treat pregnant women, for example, since it presents fewer risks for a fetus than medication does, or individuals with heart disease, for whom medications can cause severe complications.

Because of the stigma attached to ECT as a result of its historical misuse and its characterization in the popular media, many physicians believe that ECT is not used as widely as it could and should be. Often, ECT is suggested as the treatment of choice, but because of its stigma, other approaches are tried first. The effect of this decision is to deprive the patient of an effective treatment and delay or prevent remission.

When ECT is indicated for the treatment of a mental disorder, it usually involves five to ten applications of ECT administered at a rate of two or three per week. The number of ECT treatments given, however, will vary depending on the individual's medical history and the severity of the presenting symptoms. ECT is always administered by a physician; it cannot be ordered by a psychologist. When ECT is applied, many medical safeguards are used to prevent or minimize adverse effects. These include the use of a muscle relaxant, anesthesia, and oxygen. These medical procedures have made the use of ECT much safer than it was during the days when the patient would thrash about the table, breaking bones.

There have been additional refinements in the use of ECT that have made it even safer. One such refinement is the application of unilateral, rather than bilateral, ECT. In unilateral ECT, the electric shock is sent through only one of the brain's two hemispheres. Usually, the shock is sent through the right hemisphere, which controls abstract thinking and creativity, rather than the left hemisphere, which controls language and rational thinking. While usually as effective as bilateral ECT, in which the shock goes through the entire brain, unilateral ECT has been shown to cause fewer adverse side effects.

Despite the refinements in ECT and the caution exercised in its use, there are several documented potential adverse side effects. Although most research indicates that these effects are temporary, some researchers suggest that ECT can cause permanent brain damage. The major adverse effects of ECT relate to how well the patient's brain functions after the treatment. The most common effect is extreme confusion and disorientation in the patient upon awakening after an ECT treatment. Generally, this confusion will last for only a few minutes to a few hours.

Another serious concern about ECT's effects on the cognitive functioning of the patient has to do with the patient's memory. ECT can cause retrograde amnesia, the inability to remember things from the past, and anterograde amnesia, the inability to memorize new material. Both forms of amnesia are most noticeable in the first days and weeks after the ECT treatments have stopped. With the passage of time, the patient will slowly remember more from the past and will regain or strengthen the ability to remember new material. In most patients, this recovery of memory will take no more than two to six months. The patient may, however, permanently lose memories of events that occurred immediately prior to the ECT treatments or while the patient was hospitalized for the treatments. The degree of memory loss appears to be related to the number of ECT treatments the patient received.

Research investigating permanent brain damage from the use of ECT has been mixed. Some research has indicated that any application of ECT will cause brain damage and that more brain damage will occur as more treatments are applied. Long-term impairment in the patient's memory is one effect that has thus been identified as permanent. Other researchers, however, have reported that ECT does not cause permanent brain damage. In the meantime, ECT is used cautiously, and research continues into its potential adverse effects.

Perspective and Prospects

Prior to the advent of psychotropic medications, there were few effective treatments for the severely mentally ill. Numerous treatment methods were attempted to help relieve the symptoms of mental illness. Among these methods were bloodletting, the use of leeches, and immersion in water. Perhaps the most common approach was the permanent institutionalization of severely mentally ill individuals. This was done not only to control patients but also to protect others, since patients were viewed as a threat to others and themselves.

As a result of the ineffectiveness of the treatments described above and the growing concern about the institutionalization of the mentally ill, a number of new treatment approaches were developed and applied. Among these new approaches was electroconvulsive therapy. Electroconvulsive shock therapy was first used on schizophrenic patients, and the treatment met with some success. It was also tried on depressed and manic patients with even greater success. As a result of these successes and the lack of other effective treatment approaches, ECT quickly came to be a commonly used treatment for individuals who suffered from a variety of mental disorders.

There were many factors that led to ECT's falling out of favor during the late 1950's. First, the earlier applications of ECT held significant dangers for the patient. The risk of death was approximately one in one thousand, and the risk of physical damage, such as broken bones, was even greater—in fact, such damage was noted in up to 40 percent of the patients. Concerns about complications caused by the use of ECT continue today, and their focus is ECT's impact on cognitive functioning.

Another factor that led to the decline in the use of ECT was the development and introduction of psychotropic medications. These medications revolutionized the treatment of the mentally ill and led to thousands of patients being deinstitutionalized. In terms of both effectiveness and safety, it soon became evident that the use of these medications was substantially preferable to the use of ECT.

A third major influence on the decline of ECT's use was the growing civil rights movement for the mentally ill. Many community and religious leaders began to advocate the fair and humane treatment of the seriously mentally ill. These individuals saw ECT as an undesirable treatment method, used as an instrument for controlling and punishing individuals who could not defend themselves. This view of ECT as inhumane soon came to be widely held. ECT was perceived as a method to control, rather than help, patients—as a punishment rather than a therapy.

These and other factors led to the substantially decreased use of ECT. Subsequently, however, well-designed research has begun to define ECT as a relatively safe treatment method that may be the best therapy in certain situations. Additionally, refinements in the application of ECT have increased its effectiveness and reduced its complications. As a result of not only the ambiguity about its potential adverse effects but also the emotional issues related to its use, the controversy about ECT and its relative risks and benefits is likely to continue for many years.

Bibliography

Abrams, Richard. *Electroconvulsive Therapy*. 3d ed. New York: Oxford University Press, 1997. Stresses medical physiology and the application of ECT to high-risk patients. Includes bibliographical references and an index.

American Psychiatric Association. *Electroconvulsive Therapy: Report of the Task Force on Electroconvulsive Therapy of the American Psychiatric Association.* Washington, D.C.: Author, 1978. This report provides the results of a major task force charged with examining the clinical use of ECT. It thoroughly reviews the issues in a very readable format. Extensive recommendations for the use of ECT are provided.

Breggin, Peter R. *Electroshock: Its Brain-Disabling Effects*. New York: Springer, 1979. This book describes many adverse effects of ECT, but severe mental dysfunction in particular. Citing research from both animal and human research, this author makes a strong argument against the use of ECT, stating that it is no more effective than a placebo, but considerably more dangerous.

Endler, N. S., and E. Persad. *Electroconvulsive Therapy: The Myths and the Realities*. Toronto: Hans Huber, 1988. This book is written for a wide audience, from psychiatrists to patients, and therefore it provides a very readable review of the topic. Much space is devoted to exploring nontechnical issues, including the myths about using ECT, the stigma attached to it, and legal and ethical concerns. An extensive bibliography is included.

Fink, Max. *Convulsive Therapy: Theory and Practice*. New York: Raven Press, 1979. Provides a thorough review of numerous issues surrounding the use of ECT. Includes a study of its effectiveness, risks, and legal, economic, and ethical concerns, as well as a comparison of ECT with other treatment methods. Several chapters are committed to a technical review of the mechanisms of ECT.

_____. *Electroshock: Restoring the Mind*. New York: Oxford University Press, 1999. Uses case studies and testimonies from patients to reinforce the argument that ECT has been refined since its early days, making it more effective. Includes bibliographical references and an index.

Friedberg, John. *Shock Treatment Is Not Good for Your Brain*. San Francisco: Glide, 1976. Provides a strong condemnation of ECT. The author believes that mental illness is a myth and that the use of ECT is unnecessary as well as inhumane. This book, which is written in a personal, nontechnical manner, includes interviews with seven individuals who have received ECT and are opposed to its further use.

Peck, Robert E. *The Miracle of Shock Treatment*. Jericho, N.Y.: Exposition Press, 1974. This short book provides a nontechnical introduction to ECT. It is written in a very readable style and is intended for the layperson who has little knowledge of the topic. The book includes brief case examples that highlight the usefulness of ECT in certain situations.

Mark E. Johnson

See also:

FORGETTING AND FORGETFULNESS

Type of psychology: Memory
Fields of study: Cognitive processes

Forgetting is one of the many puzzling aspects of memory, and various theories have tried to explain it in different ways; among the proposed theories are the concepts of memory decay, interference, and purposeful forgetting.

Principal terms

BIT: a very small amount of data or information, such as a number, letter, or name
CHUNK: an amount of information or data
DECAY: the loss of memory traces over time
ENCODING: the learning of new material or information
INFORMATION-PROCESSING MODEL: the idea that people learn new information by performing various operations on it; the analogy is to a computer's operation
RETRIEVAL: the remembering or recalling of previously learned information or material

Overview

Although everyone has forgotten something at some point in their lives, some people seem to have better memories than others. There are several theories concerning why people forget and why some people seem to be forgetful or "absentminded." Nevertheless, it is not really known why some people forget and others have very good memories.

One theory on forgetting holds that "forgotten" material was never learned in the first place. Another possibility is that very little importance was attached to the material learned and forgotten. Sometimes people are overwhelmed by the sheer amount of information they must learn and are simply incapable of remembering the massive amount of material. Another theory about forgetting suggests that material is never really forgotten; rather, one cannot find the key to retrieve the information from the brain's filing system—its long-term memory. Nearly everyone has experienced the "tip-of-the-tongue" phenomenon (one sees someone at a party, for example, and cannot quite remember the person's name). Sometimes concentration aids memory retrieval; often association helps the process. Psychologists have also noted primacy and recency effects regarding memory; that is, one remembers what is learned first and what is learned last most efficiently. Material that is presented in the middle tends to be more easily forgotten. Aging seems to affect the retrieval process, but the reasons are not completely understood; brain deterioration and diminished care, concern, or motivation are all possible factors.

Sometimes interference can affect one's ability to remember. If one is taking classes at nine, ten, and eleven in the morning, for example, one may have difficulty remembering material because the information from each of the three classes interferes with that of the other classes; this will be especially true if the subject matter is similar. This same process can affect memories of everything from motion pictures seen to events in one's own life. The greater the number of similar films or events (such as dinners in the same type of restaurant) there have been, the more interference there may be. There are two types of interference, retroactive and proactive interference. In proactive interference, occurrences that come before an event or learning situation interfere with one's ability to learn or remember; in retroactive interference, the occurrence that interferes with remembering comes after the event or learning situation.

One's mental state, according to many psychologists, has much to do with one's ability to learn, retain, and recall information. If one is suffering from grief or loss, one's ability to remember will be severely impaired. Children who are abused often have difficulties learning and remembering, since they are preoccupied with the worries and concerns caused by their traumatic home situation. People suffering from depression also may have problems remembering. Counseling or therapy will sometimes alleviate a person's emotional concerns and therefore result in better recall. Emotional problems that may be helped in this way include depression, anxiety, and fear of failure.

There has been debate among psychologists as to whether information stored in long-term memory is stored there permanently. Some memory theorists believe that a decay or fading factor is at work when one forgets information. That is, memory traces naturally fade away and are lost simply because of the passage of time. If one is a freshman in college, one may remember many members of one's senior class in high school very well. In another ten years, however, one may be less able to remember one's classmates and may have forgotten some of those with whom one had only superficial friendships. In twenty years, more information will fade unless one actively tries to rehearse or review the people who were in the class. For example, if one takes out one's high school yearbook every June for twenty years and reminisces about the people in it, one will better be able to recall the names at a twenty-fifth high school reunion.

Some theorists believe that if one can link or associate people, places, or events with other things, one may be able to recall past people or events more effectively. This theory holds that people's minds normally tend to associate one thing with another. These "associationistic" theories are based on the idea that bonds are formed in the brain between places or bits of information. If the bonds are inadequately or poorly formed, then forgetting may occur; bonds must periodically be re-formed to guard against forgetting.

The psychoanalytic (or Freudian) perspective on forgetting emphasizes the idea that people "forget" events that are emotionally traumatic. This is motivated, or purposeful, forgetting; the Freudian term for it is "repression." An example would be a woman who, as a six-year-old girl, had been sexually molested by her father or another relative and who has since forgotten the incident. Interestingly, repression has been known to occur in both victims and perpetrators of violent crimes.

Applications

Two different types of tests are used to assess memory and learning; one type tests recognition, while the other tests recall. A multiple-choice test assesses the first type of memory, because in this type of test one needs to recognize the correct answer when one sees it. An essay examination tests recall—all the responsibility is on the learner to recall as much relevant information as he or she can.

Research on memory and forgetting can be applied in both academic and nonacademic settings. There are a number of things one can do to aid learning and protect against forgetting. Overlearning is one tactic that ensures that one has learned material and will remember it later. In this technique, a student repeats the material by rehearsing it in his or her head to ensure later recall. If one needs to learn a formula, one may repeat it over and over—perhaps writing it a hundred times. This can be tedious, which undoubtedly spurred the search for other options to learn and remember more effectively. Constant review is another strategy. In spaced practice, students study materials to be learned for one hour each night before the test. These students seem to remember the material better than those who spent eight hours studying the material the night before the test. (That type of study—"cramming"—is called massed practice.) For some students, cramming does work, but the material is easily forgotten following its use immediately after the cramming session. Cramming also creates anxiety and fatigue, which may interfere with optimal performance. It is important to eat and sleep well the night before a test.

Some students with poor organizational skills need to expend extra effort to organize the material they have learned. They may employ index cards, for example, to help group and link relevant materials. Mnemonics are memory tricks or devices that help one recall information. The poem that begins "Thirty days have September, April, June, and November," for example, helps one remember the number of days in each month. The word "homes" is frequently used as an acronym for the names of the Great Lakes—Huron, Ontario, Michigan, Erie, and Superior.

Note taking is one way to minimize forgetting; reviewing notes can help one prepare for an examination. For this to be most effective, however, one must be able to discriminate between useful and unimportant information at the time of writing the material down. The same holds true for underlining or highlighting material in books or notes. Taping lectures for later review is particularly useful in cases where a lecturer speaks very rapidly, making effective note taking difficult. Tapes are also effective and important aids in learning a foreign language. One advantage is that material can be reviewed in the car or while using a portable cassette player.

Concentration is an important part of learning and remembering, and people do not often spend enough time concentrating intensely. It has been said that thirty minutes of concentrated, uninterrupted study is better than two hours of haphazard study. The minimizing of outside stimuli is also important; one should study in a quiet place with few distractions. Studying in the same place (and at the same time) every night is also thought to be important for optimal results. Learning should also be active in order to minimize forgetting. Making decisions regarding material to be learned is a useful tool for facilitating learning; one may ask oneself questions about topics or subjects in order to learn or review. Students should be prompted to think about their own learning styles and to allot the necessary time to learn a given amount of material. Many people have their own preferred learning style. Some people learn better by seeing data and information; others assimilate information better by hearing it. Ideally, one should find and maximize one's preferred mode. There are tests designed to determine one's preferred mode of learning.

If one is trying to assimilate too much information in too short a time, one may experience "information overload." Students taking summer classes in which a semester's worth of information is compressed into a few weeks experience this, as may those taking eighteen or more hours of classes in a semester. This may also affect someone beginning a new job that involves mastering a large amount of information or technical material. Material that is meaningful to the learner has been found to be easier to remember and recall.

Perspective and Prospects

The mysteries of remembering and forgetting have certainly fascinated humankind for hundreds, even thousands, of years. In the late nineteenth century, memory was one of the areas of interest to early psychologists such as Hermann Ebbinghaus and William James. Ebbinghaus conducted an experiment in 1885 in which he tested his own memory; he graphed a "forgetting curve," illustrating how much information on a particular list he forgot over time. William James wrote about the "tip-of-the-tongue" phenomenon in 1890, evocatively describing the "gap" that exists in the place of a name one is trying to recall as "intensely active" and containing the "wraith of the name" beckoning within it.

Research on memory has explored many avenues; among them are memory losses that are attributable to physical or physiological causes. Head injuries, for example, can cause difficulties remembering certain information after an accident. In cases of brain tumor, when certain parts of the brain are removed, aspects of memory may be irreparably lost. Alcoholics who drink heavily for many years frequently encounter difficulties remembering; this condition is sometimes termed Korsakoff syndrome. Those who use drugs may also experience memory impairment; actual brain damage may occur in such cases. Older people with Alzheimer's disease or other types of dementia have trouble remembering. Strokes or internal injuries can also cause memory loss, as can epilepsy; during an epileptic seizure, oxygen is not getting to the brain, a condition that may result in brain damage and memory loss.

It is not known exactly how people learn or why they remember or forget. Some psychologists posit that the brain's chemical makeup and activity (particularly involving those substances known as neurotransmitters) are central to learning and remembering; others contend that the brain's electrical activity is crucial in determining one's memory. If there is either a chemical or an electrical abnormality in the brain, people may have difficulties learning or recalling information and events that have been learned.

With newer methodologies for brain scanning, including such noninvasive procedures as nuclear magnetic resonance (NMR) imaging, positron emission tomography (PET) scanning, and computerized axial tomography (CAT) scanning, researchers may be better able to probe various physiological reasons for forgetting. With more and more data available to be learned, research on memory and forgetting will continue to be imperative. Teachers must teach students how to learn and remember, and students must participate actively in the learning process as well as employ many of the available tactics for aiding recall.

Bibliography

Baddeley, Alan. *Human Memory: Theory and Practice*. Rev. ed. Boston: Allyn & Bacon, 1998. Retains all the chapters of the previous edition and adds three new chapters, called "Consciousness," "Implicit Learning," and "Recollective and Implicit Memory." Additional topics include failing memory, retrieval, treating memory problems, and the role of memory.

Graham, Kenneth G., and H. Alan Robinson. *Study Skills Handbook*. Newark, Del.: International Reading Association, 1984. A very practical handbook which includes many of the principles set forth by Frank Robinson (who developed the "survey, question, read, recite, and review," or SQ3R, study method). Helps to teach study skills, thereby increasing memory and helping to prevent forgetting.

Haberlandt, Karl. *Human Memory: Exploration and Application*. Boston: Allyn & Bacon, 1999. An up-to-date overview of the multifaceted study of memory. Presents advances in human memory research fully integrated within the mainstream of the cognitive approach. A variety of perspectives are presented, including psychobiological, developmental, neuropsychological, applied, and cognitive views.

Hayes, John R. *The Complete Problem Solver*. 2d ed. Hillsdale, N.J.: Lawrence Erlbaum Associates, 1989. The title of this book is somewhat deceiving: Although it does discuss problem solving, it emphasizes the role of memory in problem solving, teaches how to use memory effectively, and links memory to learning strategies.

Kail, Robert V. *The Development of Memory in Children*. 3d ed. New York: W. H. Freeman, 1990. A theoretical book dealing with issues regarding children's memory. This text discusses how children develop the capacity to remember. Good reference book on how memory develops.

Loftus, Geoffrey R., and Elizabeth F. Loftus. *Human Memory: The Processing of Information*. Hillsdale, N.J.: Lawrence Erlbaum, 1976. One of the best single books on memory available. Covers learning, remembering and forgetting, and a number of other topics regarding memory.

Stern, Leonard. *The Structures and Strategies of Human Memory*. Homewood, Ill.: Dorsey Press, 1985. This book is a good overview of memory and the applications of memory in life. Discusses long-term memory, a topic many researchers tend to avoid or downplay because of assessment problems. Contains a very systematic review of much of the research in a wide diversity of topics. A good reference book for the serious investigator of human memory in all of its complexities.

Michael F. Shaughnessy

See also:

Alzheimer's Disease; Brain Disorders; Dementia; Memory Loss.

GERIATRIC PSYCHIATRY

Type of psychology: Developmental psychology
Fields of study: Adulthood; interpersonal relations

This subspecialty of psychiatry deals with the diagnosis and treatment of psychiatric syndromes experienced by older people.

Principal terms

ACUTE CONFUSION SYNDROME: a transient condition caused by the action of various biological stressors on vulnerable older persons, who may experience inattention, disorganized thinking, other cognitive impairments, and emotional problems

ANXIETY: a condition characterized by nervousness or agitation; in older people, it is often caused by the existence of a psychiatric disorder such as depression, a general medical condition such as hypothyroidism, or a side effect of medication

DEPRESSION: a condition characterized by a persistent mood of sadness, weight loss, greatly decreased interest in life, and sometimes psychotic episodes; biological factors, family history of depression, underlying medical problems, and medication side effects all can contribute to these symptoms

HYPOCHONDRIASIS: a condition in which the patients believe strongly that they are suffering from one or more serious illnesses, even when this belief is unsupported by medical evidence

INSOMNIA: disturbed sleep, which occurs in older people more often than in any other age group; insomnia in older people can be caused by many factors, such as dysfunctional sleep cycle, breathing problems, leg jerking, underlying medical and psychiatric disorders, and the side effects of medication

MEMORY LOSS SYNDROME: a condition in which a person gradually but progressively loses capacity in many cognitive areas, but especially in the ability to remember; Alzheimer's disease is considered the most common factor causing serious memory loss in older people

SUSPICIOUSNESS: a range of symptoms from increasing distrust of others to paranoid delusions of conspiracies; changes related to aging are thought to be major factors causing increased suspiciousness in older people

Overview

Growing numbers of old and very old people and the increased complexity of diagnosis and treatment of this age group has driven the growth of geriatric psychiatry. Psychiatrists who specialize in working with the geriatric population note that the psychiatric problems experienced by older people often fit poorly in the diagnostic categories set down in the *Diagnostic and Statistical Manual of Mental Disorders* (4th ed., 1994, DSM-IV). The interplay among declining physical health, decreasing mental functioning, social withdrawal and isolation, and

The need for specialists in geriatric psychiatry has increased with rising life expectancies in the United States. (Digital Stock)

vulnerability to stress makes proper diagnosis and appropriate treatment more difficult. In response to this complexity, practitioners of geriatric psychiatry tend to take a broader approach to diagnosis and to use an interdisciplinary model in developing a treatment plan. The profession of geriatric psychiatry has developed most in Great Britain and Canada but is attracting growing numbers of practitioners in the United States and other Western countries.

Applications
Geriatric psychiatrists tend to follow the lead of specialists in geriatric medicine, who have found that taking a syndromal approach to diagnosis appears to work better with older patients. Among the psychiatric syndromes used by geriatric psychiatrists are acute confusion, anxiety, depression, hypochondriasis, insomnia, memory loss, and suspiciousness. Special attention must be given by geriatric psychiatrists to the older person's overall ability to function, general health status, social support system, family history, and preexisting conditions. Geriatric psychiatrists are forced to acknowledge the role played by changes in the brain as it ages and to separate changes that are relatively benign from those that pose real threats to the patient. Hospitalization and significant medical intervention tend to occur more often in the later stages of a person's life, and geriatric psychiatrists are aware that these events can have a great impact on the patient's mental well-being.

When they can, geriatric psychiatrists draw readily upon the help of other health care providers in treating the older person, including the use of specially qualified clinical psychologists, social workers, nurses, occupational therapists, speech pathologists, dietitians, and physical therapists. Improving the understanding of family members and providing them with supportive advice and services can be an important part of the overall treatment plan.

Perspective and Prospects
In the United States, federal funding has expanded for qualified providers, such as clinical psychologists and social workers, to render mental health services for older people, especially those who live in long-term care facilities. Funds have increased for the proper training of those who provide mental health services to older people. Examinations have been established to show evidence of "added qualifications" in geriatric medicine and psychiatry. More textbooks and specialty journals devoted to geriatric mental health are now in circulation. The federal government has sponsored important national conferences on various aspects of geriatric mental health. With the cost of hospitalized and long-term care continuing to rise, more emphasis has been given to preventive services and day care services.

Furthermore, some hospitals have established specialized geropsychiatric units to improve diagnosis and treatment and to decrease the time that older people spend in the hospital. Services are expected to increase for adult children who care for older parents with mental illnesses. Research efforts have increased concerning the causes and appropriate treatment of psychiatric problems in older people. Older people are becoming healthier as they learn more about how mental and physical health are affected by the way in which one lives: Older people are advised to stop smoking, eat a better diet, exercise more, and continue to take an active part in family and community life. All these trends are expected to continue in the future.

Bibliography

Birren, James E., Ronald P. Abeles, and K. Warner Schaie, eds. *Handbook of the Psychology of Aging.* 4th ed. New York: Academic Press, 1996. This edition reviews recent developments in research on social and biological influences on behavior, cognitive functions in the aging individual, and motivational and personality changes with age.

Busse, Ewald W., and Dan G. Blazer, eds. *The American Psychiatric Press Textbook of Geriatric Psychiatry.* 2d ed. Washington, D.C.: American Psychiatric Press, 1996. Offers basic scientific knowledge essential to treating mental disorders of late life. Covers biological and behavioral changes that occur in normal aging.

Lenze, Eric J., et al. "Comorbid Anxiety Disorders in Depressed Elderly Patients." *The American Journal of Psychiatry* 157, no. 5 (May, 2000): 722-728. A cross-cultural study that measured current and lifetime rates and associated clinical features of anxiety disorders in depressed elderly patients.

Schneider, Lon S. *Developments in Geriatric Psychiatry.* San Francisco: Jossey-Bass, 1997. Includes late-life suicide and depression in primary care settings, the use of antidepressants, the assessing of competency, and dementia. Includes bibliographical references and indexes.

Spar, James E., and Asenath La Rue. *Concise Guide to Geriatric Psychiatry.* 2d ed. Washington, D.C.: American Psychiatric Press, 1997. Covers the psychiatric aspects of normal aging and the diagnosis and treatment of mood disorders, dementia, delirium, anxiety, and psychoses. Includes bibliographical references and an index.

Russell Williams

See also:

Alcoholism; Alzheimer's Disease; Anxiety Disorders; Brain Disorders; Dementia; Depression; Domestic Violence; Grief and Guilt; Hypochondriasis, Conversion, Somatization, and Somatoform Pain; Memory Loss; Neurosis; Paranoia; Phobias; Psychosomatic Disorders; Sexual Dysfunction; Sleep Apnea Syndromes and Narcolepsy; Stress; Suicide.

GESTALT THERAPY

Type of psychology: Psychotherapy
Fields of study: Humanistic therapies

Gestalt therapy, founded by Fritz Perls, is an outgrowth of the existential-humanistic approach to psychotherapy. It focuses on nonverbal behaviors, dreams, and current thoughts and emotions; as clients become more aware of denied feelings, their innate healing powers are activated.

Principal terms

DREAMWORK: the Gestalt process of determining the meaning of one's dreams by role-playing the various parts of the dream

EMPTY-CHAIR TECHNIQUE: a Gestalt procedure in which one discusses an interpersonal conflict by addressing an empty chair as though the other person were seated in it

EXISTENTIAL-HUMANISTIC PSYCHOTHERAPY: an approach to psychotherapy that stresses one's freedom to make choices, responsibility, and the innate goodness of human beings

HERE AND NOW: a term used in Gestalt therapy that refers to allowing the client to focus only on present thoughts and feelings

HOT SEAT: a term used in Gestalt group therapy for the situation in which one of the clients sits in front of the therapist

Overview

Gestalt therapy emerged during the 1960's as a powerful alternative to the main two available therapeutic techniques, psychoanalysis and behavioral therapy. This approach to therapy, founded by Frederick (Fritz) Perls, attempts to integrate clients' thoughts, feelings, and actions into a unified whole; *Gestalt*, in fact, is the German word for "whole." Gestalt therapists believe that emotional problems as well as some of the dissatisfactions experienced by ordinary individuals are attributable to a lack of recognizing and understanding one's feelings. The fast pace of technological society and the general loss of purpose in individuals' lives has led to a numbing of emotions. Gestaltists believe that many people deny or lose parts of themselves when they are faced with the overwhelming task of coping in society; for example, a person may deny anger toward a loved one.

The role for the Gestalt therapist is to help the client become more aware of the split-off emotions. The therapist takes an active role by requiring the patient to talk about current experiences and feelings. The patient is neither allowed to look for explanations or problems from the past nor expected to talk about future plans. Gestaltists believe that anxiety is the result of an excessive focus on the future. The client is expected to attend to current feelings and experiences—to stay in the "here and now."

Gestalt therapy arose from the existential-humanistic school of psychology.

Prior schools had portrayed individuals rather pessimistically, believing that human beings are relatively evil creatures whose actions are determined by forces outside their control (such as instincts or the environment). People were seen as adaptive hedonists trying to receive the greatest amount of pleasure for the least amount of effort. The existential-humanistic school of psychology portrays individuals more optimistically, believing people innately strive to achieve their fullest human potential. Failure to do so is not the result of an evil nature but rather the fault of obstacles on this path to perfection. Gestalt therapists agree with the existential-humanistic focus on individual responsibility. One freely chooses one's actions and therefore is responsible for them. There is no provision for blaming a past situation or one's current environment. Gestalt therapists encourage independence and uniqueness in their clients. They push them to be themselves rather than adopting the "shoulds" and "oughts" recommended by society. Perls emphasized this focus on independence and responsibility by stating that the process of maturation is moving from environmental support to self-support.

Probably the greatest contribution of the Gestalt style of therapy has been the techniques developed to increase individual self-awareness. These techniques are consistent with the belief that emotional problems stem from avoidance of or failure to recognize one's feelings. The Gestalt therapist is very active and confrontational during the therapy session (in fact, in a group setting, talking to the therapist is called taking the "hot seat") and frequently interprets and questions the client's statements. The goal is a genuine relationship between two individuals, free of normal social conventions, in which a free exchange of thoughts and feelings can take place.

In one technique of Gestalt therapy, called the "dreamwork," the client reports a recent dream. The Gestalt school believes that the events in a dream represent fragmented and denied parts of the personality. Rather than search for explanations in one's childhood, as in the approach of dream analysis originated by Sigmund Freud, clients are encouraged to bring the dream into the present by acting out different parts of the dream. Rather than say "There was a train in my dream," they are required to act out the part of the train. They might say "I am a train. I am very powerful and useful as long as I stay on track." This moves the focus of the dream into the here and now.

Another therapeutic technique used by Gestalt therapists involves a focus on and exaggeration of nonverbal behaviors. Gestaltists believe that much denied information is accessible through body language. For example, a client may state that she is happy and content in a relationship, while she is scowling and keeping her arms and legs crossed in a tight and tense fashion. Gestalt therapists help their clients become aware of these feelings by getting them to exaggerate their actions. A man who is talking about his wife while clenching his hand in a fist and tapping it on the table may be told to clench his fist tighter and bang it hard on the table. This exaggeration of nonverbal behavior would be to make him acutely aware of his anger toward his wife.

Another well-known procedure developed by the Gestalt school of psychotherapy is the "empty-chair technique." This strategy is employed to bring past conflicts into the here and now, where feelings can be reexperienced. The client often will relate to the therapist a disagreement with some significant other. Rather than ask for details of the encounter (a procedure that keeps the focus in the past), the therapist will encourage the client to address an empty chair in the office as though that person were sitting in it. The client must role-play the relevant situation. The therapist may also get the client to play the part of the significant other in the empty chair. This switching back and forth of chairs and roles is a powerful technique to foster empathy, understanding, and a clarification of feelings. This technique can be used not only for conflicts between individuals but also for discrepant feelings within one person.

Applications

The Gestalt approach to psychotherapy is best explained by examples. A student once reported a dream in which she remembered a gum wrapper being dropped outside a nearby church. Rather than search for a meaning of the dream's symbols in her childhood, her friend, a clinical psychologist, asked her to become the elements in the dream. She initially chose the gum wrapper. She stated that as a gum wrapper she concealed something very good and appealing and that most people took the good part from inside her and then threw her away. She stated that she felt like trash littered on a beautiful lawn and that eventually some caring person would come and throw her away.

The student then began to play the role of the church in the dream. She stated that as a church she was a beautiful building constructed from caring hands. She indicated that good things happened inside her but that she was used too infrequently. Many people were afraid or disliked coming to her, she said, and most of the time she was empty inside. The student was surprised as she completed this description of the dream. She talked about the similarity of her explanations of the two elements in the dream. When asked if she felt this way, she stated that this idea at first surprised her somewhat; however, as she continued to elaborate, she became more aware of her feelings of emptiness and loneliness. She had become aware of denied aspects of her emotions.

Gestalt therapy's active focus on nonverbal behavior and denied portions of the personality often can be quite dramatic. The judicious use of these techniques may allow insights into dynamics that are not available through ordinary interpersonal interactions. In one case, a family was being seen by co-therapists in family therapy. The family consisted of a mother, father, son, and daughter. The son was the identified troublemaker in the family, and he demonstrated a wide range of symptoms that caused the family much pain and suffering. During the course of therapy, it became apparent that the mother was an unwitting co-conspirator in these troubles. She often would rescue her son from his precarious and often dangerous situation and restore matters to normal. This served the function of ensuring her role as a "good mother," while providing the son with the reassurance that he was loved by her. Whenever she threatened not to rescue him, he accused her of not caring for him. She inevitably crumbled and provided for his needs. The father and daughter had their own alliance in the family and, although they complained, they did not interfere in this dysfunctional family pattern that frequently ended in severe problems.

The two therapists hypothesized the pathological nature of this interaction and periodically attempted to present it to the family; however, the pattern was so important and so entrenched in the family's style of interaction that any mention of it led to vehement protests and denials that it was an issue of importance. During a therapy session, one of the therapists noticed the pattern in which the family members usually seated themselves. The mother and son sat close to each other on one side of the therapy room, while the father and daughter sat near each other across from them. The two therapists sat across from each other on the other sides of the room. One therapist, taking a cue from the Gestalt emphasis on the importance of nonverbal behaviors, moved his chair and sat in the small space between the mother and son. A stunned silence ensued. The mother and son began to show agitation, while the father and daughter, from across the room, became increasingly amused at the nature of this interaction. The therapists elicited the reactions and analyses of the family to this new seating arrangement. The mother and son continued to display uncertainty and bewilderment, while the father and daughter immediately identified that someone had dared to come between "Mom and her boy." This led to a more open discussion of the pathological nature of the family interactions. The father and daughter could see that they had allowed this damaging pattern to continue. The mother and son, while not quite as open to this discovery because of the threatening nature of the disclosure, could not deny the emotions that were aroused from someone physically invading their territory. The insights that resulted from this simple Gestalt technique moved therapy along much faster than had previous verbal interactions. It demonstrates the Gestalt tenet that a focus on nonverbal patterns of communication may allow clients to become aware of previously denied aspects of their personalities.

Perspective and Prospects

Gestalt therapy emerged during a period of increased popularity for the existential-humanistic position in psychology. This approach, sometimes known as the "third force" in psychology, came from opposition to the earlier forces of psychoanalysis and behaviorism. Existential-humanistic proponents objected to the pessimistic psychoanalytic view of humans as vile creatures held captive by primitive, unconscious desires. They also differed from the environmental determinism set forth by the behavioral school that people are simply products of past punishments and rewards. The existential-humanistic therapists focused on the human freedom to choose one's actions (regardless of unconscious desires and past consequences), the relative goodness of the human species, and people's innate desire to reach their fullest potential. This approach fit well with the period of great social upheaval and change following World War II.

The Gestalt approach often is compared to the client-centered (or person-centered) therapy of Carl Rogers. Both types of psychotherapy endorse the basic assumptions of the existential-humanistic school; however, they differ considerably in their approach and techniques. In client-centered therapy, the client is encouraged to express his or her thoughts and feelings about a situation. The therapist remains relatively passive, giving minimal verbal prompts or paraphrasing the client's statements. The client is responsible for the direction and content of the therapy session; the therapist provides only a clarification of unclear statements or feelings. The idea behind this approach is that the therapist is providing an atmosphere of unconditional acceptance in which the client can explore his or her emotional issues. Eventually, the client's innate curative ability will take over. The Gestalt therapist, in contrast, is much more confrontational in interpreting statements and asking questions. The Gestalt approach places a greater emphasis on the interpretation of nonverbal behaviors and the usefulness of dreams. Although different in technique, both approaches point to the freedom to choose, the innate goodness of the client, and the strength of the therapeutic relationship as curative factors.

The influence of the Gestalt approach to psychotherapy diminished with the death of Fritz Perls in 1970. He was the emotional and spiritual leader of the group, and his charisma was not replaced easily. Gestalt therapy is not considered a mainstream psychotherapy; however, it does have numerous enthusiastic followers. The greatest contribution of the Gestalt orientation has been the techniques developed to assist clients in becoming more aware of hidden thoughts and emotions. Therapists from a wide variety of orientations have adapted and applied these procedures within their own theoretical framework. The impact of dreamwork, the hot seat, nonverbal interpretations, and the empty-chair techniques seems to have outlasted the theory from which they came.

Bibliography

Davison, Gerald C., and John M. Neale. *Abnormal Psychology*. 8th ed. New York: John Wiley & Sons, 2000. A frequently used textbook in the field of abnormal psychology. It gives an interesting overview of Gestalt therapy practice as well as an explanation of how these techniques may be applied to abnormal behaviors. The authors present a balanced critique of Gestalt therapy and of how it fits with the existential-humanistic approach to abnormality.

Ivey, Allen E., and Lynn Simek-Downing. *Counseling and Psychotherapy: Skills, Theories, and Practice*. 2d ed. Englewood Cliffs, N.J.: Prentice-Hall, 1980. This popular textbook on psychotherapy gives a brief overview of Gestalt therapy. It includes examples of Gestalt therapists working with clients and analyzes each statement in terms of type of approach (confrontation, question, or empathy).

Karp, H. B. *The Change Leader: Using a Gestalt Approach with Work Groups*. San Diego: Pfeiffer, 1996. Discusses Gestalt therapy in relation to organizational change and teams in the workplace. Includes bibliographical references and an index.

Mackewn, Jennifer. *Developing Gestalt Counselling*. Thousand Oaks, Calif.: Sage Publications, 1997. A field theoretical and relational model of contemporary Gestalt counseling and psychotherapy. Includes bibliographical references and an index.

Perls, Frederick S. *The Gestalt Approach and Eye Witness to Therapy*. Ben

Lomond, Calif.: Science & Behavior Books, 1973. Two short pieces printed in one volume. *The Gestalt Approach* was Perls's last attempt to rework Gestalt therapy and is one of his most complete attempts to do so. *Eye Witness to Therapy* is a collection of verbatim therapy transcripts. They are easily readable and present excellent examples of practical applications of Gestalt theories.

_____. *Gestalt Therapy Verbatim.* Toronto: Bantam Books, 1959. This book is easy to read and contains a good balance of theory and case examples. Many of the examples come from group dreamwork seminars and portray the Gestalt approach to dream analysis.

_____. *In and Out the Garbage Pail.* Toronto: Bantam Books, 1969. This is a humorous and free-floating autobiography by the founder of Gestalt therapy. Often entertaining, Perls uses his memories and experiences to illuminate principles of his theory.

Brett L. Beck

See also:

Abnormality: Humanistic-Existential Models; Group Therapy; Person-Centered Therapy; Psychotherapy: Goals and Techniques.

GRIEF AND GUILT

Type of psychology: Social psychology; stress
Fields of study: Coping; critical issues in stress; interpersonal relations

Grief and accompanying guilt are common reactions to the fact or eventuality of serious losses of various kinds, especially death; every person eventually experiences grief, and while grief is normal, its effects can be incapacitating.

Principal terms

ABNORMAL GRIEF: an unhealthy response to a loss, which may include anger, an inability to feel loss, withdrawal, and deterioration in health

GRIEF: a multifaceted physical, emotional, psychological, spiritual, and social reaction to loss

GUILT: a cognitive and emotional response often associated with the grief experience in which a person feels a sense of remorse, responsibility, and/or shame regarding the loss

LOSS: the sudden lack of a previously held possession, physical state, or social position or the death of a loved one

Causes and Symptoms

During life, people unavoidably experience a variety of losses. These may include the loss of loved ones, important possessions or status, health and vitality, and ultimately the loss of self through death. "Grief" is the word commonly used to refer to an individual's or group's shared experience following a loss. The experience of grief is not a momentary or singular phenomenon. Instead, it is a variable, and somewhat predictable, process of life. Also, as with many phenomena within the range of human experience, it is a multidimensional process including biological, psychological, spiritual, and social components.

The biological level of the grief experience includes the neurological and physiological processes that take place in the various organ systems of the body in response to the recognition of loss. These processes, in turn, form the basis for emotional and psychological reactions. Various organs and organ systems interact with one another in response to the cognitive stimulation resulting from this recognition. Human beings are self-reflective creatures with the capacity for experiencing, reflecting upon, and giving meaning to sensations, both physical and emotional. Consequently, the physiological reactions of grief that take place in the body are given meaning by those experiencing them.

The cognitive and emotional meanings attributed to the experience of grief are shaped by and influence interactions within the social dimensions of life. In other words, how someone feels or thinks about grief influences and is influenced by interactions with family, friends, and helping professionals. In addition, the individual's religious or spiritual frame of reference may have a significant influence on the subjective experience and cognitive-emotional meaning attributed to grief.

The loss of a life partner, particularly after a lengthy relationship, is a source of intense grief and may trigger guilt in the survivor. (PhotoDisc)

The grief reactions associated with a loss such as death vary widely. While it is very difficult and perhaps unfair to generalize about such an intensely personal experience, several predictors of the intensity of grief have become evident. The amount of grief experienced seems to depend on the significance of the loss, or the degree to which the individual subjectively experiences a sense of loss. This subjective experience is partially dependent on the meaning attributed to the loss by the survivors and others in the surrounding social context. This meaning is in turn shaped by underlying belief systems, such as religious faith. Clear cognitive, emotional, and/or spiritual frameworks are helpful in guiding people constructively through the grief process.

People in every culture around the world and throughout history have developed expectations about life, and these beliefs influence the grief process. Common questions in many cultures include "Why do people die?" "Is death a part of life, or a sign of weakness or failure?" "Is death always a tragedy, or is it sometimes a welcome relief from suffering?" and "Is there life after death, and if so, what is necessary to attain this afterlife?" The answers to these and other questions help shape people's experience of the grief process. As Elisabeth Kübler-Ross states in *Death: The Final Stage of Growth* (1975), the way in which a society or subculture explains death will have a significant impact on the way in which its members view and experience life.

Another factor that influences the experience of grief is whether a loss was anticipated. Sudden and/or unanticipated losses are more traumatic and more difficult to explain because they tend to violate the meaning systems mentioned above. The cognitive and emotional shock of this violation exacerbates the grief process. For example, it is usually assumed that youngsters will not die before the older members of the family. Therefore, the shock of a child dying in an automobile crash may be more traumatic than the impact of the death of an older person following a long illness.

Death and grief are often distasteful to human beings, at least in Western Judeo-Christian cultures. These negative, fearful reactions are, in part, the result of an individual's difficulty accepting the inevitability of his or her own death. Nevertheless, in cultures which have less difficulty accepting death and loss as normal, people generally experience more complicated grief experiences. The Micronesian society of Truk is a death-affirming society. The members of the Truk society believe that a person is not really grown up until the age of forty. At that point, the individual begins to prepare for death. Similarly, some native Alaskan groups teach their members to approach death intentionally. The person about to die plans for death and makes provisions for the grief process of those left behind.

In every culture, however, the grief-stricken strive to make sense out of their experience of loss. Some attribute death to a malicious intervention from the outside by someone or something else; death becomes frightening. For others, death is in response to divine intervention or is simply the completion of "the circle of life" for that person. Yet for most people in Western societies, even those who come to believe that death is a part of life, grief may be an emotional mixture of loss, shock, shame, sadness, rage, numbness, relief, anger, and/or guilt.

Kübler-Ross points out in her timeless discourse "On the Fear of Dying" (*On Death and Dying*, 1969) that guilt is perhaps the most painful companion of death and grief. The grief process is often complicated by the individual's perception that he or she should have prevented the loss. This feeling of being responsible for the death or other loss is common among those connected to the deceased. For example, parents or health care providers may believe that they should have done something differently in order to detect the eventual cause of death sooner or to prevent it once the disease process was detected.

Guilt associated with grief is often partly or completely irrational. For example, there may be no way that a physician could have detected an aneurysm in her patient's brain prior to a sudden and fatal stroke. Similarly, a father cannot monitor the minute-by-minute activities of his adolescent children to prevent lethal accidents. Kübler-Ross explains a related phenomenon among children who have lost a parent by pointing out the difficulty in separating wishes from deeds. A child whose wishes are not gratified by a parent may become angry. If the parent subsequently dies, the child may feel guilty, even if the death is some distance in time away from the event in question.

The guilt may also involve remorse over surviving someone else's loss. People who survive an ordeal in which others die often experience "survivor's guilt." Survivors may wonder why they survived and how the deceased person's family members feel about their survival, whether they blame the survivors or wish that they had died instead. As a result, survivors have difficulty integrating the experience with the rest of their lives in order to move on. The feelings of grief and guilt may be exacerbated further if survivors believe that they somehow benefited from someone else's death. A widow who is suddenly the beneficiary of a large sum of money attached to her husband's life insurance policy may feel guilty about doing some of the things that they had always planned but were unable to do precisely because of a lack of money.

Lastly, guilt may result when people believe that they did not pay enough attention to, care well enough for, or deserve the love of the person who died. These feelings and thoughts are prompted by loss—loss of an ongoing relationship with the one who died, as well as part of the empathetic response to what it might be like to die oneself.

Feelings of guilt are not always present, even if the reaction is extreme. If individuals experience guilt, however, they may "bargain" with themselves or a higher power, review their actions to find what they did wrong, take a moral inventory to see where they could have been more loving or understanding, or even begin to act self-destructively. Attempting to resolve guilt while grieving loss is doubly complicated and may contribute to the development of what is considered an abnormal grief reaction.

The distinctions between normal and abnormal grief processes are not clear-cut and are largely context-dependent; that is, what is normal depends on standards that vary among different social groups and historical periods. In addition, at any particular time the variety of manifestations of grief depend on the individual's personality and temperament; family, social, and cultural contexts; resources for coping with and resolving problems; and experiences with the successful resolution of grief.

Despite this diversity, the symptoms that are manifested by individuals experiencing grief are generally grouped into two different but related diagnostic categories: depression and anxiety. It is normal for the grieving individual to manifest symptoms related to anxiety and/or depression to some degree. For example, a surviving relative or close friend may temporarily have difficulty sleeping, or feel sad or that life has lost its meaning. Relative extremes of these symptoms, however, in either duration or intensity, signal the possibility of an abnormal grief reaction.

In *Families and Health* (1988), family therapist William Doherty and family physician Thomas Campbell identify the signs of abnormal grief reactions as including periods of compulsive overactivity without a sense of loss; identification with the deceased; acquisition of symptoms belonging to the last illness of the deceased; deterioration of health in the survivors; social isolation, withdrawal, or alienation; and severe depression. These signs may also include severe anxiety, abuse of substances, work or school problems, extreme or persistent anger, or an inability to feel loss.

Treatment and Therapy

There is no set time schedule for the grief process. While various ethnic, cultural, religious, and political groups define the limits of the period of mourning, they cannot prescribe the experience of grief. Yet established norms do influence the grief experience inasmuch as the grieving individuals have internalized these expectations and standards. For example, the typical benefit package of a professional working in the United States offers up to one week of paid "funeral" leave in the event of the death of a significant family member. On the surface, this policy begins to prescribe or define the limits of the grief process.

Such a policy suggests, for example, that a mother or father stricken with grief at the untimely death of a child ought to be able to return to work and function reasonably well once a week has passed. Most individuals will attempt to do so, even if they are harboring unresolved feelings about the child's death. Coworkers, uncomfortable with responding to such a situation and conditioned to believe that people need to "get on with life," may support the lack of expression of grief.

Helpful responses to grief are as multifaceted as is grief itself. Ultimately, several factors ease the grief process. These include validating responses from significant others, socially sanctioned expression of the experience, self-care, social or religious rituals, and possibly professional assistance. Each person responds to grief differently and requires or is able to use different forms of assistance.

Most reactions to loss run a natural, although varied, course. Since grief involves coming to grips with the reality of death, acceptance must eventually be both intellectual and emotional. Therefore, it is important to allow for the complete expression of both thoughts and feelings. Those attempting to assist grief-stricken individuals are more effective if they have come to terms with their own feelings, beliefs, and conflicts about death, and any losses they personally have experienced.

Much of what is helpful in working through grief involves accepting grief as a normal phenomenon. Grief-related feelings should not be judged or overly scrutinized. Supportive conversations include time for ventilation, empathic responses, and sharing of sympathetic experiences. Helpful responses may take the form of "To feel pain and sadness at this time is a normal, healthy response" or "I don't know what it is like to have a child die, but it looks like it really hurts" or "It is understandable if you find yourself thinking that life has lost its purpose." In short, people must be given permission to grieve. When it becomes clear that the person is struggling with an inordinate amount of feelings based on irrational beliefs, these underlying beliefs—not the feelings—may need to be challenged.

People tend to have difficulty concentrating and focusing in the aftermath of a significant loss. The symptoms of anxiety and depression associated with grief may be experienced, and many of the basic functions of life may be interrupted. Consequently, paying attention to healthy eating and sleeping schedules, establishing small goals, and being realistic about how long it may take before "life returns to normal" are important.

While the prescription of medication for the grief-stricken is fairly common, its use is recommended only in extreme situations. Antianxiety agents or antidepressants can interfere with the normal experiences of grief that involve feeling and coming to terms with loss. Sedatives can help bereaved family members and other loved ones feel better over the short term, with less overt distress and crying. Many experts believe, however, that they inhibit the normal grieving process and lead to unresolved grief reactions. In addition, studies suggest that those who start on psychotropic medication during periods of grief stay on them for at least two years.

The grief process is also eased by ritual practices that serve as milestones to mark progress along the way. Some cultures have very clearly defined and well-established rituals associated with grief. In the United States, the rituals practiced continue to be somewhat influenced by family, ethnic, and regional cultures. Very often, however, the rituals are confined to the procedures surrounding the preparation and burial of the body (for example, viewing the body at the mortuary, a memorial service, and interment). As limited as these experiences might be, they are designed to ease people's grief. Yet the grief process is often just beginning with the death and burial of the loved one. Consequently, survivors are often left without useful guidelines to help them on their way.

Another common, although unhelpful, phenomenon associated with the process is for the grief-stricken person initially to receive a considerable amount of empathy and support from family, friends, and possibly professionals (such as a minister or physician) only to have this attention drop off sharply after about a month. The resources available through family and other social support systems diminish with the increasing expectation that the bereaved should stop grieving and "get on with living." If this is the case, or if an individual never did experience a significantly supportive response from members of his or her social system, the role of psychotherapy and/or support groups should be explored. Many public and private agencies offer individual and family therapy. In addition, in many communities there are a variety of self-help support groups devoted to growth and healing in the aftermath of loss.

Perspective and Prospects
The grief process, however it is shaped by particular religious, ethnic, or cultural contexts, is reflective of the human need to form attachments. Grief thus reflects

the importance of relationships in one's life, and therefore it is likely that people will always experience grief (including occasional feelings of guilt). Processes such as the grief experience, with its cognitive, emotional, social, and spiritual dimensions, may affect an individual's psychological and physical well-being. Consequently, medical and other health care and human service professionals will probably always be called upon to investigate, interpret, diagnose, counsel, and otherwise respond to grief-stricken individuals and families.

In the effort to be helpful, however, medical science has frequently intervened too often and too invasively into death, dying, and the grief process—to the point of attempting to disallow them. For example, hospitals and other institutions such as nursing homes have become the primary place that people die. It is important to remember that it has not always been this way. Even now in some cultures around the world, people die more often in their own homes than in a "foreign" institution.

In the early phases of the development of the field of medicine, hospitals as institutions were primarily devoted to the care of the dying and the indigent. Managing the dying process was a primary focus. More recently, however, techno-logical advances and specialty development have shifted the mission of the hospi-tal to being an institution devoted to healing and curing. The focus on the recovery process has left dying in the shadows. Death has become equated with failure and associated with professional guilt.

It is more difficult for health care professionals to involve themselves or at least constructively support the grief process of individuals and families if it is happen-ing as a result of the health care team's "failure." In a parallel fashion, society has become unduly fixated on avoiding death, or at least prolonging its inevitability to the greatest possible extent. The focus of the larger culture is on being young, staying young, and recoiling from the effects of age. As a result, healthy grief over the loss of youthful looks, stamina, health, and eventually life is not supported.

Medical science can make an important contribution in this area by continuing to define the appropriate limits of technology and intervention. The struggle to balance quantity of life with quality of life (and death) must continue. In addition, medical science professionals need to redouble their efforts toward embracing the patient, not simply the disease; the person, not simply the patient; and the com-plexities of grief in death and dying, not simply the joy in healing and living.

Bibliography

Archer, John. *The Nature of Grief: The Evolution and Psychology of Reactions to Loss*. New York: Routledge, 1999. A synthesis of material from evolutionary psychology, ethology, and experimental psychology on the process of grief. Argues that grief is not an illness or a disorder but a natural reaction to losses of many kinds.

Cook, Alicia Skinner, and Kevin Oltjenbruns. *Dying and Grieving: Lifespan and Family Perspectives*. 2d ed. Fort Worth, Tex.: Harcourt Brace College Publish-ers, 1998. Addresses the psychological aspects of death and its effect on the family. Includes bibliographical references and indexes.

Doka, Kenneth J., ed. *Living with Grief After Sudden Loss: Suicide, Homicide,*

Accident, Heart Attack, Stroke. Washington, D.C.: Taylor & Francis, Hospice Foundation of America, 1997. Provides information that will be useful for individuals dealing with the different kinds of adjustment related to the death of a loved one or the loss of functioning or abilities.

Goldman, Linda. *Life and Loss: A Guide to Help Grieving Children.* 2d ed. Philadelphia: Accelerated Development, 2000. Appropriate for health care professionals and parents. Includes bibliographical references and an index.

Klass, Dennis, Phyllis R. Silverman, and Steven L. Nickman, eds. *Continuing Bonds: New Understandings of Grief.* Washington, D.C.: Taylor & Francis, 1996. Examines cross-cultural manifestations of bereavement, particularly the psychological aspects. Includes a bibliography and an index.

Kübler-Ross, Elisabeth, ed. *Death: The Final Stage of Growth.* Englewood Cliffs, N.J.: Prentice Hall, 1975. A valuable companion to Kübler-Ross's earlier work, this book contains insightful perspectives on variations in culture, the impact of institutions, and the importance of ritual in the dying and grieving processes.

_____. *On Death and Dying.* New York: Macmillan, 1969. This book is, and will remain, a classic in the field. Kübler-Ross shares the experience of many years working with dying patients and their families. In addition to discussing the typical stages through which people progress in the death and dying process, she details the many specifics and variations of people's grief and guilt reactions to death and dying.

Staudacher, Carol. *Beyond Grief: A Guide for Recovering from the Death of a Loved One.* Oakland, Calif.: New Harbinger, 1987. A clear and readable guide to the grief process. The author provides specific examples relevant for some of the most painful grief experiences: those following the death of a spouse, child, or parent at an early age.

Layne A. Prest

See also:

Child and Adolescent Psychiatry; Depression; Geriatric Psychiatry; Neurosis; Phobias; Psychiatry; Stress; Suicide; Teen Suicide.

PSYCHOLOGY
AND
MENTAL HEALTH

CATEGORY LIST

Abnormality
Abnormality
Abnormality: Behavioral Models
Abnormality: Biomedical Models
Abnormality: Cognitive Models
Abnormality: Family Models
Abnormality: Humanistic-Existential
　Models
Abnormality: Legal Models
Abnormality: Psychodynamic Models
Abnormality: Sociocultural Models
Diagnosis and Classification
Madness: Historical Concepts

Anxiety Disorders
Agoraphobia and Panic Disorders
Amnesia, Fugue, and Multiple Personality
Anxiety Disorders
Aversion, Implosion, and Systematic
　Desensitization Therapies
Eating Disorders
Hypochondriasis, Conversion,
　Somatization, and Somatoform Pain
Insomnia
Lobotomy
Neurosis
Obsessive-Compulsive Disorder
Paranoia
Phobias
Psychoactive Drug Therapy
Psychosurgery

Childhood and Adolescent Disorders
Anorexia Nervosa and Bulimia Nervosa
Attention-Deficit Disorder
Autism
Bed-Wetting
Child Abuse
Child and Adolescent Psychiatry
Divorce and Separation: Children's Issues
Down Syndrome
Eating Disorders
Identity Crises
Juvenile Delinquency
Phobias
Play Therapy

Psychotherapy: Children
Schizophrenia: High-Risk Children
Sibling Rivalry
Teenage Suicide

Depression
Depression
Electroconvulsive Therapy
Grief and Guilt
Manic-Depressive Disorder
Psychoactive Drug Therapy
Seasonal Affective Disorder
Suicide
Teenage Suicide

Developmental Issues
Behavioral Family Therapy
Child Abuse
Child and Adolescent Psychiatry
Couples Therapy
Divorce and Separation: Adult Issues
Divorce and Separation: Children's Issues
Domestic Violence
Geriatric Psychiatry
Identity Crises
Juvenile Delinquency
Midlife Crises
Sexual Variants and Paraphilias
Sibling Rivalry
Strategic Family Therapy

Diagnosis
Behavioral Assessment and Personality
　Rating Scales
Diagnosis and Classification
Personality: Psychophysiological Measures

Emotional Disorders
Agoraphobia and Panic Disorders
Aggression: Definitions and Theoretical
　Explanations
Aggression: Reduction and Control
Amnesia, Fugue, and Multiple Personality
Anxiety Disorders
Child Abuse
Child and Adolescent Psychiatry

Divorce and Separation: Adult Issues
Divorce and Separation: Children's Issues
Domestic Violence
Grief and Guilt
Hypochondriasis, Conversion,
    Somatization, and Somatoform Pain
Identity Crises
Jealousy
Juvenile Delinquency
Manic-Depressive Disorder
Midlife Crises
Neurosis
Obsessive-Compulsive Disorder
Paranoia
Phobias
Psychoactive Drug Therapy
Psychosomatic Disorders
Sexual Dysfunction
Sibling Rivalry
Type A Behavior Pattern

Learning Disorders
Aphasias
Attention-Deficit Disorder
Autism
Dyslexia
Learning Disabilities
Mental Retardation

Organic Disorders
Alzheimer's Disease
Aphasias
Attention-Deficit Disorder
Autism
Brain Disorders
Dementia
Down Syndrome
Dyslexia
Forgetting and Forgetfulness
Memory Loss
Mental Retardation
Psychosomatic Disorders
Seasonal Affective Disorder
Sleep Apnea and Narcolepsy
Type A Behavior Pattern

Personality Disorders
Addictive Personality and Behaviors
Aggression: Definitions and Theoretical
    Explanations

Aggression: Reduction and Control
Amnesia, Fugue, and Multiple Personality
Antisocial Personality
Behavioral Assessment and Personality
    Rating Scales
Borderline, Histrionic, and Narcissistic
    Personalities
Codependent Personality
Personality: Psychophysiological
    Measures
Projective Personality Traits
Psychosis
Type A Behavior Pattern

Schizophrenias
Lobotomy
Paranoia
Psychoactive Drug Therapy
Psychosurgery
Schizophrenia
Schizophrenia: High-Risk Children

Sexual Disorders
Sexual Dysfunction
Sexual Variants and Paraphilias

Sleep Disorders
Biofeedback and Relaxation
Insomnia
Sleep Apnea and Narcolepsy

Stress
Anxiety Disorders
Biofeedback and Relaxation
Insomnia
Phobias
Post-traumatic Stress
Stress
Stress: Behavioral and Psychological
    Responses
Stress: Coping Strategies
Stress: Physiological Responses
Stress: Prediction and Control
Type A Behavior Pattern

Substance Abuse
Addictive Personality and Behaviors
Alcoholism
Codependent Personality
Substance Abuse

Treatments
Analytical Psychotherapy
Aversion, Implosion, and Systematic
   Desensitization Therapies
Behavioral Family Therapy
Biofeedback and Relaxation
Cognitive Behavior Therapy
Cognitive Therapy
Community Psychology
Couples Therapy
Electroconvulsive Therapy
Gestalt Therapy
Group Therapy
Lobotomy
Mental Health Practitioners
Modeling Therapies
Music, Dance, and Theater Therapy

Operant Conditioning Therapies
Person-Centered Therapy
Play Therapy
Psychiatry
Psychoactive Drug Therapy
Psychoanalysis: Classical Versus Modern
Psychosurgery
Psychotherapy: Children
Psychotherapy: Effectiveness
Psychotherapy: Goals and Techniques
Psychotherapy: Historical Approaches to
   Treatment
Rational-Emotive Therapy
Reality Therapy
Strategic Family Therapy
Transactional Analysis